Timber Castles

Timber Castles

Robert Higham
and
Philip Barker

STACKPOLE
BOOKS

Dedicated to the memory of
R. Allen Brown and D. J. Cathcart King

Published by
Stackpole Books
5067 Ritter Road
Mechanicsburg, PA 17055

First U.S. Edition 1995

Published by arrangement with
B. T. Batsford Ltd.
4 Fitzhardinge Street
London, W1H 0AH, Great Britain

Copyright © Robert Higham and Philip Barker 1992

First published in Great Britain by B. T. Batsford Ltd. in 1992

Typeset in Hong Kong

Printed in Great Britain

Library of Congress Cataloging-in-Publication Data
Higham, Robert.
Timber castles / Robert Higham and Philip Barker. — 1st U.S. ed.
p.   cm.
Originally published: London : B. T. Batsford, 1992
Includes bibliographical references and index.
ISBN 0-8117-1747-X
1. Timber castles.   I. Barker, Philip, 1920–   .   II. Title.
UG405.H54   1995
256.7'094'0902—dc20
94-19557
CIP

Contents

List of illustrations 7

Preface 11

Acknowledgements 13

List of abbreviations 15

1 Timber castles: their study and background 17

2 Origins of timber castles in the British Isles 36

3 Origins of timber castles in Europe 78

4 The documentary contribution 114

5 The pictorial evidence 147

6 Stone and timber 171

7 The earthworks of timber castles 194

8 The structures of timber castles: the excavated evidence and its interpretation 244

9 Hen Domen, Montgomery: a case-study 326

10 Epilogue 348

11 Gazetteer of excavations in Great Britain and Ireland 353

Appendices:
A Timber castle vocabulary 361
B *Castel* 362

Notes 365

Further reading 383

Index 385

Illustrations

1.1	Caernarfon castle	18
1.2	Survey of Stafford castle	19
1.3	Pitt-Rivers' plan of Caesar's Camp	22
1.4	Morgan's excavation of Bishopston	23
1.5	Castle earthworks: Wembworthy	24
1.6	Castle earthworks: Blackdown Rings	25
1.7	Burh and castle plans: Wallingford and Wareham	25
1.8	Distribution map of British mottes	27
1.9	The Montgomery region of the English-Welsh border	29
1.10	Ramparts and fighting platforms of a Maori pa	33
1.11	Plan of a timber fort at Wolstenholme Town, Virginia	34
1.12	Nagoya castle, Japan	35
2.1	Documented castles in England and the Welsh border before 1086	41
2.2	Plan of Cheddar royal palace	42
2.3	Plan of royal palace at Yeavering	42
2.4	Documented castles of 1051	43
2.5	Richard's Castle	44
2.6	Hereford castle	44
2.7	Ewyas Harold	45
2.8	Distribution of (a) ringworks and (b) mottes in England	46
2.9	Proportions of mottes and ringworks in England and Wales	48
2.10	Castle Neroche	49
2.11	Earl's Barton	50
2.12	Sulgrave	50
2.13	Late Saxon buildings at Sulgrave	51
2.14	Late Saxon buildings at Portchester	52
2.15	Stone building at Winchester	53
2.16	Eynsford	54
2.17	Late Saxon Goltho	55
2.18	Reconstruction of Goltho	56
2.19	Documented castles of the immediately post-Conquest period	59
2.20	Aldingham	61
2.21	Possible pre-Norman enclosures in the central Welsh marches	63
2.22	Timber castles and geology in Glamorgan	65
2.23	Distribution of mottes in Wales	66
2.24	Distribution of ringworks in Wales	66
2.25	Cruggleton	68
2.26	Crookston	69
2.27	Mote of Urr	69
2.28	Distribution of mottes in Scotland	70
2.29	Possible castle ringworks in Ireland	72
2.30	Distribution of mottes in Ireland	73
2.31	Motte at Knockgraffon	74
2.32	Rath converted into a motte and bailey, Castleskreen	75
2.33	Section through rath, Rathmullan	75
2.34	Gransha	76
3.1	The Danish geometrical fortresses	80–1
3.2	A Danish motte and manor house	82
3.3	Section through a defended crannog	83
3.4	Timber defences of a Slav fortress	84
3.5	Timber and earth defences around stone donjons in Romania	85
3.6	Bipartite plans, Poland	86
3.7	Lakeside Slav settlement	86
3.8	Section through motte at Plemięta, Poland	87
3.9	Bipartite fortification, Hofe	89
3.10	(a) Distribution of mottes in the Rhineland; (b) schematic development of der Husterknupp	90–1
3.11	Distribution of mottes in the Netherlands	92
3.12	A *terp* raised into a motte	93
3.13	Distribution of circular earthworks in France	94
3.14	The donjon at Langeais	98
3.15	Mottes in Finistère	99

ILLUSTRATIONS

3.16 Arques-la-Bataille 101
3.17 Castles in Normandy documented before 1066 102
3.18 Small enclosures in Normandy 102–4
3.19 Earthworks at Sebecourt 105
3.20 Earthworks at Mirville 106
3.21 Earthworks at Notre-Dame-de-Gravenchon 107–10
3.22 Earthworks at Grimbosq 111
3.23 Earthworks at St Foy de Montgomery and St Germain de Montgomery 112
3.24 The lands of Roger de Montgomery in 1086 113

4.1 A survey of the castle at Ardres 117
4.2 The motte and shell-keep at Durham 119
4.3 Plan of the earthworks at Le Puiset 124
4.4 Earthworks at Mount Ferrant 125
4.5 Exeter castle gatehouse 130
4.6 Plympton castle 131
4.7 The Rings, Corfe 132
4.8 Bentley and Powderham 133
4.9 Earthworks at Huntingdon castle 134
4.10 Clifford's Tower, York 138
4.11 An eighteenth-century view of the motte at Shrewsbury 139
4.12 Linlithgow Palace 140
4.13 Selkirk motte and bailey 141
4.14 Aerial view of Sycharth 145

5.1 The Bayeux Tapestry: Dol 148
5.2 The Bayeux Tapestry: Dinan 148
5.3 The Bayeux Tapestry: Rennes 149
5.4 The Bayeux Tapestry: Bayeux 149
5.5 The Bayeux Tapestry: Hastings 154
5.6 The Bayeux Tapestry: Hastings 155
5.7 Hastings castle earthworks 156
5.8 Capital from Westminster 157
5.9 a & b) Carving from Modena cathedral 160
    c) Column capital from Abbaye aux Dames, Caen 161
5.10 Timber and stone castles from a fourteenth-century manuscript 162–3
5.11 a) Carving from New Buckenham
    b) & c) Plans of Old and New Buckenham 164
5.12 Timber outworks of stone castles by Simone Martini 165
5.13 The Old Shepherd by Guilio Campagnola 166
5.14 Dampierre le Château 168
5.15 Detail of Castlemilk 169
5.16 A sixteenth-century artillery fort of earth and timber 169

6.1 Harlech Castle 174
6.2 Timber-framed lodgings at Windsor castle 175
6.3 Hollar's view of Windsor castle 176
6.4 A recent survey of Windsor Round Tower 177
6.5 Surviving twelfth-century detail from Farnham Castle 178
6.6 Leicester castle great hall 179
6.7 Hereford bishop's palace hall 179
6.8 Tamworth castle 180
6.9 Reconstruction of timber hourde 181
6.10 Timberwork on north tower at Stokesay 182
6.11 View of north tower at Stokesay 183
6.12 Timber reinforcement at three castles 185
6.13 Timber reinforcement in shell keep at Plympton 186
6.14 Tower at Lorch 186
6.15 Stone footings at Rathmullan 188
6.16 Stone foundation at Totnes 189
6.17 Reconstruction of motte at Farnham 190
6.18 Notre-Dame-de-Gravenchon 192
6.19 Timber and stone walls: a comparison 193

7.1 Y Gaer, St Nicholas 203
7.2 Coed Caeau, Erwood 204
7.3 Hawcock's Mount, Westbury 205
7.4 Bishopston Old Castle 206
7.5 Amaston, Alberbury 207
7.6 Acton Bank, Lydbury North 208
7.7 Cefn Bryntalch, Llandyssil 209
7.8 Tenbury Wells 210
7.9 Cwm Camlais Castle, Trallerg 211
7.10 Eglwys Cross (or Mount Cop), Bronington 212
7.11 Tomen Castell, New Radnor 213
7.12 Bishop's Moat, Castlewright 214–15
7.13 Pains Castle 216
7.14 Tomen Y Rhodwydd, Llandegla 217
7.15 Hen Domen, Montgomery 217
7.16 a) & b) Hockleton, Chirbury 218–19
7.17 Moel Frochas, Llanrhaeadr-ym-Mochnant 220
7.18 Wilmington, Chirbury 221
7.19 a) & b) Castell Crugerydd, New Radnor 222–3
7.20 Tomen Bedd Ugre, Llandewi Ystradenny 224
7.21 Rhyd Yr Onen, Llangurig 225
7.22 a) & b) Moat, Llandinam 226–7
7.23 Aberllynfi Castle, Gwennyfed 228
7.24 Kingsland 229
7.25 a) & b) Lingen 230–1
7.26 More, near Lydham 232–3
7.27 a) & b) Castell foel Allt, Pilleth 234–5

7.28 Caer Penrhos, Castell Cadwaladr, Llanrhystyd   236
7.29 Caus Castle, Westbury   237
7.30 Colwyn Castle, Glascwm   238
7.31 British Camp, Malvern   239
7.32 Chartley Castle, Stafford   240
7.33 Twt Hill, Rhuddlan   241
7.34 Powys Castle and Lady's Mount   242
7.35 Castell Cwm-Aron, Llanddewi, Ystradenny   243

8.1 Tandslet plan and elevation   246
8.2 Nes stave church, Norway   247
8.3 Plans of Nes stave church   248
8.4 Nes stave church   249
8.5 Isometric drawing of Nes stave church   250
8.6 Foundations of the church at Nes   251
8.7 Wooden window opening at Nes   252
8.8 St Peter's church, Pirton: tower   253
8.9 Pembridge bell tower   255
8.10 Interior of Pembridge bell tower   254
8.11 Interior of Pembridge bell tower   254
8.12 Mamble church tower, isometric drawing   256
8.13 Mamble church tower   256
8.14 Mamble church tower   257
8.15 Navestock belfry   258
8.16 Timber belfry, Brookland   259
8.17 Interior of Yarpole bell tower   260
8.18 Yarpole bell tower   260
8.19 Detail of Yarpole bell tower   262
8.20 Detail of Yarpole bell tower   262
8.21 Pembridge market hall   263
8.22 Posts of Pembridge market hall   263
8.23 a) & b) Mirville, France   264
8.24 Mirville: phases VII, VIII and IX   265
8.25 Mirville: reconstruction of house VII   266
8.26 Mirville: wooden tower with stone foundations   266
8.27 Comparison of plans from Notre-Dame-de-Gravenchon and Mirville   267
8.28 Der Husterknupp, Germany, period I   268
8.29 Der Husterknupp, period II   269
8.30 Der Husterknupp, period IIIA   269
8.31 House 3, Der Husterknupp   270
8.32 House 3, Der Husterknupp   271
8.33 Reconstruction of periods I, II and III at Der Husterknupp   272
8.34 Plan of Hoverberg, Germany   274
8.35 Launceston   275
8.36 Launceston SW bailey   276
8.37 Lydford, Devon   277
8.38 Barnard Castle ringwork   278

8.39 South Mimms, reconstruction of the motte   279
8.40 Therfield   280
8.41 Goltho: plan of period 6   282
8.42 Goltho: reconstruction of the motte   283
8.43 Goltho: motte and bailey castle plan   283
8.44 Goltho: reconstruction of the motte and bailey castle   284
8.45 Goltho: period 7   285
8.46 Goltho: reconstruction of the hall, c.1150   286
8.47 Prudhoe castle, phase 3   287
8.48 Reconstruction of Stafford castle   289
8.49 Detail of reconstruction, Stafford castle   290
8.50 Detail of reconstruction, Stafford castle   290
8.51 Detail of reconstruction, Stafford castle   291
8.52 a) Tamworth, isometric drawing of bailey defences   292
     b) Reconstruction of rampart at Tamworth   294
8.53 a) Abinger motte b) Plan of Abinger motte top   295
8.54 Reconstruction of structures on Abinger motte   296
8.55 Castle Bromwich plan of structures   297
8.56 Plan of Sandal castle   299
8.57 Great Hall and kitchen, Sandal   300−1
8.58 a) & b) Sycharth   302
8.59 Llantrithyd castle ringwork   304
8.60 Cae Castell phases   305
8.61 Cae Castell, period I   306
8.62 Cae Castell, period II   306
8.63 Cae Castell, period III   307
8.64 Cae Castell, period IV   307
8.65 Cae Castell, period V   308
8.66 Cae Castell, period VI   309
8.67 Castle Tower, Penmaen   311
8.68 Keir Knowe of Drum   313
8.69 Castlehill of Strachan   314
8.70 Peebles Castle Hill   316
8.71 Barton Hill, Kinnaird   317
8.72 Clough Castle   319
8.73 Lismahon, Co. Down   321
8.74 Lismahon, sequence of structures   322
8.75 Lismahon, reconstruction of house and tower   323
8.76 Weoley Castle, Birmingham   324
8.77 Weoley Castle, development of wooden building   325

9.1 Provisional plan of Hen Domen   327
9.2 Hen Domen: the context of the site   327
9.3 Location map of Hen Domen   328

ILLUSTRATIONS

9.4 Hen Domen: the earliest castle   332
9.5 Hen Domen: Phase X, *c.*1150   336
9.6 Reconstruction of Phase X, Hen Domen,
     *c.*1150   337
9.7 Hen Domen: Phase Y, late twelfth to
     early thirteenth century   339

9.8 Hen Domen: Phase Z, *c.*1223–1300   340
9.9 Hen Domen, provisional plan of the
     motte top   342

11.1 Numbers of excavated sites in Great
     Britain and Ireland   354

Preface

The purpose of this book is to restore timber castles to their rightful place in the history of fortification; to show that they were not temporary versions of stone castles, but were formidable strongholds which dominated their surrounding landscapes, sometimes for centuries. Because they have, without exception, disappeared, leaving only their earthworks and the elusive traces of their timber foundations, they have been little understood, even by the most eminent historians of the medieval period. A reassessment has depended chiefly on detailed excavated evidence, almost all of which has only become available within the last thirty years.

Although timber castles were both numerous and widespread, explaining and illustrating their importance involves some difficulties. All the relevant categories of evidence – in the field, below ground, in documentary and pictorial sources – are deficient in some way. The authors' familiarity with this evidence varies, from that literally dug up with our own hands to that known only indirectly through the work of others. The danger of writing from a wide array of secondary sources in several languages, mixed with published (and sometimes unpublished) primary evidence, is considerable. If sometimes we have misconstrued, or omitted, the results of work carried out by colleagues, often working far away, then the fault is ours, not theirs. In conception this is a work of collaboration, and we have both con-

tributed in some measure to all parts of it. More specifically, chapters 1–6 and 10–11 are by RAH, and chapters 7–9 by PAB.

Relevant work has been published since we stopped gathering information. On Germany, of which our treatment is brief, there is a two-volume survey of German castellology, *Burgen der Salierzeit* (Thorbecke, Sigmaringen 1991) and the July–September 1991 issue of *Archäologie in Deutschland*, some of which concerns castle research. On the British Isles, there is Norman Pounds' *The Medieval Castle in England and Wales* (Cambridge 1990), Michael Thompson's *The Rise of the Castle* (Cambridge 1991) and Brian Graham's 'Twelfth and Thirteenth Century Castles in Ireland', *Fortress*, 9 (May 1991). The fruits of the Royal Commission's labours on castles in South Wales have also now been published: *RCAHM (Wales). Glamorgan, vol. III, part 1a. Medieval Secular Monuments: the Early Castles from the Norman Conquest to 1217* (HMSO 1991).

We hope that this book will be readable in two ways. The text is self-contained, and may be followed by some readers without constant reference to the notes. For such readers, a few of the more important published items are listed as 'further reading' at the end of the book (though in some chapters the material does not lend itself easily to this). For readers who do wish to use them, the notes identify the published evidence and indicate where particular points may be pursued. Unless otherwise stated, the place of publication of works cited is London. Some repetition in the notes of different chapters has been tolerated to save the interested reader the chore of constant cross-reference.

We have inherited a much-respected tradition of castle authorship published by Batsford. Hugh Braun's *The English Castle* (1936, 1943) and R. Allen Brown's *English Medieval Castles* (1954), which appeared in later editions (3rd and final, 1976) as *English Castles*, became deservedly famous works. Both covered the whole subject in a broad way. More recently has been published Tom McNeill's *The English Heritage Book of Castles* (1992). Ours is a more specialized contribution, in a field which, appropriately, all our predecessors recognized as important.

Acknowledgements

Without the help of numerous friends and colleagues this book would not have been published. C.R. Musson and C.J. Spurgeon respectively made available the aerial photographs and site surveys for chapter 7. The late R. Allen Brown offered his translations of various chronicle passages as the basis for ours, and D. Trotter advised on, including translation of, the poet Wace. H.M. Colvin, A.D. Saunders and J.R. Kenyon helped with sixteenth-century sources. On English and French matters we are indebted to B.K. Davison; on Wales to C.J. Spurgeon, C.R. Musson and J.R. Kenyon; on Scotland to G. Stell, C. Tabraham and D. Pringle; on Ireland to T. Barry, A. Hamlin, C. Lynn and T. McNeill; on Normandy to D. Bates, J. le Maho and J. Decaens; on Spain to P. Banks, R. Hitchcock and A. Longhurst; on Poland to W. Piotrowski and L. Kajzer; on Germany to D. Barz; on Japan to J. Critchley; and on America to D. Croes. B. Morley, C. Currie, B. Kerr and J. Pidgeon advised on some surviving timber structures. J. West, L. Grant, E. Rose, P. Rutledge and M. de Bur made invaluable comments on some of the pictorial evidence. Further assistance with points of detail is acknowledged in the notes. Our friend and colleague John Allan read most of the text at a late stage in its development and made many valuable comments. Despite all this assistance, shortcomings undoubtedly remain: they are wholly are own.

Many have unknowingly contributed in different ways through discussion spread over many years, and countless excavators have contributed to three decades of work at Hen Domen. The text and illustrations of chapter 9 are an amalgamation and revision of two earlier publications: P.A. Barker & R.A. Higham, *Hen Domen, Montgomery: A Timber Castle on the English-Welsh Border. Excavations 1960–1988: A Summary Report* (Hen Domen Archaeological Project 1988); and P.A. Barker, 'Hen Domen revisited', in *Castles in Wales and the Marches: Essays in Honour of D.J. Cathcart King* (eds. J.R. Kenyon, R. Avent, Cardiff 1987), 51–4.

We are grateful to A.D. Saunders, editor of the journal *Fortress*, for providing an opportunity to discuss in advance the material and ideas of this book in R.A. Higham. 'Timber Castles – a Reassessment', *Fortress*, 1 (May 1989), 50–60.

Peter and Pamela Scholefield drew the plans for chapters 7 and 8, and Sean Goddard drew all remaining figures which are not direct reproductions from earlier publications. Lesley Bryant organized and edited the information in the Gazetteer, and David Hill, of Exeter University's Project Pallas, produced its computer-generated diagram. Jennifer Warren, Lesley Botham and Christine Priddy word-processed various drafts of several chapters. To all these we express our gratitude.

Thanks are due to all those authors, editors and publishers who have permitted the reproduction of their published illustrations.

Brief ascriptions are given in the captions, and full publication details in the notes and Gazetteer.

Thanks are also due to the following for permission to reproduce unpublished material, for which full details are given in the captions and notes: British Library; Royal Library, Windsor; Ashmolean Museum, Oxford; Courtauld Institute of Art; English Heritage; CADW; Scottish Monuments; RCAHM, Wales; RCAHM, Scotland; RCHM, England; The Archaeological Survey, Dept. of Environment, Northern Ireland; Stafford Borough Council; Exeter Museum Archaeological Field Unit; Brian K. Davison.

Abbreviations

Antiq. J.   Antiquaries Journal
Archaeol. Aeliana   Archaeologia Aeliana
Archaeol. Camb.   Archaeologia Cambrensis
Archaeol. Cant.   Archaeologia Cantiana
Archaeol. J.   Archaeological Journal
Armitage 1912   E. Armitage, *Early Norman Castles of the British Isles* (1912)

BAR   British Archaeological Reports
Barker and Higham 1982   P.A. Barker, R.A. Higham, *Hen Domen, Montgomery: A Timber Castle on the English-Welsh Border* (Royal Archaeol. Institute Monograph, 1982)
Beds. Archaeol. J.   Bedfordshire Archaeological Journal
Berks. Archaeol. J.   Berkshire Archaeological Journal
Brown 1976   R. Allen Brown, *English Castles* (3rd ed. 1976)

Ch.G.   Château Gaillard: études de castellologie médiévale (Vol. I Caen, Vol. II Cologne, Vol. III London & Chichester, Vol. IV Ghent, Vols. V–XIII Caen) (dates cited are year of publication, not conference)
Cornish Archaeol.   Cornish Archaeology
Curr. Archaeol.   Current Archaeology

EHD   English Historical Documents
EHR   English Historical Review

Fournier 1978   G. Fournier, *Le château dans la France médiévale: essai de sociologie monumental* (Paris 1978)

J. Brit. Archaeol. Ass.   Journal of the British Archaeological Association

Kenyon and Avent 1987   J.R. Kenyon and R. Avent (eds), *Castles in Wales and the Marches: Essays in Honour of D.J. Cathcart King* (Cardiff, 1987)
King 1983   D.J.C. King, *Castellarium Anglicanum: An Index and Bibliography of the Castles in England, Wales and the Islands* (2 Vols., New York, 1983)
KW I, II   The History of the Kings Works: Vols. I and II: the middle ages, eds. H.M. Colvin, R.A. Brown, A.J. Taylor

(2 Vols. and plans, 1963).
Vol. III: 1485–1660 (Part I), eds. H.M. Colvin, D.R. Ransome, J. Summerson (1975)
Vol. IV: 1485–1660 (Part II), eds. H.M. Colvin, J. Summerson, M. Biddle, J.R. Hale, M. Merriman (1982)

Med. Archaeol.   Medieval Archaeology
Mortet and Deschamps   V. Mortet, P. Deschamps, *Recueil des textes relatifs à l'histoire de l'architecture et la condition des architectes en France au moyen âge* (Paris, 2 Vols. 1911, 1929)

Proc. Battle Conf.   Proceedings of the Battle Conference on Anglo-Norman studies
Proc. Brit. Acad.   Proceedings of the British Academy
Proc. Cambs. Antiq. Soc.   Proceedings of the Cambridge Antiquaries Society
Proc. Devon Archaeol. Soc.   Proceedings of the Devon Archaeological Society
Proc. Hants. Field Club Archaeol. Soc.   Proceedings of the Hampshire Field Club and Archaeological Society
Proc. Soc. Antiq. Scot.   Proceedings of the Society of Antiquaries of Scotland
Proc. Somerset Archaeol. Nat. Hist. Soc.   Proceedings of the Somerset Archaeology and Natural History Society
Proc. Suffolk Inst. Nat. Hist. Archaeol.   Proceedings of the Suffolk Institute of Natural History & Archaeology

R.C.A.H.M.   Royal Commission on Ancient and Historical Monuments
R.C.H.M.   Royal Commission on Historical Monuments
Renn 1973   D.F. Renn, *Norman Castles in Britain* (2nd ed., 1973)

Salch 1979   C.L. Salch, *Dictionnaire des Châteaux et des Fortifications du Moyen Age en France* (Strasbourg, 1979)
Soc. Antiq. Res. Reps.   The Society of Antiquaries of London Research Reports

Trans. Bristol Gloucs. Archaeol. Soc.   Bristol and Glouces-

15

tershire Archaeological Society Transactions

Trans. Devonshire. Ass. *Transactions of the Devonshire Association*

Trans. Dumfries. Galloway Nat. Hist. Antiq. Soc. *Transactions of the Dumfriesshire and Galloway Natural History and Antiquaries Society*

Trans. Essex Archaeol. Soc. *Transactions of the Essex Archaeological Society*

Trans. Glasgow Archaeol. Soc. *Transactions of the Glasgow Archaeological Society*

Trans. Shrops. Archaeol. Soc. *Transactions of the Shropshire Archaeological Society*

Ulster. J. Archaeol. *Ulster Journal of Archaeology*

V.C.H. *Victoria County History*

— 1 —

Timber castles: their study and background

Archaeology

Castles are among the best known and most studied archaeological features of the landscape. Scholarly research into their history and archaeology has developed continuously from the nineteenth century, and in particular instances even earlier, to the present day. Few medieval subjects (churches being the obvious comparison) have been so commonly chosen by the authors of 'popular' works. Books on castles proliferate. What then, is the justification for the appearance of yet another? We believe the quantity of publication to be misleading, for large numbers of volumes say more or less the same thing, their contents deriving from earlier works and from field examination of the obvious and better known monuments. Out of the general volumes available the serious student turns largely to the work of only a handful of modern authors. Moreover, it seems to us that there is an imbalance in virtually all general treatments of the subject, which favour the better preserved stone-built sites to the neglect of many others. To some extent this is understandable. The stone castles are easier to illustrate, to analyse in physical terms and to arrange in a sequence of development over the centuries. They are commonly better documented, making it easier to explain their origins and histories. Such castles, however, owe their prominence in modern literature largely to the fact that they were built of stone

and are consequently better preserved above ground. The same accident of history is responsible for the grand image of stone which is the prevailing popular idea of the castle (fig. 1.1). But, up to the thirteenth century, and sometimes beyond, large numbers of castles, perhaps even a majority, were not built of stone, but of timber, clay, cob, wattle and daub, thatch and shingle, none of which materials leaves positive traces except under particular (and in the British climate, rare) conditions of preservation. For castles built in any or all of these materials the inadequate phrase 'timber castle' will be used throughout.

It would be wrong to imply that timber castles have received no attention whatever from the authors of general books. Two recent continental publications, by Hermann Hinz, *Motte und Donjon* (Cologne 1981), and W. Hermann, *Le Château Préfabriqué au Moyen Age* (Strasbourg 1989) treated some aspects of timber castles more fully than is usual. In Britain there have been some relevant publications since the important work carried out at the beginning of this century (see below). For example, in *The English Castle* (1936), Hugh Braun pointed out the importance and variety of 'castles of earth' as he called them, and in 1937 he published a separate article on the subject. The influential excavation at Abinger (Surrey) by Brian Hope-Taylor resulted not only in a published excavation report (1950) but also in an article (1956)

1.1 Places such as Caernarfon, built by Edward I in the late thirteenth century, provide much of the castle's popular image.

which ranged more widely in the subject.[1] It is not, however, unfair to say that they have received compressed treatment in comparison with other castles, and sometimes the timber castle offered to the reader has been more or less imaginary, or at least concocted from minimal evidence. Modern works on castles have neglected this aspect of the subject relative to their treatment of stone castles, though some do acknowledge its importance, notably the late R. Allen Brown in his *English Castles* (3rd ed. 1976). A book in which timber sites are given adequate attention is J.R. Kenyon's *Medieval Fortifications* (Leicester 1990), an excellent recent survey which analyses the archaeology of castles rather than their architecture, and H. Clarke's *The Archaeology of Medieval England* (1984, chapter 4) provides a better-than-average discussion of the subject.

An important distinction must be made,

however, between published discussion of the structural evidence of timber castles on the one hand and of the earthworks which commonly accompanied them on the other. The latter subject has indeed received considerable attention both from individual writers and from organizations such as the Royal Commissions on Historic Monuments. The present book is not primarily about the fieldwork of castle earthworks, partly because their classification has been relatively well treated, but also because earthworks were common components in castles of all sorts, stone as well as timber, late as well as early. Discussion of earthworks is not, of course, excluded since they normally provided the framework within which the builders of a timber castle were working and since some structures (a motte or a rampart, for example) might be a mixture of earthwork and timber construction. In some excavations discussed below important information has been retrieved from within the earthworks. Accordingly, a chapter (7) is devoted to the earthworks, not least to emphasize how varied in shape and size the sites could be.

Their study also helps reveal the landscape context of timber castle sites, as well as their relationship with adjacent settlements. Recent survey of the extensive earthworks at Stafford castle, for example, reveals not only the enormous extent of this initially timber castle, to whose motte-top was eventually added a stone keep, but also the fact that it incorporated an outer settlement (fig. 1.2).

A major concern here has been to bring together the structural evidence for timber castles which is at present scattered in numerous publications (chapter 8). The bulk of this evidence has been recovered in excavation, and much of it is the 'negative' or 'ghost' evidence of post-holes and comparable features. Sometimes timber survives in the ground, but not commonly. Also uncommon,

but nevertheless important, is the survival of some early timberwork above ground which helps in the process of general reconstruction (chapter 6). Non-archaeological sources include a small amount of pictorial evidence (chapter 5), and a body of documentary material which helps particularly in problems of dating and identifying sites but which also contains useful descriptions (chapter 4). Nevertheless, we should not be surprised to discover that many of the sites in question have little documented history, a further

1.2 Detailed surveys of sites built originally of timber, such as Stafford, can reveal not only the complexity of the castles themselves, but also their relationship with adjacent settlements (courtesy of Stafford Borough Council).

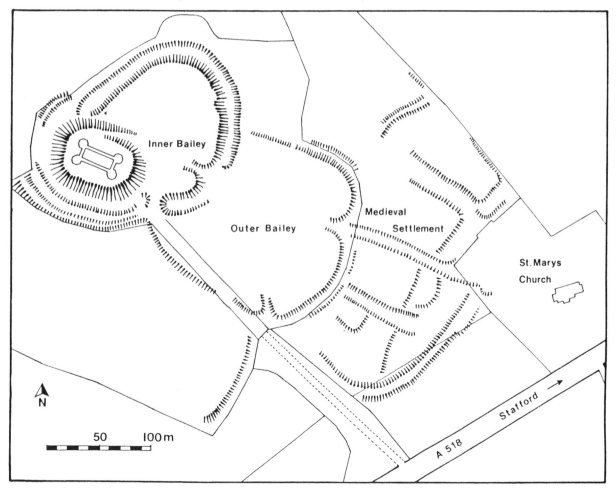

reason for giving attention to their physical analysis.

The authors' interest in this subject arose from the excavation at Hen Domen, Montgomery (Powys), a timber and clay castle on the Welsh border (see chapter 9). We were impressed by the diversity of the evidence available from this and other sites which suggested from the start that timber castles were no less fascinating and individual than stone ones. We were, in contrast, unimpressed by the absence of any general treatment of this evidence and concluded that there was a gap in the enormous literature on castles which needed filling. We hope this book goes some way towards filling that gap. Since, however, the timber castle was a widespread phenomenon in the medieval world the task of filling it comprehensively would be an enormous undertaking. The evidence is found as far afield as Ireland and Poland, Denmark and Italy, and the potentially available material is much greater than we have been able to assemble here. We have tried to be reasonably thorough within the British Isles, but our inclusion of European material is highly selective. Nevertheless we feel some European perspective is better than none at all. We have, in any case, taken the view that the most important requirement is to include those sites upon which some discussion and interpretation can be offered, rather than provide a comprehensive catalogue of Euro-post-holes. There is, it must be admitted, no rationality in the geographical or chronological spread of the available structural evidence. With few exceptions there has been little general research strategy. In the 1950s and 1960s A. Herrnbrodt, M. Müller-Wille and others carried out excavation and fieldwork on mottes and other sites in the Rhineland, including der Husterknupp, der Hoverberg and Haus Meer (Büderich). This work, mainly associated with the Rheinisches Landesmuseum at Bonn, led to a number of important publications.[2] In the same period, D. Waterman undertook investigations on mottes in Northern Ireland. These excavations, at such sites as Lismahon and Clough, were published individually[3] as well as in more summary form in the deservedly famous An Archaeological Survey of County Down (Belfast, HMSO 1966). His work created an interest in the subject which is still actively pursued by his successors in that area. In England, the 900th anniversary of the Norman Conquest led to renewed discussion of castle origins, and in 1967 the Royal Archaeological Institute established a research project on 'The Origins of the Castle in England'. The excavations carried out at Bramber, Hastings, Hen Domen, Sulgrave and Baile Hill (York) were published a decade later, though at that date work remained incomplete at some of the sites.[4] Finally, while excavations in Northern France were being pursued in the 1960s, it is the more recent work at such places as Mirville and Gravenchon (Seine Maritime), and Grimbosq (Calvados) which have revealed the complexity of sites in this area, so crucial to the development of the early castle. In 1980, a major colloquium at Caen was devoted to the subject of medieval earth and timber fortifications.[5] Despite all this effort, the researches so far undertaken have not collectively tackled the problems of timber castles' origins, physical forms, development and decline.

Much larger is the number of sites from which some evidence has been recovered. Over 100 are listed in the Gazetteer for Great Britain and Ireland (chapter 11), itself probably not comprehensive. Yet these are only a small minority of the total number of monuments whose earthworks represent castles which were always, or were at least initially, built of timber. Even within the numbers excavated, much of the evidence has been recovered on a small scale and the sites from which any general picture of timber castles emerges are relatively few.

We have largely confined ourselves to what

most people would understand by the word 'castle', that is the private defended residence of the kings and ruling classes of medieval society. Full treatment of, for example, the early Irish rath or the later medieval 'moated site' is not included. Similarly excluded are Carolingian fortifications built against Saxons and Northmen, or German ones built against Magyar and Slav. From time to time, however, reference is made to such sites where comparisons seem helpful. In our discussion of the origins of timber castles we have inevitably touched upon some controversial matters about the origins of the castle itself. We are, however, concerned primarily with a particular sort (or rather sorts) of site. The evidence suggests that a variety of forms was built from the earliest days of the castle to the last, and the demonstration of this variety seems to us to be more important than arguing about whether the earliest castle ever built was of stone or of timber, or whether or not it had a motte. There will, in any case, never be reliable answers to such questions. Finally, our title deliberately omits the word 'the'. We are aware that despite the importance of these sites they were not a category wholly separate from other sorts of castle, a point which is treated more fully in the discussions on origins and the relationship of timber and stone castles. Builders of castles tried to achieve similar defensive and residential ends, though on widely differing scales. Their choice of building technique was influenced by a number of considerations: time and resources for building, permanence of use and available raw materials. Whatever the end result, whether a tiny earth and timber motte or a massive stone keep, it was a castle. There is little evidence that contemporaries were interested in, or even recognized, the physical categorization to which modern archaeologists and historians are accustomed. The endless variety in detail, which close examination of castles reveals, suggests it was their individuality which

concerned their designers and which struck observers. The sites dealt with here represent part of that broad spectrum of individuality.

Extensive excavation of timber castles is a relatively modern development, essentially post-Second World War, though earlier examples of motte explorations can be found. In the 1920s Bruce Oliver excavated (stone) structures on the motte at Barnstaple (Devon). In 1935, Gerald Dunning examined the entire motte-top at Alstoe Mount, Burley (Rutland), though the results were unrewarding. Soon after, Gordon Childe found evidence of a thirteenth-century timber palisade and tower on a rocky motte at Doonmore (Co. Antrim). From 1935–9, F. Jervoise examined some two thirds of the motte surface at West Woodhay (Berkshire) though the work was not published until many years later and the evidence suggested a stone rather than a timber structure.[6] The general appreciation of such sites has, however, a much longer ancestry and some excavations took place in the nineteenth century. General Pitt-Rivers dug the earthworks at Caesar's Camp, Folkestone, in 1878, and Colonel Morgan dug those at Bishopston, Gower, a few years later (figs 1.3, 1.4 and 7.4). Morgan also recognized the motte at Swansea for what it was and carried out rescue work during its destruction in 1913. One of the earliest explorations was perhaps at Penwortham (Lancashire), where a timber structure within a probable motte was explored in the 1850s. Elsewhere, mottes were sometimes excavated when mistakenly identified as prehistoric barrows, as at Twmpath, Rhiwbina (South Glamorgan) which was examined by the Cambrian Archaeological Association in the previous decade. In Germany, the establishment of a medieval date for some earthworks was beginning, for example at the excavation of Hilden, near Düsseldorf, published in 1888.[7]

Another early contribution to timber castle studies came not, however, from excavation, but from the general acceptance, around the

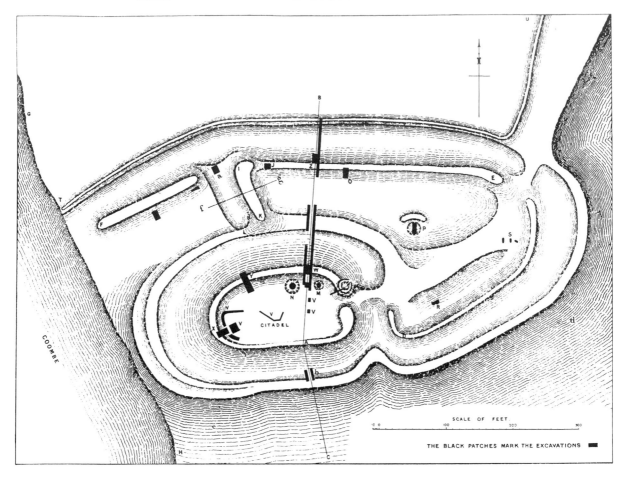

1.3 Pitt-Rivers' plan of his excavation at Caesar's Camp, Folkestone (Kent) (after *Archaeologia*, 47, 1883).

turn of the century, of the medieval date of large numbers of earthworks which previous generations had often supposed to be pre-historic, Roman, Anglo-Saxon or Viking. Excavation naturally helped advance this proposition, by demonstrating their date, as at Caesar's Camp and Bishopston, through the recovery of medieval artefacts. Of Caesar's Camp, Pitt-Rivers wrote, 'the general char-acter of this earthwork, with a citadel in one corner, is Norman, and the fact of its being unwalled is no reason for considering it earlier than that period.' But in more general terms, the systematic description and illustration of

large numbers of earthwork sites, mottes and enclosures, put timber castles on the map for all time. Important English publications in-cluded Adrian Allcroft's *Earthwork of England* (1908) and J.P. Williams-Freeman's *An Introduction to Field Archaeology as Illustrated by Hampshire* (1915). In the same period the *Victoria County Histories* were employing, together with simple plans, the classification of earthworks proposed by the Congress of Archaeological Societies in 1903, which included mottes, with or without baileys, and a variety of enclosure sites (fig. 1.5). In 1908 a Royal Commission was issued for the making of an inventory of 'Ancient and Historical Monuments and Constructions' in England. The resulting surveys, and their subsequent counterparts elsewhere in Britain, stimulated

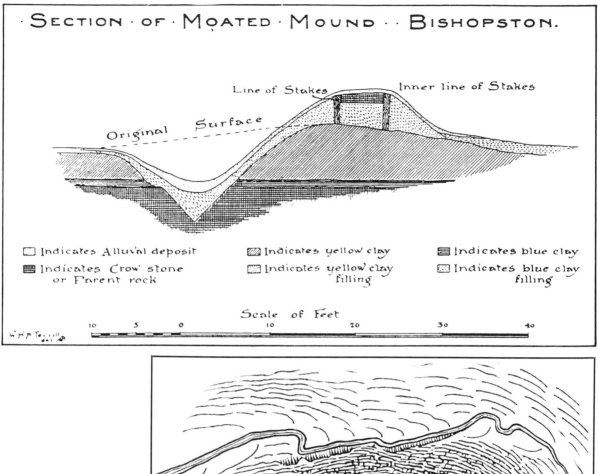

·SECTION·OF·MOATED·MOUND··BISHOPSTON·

Line of Stakes   Inner line of Stakes

Original   Surface

☐ Indicates Alluvial deposit
☰ Indicates Crow' stone or Parent rock
▨ Indicates yellow clay
▦ Indicates yellow clay filling
☰ Indicates blue clay
▦ Indicates blue clay filling

Scale of Feet

10   5   0   10   20   30   40

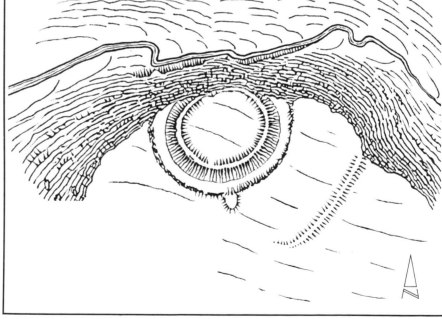

1.4 Morgan's sketch survey of the ringwork at Bishopston and his section of the rampart showing positions of internal timbers. The exact location of the section is not known, but it is probably in the centre of the southern arc of the rampart (*Arch. Camb.*, 16, 1899).

critical fieldwork on castle earthworks which still continues (fig. 1.6). The RCAHM in Wales, for example, has compiled comprehensive information on early castles of all sorts as part of its coverage of Glamorgan. This

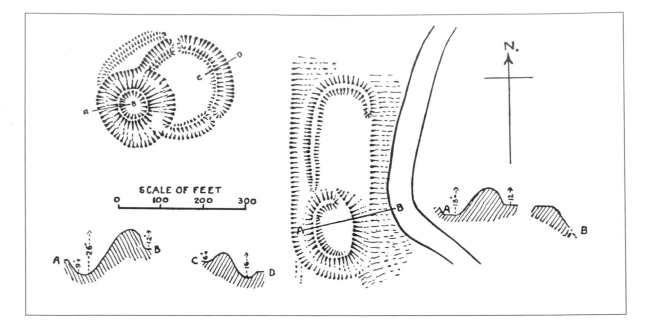

1.5 Early-twentieth-century survey of castle earthworks at Wembworthy (Devon) (*Victoria County History of Devon*, 1905).

comprises fieldwork and survey, combined with documentary study and (where available) excavated evidence, the whole set against its geographical and historical background. The data used in this, and other RCAHM work in Wales, has been drawn upon in the compilation of chapter 7.[8] Similarly, in the Republic of Ireland, the office of Public Works treats castle earthworks in its county survey programme, of which the most recent product is the *Archaeological Survey of County Louth* (Dublin 1991).

The work carried out around the turn of the last century emphasized the importance of castles other than the great stone monuments whose architectural study was already well established. Earlier exponents of fieldwork and topographical study seem not to have been very interested in castle earthworks *per se*, perhaps because so many had no documented history. Mottes and other earthworks which carried obviously medieval masonry were, however, noted. Of the motte at

Tamworth, for example, John Leland wrote: 'the dungeon hille yet standith, and a great round tower of stone on it'.[9] When, in the later nineteenth century, castle earthworks received more critical treatment, their medieval date was revealed through excavation in only a few cases. For the most part their dating depended upon a typological argument, which in turn had a documentary basis: a sufficient number of sites had documentary dating to make it probable beyond reasonable doubt that others with broadly similar plans were also of similar date. Crucial to the promotion of this line of argument was the work of Mrs Ella Armitage, whose published articles, culminating in her renowned *The Early Norman Castles of the British Isles* (1912), refined the dating of castles generally and in particular showed that mottes were Norman castles, not, as previously argued by some, the *burhs* of the *Anglo-Saxon Chronicle* (fig. 1.7). This great book, which acknowledged the debts owed to Pitt-Rivers, Allcroft and other earlier workers, laid the general foundations of timber castle studies by putting their earthworks in a proper historical context and arguing the likely timber origins of many

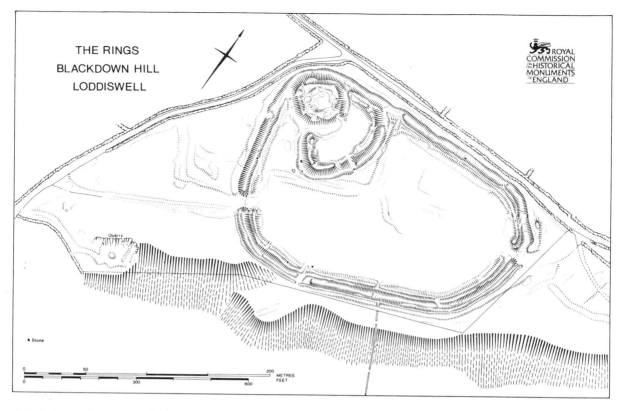

1.6 (*Above*) A late twentieth-century castle earthwork survey – Blackdown Rings, Loddiswell (Devon) (courtesy of C. Dunn and RCHM, England).

1.7 (*Below*) Contrasting burh and castle plans as presented by Ella Armitage for (a) Wallingford and (b) Wareham (Armitage 1912).

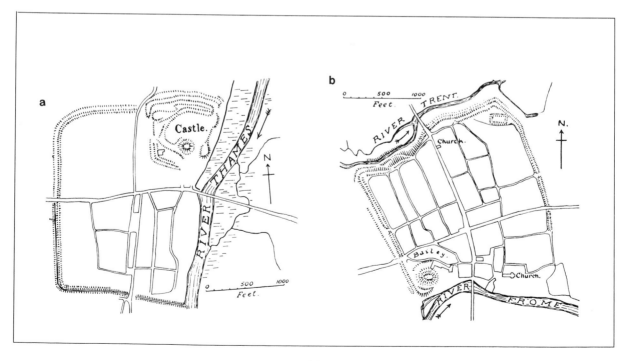

castles whose visible remains are of stone. 'These earthworks', wrote Mrs Armitage, 'are castles, in the usual sense of the word; that is the private fortified residences of great landowners.' In passing, Mrs Armitage also observed other points crucial to the subject. For example, despite her insistence on the importance of mottes she also recognized the importance of enclosure castles. And despite her keenness to explain the origin of castles (of all sorts) she also recognized that timber castles had a long history stretching up to the thirteenth century and even later. Not the least of her achievements was pointing out the relevance of contemporary documentary and pictorial evidence to the study of sites whose timber superstructures had long vanished. All these lines of enquiry are pursued below.[10]

History

Like so much of the archaeology of the Middle Ages timber castles have an historical as well as an archaeological side to their study. In the sense that the 'history' of a subject is the study of its documented record, the concept of the 'history' of the timber castle is a limited one. The evidence comprises a patchy and scattered series of references in sources which were never designed to convey to contemporaries, let alone to posterity, a general picture of the subject. This is hardly a topic which a medieval historian would choose to study for its own sake. The interest of the documentary evidence stems from the contribution it makes to a multi-disciplinary study of a difficult subject. The problem lies not simply in the inadequate quantity of this evidence, but also in its inconsistent coverage of the surviving sites. Many, probably a majority, of the earthworks representing timber castles have no documentary history at all. As archaeological monuments they may as well be prehistoric. In many cases probable ownership and approximate date are worked out by studying the documented history of land ownership for the place in which they are situated; the sites themselves may never figure in a documentary source.

This incomplete documentary coverage has broader implications for the dating of the field monuments generally. The motte and bailey is a form of earthwork recognized as medieval in date wherever it is observed in the British Isles and mainland Europe. This recognition relies on the fact that some sites are well dated by documentary record: they may appear in a medieval chronicle, for example, or in some administrative record. In the British context the relevant date range is broadly from the later eleventh to the thirteenth centuries. Using this sample as the framework for dating by typology or classification, a similar date range is inferred for a larger number of other, physically comparable, sites which themselves lack documentation. A similar process applies to the dating of other earthwork forms, notably the heavily embanked enclosures with defended entrances commonly referred to as 'ringworks'. In recent years dating by scientific methods such as radiocarbon assay, dendrochronology and thermo-remanent magnetism has also made an impact on castle studies, though the considerable evidence for reuse of timber in castles (below, especially chapter 4) should act as a warning about over-reliance on individual dendrochronological dates. The application of scientific dating, though important in principle, has so far been relatively infrequent in practice. Broadly speaking the chronology of the subject is still based on the documentary sources, with pottery and other artefacts providing additional evidence from excavated sites.[11] Dating then, is the most common application of documentation to the study of timber (as of other) castles, whether by a direct reference, by the association of known land-ownership or more indirectly by typology.

Closely related to the dating of sites is studying them in their political and social contexts, from the details of individual family histories to broader considerations of regional and national history. No more graphic illustration of this point could be found than in the dense distribution of mottes along the Welsh border (fig. 1.8), the greatest single concentration in the British Isles.[12] Allowance must be made for the inherent deficiency in any such maps, which exaggerate the quantity of activity in the landscape by putting together sites which may not all have been in contemporary use. Nevertheless, the mottes of this area reflect its continuing instability over many generations from the eleventh century onwards. The kings of England, the earls of Chester, Shrewsbury and Hereford and their followers, the marcher lords who succeeded them, the princes of Powys and of other Welsh territories, all these at one time or another competed for supremacy here and created a society in which hostility and insecurity were features of everyday life. Castles large and small proliferated, sometimes of stone but more often of timber, a means both of defending land and property and extending their builders' authority into neighbouring areas. Large numbers of these sites have no specific documentary history. They are assumed to be medieval on the typological argument discussed earlier and their political and social context is studied with reference to the documented history of the region in which they are situated. This can be applied in broad terms, and also in microcosm.

In the Vale of Montgomery (fig. 1.9) a series of small undocumented mottes has been studied against the background of Domesday Book and the resettlement of this troubled area by the tenants of Roger de Montgomery, earl of Shrewsbury, in the late eleventh century. This area also provides more detailed examples of available documentary help in establishing the context of castle-building. The shift of site from the timber castle at Old Montgomery (Hen Domen) to the stone castle at New Montgomery in 1223 is well known,

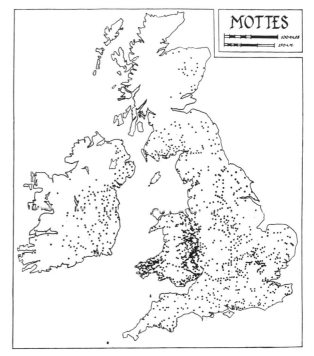

1.8 Derek Renn's famous distribution map of British mottes (Renn 1973).

being attested in both chronicle and administrative sources. Further east along the valley is another pair of sites near Westbury. Caus castle, as it is now known, is a stone-built hilltop castle belonging to the Corbets, one of the marcher families who succeeded to the borderlands of the Norman earldom of Shrewsbury after 1102. Nearby, on lower ground, is the ringwork site of a former timber castle known as Hawcock's Mount, a name which is a corruption of 'Old Caus' (fig. 7.3). Here, as at Montgomery, a stone castle has succeeded a timber one. The date of the move may be suggested by the documented Welsh attack (in either 1134 or 1140), in which Caus was burned, though this cannot be proved with the precision available for Montgomery. Similarly, whereas the foundation date for Old Montgomery is known (between 1070 and 1086), the origin of Old Caus is not. Once

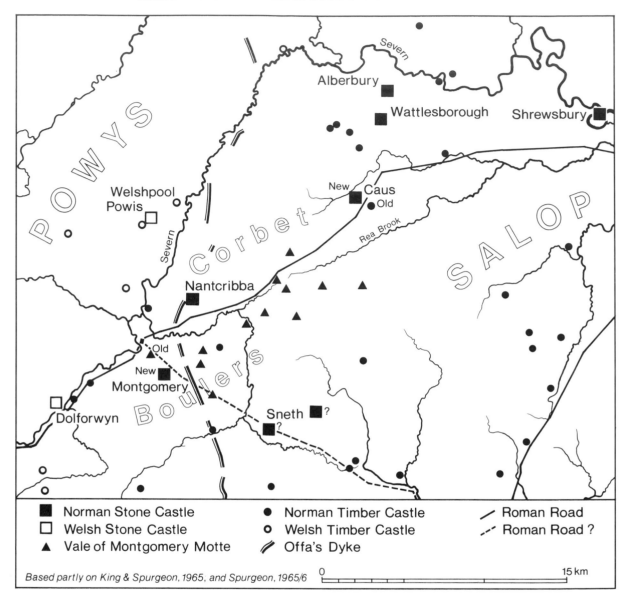

1.9 A local landscape of castles – the Montgomery region of the English-Welsh border, where timber castles proliferated (Barker and Higham 1982).

again, the likely context has to be sought in the political and tenurial history. In the late eleventh century, the Corbets were the most powerful tenants of the earls of Shrewsbury in this area, and Old Caus was probably built as part of the initial Norman settlement of the area. Just as Roger de Montgomery named his new castle after his place of origin in Normandy, so also the Corbets adopted a nostalgic name, derived from the Pays de Caux, for their castle.[13]

In more specific respects, however, the documentary study of timber castles can be rather disappointing, not simply because so many sites are more or less undocumented, but also because the sources reveal little physical detail. Some famous descriptive passages from medieval chronicles will be quoted. These are not, however, typical of the written record. Like so much of the physical side of medieval culture, all but the most spectacular castles were largely taken for granted by contemporaries. The problem is more acute for timber castles than for castles generally, since the relatively early date of so many means they do not figure significantly in the administrative records whose quantity increased from the later twelfth century. The occurrence of timber castles in pictorial sources of various kinds is equally disappointing. Discussion inevitably centres on the famous representations in the Bayeux Tapestry, though an attempt is made below to include other, less well-known examples. The fact is that, were it not for the evidence produced by the excavation of timber castles our knowledge of their general planning, of individual buildings, of building technology and of defensive construction would be negligible.

The case of Hen Domen, Montgomery (Powys), discussed in chapter 9 in detail, demonstrates this argument. It was established by an earl (Roger de Montgomery), occupied for most of its life by a family of marcher lords (de Boulers) and finally taken over by Henry III, an English king: it was a physical product of the top ranks of medieval society. Yet the quantity of direct documentation, as opposed to the more general documentation of the castle's ownership, is very disappointing. There are a few brief references to the site's existence in the late eleventh century and a few equally brief references to its royal occupation and succession by New Montgomery castle in the early thirteenth century. In the longest period of its existence, the twelfth century, there is not a single direct contemporary reference. Some details of this period, mainly of the castle's social organization but also touching on its buildings, can be reconstructed retrospectively from sources produced in the thirteenth century for quite different pur-

poses. But were this site to have been totally destroyed we would not even know from the documentary evidence that it was a motte and bailey, nor would we know that it was entirely built of timber and clay. We would have no idea whatever of the profusion of structures and of the various rebuildings which excavation has revealed.

This line of argument could too easily become a general dismissal of documentary sources in the study of timber castles. This would be quite unfair. Not only is the written evidence crucial to understanding the date and social context of the archaeological sites, it also provides fascinating information from a number of categories of record discussed below. Despite the qualifications made earlier, there is more of this evidence than is sometimes recognized.

Although it is generally excavation which reveals the detail of these sites, this is not always the case, as is demonstrated by two contrasting examples. First the well-known descriptions from twelfth-century chronicles contain information on the superstructure of buildings such as Ardres, near Calais. This information would not necessarily be inferred from excavated ground-plans alone. The latter are notoriously easy to 'under-interpret' in that the potential complexity of internal planning, of elevation and of decorative finish can easily be forgotten. The documentary sources serve to remind us that though timber castles above ground have disappeared, they fulfilled the same functions as the stone castles which still survive and were produced by the same castle-building society. The limited pictorial and structural evidence discussed below emphasizes the same point. Second, excavated evidence does not necessarily amplify all the themes suggested by the documentary evidence. At Hen Domen, while excavation has revealed a mass of structural evidence not even hinted at in the written record, it has not so far revealed much evidence (apart from its heavy defences and one or two of its buildings) which reflects the aristocratic nature of its occupation. The impression given by most of the artefacts is, for whatever reason, a fairly poor one. The documentary evidence provides a vital reminder of the social status of the site which might not be inferred from the results of excavation alone.[14]

The tradition of timber building and defences

Although this book deals essentially with the medieval period, it is necessary also to emphasize the long and widespread nature of the timber-building tradition as a whole, within which timber castles played a part. The application of timber and related materials, as well as of earthworks, to a wide variety of residential and domestic needs is a basic cultural feature of northern and western Europe, of the Slavic lands further east, and of some areas far removed from Europe. In this sense, timber castles were a medieval adaptation of a tradition deeply rooted in prehistory. There has been little attempt, however, to put them in a broader context, except for a chapter entitled 'Forts and Castles' in F.H. Crossley's book *Timber Building in England* (1951).

The differential rate of survival of the various materials available has produced within our present environment a very unbalanced reflection of the medieval landscape of buildings. The twelfth- or thirteenth-century European traveller viewed his or her contemporary scene quite differently. The great castles and churches of stone stood out, then as now. Indeed, they stood out more because the scale of the buildings which accompanied them was generally smaller than today. However, many, and in some areas and periods most, of the other buildings to be seen were not 'stone' structures at all. There were certainly stone buildings to be found – some manor houses, some town houses, and some peasant houses. Nevertheless, building in timber, wattle and daub, clay, cob, turf, thatch and shingles was widespread. Structures made of such materials formed by far the majority and provided an essential characteristic of the landscape which stretched back in unbroken tradition to prehistoric times. Clearly, the use of these materials varied from one area to another according to local conditions of wealth, of culturally transmitted building 'style', and of available physical resources. Where stone was more readily available, then stone building technology might have an earlier impact than in areas where it was rarer, though not necessarily so. If, however, we take a broad European perspective, it is probable that the majority of buildings ever erected, until relatively modern times, were of timber or other perishable materials. Moreover, it is obvious that even 'stone buildings' had important timber components such as roofs.

The importance of this tradition cannot be over-emphasized. It became entrenched in the culture of some areas and transcended other considerations of wealth and available physical resources. Anglo-Saxon England provides a good example. Building stone is not rare in England, though it is not uniformly distributed across the country. The builders of churches exploited it, as well as reusing Romano-British materials. But the evidence of stone churches is not wholly representative, since there were numerous timber versions which have not survived, Greenstead (Essex) being the famous exception. Some timber churches have been excavated, and there are regular documentary references to them up to *c.*1100. They could be fine structures, as a written description of the late pre-Conquest church at Wilton (Wilts) testifies. William of Malmesbury described Alfred's church at Athelney as a centrally-planned timber structure of small area whose main element was supported by four ground-fast uprights. Features of stone church towers such as pilaster strips may reflect the background of timber technology.[15] The secular building tradition remained almost exclusively one of timber. Known exceptions are very few (see below, chapter 2). Stone was used in the royal palace site at Northampton, and a probable royal building at Old Windsor (Berks), in the tower-like structures beside houses of high status at Portchester and Winchester (Hants) and Sulgrave (Northants), and in the recently reassessed late Saxon phase at Eynsford (Kent). In a peasant context there are only the longhouses at Mawgan Porth, which, being in Cornwall, were peripheral to the mainstream of Anglo-Saxon tradition.[16] The inescapable conclusion, drawn from extensive excavation, is that timber was the preferred material of society as a whole. Had kings, in particular, wished to build residences of stone on a regular basis they could have done so: the craftsmen, the raw materials, the directive power and wealth were all available. Although Asser spoke of the halls and chambers built by Alfred of stone and timber, the palaces at Yeavering and Cheddar (in its early phases), as well as numerous rural settlements bear witness to the cultural ascendancy of timber. The normal Old English verb for 'to build' was *timbrian* and the noun *timber* was also a synonym for 'a building'.[17]

The Anglo-Saxons also employed timber and earthworks in fortifications, though here the situation was modified by the survival, reuse and repair of Roman stone walls. But the builders of the great linear earthworks — Offa's Dyke, East and West Wansdyke, the East Anglian dykes — eschewed the use of stone. The new burghal defences of Wessex, and the Mercian examples which preceded them also relied in the first instance on the same technology. Their revetment in stone in some cases was a secondary development which took place later in the pre-Conquest period. When Aethelflaed, Lady of the Mercians, established a base at Chirbury near the border with Powys in 915, the *Anglo-Saxon Chronicle* recorded that she 'timbered the *burh*'.[18] It is hard to escape the conclusion that the Anglo-Saxon adherence to timber building resulted not from restrictions of resources or limited outlook. It resulted instead from a positive commitment to a deeply-rooted cultural tradition, a literary reflection of which can be seen in the halls of Beowulf. It also involved a constructive response to a resource which the English countryside provided in both quality and quantity.

It is, therefore, hardly surprising that timber castles were to flourish in England: the cultural and technological context for their diffusion and maintenance was already well established. But the patterns of post-holes, which are all that remain of most timber buildings until fairly late in the Middle Ages, are a poor reflection of the sophistication which carpenters could achieve. Although fragments survive in otherwise stone sites, no timber castle stands above ground for us to study.

Careful use can be made of surviving timber buildings of other forms — bell-towers, for example — which might convey something of the character of timber castles. Such structures, which are discussed below (chapter 8), are also part of the long tradition of timber building. Other late medieval timber buildings remind us that this technology was not unprogressive. Despite the increasing use of stone in this period, it also saw a blossoming of carpentry techniques, seen, for example, in the development of better roofs and of fully-framed buildings. By the end of the Middle Ages we can see surviving above ground the culmination of a centuries-long tradition. For a substantial period, one of its products had been timber castles.

Other areas of Europe had an equally important timber tradition. In Norway, vernacular architecture remained extensively timber down to the nineteenth century, and at least 200 medieval secular buildings survive, despite the continuous process of renewal. Better known are the timber 'stave churches' (see figs 8.1–7), of which there are about 30 medieval examples in south central Norway, an area which saw less development of stone church architecture than other parts of the country. In southern Scandinavia the fortresses, such as Trelleborg (see fig 3.1), and the trading settlements, such as Hedeby, employed a timber tradition. Northern Europe saw a greater variety of materials used in the early Middle Ages than was the case in England. Stone was employed, for example, in the buildings and enclosures of the fortified island sites of Sweden such as Eketorp. In the Viking world of the north Atlantic and northern British Isles, turf and stone were much used in house construction. This practice was a cultural response to a cold and windswept environment which lacked good building timber.[19] Further east, timber building of all sorts, including churches, was a characteristic feature of Russian culture. The Moscow kremlin, founded in the twelfth century, was a timber fortification until the fourteenth. Apart from its stone kremlin and cathedral, Novgorod was still essentially timber in the seventeenth century, as were the majority of Russian fortress-towns at this date. Some settlements, such as Staraja Ladoga, whose timber fortress was established in the ninth century, were of mixed Viking and Slav origin.[20]

In Germany and the Low Countries timber building was common, as in villages such as Warendorf and the trading centre at Dorestad. Carolingian or other residences, such as the Ottonian palace at Tilleda, employed both timber and stone construction.[21] The situation in France, straddling different cultural zones, was complex, with both timber and stone traditions. On the one hand, there is plentiful early medieval documentary evidence for timber buildings. On the other, the more southerly areas tended to share the Mediterranean stone technology, as is illustrated by the emergence from the later twelfth century of stone-built hilltop settlements, such as the Provençal village of Rougiers (Var), comparable with those produced by the process of incastellamento in Italy.[22] However, it would be very misleading to suggest a simple division into a timber-using north and a stone-using south, as some of the examples quoted above illustrate. The situation was complicated by localized variations and responses to environment, as well as by the growing use of stone by peasant communities in all areas from the twelfth century. Equally, the notion of stone building is itself an over-simplification, disguising important distinctions: between stone buildings proper and those with stone dwarf-walls; and between stone bonded with lime mortar and stone bonded with clay or bedded dry. In these last respects the north-south distinction does have some relevance, the former technique in each case being more characteristically southern.[23]

The traditions of timber and earthwork did not die at the end of the Middle Ages. Earthworks were an important part of artillery fortresses from the sixteenth century, and in addition to the major works, lesser sites continued to be built. Between the Kentish fortresses of Deal, Sandown and Walmer were originally situated circular, ditched earthworks in the ancient ringwork tradition. In Ireland, the early seventeenth century English plantation settlements were frequently defended in timber and earthwork, and some Irish crannogs were also occupied in this period. In Russia, particularly Asiatic Russia, timber fortifications were built into the eighteenth century, sometimes even in the nineteenth.[24] In very recent times, fighting from trenches and dug-outs, reinforced by timber and sandbags (a portable form of earthwork) has been a prominent feature of warfare.

Examples of timber fortification which could be listed span a long period, from prehistoric to modern times. It is not possible here to discuss them all; they are too numerous and widespread. In New Zealand, for example, the Maoris built *pa*, villages defended by earthworks, timber palisades and fighting platforms, from the fourteenth century AD, when castles were flourishing in Europe (fig. 1.10).[25] From the European standpoint, however, two areas are of particular, but contrasting, interest. In America, European settlers frequently employed timber for domestic and defensive building, and found the same tradition among some of the Native American cultures. Although many permanent fortifications, particularly in the east and south, were eventually built of stone, brick or adobe, the timber tradition continued in frontier zones until the second half of the nineteenth century.[26] Earliest among the excavated colonial sites are those at Martins Hundred, an area of English settlement on the James River, near Virginia's original capital at Jamestown (later moved to Williamsburg). Established in 1619, and not occupied after the middle of the seventeenth century, these sites were built exclusively of timber (as was contemporary Jamestown). The main centre, Wolstenholme Town (fig. 1.11), comprised a strong palisaded fort with an adjacent settlement enclosed by more lightly-built fences. The excavated ground evidence, mainly post-holes and construction trenches, was no different in character from that of a medieval timber-built site in Europe. It conformed well with a contemporary description of the Jamestown fort, said to have been defended with a palisade of strong posts and planks, with a tower and gate at each corner.

Second, in late medieval and early modern Japan there developed a castle-building tradition, the social inspiration of which was not dissimilar to that of medieval Europe.[27] Japanese society received some European influence in the later sixteenth century, but Japan's subsequent self-imposed isolation preserved many of its ancient institutions until the mid-nineteenth century. Fast developing by the later twelfth century, Japanese feudalism rested upon familiar foundations – a manorial system, and a noble, mounted, military class of landowners. By the later Middle Ages, castles proliferated in the properties of these landed warriors. Earthen and timber-built enclosures, sometimes with a central tower, overlooked their agricultural

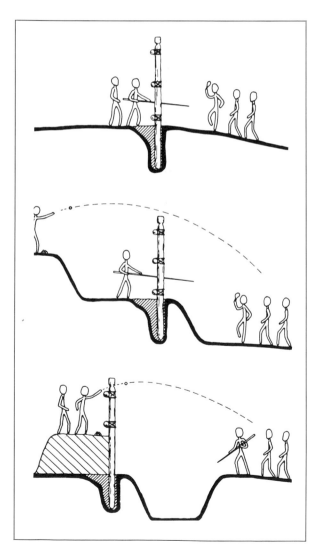

1.10 Ramparts and fighting platforms of a Maori pa (A. Fox, *Prehistoric Maori Fortifications in the North Island of New Zealand*, 1976).

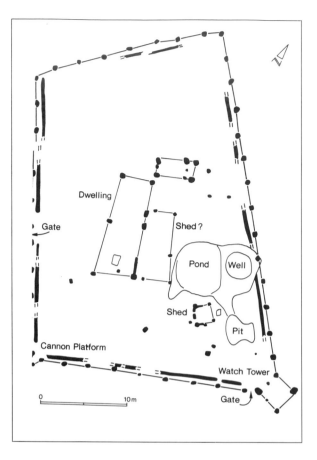

1.11 Plan of a timber fort built by settlers at Wolstenholme Town, Martin's Hundred, Virginia (after I. Noel-Hulme, *Martin's Hundred*, 1982).

estates from a nearby hilltop. Frequently, they were used only in a military crisis, and the lord's permanent residence lay in a more sheltered position. More spectacular, however, were the castles built in the late sixteenth and seventeenth centuries, when smaller numbers of much larger, residential fortresses were built as new centres of military and economic power. These sites, frequently palatial in scale with landscaped interiors, were often a component of new urban developments. They might be accompanied by outer defences of stone and earthwork, made necessary by the introduction of artillery, and the lower parts of major buildings were also of

stone. But their superstructures, commonly of light timber and plasterwork with much decoration, created a distinctly non-European type of timber castle. Tower keeps, in particular, represented the height of contemporary Japanese secular architecture (fig. 1.12).

Conclusion

The traditions of building in timber employed in different periods and places were not all identical. In some parts of the world, where straight-growing trees were abundant and could be trimmed whole or in part, timber was employed as logs. This technique was developed long ago for houses and defences in northern and eastern Europe, as well as more recently in North America. Such structures, in which the logs were often laid horizontally with simple halved joints, were literally 'timber' – they included no significant use of other materials. Elsewhere, where such supplies were less abundant, trees could be split to make massive planks. In stave construction a wall was built of contiguous vertical members, again consuming much raw material. This technique was extensively used in western Europe in the early Middle Ages. Alternatively, principal posts could be spaced at wider intervals, infilled with panels of wattle and daub or clay. While less suitable for defensive purposes than for domestic, nevertheless excavation has revealed significant use of clay construction in timber castles. Finally, a distinction should be made between timber buildings with earthfast posts set in post-holes or trenches and those with a framed superstructure resting upon sill beams or even a dwarf-wall of stone. The latter require more sophisticated carpentry and in domestic buildings in western Europe seem to be a twelfth-century and later development. The construction of timber defences may have followed a similar evolution. But at Hen Domen there is evidence, both from the ground and from some preserved timbers, of framed construction early as well as late in the site's occupation. In the documentary discussion (chapter 4) there is considerable evidence of prefabrication from the twelfth century, with some possibly earlier examples.

The long-lasting and widespread nature of these timber building traditions provides a clear context for the study of timber castles. The following chapters are a demonstration that timber was not, as sometimes argued, 'an unsuitable material for permanent fortification'.[28] Timber defence was regarded as normal, not necessarily a second choice to stone. We are concerned here firstly to demonstrate the importance of timber castles in terms of numbers, as a proportion of the total landscape of castles. Second, we aim to show that timber castles played a major role in the castle's general history over a long period. Timber castles were not second-rate, temporary fortifications, superseded quickly and comprehensively by stone ones. Early timber castles could be long-lived, rebuilt many times (and perhaps never in stone), and new ones were still being built when massive and sophisticated stone castles were increasingly common. A general rehabilitation of timber castles is long overdue.

1.12 Timber castle on stone foundations at Nagoya, Japan (after P. Orui, M. Toba, *Castles in Japan*, 1935; drawn by Mike Rouillard).

— 2 —

Origins of timber castles in the British Isles

Wider problems

The titles of this and the following chapter are carefully phrased. The available evidence, historical and archaeological, will not provide simple answers to the questions: how, when, and why did timber castles first appear? The discovery of major new documentary sources is improbable and the available accounts are uneven in coverage. Sizeable though the total quantity of historical references to timber castles is, the majority of such references are irrelevant to the problem of their first appearance. Commonly we are told that a castle existed at a certain time, but less often exactly when it had been first established. Infrequent, too, is documentary information on the physical form which early sites took. Neither can the data accumulated from numerous excavations be offered in general explanation of the problem. The experience of excavation suggests very strongly that the physical character of timber castles was no less individual than that of their substantially stone counterparts. Just as excavation reveals an array of structural design and detail, it also reveals a wide variety of development, from sites' first foundations to their eventual abandonment. A further problem with the excavational approach is that the survival of a castle's earliest phase, so crucial to an understanding of origins, cannot be guaranteed. It may well have been largely destroyed during later works. The survival and uncovering of the early, and sometimes pre-castle levels at several sites has been a bonus which could not be assumed in the advance planning of any excavation. Even where early phases do survive, they may not be datable within the critical limits required. There will never be sufficient evidence, historical or archaeological, to address adequately such questions as when *exactly* was the motte added to *this* site, or (in an English context) from which side of 1066 does *this* phase originate?

Assumptions about chronology based on fieldwork alone have been shown on numerous occasions to be quite wrong. The surviving field monument represents the sum of the site's total development. Not only may later phases have masked or destroyed earlier ones, but also non-contemporary stages of development may be indistinguishable from each other, the long process of erosion and decay having brought about an apparently uniform, single-phase site. This is particularly a danger with timber castles never rebuilt in stone, which lack the helpful evidence of datable architectural features. The classic example is where a motte looks like a primary feature of a site, but is shown by excavation to be either a secondary addition or a gradual growth. Also dangerous are assumptions about field monuments based upon a perceived historical context rather than actual documentary or archaeological dating. Some sites in Normandy formerly thought to be early eleventh century in date have been shown by excavation to have reached their final (and therefore visible) form nearly a century later. Some Irish sites which looked like Norman mottes turned out on excavation to be earlier, native mounds.

Just as there was no single 'type' of timber castle (as indeed the timber castle itself was hardly a 'type' of castle) they are unlikely to have had a single point of origin and certainly had no single line of development. In the same way that the title of this volume is 'timber castles' rather than 'the timber castle' so also we must think of 'origins' rather than 'the origin'. Understanding the varied origins of timber castles is one of the most challenging aspects of their study, and we can only at present consider their general historical contexts, rehearse the relevant documentary references and describe those excavations where crucial information has been re-covered. This evidence does little more than illustrate possible lines of development, and there is room for much more research on this topic.

A point of great importance is that timber castles emerged in separate areas over a long span of time. It is therefore necessary to examine, both socially and physically, dif-ferent origins in different places. This in turn raises another important issue: the relation-ship of timber castles with the traditions of defence already prevailing in each area. This relationship could be specific, where an existing site was transformed into a timber castle; it could also be more general, where the prevailing tradition affected the ease with which timber castle building was adopted or the general form which it took. In what follows these points will be considered territory by territory.

The distribution of sites in these various areas is clearly relevant to their social origins. In broader terms the eventual overall distri-bution of timber castles is also a reflection of environmental influences. In his *Earthwork of England* (1908) Adrian Allcroft showed not

only a very good appreciation of the varied form of timber and earth castles but also a sound grasp of their distribution in the British Isles, north-west France, and parts of Germany, Denmark and Italy. In a charac-teristically useful passage in *Early Norman Castles of the British Isles* (1912) Ella Armitage made similar observations, adding that where we find mottes in more southerly areas they are often adapted natural outcrops rather than conventional man-made mounds.[1]

Although more recent research has refined our distribution maps, extending the known distribution of sites eastwards in particular, this picture is still essentially true. A simple illustration of the environmental influence is to be found in the westerners' crusading experience. Despite their familiarity with timber castles at home, the permanent (as opposed to siege) fortifications they built in the Near East were substantially of stone from the start: stone was plentiful, whereas good timber was scarce.[2]

The environmental influence on castle building traditions was also at work in more localized ways. The Low Countries, while not lacking stone castles, suffered a relative lack of building stone which encouraged the use of timber at an early date and subsequently the use of brick, which was employed on castles from the thirteenth century.[3] South-west England, on the other hand, while not lacking timber castles, did not enjoy such a wide-spread rural timber building industry as did English areas further east. Here some of the very earliest castles made use of stone tech-nology, as well as of mottes erected on natural rock outcrops, and the subsequent popularity of circular keeps and shell-keeps may have reflected (as in South Wales, where the fashion was similar) a relative lack of ashlar for good quoins.[4] More generally, however, north-west Europe and the British Isles provided an environment well endowed with the raw materials of timber fortification. And, equally important, their centuries-old employment of this tradition created a context in which timber castles could flourish.

The origins and early history of castles generally are likely to remain veiled in a good degree of obscurity. And since timber castles were among the earliest, possibly *the* earliest castles, a study of their origins becomes partly a study of the wider subject. In the traditional view of castles, their origins are inextricably linked with the development of what, since the seventeenth century, has been called 'feudalism'.[5] The technology of building in timber and earth was, however, enjoyed by many societies, not only in 'feudal' Europe. Although military technology is sometimes viewed as a major indicator of cultural differences – the traditionally accepted view of mottes is an example – the study of timber castles, in all their forms, tends to emphasize broad similarities of habit rather than differences of principle. The organization of warfare by similar higher social classes wielding power across widespread territories ensured a willingness to adapt or even copy neighbouring practices: the Welsh princes, for example, did not forgo the advantages of castle-building on the basis of their Celtic, 'non feudal' ancestry.

Nevertheless it is interesting to observe not only the similarities but also the differences of detail between one area and another. Such comparisons, both social and physical, will become apparent in what follows, and sometimes they touch upon issues crucial to the origins of timber castles. This emerges, for example, in the discussion of Ireland, where raised-earthwork and timber sites may have developed independently of northern French 'feudal' influence. This in turn raises the (rather unanswerable) question: did such an area develop *castles* independently, or are we not to regard such sites as *castles* until a later date when they were more strictly comparable with others elsewhere and part of a more widespread social and political system which historians define as feudal? In provoking such issues, the study of timber castles may help

create a broader cultural perspective than does that of stone castles whose surviving architecture dates mainly from the period when castles were already well established. In this sense, the study of timber castles can stimulate the most basic of all debates to be found in castle studies: what is a castle? Can it be defined by its purely physical attributes regardless of social context? Or is the social context the essential criterion, the physical attributes merely the by-product of available technology and building tradition?

It is for this reason that the following discussion begins not with France, the home of the castle in the traditional view, but with the British Isles. Here the interplay of native and imported culture, and the problems this raises for the study of castles, can be examined better than anywhere else. Moreover, the varied experience of England, Wales, Scotland and Ireland, in their earlier development as well as in their confrontation with Norman invaders and settlers, provides useful contrasts between immediately neighbouring areas.

England

The Norman Conquest and English castle origins have become so closely connected in the customary view of the subject that it is difficult to avoid starting a discussion with the Norman Conquest. While it is undeniable that this led to major English developments, the tendency to link the two automatically together can blur other, equally important themes. It has been normal to argue, for virtually the past century, that Anglo-Saxon and Norman attitudes to defence were quite distinct. Anglo-Saxon *burhs* were communal fortifications for the common good, often used in defence against the Vikings. Norman castles, on the other hand, were private fortifications, not only instruments of conquest, but also physical expressions of a society organized for war against constant external threats and internal tensions. This sharply defined antithesis, whose best known exposition is in the work of Ella Armitage, marked a major step forward when first developed, replacing a muddled view of the subject in which mottes had often been identified with Anglo-Saxon *burhs*. It has been of enormous influence ever since, and is still, with remarkably few refinements, the accepted orthodoxy.[6] But, as is often the case, the original statement had in places a subtlety lost in its subsequent repetition. Careful reading of *The Early Norman Castles of the British Isles* reveals an awareness that Norman society and its castles were still developing at the time of the Conquest.[7] Later, the thesis simply became that of a fully feudal Norman society imposing its ideas, normally in the form of mottes and a few spectacular stone castles, on a more centrally-organized Germanic society.

It is a fascinating, if somewhat unproductive exercise to speculate how English society might have developed had the Norman Conquest not occurred. The 'counterfactual' view of history argues that in order to understand the effects of one thing upon another one has to 'undo' the known effects. According to R.W. Fogel's *Railroads and American Economic Growth* (Baltimore 1964), for example, in order to understand the impact of the introduction of railways upon the modern American economy one must consider this economy without the railways: other possible ways in which it might have evolved must be envisaged.

In an age when the 'invasion hypothesis' is less favoured as an explanation of change than it was when clear ideas on castle origins were first developed, it is interesting to apply this 'counterfactual' notion to Anglo-Norman England. The Norman impact on England, and eventually on Wales, Scotland and Ireland, was profound in some respects, negligible in others. The top end of society was transformed. The substratum of society, and the bulk of its material culture, was affected

much less. Because castles were a product of the upper levels of society, any discussion of early castles in England will have a 'Norman' flavour. It is impossible, to pursue the railroads analogy, to reconstruct an early-twelfth-century England without the Normans. Nevertheless, one or two general considerations are relevant. First, there is an (albeit limited) amount of archaeological evidence for defended private residences in late Saxon England. The crucial phases at a small number of excavated sites, to be discussed fully below, could be the surface of a much larger quantity of evidence lying concealed beneath sites which as field monuments appear to be 'post-Conquest'. Second, despite the traditional view that strong English kingship resisted the political fragmentation prevailing in the former Carolingian empire, there is also an increasing view of late Saxon England as a society dominated rather by lordship, lordship which had essential components of land-holding, of military service and of personal fealty.[8] Although 'private warfare' did not characterize late Saxon England, the circumstances which might have led to a desire for private security were certainly not lacking. The problem of the Vikings, though first resolved by the 950s through the reconquest of the Danelaw, was reopened in the wars of Ethelred II's reign. And England's unity under Edward the Confessor is easily exaggerated: the far north remained separatist, the earldoms created by Cnut grew in power and sometimes challenged the king, and tensions between the native and Norman elements at court created a major political crisis in the early 1050s.[9]

From the late Saxon period there is also growing evidence for reorganization of rural estates, at least in some parts of England, into the more organized manorial system of later times. This had implications not only for the idea of lordship, but also perhaps for the pattern of residence of the land-holding class.[10] In other words, if we take a European view rather than a narrower Norman-English comparison, we might find in late Saxon England a society developing along lines which elsewhere we would regard as 'feudal' – in fact one regional variant in a feudal Europe which was by no means uniform – and in which the 'castle' would be perfectly acceptable. Though the hypothesis is quite unprovable, England may have been moving gradually in a direction in which it was suddenly pushed at a far greater rate by the Norman Conquest and its aftermath. Nor should we forget that conquests are not the only means by which ideas and practices are transmitted. The Norman Romanesque style first came to England through the peaceful medium of royal patronage, in the reign of Edward the Confessor. Comparable in scale and design to Jumièges and other Norman churches, the rebuilding of Westminster was probably conceived around 1050, when Norman influence at Edward's court was strong. Sufficiently advanced to be dedicated in 1065, it was completed in the Conqueror's reign.[11] It is also possible, therefore, that, without a Norman Conquest, English kings and their noble followers would have adopted the castle-building and other habits of their European neighbours, though with what speed and in what manner it is impossible to guess.

Late Saxon England certainly displayed features conducive to the eventual spread of castles. There was already a tradition of labour provision for work on fortifications as well as of the earth and timber technology which so many castles employed. Even the distinction between *burh* and castle may not always have been as significant as normally supposed. Although they were very different in size and form, their functions were sometimes similar. Late Saxon kings used *burhs* not only in defence but also in attack and colonization, as in the reconquest of the Danelaw. The Normans made a similar use of castles, which, together with monasteries and new boroughs, became a means not only of conquest but also of colonization, of extension of influence.[12] Although we are accustomed to think of *burhs* as 'public' and castles as 'private', the distinction is not always as clear in practice as in principle. Late Saxon town defences certainly protected people, sometimes with notable success, as in Exeter's 18-day resistance to the Conqueror himself, but the West Saxon *burhs* had initially been royal military sites, with garrisons raised through obligations to the kings. Many royal castles of later centuries, 'private' according to the accepted view, were also primarily military strongholds, and their provision of sometimes lavish residences does not alter this fact. In another sense, too, the *burh*–castle parallel in function, though not in form, is striking: *burhs* were ultimately royal, even if, as in the foundation of Worcester in the 890s by the ealdorman Ethelred, someone acted on the king's behalf. Later on, despite the proliferation of castles in England, there was also a strong belief that all fortifications were ultimately royal and that castles not established personally by kings should be sanctioned by royal authority. The same theory applied in Europe, where the kings of France, and the counts and dukes of former Carolingian territories, also regarded themselves as overlords of all castles. In this respect, the notion of the so-called 'private' castle begins to break down, though it meant a great deal when castles were built, or held, by their occupants against their overlords.[13]

When more specific documentary and archaeological evidence is examined, however, these aspects of possible continuity run into difficulties. It is undoubtedly a fact that the Normans built large numbers of castles in a short time. Domesday Book mentions about 50, others appear in a variety of other written sources (fig. 2.1), and an unknown number of undocumented sites in the landscape also belongs to this period. In contrast, docu-

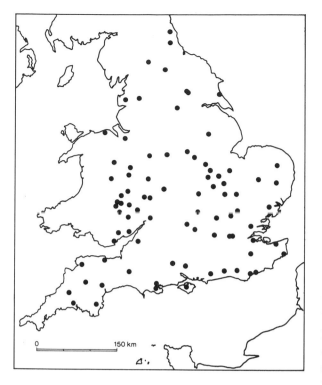

2.1 Castles in England and the Welsh border with documentary evidence before 1086 (after Renn 1973).

to be held (for a time) against attack. Moreover, the site as a whole, within which this building stood, was also defensible, since its gates were closed against the attackers. It is referred to as a *burh*, a word which despite its better known connotation as a defended town could mean any sort of enclosed place. The late seventh-century laws of Ine of Wessex refer to enclosed residences belonging to both ceorl and king, and the laws of Alfred cater for sieges of private houses in warfare. Place-names containing the *burh* element abound, and deserve greater study. Many of them are irrelevant to this theme, referring to ancient fortifications near the places concerned. Others were Middle English formations of later date, when 'bury' came to mean manor house, fortified or not. Many other *burh* elements in compound names, however, are likely to denote Anglo-Saxon enclosed houses.[16] The second passage, for the year 900, concerns a West Saxon royal residence at Wimborne (Dorset). This, too, was at least partly defensible, for in the incident described the gates could be securely barricaded against its opponents.

We might expect royal residences at the very least to have been defensible as matters of practicality and prestige, but the archaeological evidence suggests this was not necessarily the case. At Cheddar (Somerset) (fig. 2.2) the successive ditches to one side of the site were primarily for drainage, and the tenth-century ditch and fence which flanked another side of the site seem to have had little defensive capability. But it is not impossible to imagine the action at *Meretun* taking place there. At Yeavering (Northumberland) (fig. 2.3) the Anglian palace buildings lay outside the adjacent palisaded enclosure, whose true purpose and relationship with the rest of the site remain somewhat enigmatic: it seems to have been a much-rebuilt survival from the British phase of the site.

At Doon Hill, Dunbar, 40 km (25 miles)

mentation and excavated evidence for pre-Conquest private castles is sparse, and the orthodox view of the Norman origin of English castles still holds sway. Nevertheless, the 1960s saw a stimulating challenge to the orthodoxy, led particularly by Brian Davison, and some of the ideas which emerged are incorporated here.[14]

There is, admittedly, a distinct shortage of helpful pre-Conquest documentary evidence. Two passages in the *Anglo-Saxon Chronicle* are, however, of great interest.[15] The first, for the year 757, contains an account of a skirmish at a West Saxon royal residence called *Meretun*. The unusual length of this passage arises from its origin in a piece of prose saga, orally transmitted and eventually written down. It is clear that this residence contained a building (*bur*, bower) which was individually strong enough

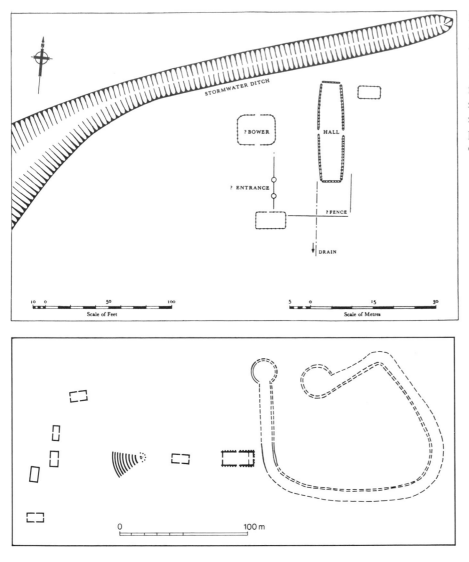

2.2 Simplified plan of late-ninth-century phase at Cheddar royal palace (Somerset) (after *KW I,* 1963). The tenth-century fence and gateway were situated on the eastern side. (2.2 and 2.3 with permission of the controller of HMSO.)

2.3 Simplified plan of late-seventh-century royal palace at Yeavering (Northumberland) (after *KW I,* 1963).

from Edinburgh, a British site was redesigned as a palisaded enclosure. It contained a timber hall of such similarity to those at Yeavering that it may reasonably be associated with the Northumbrian expansion to the Forth in the seventh century.[17] At Tamworth (Staffs), the ditched enclosure pre-dating the tenth-century *burh* defences may represent the lightly-defended perimeter of the presumed Mercian royal palace. The urban royal palaces in London (moved to Westminster by Edward the Confessor),

Gloucester and Winchester are not known to have been defended, though presumably they were enclosed in some way. The Bernician kings had a stronghold on the promontory at Bamburgh. Although its form is not known, it was remembered in later tradition as a place originally fortified in timber.[18]

The *Anglo-Saxon Chronicle* is more forthcoming, however, in its account of certain fortifications associated with the Norman 'favourites' of Edward the Confessor. In the troubled period of English court politics from

1051–2, reference is made to certain establishments normally assumed to be castles as conventionally defined because the word used for them was *castel* (see Appendix B). Although the identification of the places referred to is far from certain, two are commonly equated with Clavering (Essex) and Ewyas Harold (Hereford and Worcester). There was at least one more (anonymous) example in Herefordshire, and in the same county a case can also be made for Hereford itself and also for Richard's Castle. This evidence has been interpreted as a deliberate royal plantation of castle-building Normans, mainly near the Welsh border, whose (presumably new) fortifications so impressed the native English that they were singled out for special mention (fig. 2.4). They have become, in the traditional argument, the exception which proves the rule: foreign castles in an English landscape otherwise devoid of them.[19] While not denying the impression which these men and their 'castles' made on contemporaries, this evidence needs a more cautious approach than it is normally given. All it 'proves' is that whatever these men built struck the English as notable. It does not prove that the English themselves were never in the habit of living in defensible residences. What may have been very different, however, was the physical form that the buildings of these 'foreigners' took, whether experimental, or already traditional across the Channel.

The English word *burh*, in any of its shades of meaning, was apparently not appropriate for them. Though it is tempting to speculate whether the unusual feature of these sites was a motte (and it was about now that mottes were apparently emerging in Normandy – see below, chapter 3), their archaeology is not particularly helpful (figs 2.5–7). Excavation on the motte at Richard's Castle produced

evidence only of a much later date, and its origin was not established. Hereford castle was extensively destroyed in the eighteenth century. Recent excavation there stimulated speculation on the whereabouts of the earlier site. It seems either to have been under the massive castle created by Henry III, or astride the pre-Conquest town defences on the mound now known as Hogg's Mount. The castle at Ewyas Harold has a motte, but this demonstrates nothing since without excavation it cannot be shown to be a primary feature. The early work may in any case have been lost in the rebuilding of the site to which Domesday Book refers.[20] The whole issue of these early castles, though much discussed and heavily relied on in support of the

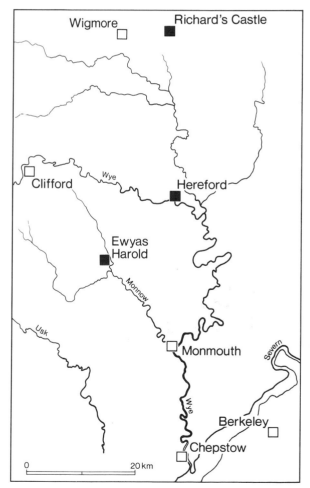

2.4 Documented castles of 1051 (■), together with those of the immediately post-Conquest years in the earldom of Hereford (after D. Renn, in *Ch.G.* I, 1962).

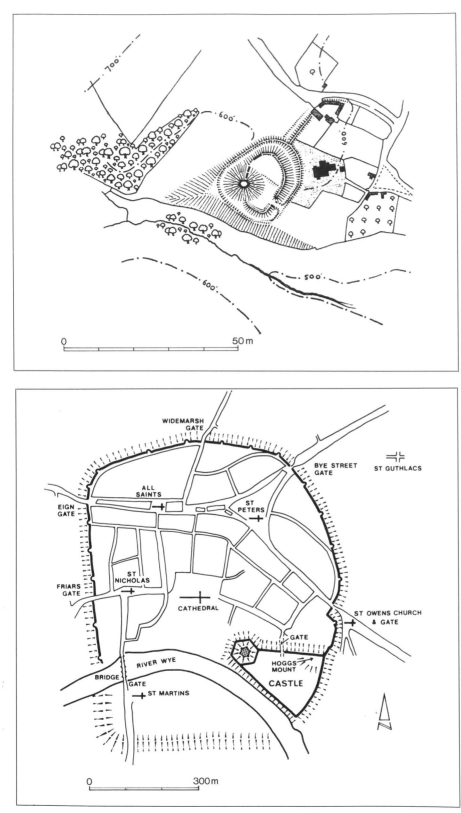

2.5 Richard's Castle (Hereford and Worcester), which perhaps overlies a site of *c*.1050 (after *RCHM. Herefordshire*, vol. III, 1934).

2.6 Thirteenth-century Hereford. The pre-Conquest castle may have been under the later castle mound or at Hogg's Mount (R. Shoesmith, *Hereford City Excavations*, vol. I, 1980; courtesy of City of Hereford Archaeology Committee).

'Norman' interpretation of English castle origins, remains undecided. We know nothing about the sites, assuming their accepted identities to be correct, at all. Given the prevailing tradition of late Saxon secular building technology, upon which their construction would have depended, we can, however, reasonably presume them to have been mainly of timber.

A further piece of pre-Conquest evidence comes from a compilation about social status dating from the early eleventh century.[21] It contains a passage explaining how a freeman (ceorl) might become a noble (thegn): 'And if a ceorl prospered, that he possessed fully five hides of land of his own, a bell and a *burhgeat*, a seat and a special office in the king's hall, then was he thenceforth entitled to the rights of a thegn.'

Although available in published form since early in this century, the possible relevance of this source was drawn into the debate about castle origins only in the 1960s. It was argued that the *burhgeat* could be the entrance to a defended residence, the elusive private *burh* of the thegnly class.[22] One version of the text includes also a church as a thegnly attribute, which certainly makes sense – parish churches often originated as private churches on secular estates. On the other hand, is it revealing anything about the early eleventh century? The whole piece is written in the past tense and its opening words are 'Once it used to be that people and rights went by dignities, and councillors of the people were then entitled to honour, each according to his rank, noble or peasant, retainer or lord.' It might be a nostalgic record of conditions long since past. And where had those conditions applied? The compilation, comprising five texts, is thought to have been a private one, associated with Wulfstan, Archbishop of York (1002–23). It may therefore have

Northumbrian, but not general significance. Another of the associated texts related to Northumbria specifically, and two to Mercia. It was certainly not part of a royal law-code. Also worrying is the somewhat 'ritual' character of the phrase 'bell and burhgeat' (which continued to occur, together with other Anglo-Saxon phrases, in Latin charters of the twelfth century). Could this refer to the line of social demarcation associated with the entrance to the aristocratic residence, even the dispensation of justice at the thegn's door, rather than to any defensive qualities? The notion, embodied in the well-known Victorian hymn, of 'the rich man in his castle, the poor man at his gate' has been of long-lasting impact. At this time, however, it was not the case that 'God made them high or lowly, and ordered their estate', as the text shows. Prosperous ceorls could become thegns, and a further passage reveals that prosperous merchants could do the same.[23]

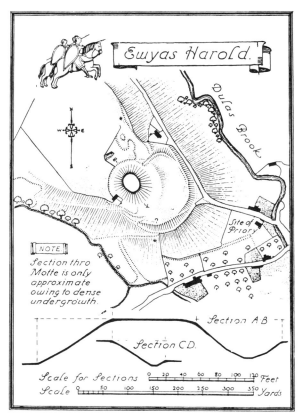

2.7 Ewyas Harold (Hereford and Worcester), which perhaps incorporates a pre-Conquest castle (*RCHM. Herefordshire*, vol. I, 1931).

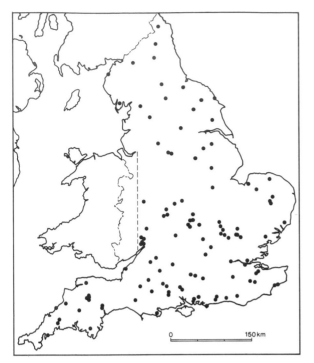 

2.8 (*Left*) Distribution of ringworks in England; (*Right*) Distribution of mottes in England (after D.J.C. King, L. Alcock, in *Ch.G.* III, 1969).

It is not necessary to look in comparable documentary detail at immediately post-Conquest England. The evidence for the widespread building of castles is incontrovertible. The narratives of William of Poitiers, whose panegyric account of William the Conqueror's career was written within a few years of the Conquest, and the *Anglo-Saxon Chronicle*, which continued to reflect English attitudes, relate the consistent use of castles from the landing of William's army onwards. Domesday Book included mention of about 50 in 1086. This is too low a figure. The great survey was not particularly concerned with castles, and other sources refer to sites not given there, bringing the documented total before c.1100 to about 90.[24] It is difficult to estimate the total number of castles, of whatever sort, built in the Conqueror's reign. There are too many undocumented castles, now surviving only as earthworks for the most part, whose exact date of origin is not known. The accompanying table and maps (figs 2.8a and b) show the approximate distribution of early castles, of mottes and of enclosure castles or ringworks, which were eventually established. Though the distributions of mottes and ringworks are not uniform, there appears to be no simple explanation of the choice between the two types of site (fig. 2.9). Apart from the apparently consistent use of enclosures in 1066–8 (see below), there appears to be no chronological significance in the distinction, which may simply have reflected the personal preferences of the builders. The period they cover extends through the twelfth century, later still in individual instances. Defining a figure for the specifically timber castles is impossible because the proportion of excavated sites is so small, but there are about 625 mottes and ringworks in England.[25]

Of particular interest is the narrative of Orderic Vitalis, whose *Ecclesiastical History* was written in the early twelfth century at the monastery of St Evroul in Normandy. His

TABLE. Numbers of mottes and ringworks in the English and Welsh counties, based on King 1983 (see also fig 2.9).

While useful in a general sense, these figures are to be treated with caution. Some sites have been destroyed, others are difficult to categorize, and at others excavation has show how a site's eventual appearance may differ from its original form. King's analysis recognizes that some timber castle sites are neither mottes nor ringworks, and defy classification. Neither do these earthwork forms necessarily represent only timber castles – at some stone remains are evident, and such sites are included in these numbers since they probably started as timber castles. The reader is referred to King's decriptions of the sites themselves. The figures include sites with and without baileys.

County	Motte	R'work	County	Motte	R'work
Anglesey	1	1	Lincolnshire	14	4
Bedfordshire	15	4	London/M'sex	3	0
Berkshire	11	0	Merionethshire	12	1
Brecknockshire	19	6	Monmouthshire	30	5
Buckinghamshire	17	2	Montgomeryshire	32	4
Caernarvonshire	7	1	Norfolk	9	7
Cambridgeshire	2	8	Northamptonshire	13	7
Cardiganshire	20	7	Northumberland	15	3
Carmarthenshire	30	7	Nottinghamshire	7	1
Cheshire	10	1	Oxfordshire	6	1
Cornwall	3	5	Pembrokeshire	18	19
Cumberland	5	2	Radnorshire	31	2
Denbigh	6	4	Rutland	5	0
Derbyshire	5	2	Shropshire	70	15
Devonshire	14	9	Somerset	11	3
Dorset	1	3	Staffordshire	6	0
Durham	3	1	Suffolk	15	2
Essex	16	6	Surrey	6	1
Flintshire	13	0	Sussex	11	6
Glamorganshire	18	17	Warwickshire	12	2
Gloucestershire	15	5	Westmorland	3	0
Hants/Wight	5	10	Wiltshire	9	8
Herefordshire	66	7	Worcestershire	5	0
Hertfordshire	12	3	Yorkshire	41	10
Huntingdonshire	4	0	Channel Islands	1	1
Kent	10	6	Isle of Man	2	0
Lancashire	13	2	Scilly Isles	0	0
Leicestershire	14	1	Lundy Island	0	0

Anglo-French parentage, together with the passage of time since the events of the Conquest, gave him a sense of the historian's detachment. He included in his treatment of these years, in particular the events of 1068, a much-quoted passage:

To meet the danger the king rode to all the remote parts of the kingdom and fortified strategic sites against enemy attacks. For the fortresses [*munitiones*] which the French call castles [*castella*] were scarcely known in the English provinces, and so the English, in spite of their courage and love of fighting – could put up only a weak resistance to their enemies.

This clear statement has normally been given much credence, and the 'very few' castles to which he referred are often identified with those, discussed above, associated with various Frenchmen in 1051–2. This association may be reasonable, but Orderic's partly-English background (his father was a chaplain to Roger de Montgomery, earl of Shrewsbury,

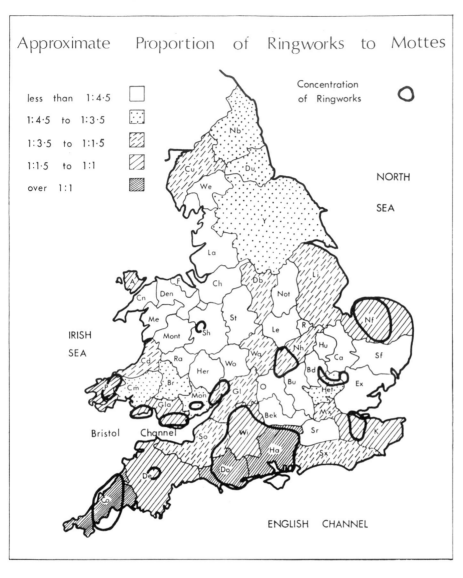

2.9 Proportions of mottes and ringworks in the English and Welsh counties (source as for 2.8).

his mother a Shropshire Englishwoman) could also have given him memories of other traditions. There is also the problem of Orderic's source, which may have been the earlier Norman writer, William of Poitiers. The original ending of the latter's text does not survive, though much of it is preserved in Orderic's work. The detail in question may simply have been quoted by Orderic from this source.[26] The precise significance of Orderic's statement is also bedevilled by its precision: that he distinguished what the French called castles may imply he knew the English also had fortifications, but that they were of different form, or known by a different name. These may simply have been the town defences which occur in his descriptions of William's campaigns against the English. Could they, alternatively, have been defended private residences, which, in the largely vernacular culture of late Saxon England, would not, of course, have been called *castella*?

Turning to the archaeology of the subject, we find that a number of sites have produced interesting evidence from the generations either side of the Norman Conquest. Some of these sites are specific in their implications, particularly Goltho (Lincs) (see pp. 54–6 and 281) and Sulgrave (Northants) (see p. 50). Elsewhere the evidence is less clear in its message. Excavation sometimes reveals phases beneath later castles which are certainly, or most probably, Saxon in date, but where the historical relationship with the sucessor site is not clear. For example, at Middleton Stoney (Oxon), the (largely stone) twelfth century castle incorporated in its earthworks an enclosure of much earlier date, with which only residual Roman and some mid-Saxon material was associated. But the precise date and purpose of this enclosure are not known. At Prudhoe (Northumberland) the date of the first phase is not wholly clear, and could be either side of the Norman Conquest (see p. 284).

A similar situation occurs at Castle Neroche (Somerset), where the initial, large enclosure was superseded by more complex earthworks covering a smaller area. Unfortunately, the first phase was undatable. It was earlier than the medieval works which succeeded it (fig. 2.10), but could have been prehistoric as easily as early medieval. At Castle Bromwich (West Midlands) (see p. 296), the twelfth-century motte stood on top of a possibly late eleventh-century motte beneath which again lay an earlier palisade enclosure. Here also, the sequence seems to have a pre-Conquest origin. At Chalgrave (Beds), the partial plan of a timber building was recovered from beneath the motte, though it remains unclear whether this was a manor house, a social precursor to the castle. At Stamford (Lincs), excavations at the castle revealed a pre-Conquest phase, consisting of a double-ditched enclosure with timber palisades. Although its precise character could not be demonstrated it

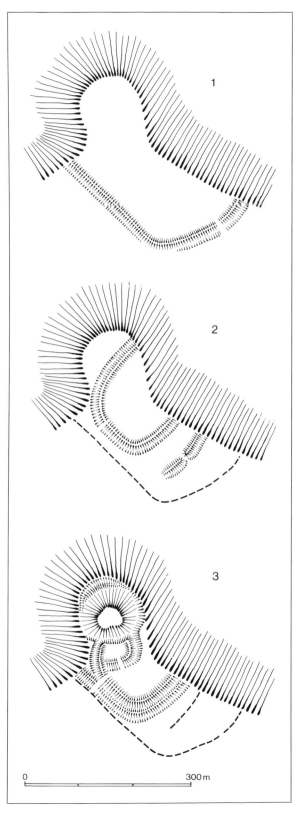

2.10 Castle Neroche (Somerset). Period 1, pre-Conquest. Period 2, early Norman. Period 3, twelfth century (B.K. Davison, in *Ch.G.* II, 1967).

seemed too small for an urban *burh*, too large for a single house enclosure, and it has been described as a possible late Saxon precursor of the castle, perhaps containing a church and a hall belonging to a royal estate. In some other towns which were to have Norman castles, the topography seems almost to demand some pre-Conquest use, for example, of the outcrop at the north-east corner of Exeter, later to become Rougemont castle.

At Earls Barton (Northants), the juxta-position of a late Saxon church and a substantial earthwork raises the possibility that the latter is itself pre-Conquest in date (fig. 2.11). The church may, of course, simply have taken advantage of the security of a much earlier, perhaps prehistoric site. Alternatively, Earls Barton may provide a tantalizing glimpse of a private *burh* with its seignurial church inside its defences. The church was dominated by a tower, which may itself have had some defensive quality. Another late Saxon tower-dominated church, at Barton-on-Humber (Lincs), also stood beside an enclosure, another potential thegnly residence.[27]

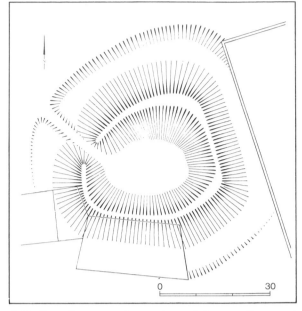

2.12 Post-Conquest ringwork overlying pre-Conquest site at Sulgrave (Northants) (B.K. Davison, in *Archaeol. J.* 134, 1977).

2.11 Pre-Conquest church and possibly pre-Conquest enclosure at Earls Barton (Northants) (B.K. Davison, in *Archaeol. J.* 124, 1967).

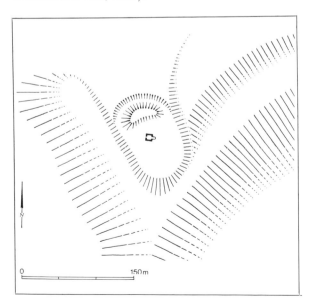

The site at Sulgrave provided no clue, prior to excavation, of its pre-Conquest origins. A small but heavily defended enclosure castle of ringwork form (fig. 2.12) produced evidence of mixed stone and timber building technology dating from the tenth to the twelfth centuries. In the tenth century, a large timber hall with a service room occupied the site, and a detached timber building, perhaps a kitchen, lay next to one end. At the other end a stone-built extension of unknown extent may have been a cross-wing. Around 1000 the hall was partly rebuilt on drystone footings and its service room demolished. To the north was added a stone building whose walls were more than 2 m (6½ ft) high at the time of excavation. Although its function is not known, some comparison with the stone tower alongside the hall at Portchester (see below) may be in order. To the same building phase, or soon after, belonged the construction of a turf bank 1 m (3¼ ft) high, with a flat-bottomed ditch 1 m (3¼ ft) deep and almost 5 m (16 ft) wide. Terminating abruptly

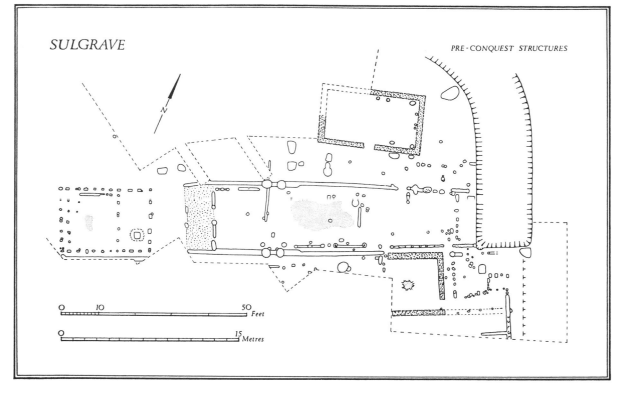

SULGRAVE

PRE-CONQUEST STRUCTURES

0   10   50 Feet

0   15 Metres

2.13 Late Saxon buildings and enclosure at Sulgrave (source as for 2.12).

at the end of the hall, they seem to represent unfinished defences (fig. 2.13).

Later in the eleventh century, probably soon after the Conquest, the hall was replaced by a new stone building and a much more massive rampart replaced the earlier one. For a time the early 'tower' was incorporated in the new defences, but it was later lost in an enlargement of the rampart and accompanying alterations to the hall range.[28] The incomplete nature of this excavation makes overall interpretation difficult, but there is at least some evidence of the late Saxon hall being defended. What is equally significant, however, is that its defences, even allowing for their apparent incompleteness, were slight compared with those of the Norman period. Perhaps here we have a glimpse of the Anglo-Saxon private *burh*, different in character from the *castel* of the *Anglo-Saxon Chronicle*, insufficiently defensible to meet Orderic's definition of a French *castellum*, but possibly surviving in many instances to become a

domus defensabilis of Domesday Book. The high social status of the site seems beyond doubt, not only because its hall was a large building, but because the adjacent late medieval church contains a reused Saxon doorway. Here, as possibly at Earls Barton, a lord's residence and church stood side by side. It is also interesting that the defences were not primary features of the site. Whether the stimulus to enclose the hall came from a physical threat (the Danish wars of Ethelred II's reign?) or from some desire to display social status in physical form is an interesting point of speculation.

Comparable in its revelation of a timber hall with stone tower, though different in many other ways, is Portchester (Hants). Here a late Roman fort of the Saxon shore was reused as a late Saxon *burh*, and the site is among those given in the list, reflecting conditions in Alfred's reign known as the Burghal Hidage.

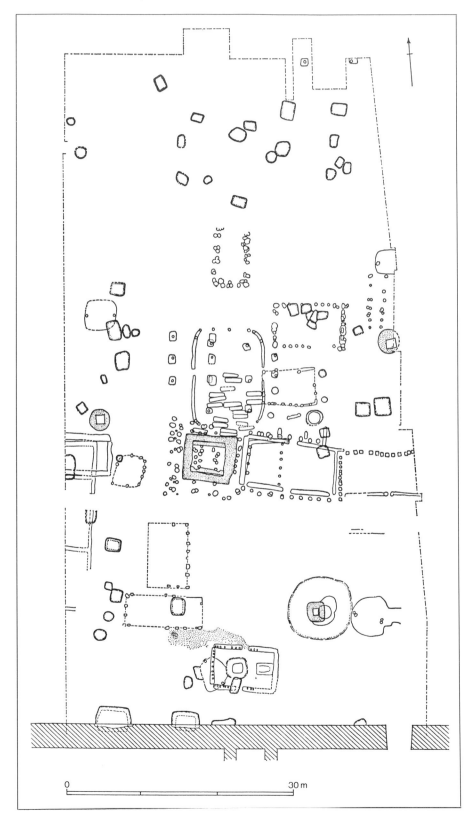

2.14 Late Saxon buildings within *burh* defences at Portchester (Hants) (B. Cunliffe, *Portchester*, II, 1976).

Unlike some other *burhs*, which were to have an urban future, Portchester's development was very individual. Excavation revealed no incipient urbanism within the former Roman fort, but instead an area of high-quality timber structures, confined to its southern side, with an overall date range of the ninth to eleventh centuries. These included an aisled hall and other buildings, and from *c.*1000 onwards a large timber hall with adjacent stone tower. The latter presumably belonged to one of the three manors into which the royal estate had been divided before the Conquest. This occupation should be interpreted as a high-status private residence. Whether or not the maintenance of the Roman defences, or of the post-Roman rampart added outside the west and north walls, continued in its original burghal sense, this high-quality residence was *de facto* a defended one. But whereas at Sulgrave and Goltho (see below) the defences were tailored to fit the residence, here the occupation seems to have been confined to one side of the enclosure (fig. 2.14). Around the mid-eleventh century the tower was re-built (as a chapel or bell-tower?) and became the focus of a cemetery which continued in use after the Norman Conquest, extending over the site of the now-abandoned hall. The later castle developed on the other side of the enclosure.[29]

Of earlier date is the enigmatic evidence from Lower Brook Street in Winchester. Here, a secular residential complex of *c.*800 consisted of a stone tower, or at least a two-storey building, with associated timber structures (fig. 2.15). The high social status of the site is suggested not only by the character of the building but also by the richness of the cemetery on to which it had encroached by this date. The building has been suggested as a thegnly residence of pre-burghal Winchester. Though extrapolation from the limited

evidence is difficult, the city may have contained a number of such residences, together with the Old Minster and the royal palace whose existence has been inferred from its appearance in later centuries. Whether any of these putative early elements in Winchester were defended, or even enclosed, is an open question, but the analogy of the stone towers at Portchester and Sulgrave, which were defended, is interesting. Moreover, the occurrence of *burh* place-names *within* some pre-Conquest towns also suggests defensible, or at least enclosed, residences: elsewhere in Winchester there was a Coitbury, at Exeter and York there was an Earlsbury, and in London there were Paulsbury, Bucklersbury, Lothbury and Aldermanbury – this last example being in the vicinity of Cripplegate fort, the traditional site of the early royal palace. There are likely to be other urban names of this type to which attention has yet to be drawn.[30]

Recent excavations at Eynsford castle (Kent) have provoked a major reassessment of evidence first published 20 years ago. Whereas previously the remains of its central stone building were interpreted as the base of a Norman tower, they have now been shown, on both stratigraphic and pottery evidence,

2.15 Stone building of *c.*800 at Winchester (Hants) (M. Biddle, in *Antiq. J.* 55, 1975).

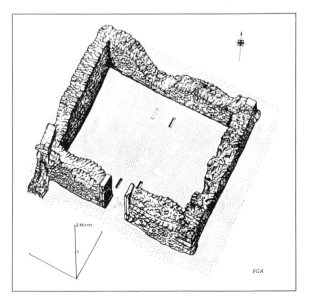

to belong to the early eleventh-century (fig. 2.16). Here, as at Sulgrave and Portchester, a stone building seems to have been a major element of a high-status residence. Its wall survived at one point to its full height of 2.4 m (8 ft), with a beam socket at its top for either an upper timber storey or simply a roof. This building, whose floor lay 1.5 m (5 ft) below the contemporary ground surface, was surrounded by a ditch of which a short stretch, 5 m (16 ft) wide and 3 m (10 ft) deep, had escaped destruction. The rest of the ditch, and its presumed rampart, had not survived the late eleventh-century building of the castle curtain wall and moat. As at Sulgrave, the site retained its high social status through the upheaval of the Norman Conquest, and the Saxon stone building may have continued in use for a short time under new ownership. If it had been accompanied by other buildings of timber, these did not survive the appearance of a new Norman domestic range.[31]

Finally, there is the fascinating evidence

from Goltho (Lincs), which has, more than any other English site, provoked debate on this theme of late Saxon private defence (see also p. 281). Here, as at Sulgrave, the field monument appeared to be a purely post-Conquest earthwork, part of a deserted medieval village whose excavation (in advance of destruction) was published separately.[32] The site which eventually became the Norman castle was first defended, according to the published account, in the middle of the ninth century. It consisted of timber domestic buildings on a courtyard plan, among which the bow-sided hall was of similar shape and size to that of the royal palace at Cheddar. The defences were considerable; though the rampart survived in only fragmentary form, it had been at least 3.6 m (12 ft) wide (figs 2.17 and 18). The defences continued in use in the tenth century but the domestic buildings were rebuilt. In the early eleventh century the courtyard was enlarged and new domestic buildings including a single-aisled hall erected. The old defences were almost flattened, with new defences enclosing the larger area. This rampart was up to 7.5 m (25 ft) wide and survived to a height of 1.5 m (5 ft) with an estimated original height of 2 m (6½ ft).

The Anglo-Saxons must have had a word to describe such a place, without doubt a defended residence of high status, and presumably it was the word *burh* in one of its applications. It is, however, most unfortunate that the later development of the site removed all traces of the defended entrance and palisade which must have accompanied this rampart and ditch. Late in the eleventh century the site became more defensible, being modified into a small motte and bailey (see chapter 8). Within the small bailey were two successive single-aisled halls. The new Norman owner

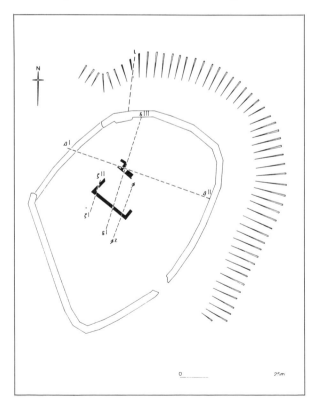

2.16 Early-eleventh-century stone building within ditched enclosure at Eynsford (Kent) (V. Horsman, in *Archaeol. Cant.* 105, 1988).

clearly needed a more defensible (or oppressive) home, and was prepared to sacrifice some of the earlier living space to achieve it. Interestingly, around the middle of the twelfth century, the site resumed something of its late Saxon character with the bailey filled in and the broader mound thus formed becoming a platform. On this was a large timber hall with aisles on all four sides. Despite the disappointing absence of struc-

tural detail in its early defences, a deficiency which persists in the motte and bailey phase because of its subsequent levelling, Goltho presents the clearest evidence to date that an Anglo-Saxon lord could find it both desirable and possible to provide his home with substantial protection. As in the case of Sulgrave,

2.17 Plan of late Saxon Goltho (Lincs) (G. Beresford, *Goltho*, 1987, following chronology given there).

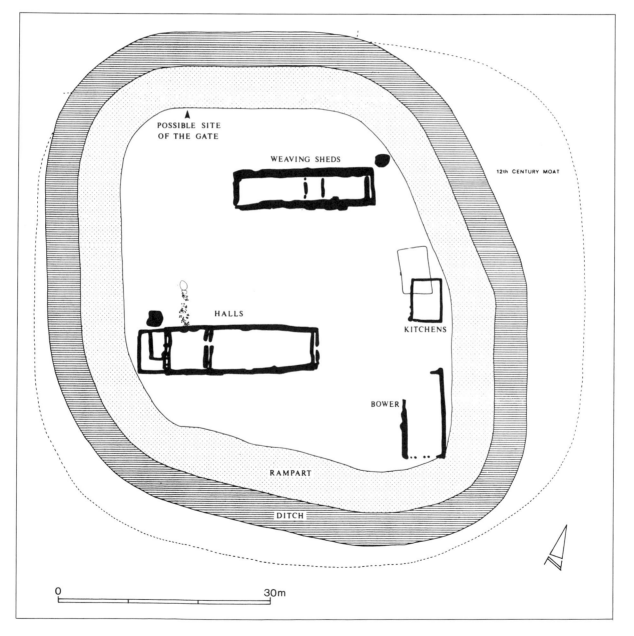

the underlying impetus cannot be explained by the archaeological evidence. The motive may have been pragmatic: the mid-ninth and the early eleventh centuries both coincided with periods of Danish aggression. Alternatively, the defences may represent a developing fashion of aristocratic residence.

It should not, however, go unnoticed that the sequence of dates suggested for Goltho has been seriously challenged. The manorial history of the area is very complex, and the

site may possibly have been misidentified. The implications of the challenge are that the motte phase may be mid-twelfth century and the last phase c.1200. If this is correct there may have been a period of abandonment (coinciding with a fragmentation of the late Saxon manor) between the Conquest and the mid-twelfth century. Alternatively – and this is most relevant to the theme under discussion – have the defended Saxon phases been dated too early (an argument also tenable on the evidence of the pottery)? Are they, in fact, of the tenth and early eleventh centuries rather than earlier? If so, the sequence of events may have been closer in date to that at Sulgrave.

2.18 Reconstruction of ninth-century buildings and defences at Goltho, based on evidence in 2.17 (source as for 2.17).

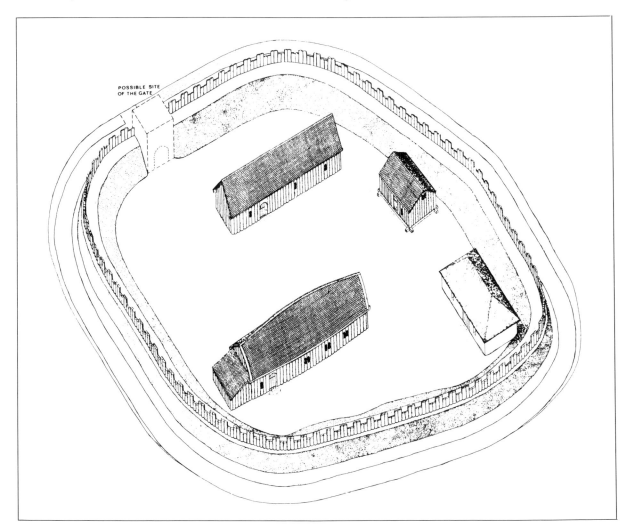

Most of the available evidence, however, suggests timber castles were a Norman development. There is certainly no evidence for pre-Conquest mottes. But negative evidence is difficult to evaluate and cannot be conclusive. For all we know, the sites of the 1050s in Herefordshire may have had mottes. So few have been excavated to great depth that, despite the strong likelihood of English mottes having only post-Conquest origins, it is not totally impossible that one day an earlier example will come to light. Equally, the silence of the English sources on matters of private residence needs careful evaluation. Why should the compilers of the *Anglo-Saxon Chronicle* be particularly concerned with the everyday dwelling habits of landholders? There is no particular reason why Goltho, Sulgrave, Eynsford and their equivalents (and they surely cannot have been the only such sites) should figure in any source at all, though they may be hinted at in the *burhgeat* of the compilation on status. If we are prepared to accept that they represent the tip of an iceberg mainly submerged beneath later castles and manorial sites, then it is possible to argue that England had its own version of the private castle which was quickly overtaken, both in numbers and massiveness of construction, by new types of site produced by a northern French conquering class fearful for its own security. In the early 1050s it was presumably the novelty of the French castles, either in their strength or design, or both, which struck the writers of the *Anglo-Saxon Chronicle*. This continued to be the case, and castles figured regularly in the post-Conquest record of the *Chronicle*. It is also of relevance to note that the enlargement of sites continued in the post-Conquest period at places which were themselves of Norman origin. At Castle Acre (Norfolk), the late eleventh-century phase consisted of a hall inside an earthwork surmounted by a timber palisade with simple entrance – no different in principle from what is presumed at Goltho and different in practice only because the hall was stone-built.[33] It was not until the twelfth century that the hall and its defences had been developed by various stages into a more formidable keep, more obviously recognizable as a castle.

The demonstration of any theory about late Saxon sites is, unfortunately, not only beyond the limits of the currently available evidence, but quite possibly beyond the limits of even the most lavishly financed research programme. Discovering earlier sites under Norman castles is, necessarily, an accidental process. Also intractable is the problem of how many of the numerous smaller enclosure sites (as opposed to hillforts and analogous sites) in the landscape may be of pre-Conquest date. We tend to assume that these are either post-Conquest or pre-Saxon, but among them may be Golthos and Sulgraves, built either by the English or by the Danes, which went out of use before or soon after the Conquest. Given the nature of the Norman Conquest and its emphasis on legitimate inheritance of land, however, we should not be surprised to find Saxon homes under Norman ones. Juxtaposition of seignurial residence and church was a common phenomenon throughout the Middle Ages. Particularly where post-Conquest sites stand next to churches, as at Sulgrave and Goltho, we may suspect that Saxon phases lie beneath. A spectacular parallel is the rebuilding of Westminster Hall by William Rufus in the 1090s. The slightly bow-sided plan of this enormous hall (the biggest in England, possibly in Europe, at the time) suggests very strongly that it was not simply on the site of Edward the Confessor's palace, but that it was a stone rebuilding *in situ* of his equally enormous timber hall. The rural palace site of Cheddar continued in use, with various rebuildings, to the thirteenth century, and the old palace outside Gloucester was maintained until the same period. At Winchester, in contrast, the Conqueror built a new hall on a different site from the earlier one.[34]

To discuss the origins of English castles one must look not only backwards into the Anglo-Saxon period but also forwards into the Anglo-Norman. Among the castles of the later eleventh or very early twelfth centuries considerable variety in both form and building technology is found. There were castles with mottes, and those with enclosure plans. There were early stone constructions, such as the gatehouses at Exeter and Ludlow, the simple tower on the motte at Okehampton (Devon), the curtains and towers at Ludlow and Richmond, as well as the more elaborate hall-keeps at Chepstow, London ('The Tower') and Colchester. There were sites with timber defences, such as the timber tower on stone footings at Totnes (Devon) (see p. 187), the first palisade and gatehouse at Castle Acre (Norfolk), or the motte tower whose fragmentary remains were discovered beneath the more famous one of twelfth-century date at Abinger (Surrey) (see pp. 292−6). There were also timber domestic buildings such as those found at Sandal (Yorks) (see pp. 299−300), Barnard Castle (Co. Durham) (see p. 299), Launceston (Cornwall) (see pp. 274−6) and Lydford (Devon) (see p. 277). There is, in addition, strong presumptive evidence for timber defences and residential buildings at the numerous unexcavated earthwork sites of the period.

By this point in time, however, the problem under discussion has taken on a new dimension. It is not only a question of whether Anglo-Saxon England provides any antecedents to these sites, but also of the wider range of influences which may have given birth to them. In the narrower conception of English castle origins, it was simply a matter of Norman importation of new ideas into a non-castle-building society. The probability, argued above, that some English pre-Conquest sites should be included in the overall tradition of private defence creates a weakness in this theory. The same is true of detailed research in Normandy (see pp. 100−6). This has shown how, apart from the early castles of the dukes and some very powerful families, the proliferation of castles in Norman society was a relatively late phenomenon. The period 1020−50 was crucial in the emergence of these powerful families, and much of their castle-building took place only towards the end of the century.[35] We thus have a more or less contemporary explosion of castle-building in both Normandy and England which makes a search for prototypes not only very difficult but perhaps fruitless.

Once the Conquest of England was a political fact, the ideas of the new ruling class circulated freely in an environment which transcended the barrier of the Channel. In addition, both the aggressive and defensive needs of the conquerors would have encouraged them to experiment with both old and new forms of fortification. The former duke was now a king, and his ambitious projects in the stone keeps at London and Colchester may have been stimulated by self-aggrandizement as well as by considerations of security. The use of stone on a massive scale, of which both sites are examples, was perhaps one reflection of this experimental and expansive mood, though it found some precedent in earlier ducal castles in Normandy. Another may have been the increasing use of mottes. While not totally unknown in northern France at an earlier date, their appearance in numbers in that region, as in England, may have been only a late eleventh-century phenomenon. The earliest Norman castles in England were not mottes, but enclosures built up against earlier defences: the Roman fort at Pevensey, the Roman and Saxon defences at London, Exeter and Winchester, and perhaps the Iron Age and Saxon defences at Hastings and Dover (fig. 2.19). The situation at Dover, however, is unclear owing to the later extensive rebuilding of the site. Though it was presumably timber-built in the Conqueror's reign there are no indications that it ever possessed a motte. The earliest

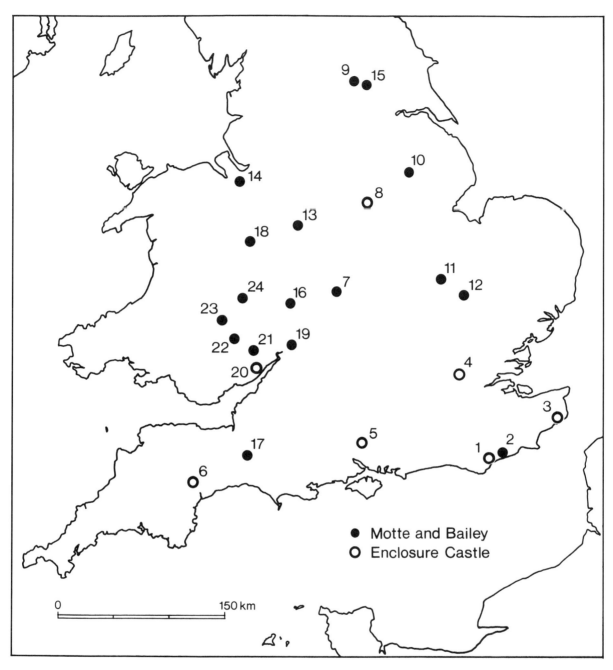

2.19 Documented castles of the immediately post-Conquest period in England and the Welsh border (B.K. Davison, in *Ch.G.* III, 1969). 1 Pevensey, September 1066. 2 Hastings, October 1066. 3 Dover, October 1066. 4 London, January 1067. 5 Winchester, summer, 1067. 6 Exeter, December 1067–early 1068. 7 Warwick, early summer, 1068. 8 Nottingham, early summer, 1068. 9 York I, mid-summer, 1068. 10 Lincoln, autumn, 1068. 11 Huntingdon, autumn, 1068. 12 Cambridge, autumn, 1068. 13 Stafford, summer, 1069. 14 Chester, summer, 1069. 15 York II, December 1069. 16 Worcester, by 1069. 17 Montacute, by 1069. 18 Shrewsbury, by 1069. 19 Berkeley, by 1070. 20 Chepstow, by 1070. 21 Monmouth, by 1070. 22 Eywas Harold, by 1070. 23 Clifford, by 1070. 24 Wigmore, by 1070.

excavated phase of the earthworks around the Saxon church, and cutting through its cemetery, may have been William's work.

Hastings poses a problem because the Bayeux Tapestry depicts the building of a motte there in the Conqueror's initial campaign in 1066. But since the Tapestry was a product of the following decade it might well contain an anachronistic portrayal of the sort of castle which by that time was common. The excavation at Hastings failed to demonstrate the date of the initial mound (which in its present form proved to be the result of an enlargement) with sufficient accuracy to solve the problem. At Castle Neroche (Somerset) the motte was shown on excavation to be a twelfth-century addition to an enclosure site dating probably from the repression of south-west England in 1068. Only with the establishment of castles from 1068 onwards, and initially those located in English towns, such as York, which resisted the Normans, was the motte a regular feature. The argument, put forward in the 1960s, that these facts suggest an actual origin of the motte in England at this time, seems in retrospect to overstretch the point.[36] A case can be made for more widespread origins of the motte generally (see below, chapter 3) and it must also be remembered that in the early campaigns speed and convenience would have been major considerations: enclosures utilizing existing defences would make good sense. Nevertheless, precise early dating of mottes is very difficult. At Baile Hill (York) excavation suggested the motte was probably primary. At Winchester, in contrast, the motte was a secondary addition of the 1070s to the initial enclosure of 1067.[37] At Hen Domen the motte was a primary feature of the castle established by 1086, probably before 1074.

What can be said in conclusion about England? It is worth recalling here the research project on English castle origins which the Royal Archaeological Institute financed in the late 1960s. By pursuing excavations at Bramber and Hastings (Sussex), Sulgrave (Northants), Baile Hill, York and Hen Domen (now Powys) it was hoped that important questions would be answered about the late Saxon period, the years of initial conquest to 1070, and the period of consolidation thereafter. In publishing some of the results from the project, its co-ordinator, Andrew Saunders, remarked that 'no generalizations nor, indeed, many broad conclusions can be drawn from the project as a whole, which may be said to have raised more questions than it has solved.' Even within the normal limitations of excavation, the individual exercises met with mixed success.[38] Nevertheless, in the context of timber castle studies, the evidence from Sulgrave (see above p. 50) and Hen Domen (see chapter 9) has proved crucial. Excavations at other sites have also made major contributions. Goltho has revealed an earth and timber ringwork tradition before the Conquest, and evidence at Portchester, Eynsford and Sulgrave suggests that the use of stone in secular Anglo-Saxon building might be related to English castle origins. At Launceston (Cornwall) (see pp. 274–6) and Lydford (Devon) (see p. 277) the simple character of the earliest timber buildings contrasts with the normal definition of a castle as a high-status residence, reminding us how castles were adaptable in campaign as well as in permanent occupation.

We must also remember that our traditional attention to Normandy in the search for the inspiration of castles is in danger of disguising not only the native English contribution, but also the contribution from other areas of France and beyond (see chapter 3). Our 'Norman' conquerors came also from Britanny, from Flanders, from the Pas de Calais (where interesting castles are documented – see chapter 4) and elsewhere. Anjou was important in the emergence of early castles, particularly stone ones, and crucial developments for the emergence of mottes took place in the Rhineland. Parallels have been drawn between English sites dominated by stone or timber towers, which were sometimes also gatehouses, and those German plans in which an enclosure is dominated by a freestanding tower or *Bergfried*.[39] It is hard to imagine Goltho or Sulgrave without gatehouses, and, in the absence of evidence for Anglo-Saxon mottes, it is perhaps to the tower tradition that we should look for the English contribution. Their construction was certainly familiar, as some surviving late Saxon churches and the hybrid English/Norman gatehouse at Exeter castle remind us.

Equally interesting is the similarity between some English sites and those Rhenish castles whose mottes grew gradually (see below p. 88). At Aldingham (Cumbria), for example, a twelfth-century ringwork was filled and heightened to become a motte (fig. 2.20), a process not dissimilar to that experienced by some Irish raths (see below pp. 70ff.). While it is impossible to demonstrate causal links in such matters, the study of castle origins and design influences clearly benefits from thinking as widely as possible.[40]

Finally, we must not forget that English timber castles continued to 'originate', in a whole variety of circumstances, down to the thirteenth century. Some of these circumstances involved the element of experimentation and improvisation which had probably characterized castles from the very beginning. In

2.20 Aldingham (Lancs – now Cumbria), a ringwork filled in and raised to form a motte during the twelfth and thirteenth centuries (after B.K. Davison, in *Med. Archaeol.* 13, 1969).

the twelfth century, the Roman amphitheatre earthworks at Silchester were adapted to contain a single-aisled hall of timber, resulting in a sort of ringwork.[41] Prehistoric earthworks could also be employed, either to take advantage of their elevated topography or to provide large outer enclosures. British Camp, on top of the Malvern Hills, is a fine example, of probably twelfth-century date (below, fig. 7.31, chapter 7).

Wales

A common medieval view of Wales, as seen in the work of Giraldus Cambrensis, for example, was a disparaging one. Giraldus saw the Welsh as a primitive rural society, incapable of building fine residences. Although less impressive than the building tradition of twelfth-century England, the Welsh legacy was not negligible, and his view was exaggerated.[42] Halls and courts for the princes and their retinues, as well as the citadels which were the centres of their political power, figure regularly in early sources. In 822, a fortress at Deganwy fell to the English, and its burning by lightning a decade earlier suggests it was mainly timber-built. A poem of *c.*900 described 'a fine fortress on the broad ocean, a mighty stronghold . . .' at *Dinbych*, the later site of Tenby castle. It was a palisaded enclosure containing accommodation for both a noble retinue and an army, as well as storage for provisions and a room for the safe-keeping of ancient writings.[43]

The lawbooks, though produced in their

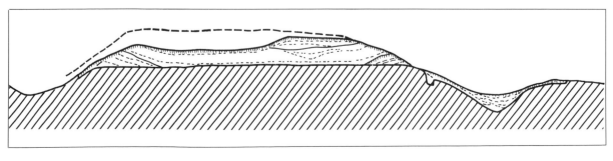

surviving form only in the late twelfth and thirteenth centuries, have been much used as a source for earlier times. Bondmen were obliged to work on royal fortifications: 'and from each bond township a man with a felling-axe and a horse to build the king's fortresses.' Such service may have been ancient, and easily converted later to support a princely *castell*. The tentative reconstruction of 'multiple estates' may suggest that Iron Age hillforts retained both military and political functions well into the early Middle Ages. Such sites had sometimes also been the location of battles between Welsh and English. Late sources also mention the lodge in front of the king's court. This may imply a gatehouse to an enclosure. In so far as any general picture emerges, it is of ancient fortifications which might shelter a population in emergency, together with others, presumably of more recent origin, associated with the political authority of powerful men. Neither was an equivalent of the classic late Saxon *burh*, nor did these sites spawn urban functions. The *burh* at *Cledemutha* (Rhuddlan), founded by Edward the Elder in 921, remains an isolated example of incipient urbanism unparalleled in Wales until the post-Conquest period. By the eleventh century, however, it was in Welsh control and a royal residence had been built: earl Harold Godwinson defeated Gruffyd ap Llywelyn there in 1063.[44]

Despite such tantalizing glimpses, the physical details of royal or noble establishments remain obscure. A recent survey has only served to emphasize the challenge of identifying early medieval Welsh sites of any sort.[45] The paucity of datable artefact evidence, the difficulty of applying Carbon 14 assessments to the period, the impossibility of distinguishing Iron Age from early medieval hillforts on purely morphological grounds, the tempting but hazardous process of equating archaeological sites with historical traditions — all these conspire to prevent an adequate reconstruction of a princely stronghold or palace. The excavated artefacts and fragmentary building plans from the hilltop sites such as Dinas Powis (Glamorgan), Dinas Emrys (Gwynedd), and Deganwy and Dinorben (both in Clywd), reflect immediately post-Roman occupation for the most part.

More recently attention has been drawn to another class of site, comprising more or less rectangular earthworks, where excavation or reliable historical tradition, or both, indicate use in the ninth and tenth centuries (fig. 2.21). These include Cwrt Llechryd, Mathrafal and various others, all in Powys. Some, situated very close to the English border, may even be Mercian works.[46] A further example is Aberffraw in Anglesey, where excavation suggests a post-Roman origin, and there is a good historical association with the princes of Gwynedd. The later use of some Roman fort sites may also be relevant to this theme. There is some artefactual evidence for this, as well as a strong historical tradition, at Segontium (Caernarfon), and at Pen Llystyn (Gwynedd), a palisaded enclosure was later built in one corner of the fort. Somewhat tantalizing, though certainly relevant to the issue of high-status residences, is the enormous aisled hall outside the fort at Forden Gaer (Powys). Discovered from the air as a crop-mark, this site was recently sampled in excavation. Its post-holes produced sherds of abraded Roman pottery, suggesting a very late Roman or post-Roman date for its construction. As always, the dearth of early medieval native occupation material makes it more or less impossible to decide how long such a site went on in use. Finally, the popularity of castle ringworks in parts of South Wales (see below) may possibly disguise some earlier Celtic fortifications which are not distinguishable by appearance alone.

As in England, the immediately post-Conquest period in Wales witnessed a Norman impact in which castle-building played a major part. In its death-tribute to the Conqueror, the *Anglo-Saxon Chronicle* noted,

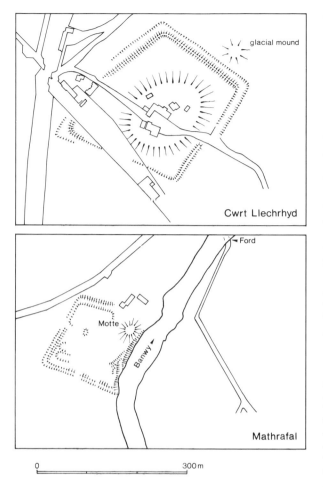

2.21 Possible pre-Norman enclosures in the central Welsh marches (C. Musson, C.J. Spurgeon, in *Med. Archaeol.* 32, 1988).

'Wales was in his power, and he built castles there, and he entirely controlled that race'. For 1087, this was certainly an exaggeration, and warfare with the Welsh was to drag on for another 200 years. Up until the final Edwardian conquest (in the late thirteenth century), however, castles established directly by English kings were not numerous. Most kings led armies into Wales at some time or another, and there were some royal foundations, such as Cardiff (by the Conqueror) or New Montgomery (by Henry III). But most were built not by the kings but by those

who actually exercised the powers of raising armies, pursuing warfare and castle-building in Wales: the earls of Chester, Shrewsbury and Hereford in the Conqueror's reign; the numerous marcher lords who had established themselves by the twelfth century; and – most important, since the great lords themselves were rarely present in person – the vassals of these men, whose main, or only, landholding interest was centred in Wales.

By the time of the Welsh revival in 1094, territories had been subjugated and castles built in conquered areas in the north, in the middle border, and in the south. In the north, for example, Hugh d'Avranches, earl of Chester, and his followers extended their powers along the coastal strip, building such castles as Rhuddlan (on royal instruction, as Orderic Vitalis related), Deganwy and Caernarfon. Roger de Montgomery, earl of Shrewsbury, penetrated the Severn valley, establishing a castle to which he gave his own name (now Hen Domen) and conquering part of central Powys beyond the river. His family was also responsible for the first castle at Pembroke. William FitzOsbern and his son, earls of the much shorter-lived earldom of Hereford, built a border stronghold at Chepstow, and further west the conquest of Glamorgan is now thought to have started with the establishment of Cardiff castle by the Conqueror himself in 1081. The process of castle-building went on for 200 years, justly earning Wales the title 'a land of castles'. The early conquests were not, however, uniformly maintained. The late eleventh-century annexations along the north coast were soon lost, as were those beyond the Severn on the central border. The 'marches' were mainly in the southern half of the country in the twelfth and thirteenth centuries, and within each lordship there was commonly a distinction between the area of heaviest Anglo-Norman influence and the remaining 'Welshry'.[47]

Although Norman castles were essentially an imposed phenomenon, they did not entirely lack links with the earlier political framework. There were no towns, as there were in England, whose subjugation would have dictated the choice of certain castle sites. On the contrary, it was often the foundation of castles which led to urban growth in Wales. Far from being randomly constituted territories, however, the lands which the Normans conquered were the commotes, the subdivisions of the cantrefs which made up the Welsh kingdoms, and the basic unit of Welsh territorial lordship. In conquering commotes, the Normans were simply perpetuating the indigenous practice of political annexation which had been going on among the Welsh kingdoms for centuries.

Significantly, it was the inheritance of lordship attached to the commotes, rather than a delegation of power from the king of England, which gave the conquerors the rights to wage war, take the resulting plunder, administer their own justice and build fortifications. Thus, the Normans, while conquerors, were also inheritors, just as they were in England. And in some parts of Wales a castle seems to have been built within each of the commotes as though to emphasize this systematic assumption of political authority.[48] Since the native centre of a commote was its *llys*, or court, maintained by the tribute paid to its lord by the men of the commote, and since the lord had the right to fortify his *llys*, it is not unreasonable to see the Norman castles, however different in physical form they may have been from a Welsh lord's court, as their institutional successors. They could also be built on the same sites in cases where the topography was suitable. Rhuddlan, whose castle was established in the late eleventh century, had an earlier royal Welsh residence (see above p. 62), and a later parallel may be found in Edward I's choice of site for Conwy castle: it was not only a physically suitable spot, but also the location of a Welsh royal palace, which was demolished to make way for the new work (see chapter 6).

In another respect, too, there was a sense of institutional continuity. By the end of the twelfth century the landscape contained not only castles built by the Normans, but also those built by the Welsh lords in areas they retained. Partly from a need to compete on equal military terms when necessary, partly from a desire to emulate their marcher neighbours socially – and these men were allies almost as often as they were enemies – the Welsh lords adopted the practice of castle-building, despite the strong association of castles with the foreigners, the 'French', which is clear from the Welsh written sources. Welsh castle-building developed probably in the aftermath of, though not apparently during, the Welsh revival of 1094, which saw the extent of Norman rule greatly reduced. The motte at Domen Castell, Welshpool was built about 1110–11 by Cadwgan ap Bleddyn. It was the first of various documented twelfth-century castles, but the documentation is not a full guide to Welsh activity.

The best preserved of the earthwork sites is the motte and bailey called Tomen y Rhodwydd, the castle built in 1149 by Owain of Gwynedd, son of Gruffyd ap Cynan, on the Powys-Gwynedd border (see fig. 7.14). The relationship of the Welsh castles to the existing *llys* sites would merit an examination which is not possible here. Presumably a new castle performed, among others, the functions of its predecessor, though there does not seem to have been a castle in every commote, as there tended to be in the marcher lordships.[49]

Frequently, a castle's Welsh or Norman origin is evident from its territorial context. But, particularly in areas which passed in and out of Welsh control, this may not always be the case, especially since castles built by the Welsh copied in most respects those built by the Normans. It has been suggested that among the stone castles a distinction may be made between Welsh and English on the basis of their masonry: the Welsh product was often, though not invariably, inferior. But in the case of earthworks representing sites of timber castles, such a distinction is difficult, if not impossible, to make. In the Severn valley west of Montgomery, for example, there are earthworks which might reflect the Norman penetration into Wales in the late eleventh century. But since in the twelfth century the area was once again part of Powys, we cannot be sure that some sites in the area are not native Welsh.[50] This problem has wider significance for the study of timber castles, since their 'Norman' character is so much a part of their traditional interpretation. The same issue emerges from the study of Irish sites (see pp. 70ff.).

Although containing numerous stone castles, among them the Edwardian castles of the north – the most famous in the British Isles, Wales was also very much a land of timber castles, as Ella Armitage insisted long ago. These were not simply an early feature of the post-Conquest landscape. There is plentiful documentary evidence for their use by both English and Welsh in the thirteenth century. A major centre of the princes of Powys, the castle near Welshpool known as Powis Castle was mainly one of timber until at least 1274, after which it underwent massive redevelopment in stone.[51]

Wales was plentifully endowed with both mottes and ringworks, the latter particularly in the south, though the builders' choice between the two types is not always explicable. It was probably a matter of personal preference in many cases. Recent work in Glamorgan, however, suggests there may have been some environmental influence, and this could be of significance for other regions (fig. 2.22). The mottes are mostly in areas covered by glacial drift, where earthworks could be more easily dug and natural glacial features such as drumlins and moraines adapted. The ringworks, in contrast, are mainly in areas unaffected by glacial activity, where much shallower soil overlying solid rock made the creation of large mounds a

2.22 Timber castles and glacial deposits in Glamorgan, South Wales (after J. Spurgeon, in Kenyon & Avent 1987).

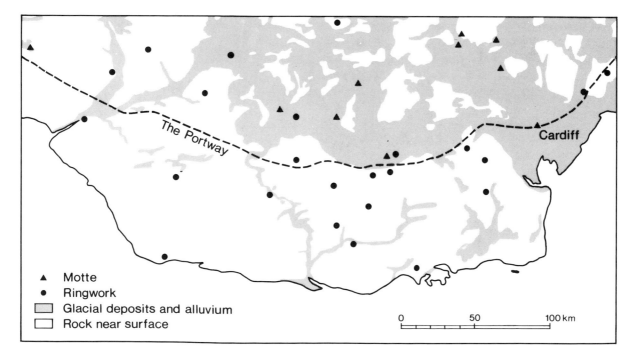

▲ Motte
● Ringwork
▨ Glacial deposits and alluvium
☐ Rock near surface

0   50   100 km

more difficult task.[52] Perhaps more than other areas of the British Isles, Wales has benefited from detailed regional studies examining the chronology and topographical context of castle foundation as well as the physical form of the sites themselves.[53] Whatever the reasons underlying the design of earthworks, mottes and ringworks seem to have been equally utilized in Wales from an early date.

On the border of the earldom of Shrewsbury, Roger Corbet, an important tenant of Roger de Montgomery, built a ringwork called Caus, whereas the earl himself built his castle, which he called Montgomery (now Hen Domen), as a motte from the start. Excavations at the latter, at the junction of the motte and bailey defences, showed that the motte was definitely a primary feature of the site. Here it may well have been a matter of personal preference, since the Montgomery properties generally had more mottes, whereas those of the Corbets had a greater proportion of ringworks.[54] Built within a few years of the Conquest, probably in the early 1070s, the primary motte at Hen Domen is of significance for English, as well as Border archaeology, in the debate about motte origins (see above p. 60). The early castles built at Rhuddlan in the north and Cardiff in the south were also mottes (that is, if their mottes were primary features). In more general terms, it has recently been argued that mottes dominated early castle-building in Wales, and that despite individually early examples, the popularity of ringworks in some areas might reflect a slightly later development, from *c.*1100.[55] The approximate total of castle earthworks in Wales, whose distribution is shown in figs 2.23 and 24, covering sites of eleventh- to thirteenth-century foundation, stands at 242 mottes and 77 ringworks.

Scotland

The experience of Scotland was very different from that of Wales. Castles appeared in Scot-

2.23 Distribution of mottes in Wales (after D.J.C. King & L. Alcock in *Ch.G.* III, 1969).

2.24 Distribution of ringworks in Wales (source as for 2.23).

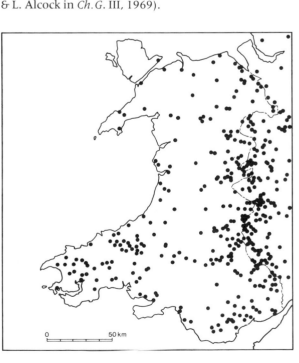

land as a result of the deliberate efforts of its twelfth-century kings to settle an immigrant feudal aristocracy. This process, which also involved the foundation of towns and monasteries, was slow, covering the reigns of David I, Malcolm IV and William I (the period 1124–1214). It suffered drawbacks from resistance within Scotland, as well as from conflict with the Angevin kings of England. Though the Scottish earls were very powerful men who sometimes challenged their kings, there was no proliferation of marcher lordships of the Welsh variety. Some of the new castles were royal ones, some were built by the Anglo-Norman newcomers and others by the native aristocracy who were assimilated to the new order.[56]

The association of castle-building with this phase of Scottish history was suggested around the beginning of this century by George Neilson. The lands of the Anglo-Norman settlers were found in many cases to bear evidence of mottes, and the correlation between the two seemed inescapable. This has always remained the accepted view, though it was later realized that among Scotland's earliest castles were also stone towers in the western, Norse areas.[57] The considerable number of surviving earthworks suggests that timber castles remained crucially important. Excavations at the Mote of Urr revealed fourteenth-century occupation above the twelfth-century phase. At Roberton (Strathclyde) and Lumphanan and Strachan (Grampian) the mottes were first constructed not earlier than the mid-thirteenth century. It is possible that other mottes, assumed to be of twelfth-century date, may also have been built in the troubled period of Scottish-English warfare.[58] Mottes also retained their social significance, as centres of baronies and symbols of seignurial justice, long after their abandonment.[59]

As in Wales and Ireland, there was already a long tradition of Celtic (as well as of Pictish) defensive works. In southern areas there are some sites which in an Irish context would be regarded as raths or ring-forts. There are also palisaded enclosures whose ancestry stretches back into prehistory. In early medieval times, there was a tradition of stone-built or timber-laced hilltop sites, as at the Mote of Mark (Dumfries and Galloway), Dunadd and Dunollie (Argyll), Dundurn (Perthshire) and Burghead (Moray). The form of these and other sites, together with the control of manpower implied by their construction, suggest they were not only the residences but also the political centres of society's most powerful men, including kings. In some cases, there are strong historical traditions pointing to the same conclusion. The evidence for such sites largely covers the period up to the eighth century, and the residences of such men on the eve of the Anglo-Norman settlement are less well understood. Sometimes there is documentary evidence for occupation in the ninth and tenth centuries, as at Edinburgh and Dundurn. Some early medieval sites were to have later castles built on top of them, as, for example, at Edinburgh, Dumbarton and Urquhart. But the significance of this for continuity of occupation or social function is not yet clear. Cruggleton (Dumfries and Galloway), with its palisaded timber hall (fig. 2.25), perhaps of eighth-century origin, beneath the later twelfth-century motte and bailey, has provided a rare glimpse of a Scottish castle's antecedents (see also p. 311).[60]

Whereas Scottish castle studies have in the past been largely directed to the (presumed) early mottes and the later stone buildings, attention has recently been drawn to earth and timber ringworks. These have been less studied than in England and Wales, but they certainly existed, for example at Crookston (Strathclyde), and a list of some 20 has been published (fig. 2.26). If they were more common than hitherto recognized, the uneven distribution (see below) of mottes may be more easily explained.[61] They are also of

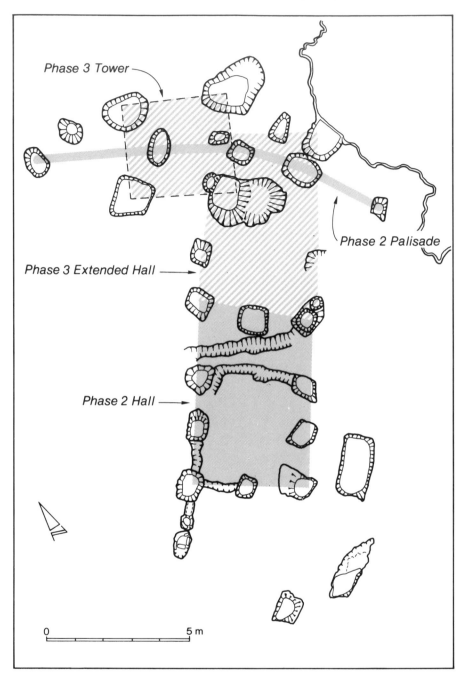

Phase 3 Tower

Phase 3 Extended Hall

Phase 2 Hall

Phase 2 Palisade

0   5 m

2.25 Cruggleton (Dumfries and Galloway). Palisaded hall of eighth to twelfth centuries (phase 2); enlarged, with tower (replacing palisade), when incorporated in a motte in the twelfth century (after G. Ewart, *Cruggleton Castle*, 1985; courtesy of Historic Scotland).

relevance to the longer theme of Scottish fortification, since they adapt a basic principle of defence which, as in Wales and Ireland, links them morphologically, if not always socially, with earlier traditions. For this simple reason, identifying a ringwork as Norman rather than early medieval can be difficult, as in the case of Castledykes, the possible predecessor to the late medieval motte at Roberton.

It is, however, the mottes which have received most attention (fig. 2.27). There are

2.26 Crookston (Strathclyde). A twelfth-century ringwork with a fifteenth-century stone tower house (courtesy of C. Tabraham and Historic Scotland).

2.27 The motte at Mote of Urr (Dumfries & Galloway), where excavation (see Gazetteer) revealed twelfth – fourteenth-century occupation and timber buildings (courtesy of G. Stell and Crown copyright RCAHM, Scotland).

now about 250 known examples, and as recently as the 1970s fieldwork has been adding to the total.[62] The traditional association of mottes with centres of royal administration and with fiefs, both large and small, of the twelfth- and thirteenth-century Anglo-Norman settlers holds true. But their unbalanced distribution is notable, at least half the total lying in the south-west. Central Scotland and parts of the north-east are also well represented, but the Highlands and most of the south-east are without mottes (fig. 2.28). This pattern may partly be due to an uneven survival and/or recognition of other types of early castle (see above). But it may also relate to the changing process of colonization. Only a small proportion of the total was connected directly with royal landholding, and in the south-east, the area of initially strong royal authority and of primary Anglo-Norman influence, there are also very few. Their main distribution lies in areas of secondary settlement, for example Galloway,

where royal authority was weaker and the settlement, often implemented against local resistance, had a correspondingly more military character. Readily defensible mottes would have a greater attraction in such areas than they did in the more secure south-east. Such analysis, however, is very tentative, and much work remains to be done on this problem. Regional studies, such as those recently published for Galloway and the north-east of Scotland, continue to reveal the form, distribution and social context of mottes, as well as their relationship with other elements in the settlement pattern.[63]

Ireland

By the later twelfth century, Anglo-Norman influence had spread also to Ireland. Here the circumstances were more akin to those in Wales at an earlier date: a piecemeal conquest by ambitious adventurers, starting in 1169, generally (though not always) with the support, and sometimes intervention, of the kings of England. But whereas in Wales there was to be a final conquest under Edward I, Anglo-Irish hostilities, as well as internal disorder among the settlers, dragged on for centuries. The Anglo-Norman settlement (for want of a better phrase – the settlers also included many Welsh and Flemings) had a fundamental and long-lasting impact on the Irish landscape. The very basis of agricultural life was affected in the creation of a manorial system, and the characteristic signs of Norman colonization, castles, towns and monasteries, sprang up in quantity.[64]

As in England, Wales and Scotland, the association of the Anglo-Normans in Ireland with sites of castles, including many mottes, was reliably established at the beginning of

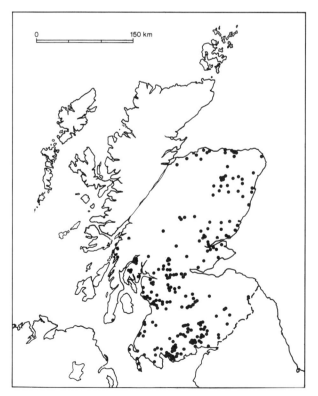

2.28 Distribution of mottes in Scotland (after G. Stell in P. McNeill, R. Nicholson (eds.), *An Historical Atlas of Scotland c.400–c.1600*, 1975, with the permission of the Trustees of the Conference of Scottish Medievalists).

this century, principally by Goddard Orpen. Prior to this, the approach to the earthwork sites in particular had been subject to a mélange of Celtic, Norse and Anglo-Norman interpretation in which nationalist sentiment played not a little part. The 'Anglo-Norman' view of castles was assisted by the apparently unequivocal statement of Gerald of Wales, whose *Conquest of Ireland* is a contemporary source for the early settlement, that the Irish were not users of castles (*castella*) but used woods and bogs for protection. Gerald also mentioned round, ditched sites, and abandoned walled sites (which he also called *castella*). These, he wrongly thought, were of Norse origin. By identifying them with the native raths and cashels of the Irish landscape, Orpen and others were able to maintain the separate, intrusive quality of the Anglo-Norman castles. Any discussion of Irish castle origins, which is complicated by the existence of these numerous earlier sites, must start from this standpoint. It is nevertheless interesting that Ella Armitage saw the possibility that this thesis would bear refinement. She recognized the likelihood of Anglo-Norman reuse (albeit in different form) of Irish sites, and she speculated whether, before 1169, the Irish might have begun to copy the earth and timber castle-building habit of their neighbours.[65] It is precisely in these matters that the now current views on Irish castle origins have diverged from the orthodox view which she helped establish.

The amount of known field evidence has grown enormously since the beginning of the twentieth century as a result of both corporate and individual efforts. Fieldwork is still active, and it seems likely that the total numbers of sites, particularly in the south, are not yet known.[66] Also much advanced is the state of historical study, where research continues to reveal the social context of castle-building in greater detail.[67] Finally, the last forty years have seen the growth of excavation on timber castles. This has not only revealed unexpected structures, but has also raised basic questions about the origins of such sites. The bulk of this work has been carried out by The Archaeological Survey of Northern Ireland, and relatively little structural detail has been recovered elsewhere.[68] It is impossible in the space available to examine adequately all lines of enquiry in this flourishing field of Irish archaeology, but those points central to the issue of origins may be briefly summarized.

In mapping the field evidence for timber castles the wider background of the Irish earthwork tradition is something of a problem. There are also thousands of raths, or ring-forts as they are now more commonly known, surviving in the landscape. Whereas a tall motte and a simple ring-fort may be easily distinguished, with other examples this is not always the case. Many Irish mottes are not the tall, conical archetype familiar in England and elsewhere. They frequently lack baileys, and their broader summits carried most of the buildings. Equally, not all raths/ring-forts were simple earthwork enclosures. There is a variant, known mainly in the north and often called the 'raised rath', whose appearance is not dissimilar from a motte. Thus, as in Wales, there is sometimes a problem of separating the works of the invaders from those of the native society: 'Anglo-Norman' and 'Gaelic' works are not always superficially distinguishable. In some cases excavation has revealed a structural sequence from rath to motte on the same site (see below p. 74). Finally (*contra* Gerald of Wales), it has been argued that raths could continue in use until after the Anglo-Norman invasions, though this is not universally accepted. In any distribution map, therefore, there is a danger of confusing different types of site.[69]

Since the more substantial ring-forts (there are also lesser examples with little defensive quality) also fade imperceptibly into what in other areas would be called ringworks, itself a category of field monument containing many medieval castles, a further complication is introduced: apart from a difference in traditional terminology, is there any significant difference between a substantial Irish ring-fort and its English or Welsh counterpart such as Sulgrave (Northants) or Hawcock's Mount, Westbury (Old Caus) (Shropshire)? Attention has now been drawn to the possibility that the medieval ringwork in this general sense has been under-represented in our view of early Irish castles, and that, in addition to extending our understanding of the Anglo-Norman settlement, this fact might explain the relative lack of mottes in areas such as Waterford, Limerick and (eastern) Cork which certainly experienced Anglo-Norman settlement. In view of the problem of making chronological distinctions amongst the almost overwhelming quantity of Irish 'ringwork' forms, pursuing this idea without numerous excavations is likely to prove very difficult. Nevertheless, it is an interesting notion and recalls the similar

view recently developed in Scotland (see above pp. 66ff.). About 20 possible examples were originally identified, on the basis of documentary or archaeological evidence, and this number has recently been raised to 45 (fig. 2.29).

It may be relevant that South Wales, an area where ringworks were popular, was a source of immigrants to Ireland in some numbers. It is certainly the case that some of the sites in question were among the earliest of all Anglo-Norman castles in Ireland, including Ferrycarrig (Wexford) and Trim (Meath). At the latter, a contemporary source actually described the building by Hugh de Lacy of a house surrounded by a ditch and palisade. Another early site was that at Baginbun Head (Wexford) which also lacked a motte. Established in 1170, this occupied the site of a much earlier promontory fort. It is hard not to recall the observations made about the earliest Norman castles in England, which also seem to have been enclosures of some sort. Mottes might have had many advantages, especially in the consolidation of conquest, but they were not the most useful type of fortification in campaign. The argument has recently been taken a stage further in relation to western Ireland, where mottes are few but where there was certainly Anglo-Norman penetration in the thirteenth century. It has been suggested that from the second quarter of that century, mottes were no longer fashionable here and ringworks were built as a matter of course: it is simply the difficulty of distinguishing them from the ring-fort tradition which has, until very recently, hampered their recognition.[70]

Despite the appearance of stone castles, such as Carrickfergus, before 1200, it is the mottes which, from the time of Goddard Orpen and Ella Armitage onwards, have

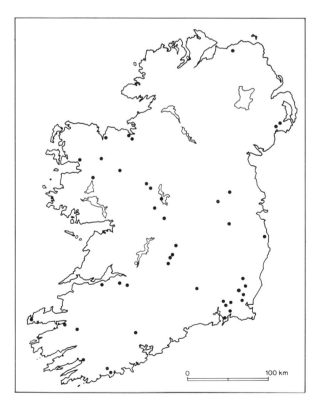

0   100 km

2.29 Possible castle ringworks in Ireland (T. Barry, *The Archaeology of Medieval Ireland*, 1987).

dominated the notion of the earliest Irish castles. Renewed attention to them as a class, as opposed to as individual field monuments, soon followed the revival of general interest in the subject from the 1960s.[71] Though an exact estimate is made impossible for the reasons discussed above, at least 350 are now known. Many seem to have been built on earlier features, such as natural rock outcrops, or on existing Irish earthworks (see below). On the whole, their distribution (fig. 2.30) reflects the areas annexed through Anglo-Norman settlement by the mid-thirteenth century. They were both partly a means of conquest and partly a symbol of the achievement of conquest (fig. 2.31). But the significance of the distribution is less obvious than was once thought, and an absence of mottes does not indicate an absence of settlement. A further complication is their occurrence in areas retained by the Irish, who, like the Welsh, emulated their neighbours. Neither do densely distributed mottes necessarily reveal the areas of heaviest settlement, which, if felt to be secure, would be in need of less defence. But areas which were frontiers at some stage did attract concentrations of mottes (which do sometimes include Irish examples), as in Antrim and Meath. Such frontier concentrations may simply indicate that in some areas, mainly northern rather than southern, the settlers faced more hostile opposition from the Irish than they did elsewhere. Mottes with baileys seem to have been situated in crucial military areas, the baileys providing space for garrisons, whereas mottes alone were more often the defended residences of the newly established manorial system. The former were more likely to give rise to market centres, even towns, whereas the latter were more likely to attract only village development.[72] The duration of motte-building is somewhat controversial. In some areas they seem not to have been built after the second quarter of the thirteenth century, but elsewhere this was not the case. Recent documentary studies and fieldwork in Leinster suggest that the settlers were still building mottes and baileys in the late thirteenth, even the fourteenth centuries. In some instances, their occupation (as well as that of sites dating from before 1200) continued to the fifteenth century.[73]

Turning to the archaeology of these sites, we can examine both the structural history of excavated examples (see chapter 8), as well as more general ideas about their relationship with the earlier ring-forts. Northern Ireland in particular has received close attention from excavators, mainly under the aegis of its Archaeological Survey. Here it is appropriate to mention those sites which have illuminated the interplay of native and intrusive works.[74] That 'mottes', with the outward appearance of purely Anglo-Norman works, could arise from

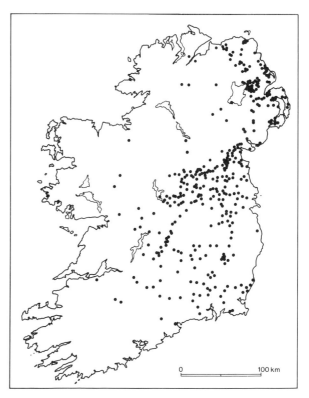

2.30 Distribution of mottes in Ireland (after T. McNeill, in *Ch.G.* XIV, 1990).

2.31 Knockgraffon motte (Co. Tipperary). One of Ireland's finest Norman mottes, with a later stone tower house in its bailey (photo. R.A. Higham).

the reuse of Irish ring-forts was established long ago in County Down (figs 2.32–33). Lismahon (see pp. 320–3) and Castleskreen, both published in the 1950s, are examples (the former a native site even in its enlarged form), and at Duneight a motte was added at one end of the site, leaving the remains of the rath, suitably strengthened, as its bailey. Rathmullan is a more recently excavated example in the same county, and examples are known also in County Antrim at Ballynarry and Dunsilly. Sometimes the Anglo-Norman phase simply represents an expedient occupation, making the motte easier to build, as it would be if a natural feature were employed.

Elsewhere, however, it appears that the ring-fort was still in use, as at Duneight where one of its buildings was retained, with some reconstruction, in the newly created bailey. At Rathmullan it was not entirely clear whether the site had been abandoned: some 'Anglo-Norman' occupation material pre-dated the heightening of the site. Such evidence not only illuminates the process of Anglo-Norman settlement in Ireland, but reminds us of what may be invisible in other parts of the British Isles where mottes have been less thoroughly dismantled. But more surprising has been the evidence from certain other sites in the north, at Gransha (Co. Down) (fig. 2.34), Big Glebe (Co. Londonderry) and Deer Park Farms (Co. Antrim). Here, motte-like mounds were found to be entirely pre-Norman in their development. They are examples of 'raised raths' which were built up by stages, achieving their final form probably in the tenth century.

Such discoveries raise the basic issue of whether an earthwork and timber castle can be defined in purely physical terms, or whether the castle was also an institutional phenomenon which can only be defined in its social context. Clearly, it is not simply a matter of dating and measuring earthworks: their potential variety on both counts is enormous. Neither were earthworks built for their own sake; they were built to be occupied. It has been rightly remarked that the excavated tops of Irish mottes, even where defended by a perimeter palisade as at Clough (Co. Down),

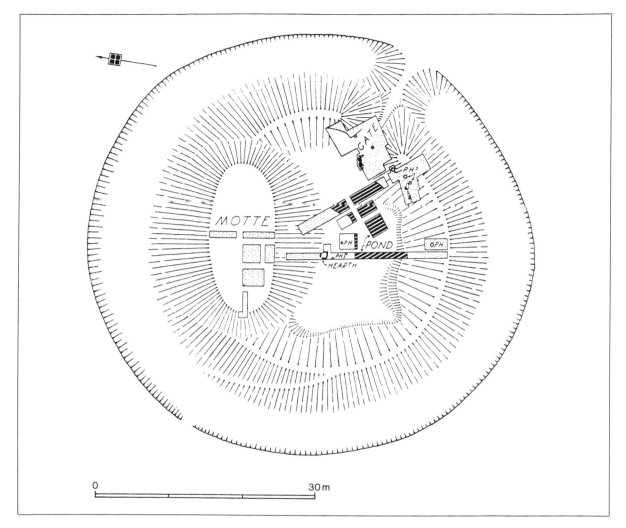

2.32 Rath converted into a motte and bailey at Castleskreen (Co. Down) (*An Archaeological Survey of County Down*, 1966; Crown copyright with permission of the Controller of HMSO).

2.33 Section through rath raised into a motte at Rathmullan (Co. Down) (C. Lynn, in *Ulster J. Archaeol.* 44–45, 1981–82; Crown copyright).

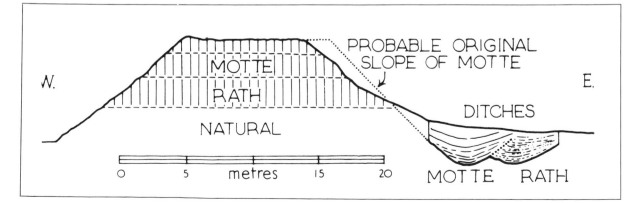

2.34 Gransha (Co. Down). A large flat-topped mound which reached its final height in the ninth or tenth century AD (C. Lynn and courtesy of The Archaeological Survey, Dept. of Environment, Northern Ireland; Crown copyright).

tend to produce normal domestic buildings rather than anything obviously military, let alone aristocratic. Structures such as the tower alongside the house at Lismahon, the possible timber predecessor of the late medieval stone tower at Clough, and the (unpublished) timber tower at Lurgankeel (Co. Louth) may not have been very typical, at least on present evidence.

The ordinariness of motte buildings may reflect the relatively low position in the social hierarchy at which some mottes were built in Ireland, as well as the possibility that whereas the mound itself was a mark of prestige, other wealth was tied up in land and livestock. The building of ordinary domestic structures on mottes has more in common with the native tradition of ring-fort occupation than with the more massive castle structures excavated and documented in other parts of the British Isles and Europe.[75] The evidence is indeed an interesting reflection of native habits, reminding us how adaptable the timber castle was. On the other hand, the discovery of

apparently blank motte-tops, as at Dunsilly and the latest phases of Castleskreen and Rathmullan, should be viewed cautiously. It seems inconceivable that anyone should heighten a motte and then not build on it, unless abandonment was enforced by some external pressure. Equally likely is that framed timber structures were erected, leaving no ground evidence. Prefabricated castles sent across the Irish Sea from England in the late twelfth century (below, chapter 4) are not likely to have left much archaeological evidence.

The discovery of raths which grew into Norman mottes, and of others which were raised into 'mottes' before the Normans ever arrived has stimulated wider debate on the origin of Irish castles. Some documentary evidence for early twelfth-century Irish royal castles, formerly dismissed as uninterpretable, has now been rehabilitated.[76] The introduction of the words *caistel* and *caislen* into the Irish annals, in reference to some half-dozen places established in the 1120s, is of great interest. The more usual word would have been *dun* or. *raith*, and the matter is to some extent paralleled by the use of *castel* in the *Anglo-Saxon Chronicle* in the 1050s (see Appendix B). These sites, several of which were constructed by Turlough O'Connor, king of Connacht, were apparently timber-built, since the annals consistently refer to their subsequent destruction by fire. They cannot be viewed archaeologically because of later developments on their sites. Occasionally these words were also used for fortifications which were not royal, hinting at the social spread of whatever it was they represented. The evidence, limited though it is, may suggest that the Irish had begun to copy, or develop for themselves, the castle-building activity of their neighbours before the invasions. Gerald of Wales, however, was adamant that the Irish did not resist the invasion from a basis of castles, which presumably means he did not see anything which he recognized as a castle by contemporary English or Welsh standards. Nevertheless, the Irish continued to call the castles of the Normans by the same two names, suggesting they may have had something in common. In more general terms, the debate has been widened to incorporate the views of historians of eleventh- and twelfth-century Ireland, who now see the period as one of increasing assimilation of outside influence by the Irish, who were perhaps less insular in outlook than previously supposed. In such a context, a view of the raised raths as an Irish form of pre-Norman castle is easier to accept, even in the traditional 'feudal' definition of the castle.[77]

The historical and archaeological aspects of these Irish sites enable the issue of timber castle origins to be raised in a more direct way than in any other part of the British Isles. This is partly the result of the ubiquitous ring-fort tradition, as well as of the late date of Norman influence, and of course the happy occurrence of some most revealing excavations. Despite being on the periphery of the Norman world, Ireland is of crucial importance to our theme. Timber castles, whether Irish or Norman, abounded and were regarded as adequate and normal fortifications and residences. In 1172–3, when Henry II of England was in Dublin, the palace built for his use was constructed of timber. This reflected not only the Irish context in which it was built, but also the wider acceptability of timber building even at the highest levels of society.[78]

—— 3 ——

Origins of timber castles in Europe

In the traditional view, castles of all sorts were born in France, from where they spread by both peaceful and military processes. In the preceding chapter, however, the origins of timber castles in the various British regions were examined within the context of their own existing defensive traditions. This approach is continued here. First, and fairly briefly, the southern, northern and central European countries are dealt with. The chapter ends with a fuller discussion of the evidence from France, which is also the most useful point of comparison with the British Isles.

Italy

Medieval Italy shared the earth and timber building tradition, and timber castle sites are known in the field, from the air, and from documentary sources. The latter suggest some timber towers existed as early as the tenth century, and in the same period began the use of 'natural mottes' on rising ground in badly-drained areas. The principle of private defence was established by the eleventh century, though a difficulty lies in interpreting the precise meaning of the vocabulary of the chronicles and charters, especially since the period also saw the process of *incastellamento*, the growth of fortified rural settlements. The evidence for the permanent use of mottes, as well as for the word *mota* itself, is mainly from the twelfth century onwards. Some were built

as late as the fourteenth century, particularly in siege warfare.[1]

The possibility of Norman importation of castle-building was noted by Ella Armitage, who discussed Norman expansion not only into the British Isles, but also into Italy and Sicily.[2] Attention has more recently been drawn to the specific chronicle evidence for castle-building by the Normans further south in the mid-eleventh century. Some of their castles utilized natural rocky sites, but at Petralia Soprana (Sicily) there is an apparently man-made, though damaged, motte. If the motte dates from the documented establishment of the castle, in 1060–6, then it is of great interest. But it is only through excavation that there would be a chance (and not a very great one, probably) of answering this question.[3] There is also evidence for the Norman castle, said by a reliable chronicle source to have been defended in timber, built on a mound in 1054 at San Marco Argentano (Cosenza). This motte, which is partly natural, is now surmounted by a later stone tower. It could be the feature first referred to, though again this is impossible to prove.[4] Excavations at Scribla, where a *castellum* was founded by the Normans in 1044 and abandoned in 1054 on the foundation of San Marco Argentano itself, have shown that the earliest defence was a timber-revetted rampart. Even when rebuilt after its re-occupation in 1064 it was not given a motte: it consisted of a platform created from a scarped hilltop, and from the twelfth century it had a stone keep. Current opinion is that mottes became common in Italy only at the end of the eleventh century, when castle-building spread more widely in society in a period of civil strife. Though some of the earlier Norman castles were timber-defended, a primary Norman importation of specifically *motte*-building is difficult to demonstrate.[5]

Spain

Spain is fundamentally a land of stone technology in fortification, and rarely has the sort of excavation been pursued which might detect possible early timber phases. Indeed, the environment is unlikely to have encouraged timber technology on the scale experienced further north. Carolingian timber watch-towers of the late eighth century have been excavated in Catalonia, where they were frontier works of the early reconquest.[6] At the major excavation of Gormaz (Soria), whose occupation stretched from the tenth to the sixteenth centuries, no complete structural phases of timber were revealed, though there were timber components of the defences and buildings.[7] In addition to the stone and mud-brick of Spanish castles, there was also the technique used in the southern regions: a mixture of pebbles in cement, sun-dried between wooden boards, known as *tapia*.[8] A well-documented agreement, on the building of a castle at Tarrega for the count of Barcelona, refers specifically to the construction of stone towers and walls. This was in 1058, when the bulk of castles in north-west Europe were certainly of timber. Here, in the marches of Christian Europe and Moslem Spain, was a territory ripe for the proliferation of castles. Castle-building in Spain generally was widespread from the 1020s, and, as elsewhere in Europe, the theory of overlordship of castles became entrenched. The practice of keeping written oaths between castellans and lords was common, and large numbers of such oaths survive from the eleventh and twelfth centuries.[9]

Denmark

In Denmark, at the other end of the continent, the situation was quite different. There was already a timber-building tradition, and this was readily applied to fortifications. The great geometrical fortifications (fig. 3.1) at Trelleborg, Aggersborg, Fyrkat and Odense/Nonnebakken were built late in the tenth century, in a period which also produced other defensive works: a major extension of the southern frontier – the Danewirke – and the ramparts of the adjacent town of Hedeby, as well as those of Århus further north, preceded them by only a few years. All were the work of king Harald Bluetooth (940–86). The frontier and urban ramparts were defensive in function, whereas the fortresses were the instrument of his internal control over the kingdom. The latter went out of use by the early eleventh century, and there were no more royal, or other works for the next hundred years.[10] Castles made their appearance only from the twelfth century, despite the frequent wars and periods of political instability which might have encouraged them. It was another period of strong royal control, under Valdemar the Great from the 1150s, which saw the development of castle-building, by kings and powerful families who supported them. The practice had not spread beyond the kings and these men by the mid-thirteenth century. There are occasional references to early timber castles, such as that built at Haraldsborg (Roskilde), and one motte, Sjørrind in North Jutland, may be a royal castle of this date. A contemporary writer commented that Danish towns and castles had timber palisades and ditches rather than stone walls, and more evidence of this period may await discovery. The known castles, however, were predominantly of stone, either curtained enclosures or great towers, in

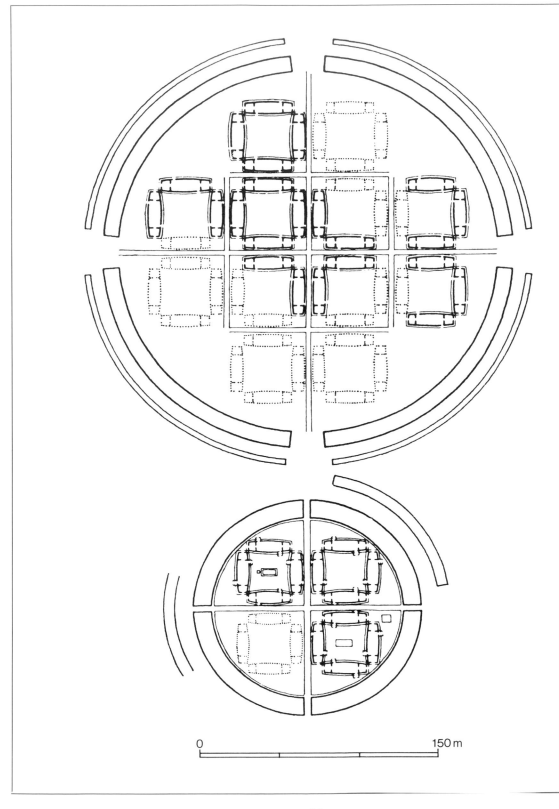

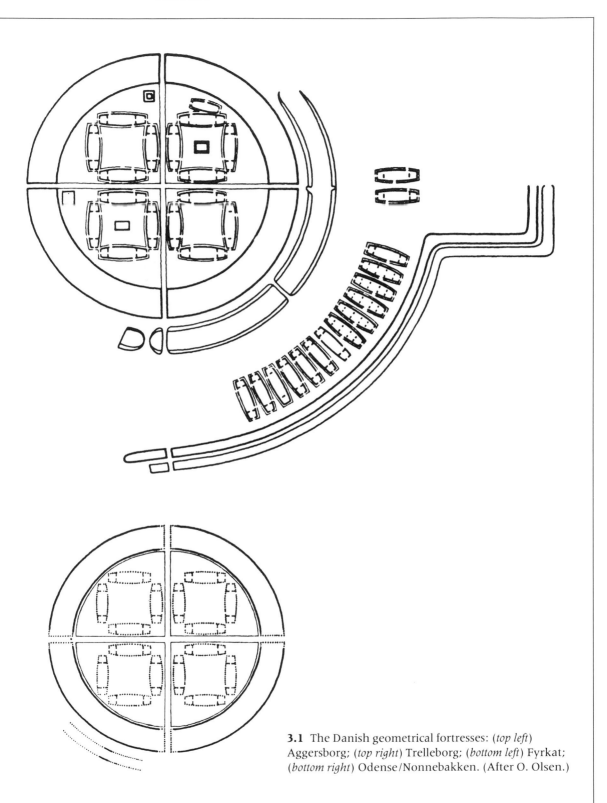

3.1 The Danish geometrical fortresses: (*top left*)
Aggersborg; (*top right*) Trelleborg; (*bottom left*) Fyrkat;
(*bottom right*) Odense/Nonnebakken. (After O. Olsen.)

3.2 A Danish motte (Diernaes) and manor house platform (Torp) of lower height (V. La Cour & H. Stiesdahl, *Danske Voldsteder fra Oldtid og Middelalder*, 2 vols. 1957, 1963).

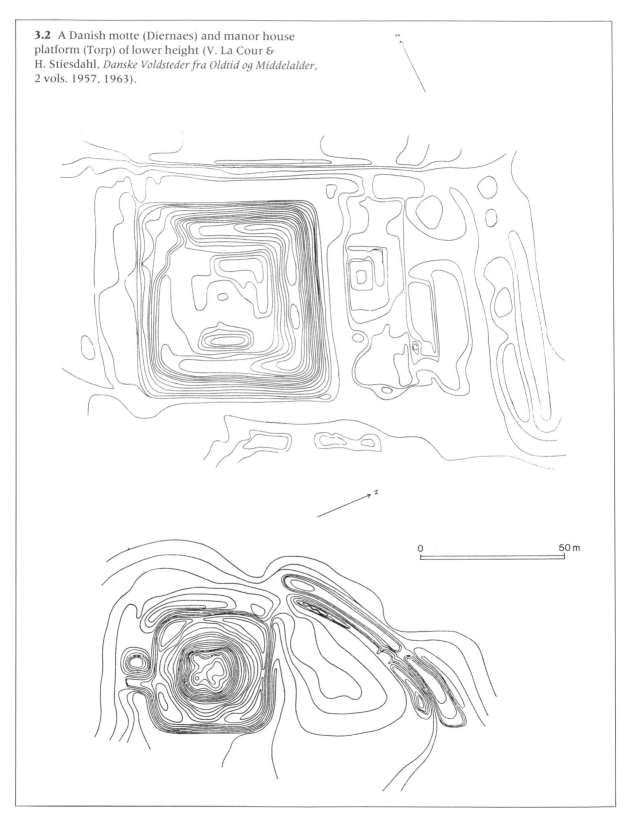

imitation of contemporary works further south.

From the end of the thirteenth century the situation changed. Renewed internal competition for the throne, peasants' revolts, external attacks and the fragmentation of the kingdom into duchies – all created the conditions in which castles were built in increasing numbers. As in other countries, the study of these castles made great progress in the later nineteenth and early twentieth centuries with, as elsewhere due regard paid to earthwork sites. Although stone castles continued to be built, it was in the fourteenth century that timber castles, often mottes (commonly squarish in plan) and baileys,

flourished (fig. 3.2). Their heyday as defensible sites was brought to an end with the re-establishment of royal control and a ban on castle-building in 1396.[11] Excavations at a number of Danish mottes, including Nørrevolde, Eriksvolde, Kaersgaard, Havrum and Jomfruhoj have produced no evidence of occupation before the fourteenth century, and plentiful evidence for timber construction. Detailed fieldwork, combined with documentary study, has shown that unfortified manor houses continued to be built within or on top of earth-works in the fifteenth and early six-

3.3 Section through defended crannog in two phases at Solvig, Denmark (after J. Hertz in *Ch.G.* VI, 1973).

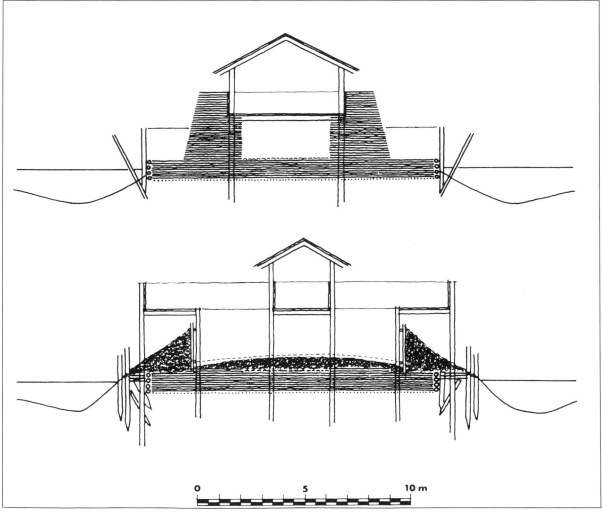

teenth centuries.[12] Another version of these sites has been revealed at Solvig, in southern Jutland, where four raised islands in a marsh were created in the fourteenth century. One of them carried an aisled timber longhouse, and collectively the settlement was a farm. But another island was a fortified nucleus carrying first a timber and turf house surrounded by a palisade, and later a timber tower with curtain wall and breastwork (fig. 3.3). Again, in undefended form, the site had later occupation in the fifteenth and sixteenth centuries.[13]

Denmark's late medieval age of timber castles makes an interesting contrast with most other areas, where, although such sites were by no means entirely obsolete at this time, they were rarely being built anew. Their late popularity reflects the dissemination of castle-building downwards through society, owing to particular political and economic circumstances. In this sense Denmark provides a microcosm of earlier developments elsewhere.

The Slavs

Among the sources of Denmark's external problems were the Slavic lands on its south-eastern borders. These were the western tip of a region stretching eastwards across Europe into present-day Russia. Timber-building technology was fundamental to this cultural zone, in domestic building and all manner of defensive works. The city of Kiev, as well as having numerous timber buildings, still had earth and timber defences when it was confronted by the Mongol army with its siege engines in 1240. So great was its destruction that it was hardly occupied again before the seventeenth century, when it was completely replanned.[14] The areas occupied by the various groups of Slavs, from their expansion

3.4 Timber defences of Slav fortress at Behren-Lübchin in the tenth century (after W. Hensel in *Ch. G.* IV, 1968).

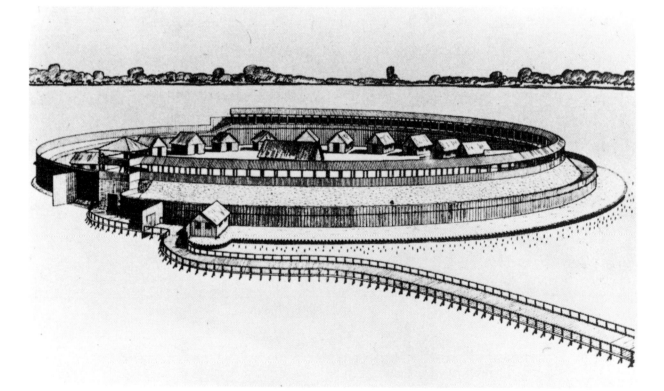

in the fifth to seventh centuries, cannot receive the treatment they deserve in the space available here.[15] It is relevant, nevertheless, to point out that the main purposes to which timber technology was put in defensive contexts were no different in principle from those found in western Europe. Timber defence was used for settlements, some of which came to have urban characteristics, for fortresses associated with warfare and expansion, and for smaller, more private establishments approximating to western 'castles'. The frequent use of complete timbers gave these works an imposing massiveness, and the building technique could also be combined with stone rubble to achieve an even more solid effect (fig. 3.4).[16]

The southern fringe of these areas came into contact with Byzantine culture, and parts of modern Romania adopted stone-building at a relatively early date. Further north, however, Transylvania was settled by the Hungarians, and here all fortifications up to the thirteenth century employed timber. In the early part of that century the use of stone was gradually introduced, but the Magyar kings tried (unsuccessfully) to restrict their subjects building to timber only. A general lack of stone fortification is thought to have contributed to the area's weakness in the face of the Mongol invasion of 1241. The small square stone donjons which grew in popularity in this period sometimes had stone curtains, but often continued to have surrounding defences of earth and timber (fig. 3.5). They are thought to have been a translation into stone of a timber tower form which was already common.[17] Another point of general interest is the emergence of settlement forms containing a defended nucleus, or citadel. This distinction between *Hauptburg* and *Vorburg* became widespread in Slavic settlements,

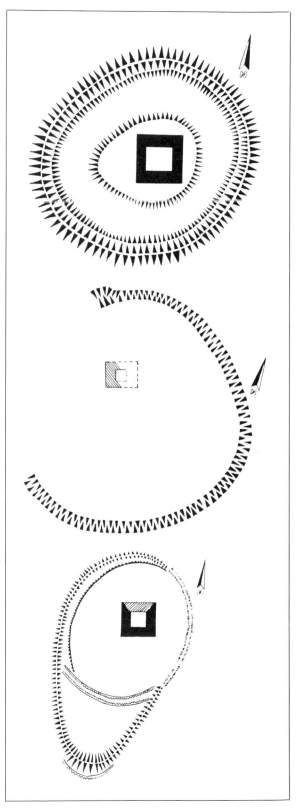

3.5 Timber and earth defences around thirteenth-century stone donjons in Romania (after G. Anghel in *Ch.G.* VIII, 1977).

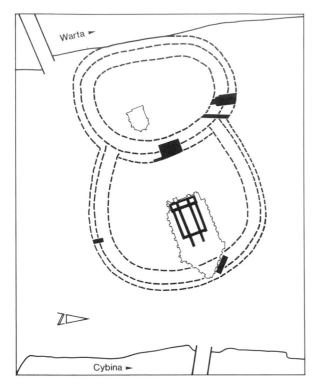

some of which became towns (figs 3.6–7), and although in some places these were replaced from the twelfth century by new market and street plans, elsewhere they were of long-lasting influence.[18]

The emergence of smaller fortified sites in the hands of the nobility, castles by western definition, also occurred in the Slavic territories, and Poland is currently the subject of much important research in this field. Here, the tradition of timber technology stretched back into prehistory – one of Poland's most famous sites is the fortified timber-built island settlement at Biskupin, which was occupied from c.700 BC onwards. The early medieval tribal fortresses were also defended in timber, as were the royal citadels such as Gniezno, which emerged from the eleventh century as royal power superseded the tribal structure. Mottes with timber defences appeared in the

3.6 Bipartite plan at Poznan, Poland (after W. Hensel, *La Naissance de la Pologne*, 1966).

3.7 Lakeside Slav settlement of the ninth century with bipartite plan, at Scharstorf, Holstein (after K.W. Struve, *Die Burgen in Schleswig-Holstein*, 1981).

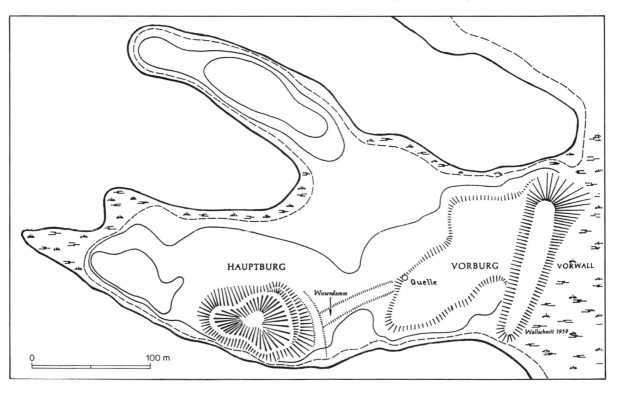

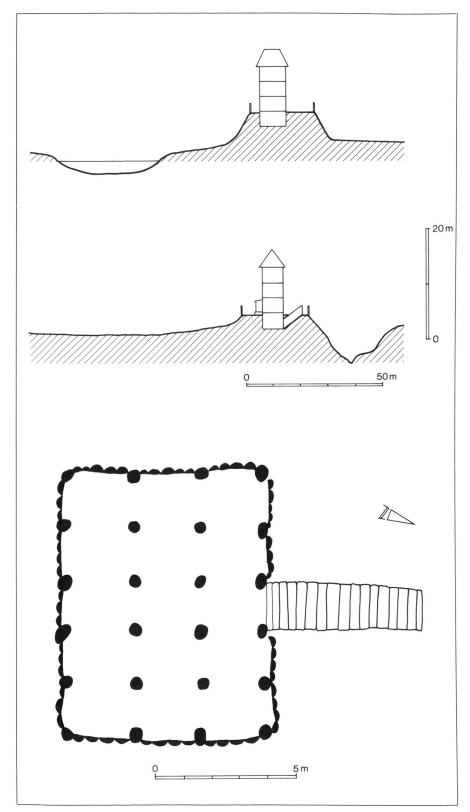

20 m

0

0   50 m

0   5 m

3.8 Section through motte and plan of timber motte tower at Plemięta, Poland (after A. Nadolskiego (ed.), *Plemięta*, 1985).

thirteenth century, becoming an increasingly common feature of Poland's developing feudal society.

By this date stone technology was also appearing, in the keeps and curtain walls built by the most powerful. At first the mottes themselves belonged only to the powerful few, but by the fourteenth century had spread to the knightly class. Excavations in the 1970s on the motte at Plemięta (Torun) recovered evidence of a stave-built rectangular residential tower, which was also partly clay-clad (fig. 3.8). The wide array of artefact evidence preserved here also revealed many domestic and military aspects of the daily life of the knightly class in the fourteenth century. Opinion is divided on the social significance of Polish mottes: were they a product of local development, or were they a direct imitation of western practice? Timber and earth technology in Poland was also long-lasting. Some fifteenth-century manor houses were surrounded by ramparts, and some timber (or stone and brick) houses continued to occupy old mottes and other earthworks. These practices survived to the seventeenth century, in some instances later.[19]

Germany

The development of castles in Germany was a long and complex process. Stone towers appeared by the tenth and eleventh centuries in private residential sites, as at Unterregenbach and Xanten (Lorraine). Other examples of similar date had timber superstructures, as at Koepfel (now in France, dep. Bas-Rhin). The tall defensive tower (*Bergfried*), circular or rectangular, eventually characterized many German castles and is perhaps the best known form.[20] But the tradition of building earthworks, in conjunction with both timber and stone, stretched back for centuries, employed in Saxon fortresses and Frankish fortresses built against the Saxons, as well as deliberately planted colonies of Franks in con-

quered areas. In some, the 'upper' and 'lower' division referred to above in Slavic contexts is apparent, for example at Hofe near Dreihausen (Hesse) (fig. 3.9), a late eighth- and ninth-century Frankish site. The attacks by Vikings, Slavs and Magyars stimulated the building of further fortifications, such as those of Henry the Fowler, in the tenth century. The numerous ringworks (*Rundwälle*) emerged at this time, in response to these outside threats. There were also, from the eighth and ninth centuries, much smaller hilltop fortifications, the precursors of the private castles. Some, such as 'Burg', Caldern (near Marburg, Hesse), already bear evidence at this date of the towers which were to proliferate later. Mottes eventually became common, sometimes on new sites and sometimes on older ringworks. Recent work in southern Germany and elsewhere suggests that mottes were first built in the eleventh century, as local noble families established residences in estates from which they also took their names. By the later twelfth century, however, the *Bergfried* within an enclosure was the more popular form. Castle fieldwork and excavation is currently very active.[21]

Rescue excavations in the Rhineland from the late 1940s showed for the first time that mottes and baileys might be more than they appear at first sight. The Rhineland is an area thickly studded with mottes, though they tend to fall at the lower end of the size range (fig. 3.10a). Their mainly low-lying situation explains the frequency of water-filled ditches, as well as the good preservation of timberwork which some excavated examples have revealed (some also bear masonry traces). They vary greatly in plan, many of the published examples bearing little resemblance to the notional text-book type. About 20 have been explored in excavation, many on a small scale.[22] Of great significance here is the discovery, made at der Husterknupp, near Frimmersdorf, 20 km (12 miles) from Düsseldorf (see also pp. 268–73), that the eventual

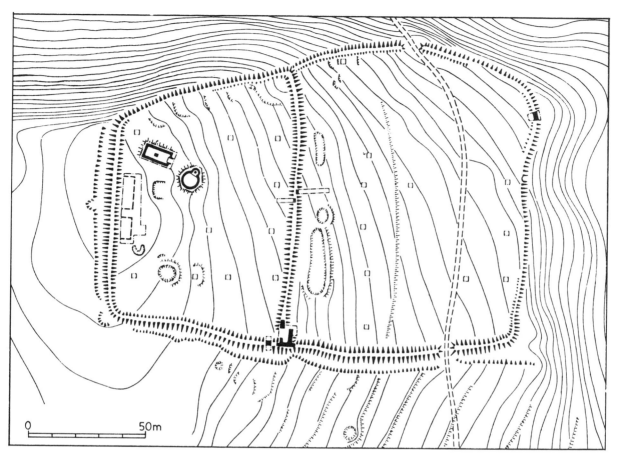

3.9 Bipartite fortification at Hofe, Driehausen (Hesse), a late eighth-ninth-century Carolingian site (after W. Schlesinger in *World Archaeol.* 7, 1976).

motte *grew* into its final shape: it was not erected *de novo* on an empty site (fig. 3.10b). The site began as a simple enclosure (*Flachsied-lung*), with slightly raised interior, wet ditch and palisade, in the late ninth or tenth century. A second enclosure was added in the late tenth century, and the original enclosure was raised to form a low mound (*Kernmotte*). Finally, between the eleventh and thirteenth centuries, the latter was raised by a number of separate operations into a higher mound, leaving the two components as a recognizable (though still not very high) motte with a bailey (*Hochmotte und Vorburg*). Though

remains of timber buildings from the earlier phases were well preserved, unfortunately all trace of whatever stood on the eventual motte had disappeared.[23]

This process of gradual growth is reminiscent of some of the Irish sites discussed above, and similar evidence has since come from Normandy (see below p. 98). It clearly indicates changing preferences, but to what were these due? It is impossible, on the basis of the archaeology alone, to distinguish the raising of a site for purposes of better drainage from a similar process stimulated by growing social differentiation or defensive needs. In its first phase, der Husterknupp was surely a lightly defended agricultural settlement, enclosing itself perhaps against a combination of floodwater and possible Viking attacks. At what point it became a 'castle', whether in the

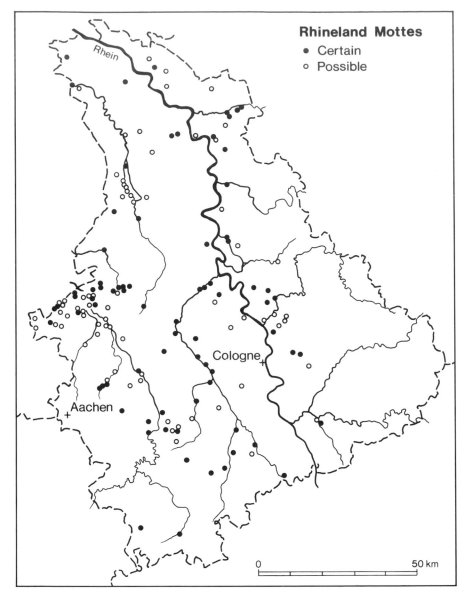

3.10 (a) (*Left*) Distribution of mottes in the Rhineland (after M. Müller-Wille, *Mittelaterliche Burghügel ('motten') im Nordlichen Rheinland*, 1966). (b) (*Right*) Schmatic development of der Husterknupp, from a simple enclosure to a motte (after A. Herrnbrodt, *Der Husterknupp*, 1958).

late tenth century or only in the eleventh, is a matter of choice. By the latter date it deserves the title not simply because of its form, but because during its final phases of development it was associated with a powerful local family. The difficulty is illustrated further by another Rhineland site. At Haus Meer, Büderich (near Düsseldorf), the artificial raising of the platform did not proceed beyond the intermediate stage, and may never have been intended as anything more than a dry platform in a wet environment.[24]

The Low Countries

Similar problems of interpreting motte origins are encountered also in the Low Countries. Here, too, the environment may have influenced the building of mottes. There was already a long tradition of raising mounds,

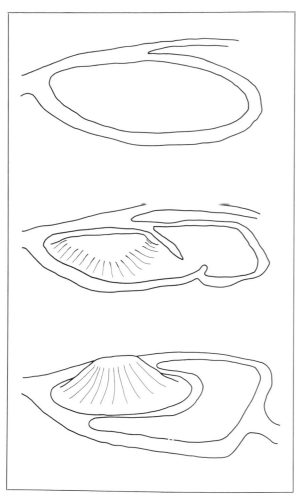

twelfth and thirteenth centuries. These, by the addition of further material, were raised into mottes 5 m (16 ft) or more high (fig. 3.12). Finally, there were mounds which were simply new mottes of this period, either wholly man-made or created from natural features.

The thirteenth century was the major period of widespread motte occupation, and the earliest evidence, documentary and archaeological, for their general building is mid-twelfth century, with occasional documentary hints at earlier ones. The twelfth-century examples were often larger and more obviously military than the more numerous thirteenth-century ones, which commonly lacked baileys.[26] The form of the very earliest Dutch castles for which there is documentary evidence, in the late eleventh century, is often difficult to reconstruct. Recent research suggests that they were dominated by stone towers rather than timber buildings and earthworks.[26]

The Dutch mounds are particularly interesting, because although the *terpen* provided a prototype, and indeed a physical foundation in some cases, the mottes themselves were not an early development by European standards generally. Dutch mottes might also be heightened during the medieval period, as excavations at Berg van Troje (Borssele) revealed. Here an earlier *terp* was raised into a motte with timber buildings *c*.1200, and a century later enlarged and revetted with a stone wall to carry a brick tower on its new summit.[28]

Of earlier date than the mottes there were some ringworks of late Carolingian origin. Some may have been similar to the Danish geometrical fortresses, as excavations at Oost-Souburg (Zeeland) revealed. At the Hunneschans (Uddel, Central Netherlands) the late ninth-century occupation was perhaps connected with the exploitation of local iron resources. The site was re-occupied in the thirteenth century and used a castle in the normal sense of a defended residence.[29]

known as *terpen*, which had begun in prehistoric times. These sites were also important in more northerly areas, as the excavations at Feddersen Wierde, near Bremerhaven in Germany, revealed.[25] In the Netherlands (fig. 3.11) there were originally very many more mounds than now survive. In Zeeland, for example, the former existence of about 170 can be deduced, as against 42 now visible. A recent analysis of such sites suggests three main lines of origin. Some are not medieval mottes at all, but well preserved *terpen* of earlier date. They had no military function, but were habitation sites raised against flooding. Second, there were early medieval *terpen*, up to about 3 m (10 ft) in height, which continued in use or which were reused, in the

3.11 Distribution of mottes in the Netherlands (after J. Bestemann in T. Hoekstra *et al.* (eds.), *Liber Castellorum*, 1981).

0   30 km

Flanders

To the south, in medieval Flanders, a recent archaeological and documentary survey examined mottes in a variety of contexts: in towns, in the rural valleys, in the reclaimed polders and in surviving marshy environments. The evidence suggests that although some castles originated at an earlier date (notably in Ghent, from the tenth century), motte building began in the eleventh century but flourished in the twelfth, and there were some later examples. The excavated evidence reveals mainly timber construction in the early phases, occasionally stone from the start, and several later replacements in stone. Apart from the urban examples, whose topography was complicated by other factors, all the mottes had attached baileys. The mottes were abandoned at various dates, often being transformed radically when incorporated in castles of later design. That at Ghent was levelled for the building of a stone donjon in the late twelfth century. Though some stone phases are known, there was a widespread timber building tradition in the area. The town defences and domestic buildings at Antwerp were solely of timber up until the thirteenth

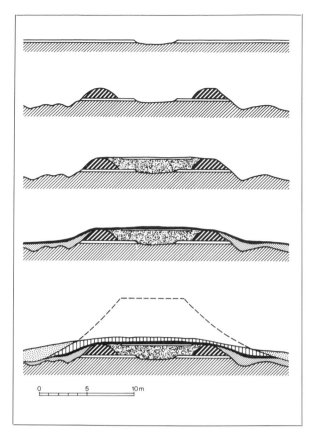

3.12 A *terp* raised by stages into a motte at Abbekinderen, Zeeland (after J.A. Trimpe-Burger in *BROB* 8, 1957).

century, when they were supplemented with stone.[30]

France

The recent identification from the air of what is possibly the castle built and destroyed within the year 979 at Vinchy (now France (Nord), then near the border between Flanders and Lotharingia), and now completely levelled, is of great interest. It has been argued that the evidence shows a former motte and bailey, though the published air photograph might equally be interpreted as two adjacent enclosures.[31] The chronicle which describes this event of 979, a reliable source of the early eleventh century, uses the words *castrum*,

agger and *turris* to describe the site at Vinchy. *Agger* has often been interpreted as 'motte', but strictly speaking meant any sort of mound. The ramparts of a heavily-defended earthwork enclosure, or ringwork, would presumably receive the same description. Without other details in a written passage to indicate more specifically that a motte was intended, the assumption is not necessarily justified.

This reflects a basic problem recurring in the discussion of castle origins generally. Rarely are the references so precise that the physical form of the site can be inferred. This has been a major hindrance to the study of early castles in France. A study of timber castle origins there is affected by two basic considerations: the long-standing argument that private castles, of any sort, were born in what is now northern France, from the Loire valley northwards; and the equally long-standing assumption that the most famous of all timber castle forms, the motte, was born in the same area at an early date, providing the prototype for mottes in all other parts of Europe. Both points have been modified by recent research. It is undoubtedly true that some private castles were emerging in the semi-autonomous provinces which succeeded the Carolingian Empire. But there is also evidence that some other areas, too, were developing their own traditions of private defence by the eleventh century. Within France itself, it has proved very difficult to show that castle-building had spread outside a very restricted social class before the same period. And a more critical view of mottes has revealed that their dissemination within France may also have been dated too early. Castles in France have been subject to more intense scrutiny in recent years than ever before, and there is room here only for the briefest outline of the evidence and the large amount of publication which its study has generated.

In 1980, a colloquium was held at Caen on the subject of earth and timber fortifications in medieval western Europe. Since the publication of that colloquium in 1981, the listing, classification and documentary study of these sites in France has been pursued by a whole team of scholars. The number of potential places is enormous – certainly many thousands.[32] The accompanying map of mottes and enclosures (fig. 3.13), which results from aerial photographic research and may also contain non-medieval sites, seems to be the only one published for France as a whole. It is inadequate in the quantity of evidence shown, but does at least reveal the character of its distribution.[33] More detailed regional studies have suggested just how many medieval earthworks there may be.

3.13 Distribution of circular earthwork forms in France (mottes, enclosures and others) published in 1965. Now much refined by regional studies, for instance 3.15 (after J. Soyer in *Annales de Normandie* 15, 1965).

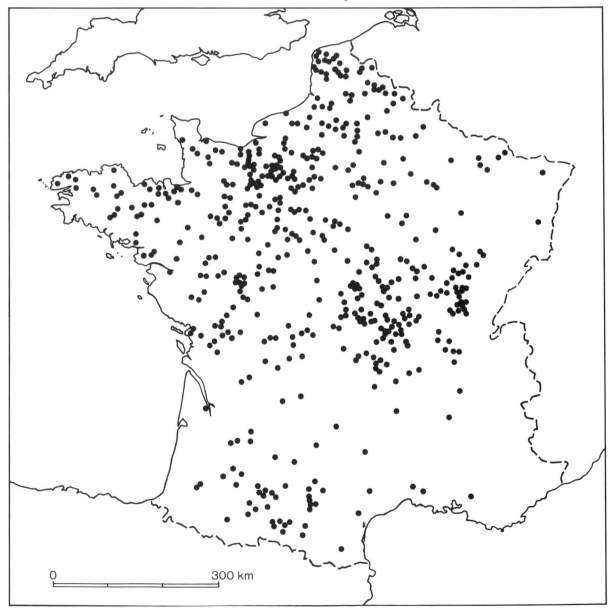

Given the likelihood that the majority were timber-built, if not throughout their existence then at least to start with, there is here a staggeringly large resource for timber castle studies. It is only in relatively recent times that the importance of enclosures of various sorts – castle ringworks, moated sites, fortified manor house sites – has been appreciated in France, and the study of such sites is now very active.[34]

Mottes, however, have had a continuous history of association with the notion of the medieval castle. Indeed, their social significance was never lost sight of. Long after its abandonment the *motte* of the old *chastel* often retained its symbolic value, as the centre of a fief and the source of lordship. Even up to the Revolution a lord might still return to the motte near his *château* to dispense justice *à cause de la motte*.[35] The word also occurs as a very common place-name element, but *motte* names need careful scrutiny: they can refer to natural as well as to man-made features.[36] The image of mottes as symbols of medieval society explains both their common description as *mottes féodales* as well as their dominant role in scholarly thought. More recently, however, awareness of evidence both for other types of early site and for the complex development of sites analogous to mottes in various areas, some well away from the feudal heart of north-west Europe, has led to the adoption of the less evocative phrase *motte castrale*, castle mound.[37]

Timber castles have long been regarded as an important ingredient of the landscape of medieval France, and, like other areas, France has an historiography in the subject going back to the nineteenth century.[38] Castles received much attention from de Caumont and Viollet le Duc, and timber castles, stone castles with timber components and timber siege machinery figured, albeit briefly, in Enlart's *Manuel d'Archéologie* published in 1904.[39] As elsewhere, the 1960s saw a growth in interest in the subject, and the *Château Gaillard* conferences emerged out of an initial meeting at Les Andelys in Normandy. A review of recent research published at that time affirmed that castles up to the later eleventh century were primarily timber ones, and that they continued in use long after this date. It was quite natural for the castles of mid and northern France to be seen as a product of the centuries-old timber building tradition of those regions.[40] Timber castles maintained their important role, in the literature of medieval archaeology in general as well of castles in particular: they were widespread, except in the southernmost parts of France, and the fact that they so often went unnoticed in early written sources was a reflection of their ordinariness. In contrast, early stone castles might receive comment simply because they were more unusual.[41]

In broad outline, this thesis can hardly be questioned. But establishing a detailed chronology for the origin of timber castles and deciding the form which the early sites took, is more problematic. The traditional starting-point is Charles the Bald's Capitulary of Pistes (Pîtres), which, issued in 864, was concerned with raising fortifications to prevent attacks up the rivers, particularly the Seine, by the Vikings. But it also insisted that those who had built *castella et firmitates et haias* without permission should demolish them.[42] What these castles, strongholds and enclosures consisted of is not clear, but there is here an indication of private works being built outside the accepted framework of royal control, and by later standards they would be called castles. Throughout the tenth and early eleventh centuries there is increasing reference to places which would be similarly defined.[43] Frequently the sources are quite unhelpful about physical matters. The writers use vocabulary derived from authors of Classical times – *castellum, castrum, firmitas, munitio, oppidum, turris, agger,* and so on – which was probably designed to create elegant prose and has generally defied attempts at archaeological analysis.[44] Sometimes we are told that a site was of timber, and the likelihood is that the vast majority were.

An older view of French castle origins saw castles as a spontaneous response by local society to problems of security created by the Viking attacks, and the implications of Charles the Bald's edict might support this view. But the conclusion from a variety of more recent regional studies is that the building of fortifications was originally within the competence only of those – the dukes and counts and their agents – who were the legitimate inheritors of imperial authority. In this sense the early castles had a 'public' as well as a 'private' quality. Castles of a less official character were built, in time of war or crisis, by the opponents of such people. In these two senses, castles were established in France during the tenth century. But, and this is an important qualification to some earlier and influential generalizations, castle-building was not yet socially widespread nor were castles very numerous.

The accumulation of research suggests that, although there were regional differences in chronology, only as the eleventh century developed, and particularly from the early twelfth century, did society, and its physical environment, become more generally 'encastled'. Though the reasons for this lie outside the scope of this discussion, it was in broad terms the result of two parallel trends. First, legitimate castle-building spread downwards through society, though always within the framework of control inherited from the Carolingians. Second, the frequent failure of the bonds of feudal society meant that castles were also built outside that framework. Although these 'adulterine' foundations were often not long in use, they nevertheless added to the landscape of castles. While castles documented at particular dates help us to see this process of castle growth, large numbers of surviving sites have no direct documentation. Their appearance can only be monitored more loosely through the history of associated lands and families. For this reason, precise

chronologies of castle origins are extremely difficult to establish.[45]

Among the sites of this period timber castles must have been numerically dominant. The earthworks, surviving in great quantity, as well as some excavated evidence, point to this conclusion. But what form did they take? As elsewhere, before excavation revealed how complex a castle's development might be, there was a tendency to equate the visible form of a French field monument with the period of its known or supposed origin. Ella Armitage, looking across the Channel for the background to English castles, often made this assumption. Some of the castles built by Theobald, count of Blois, and Fulk, count of Anjou, in the mid and late tenth century respectively, had had mottes (though not always surviving). These, she supposed, were original features of the sites.[46] This line of argument was for a long time influential among French scholars (who also developed it independently) and it led to the conclusion that the motte was an early and normal component of timber castles. It was accordingly very easy to imagine mottes being 'exported' from northern France by the Normans to the British Isles and Italy. The 'gradual' growth of mottes, by the processes which were eventually observed in the Rhineland and Low Countries, was seen as an interesting but peripheral development to their main origin in late tenth-century France. Moreover, mottes in France were seen as something new, not functional successors to residences of earlier date, even if they happened to be on top of such. This general view was still entrenched among French archaeologists and historians in the 1960s, when mottes and other early castles everywhere were coming under increasing scrutiny.[47]

The last twenty years has seen considerable development in research, and much greater allowance is now made for both chronological and regional variation. In more recent discussions, the development of French and other mottes, perhaps in different areas simultaneously, has been placed generally within an eleventh-century context.[48] In fact, despite an adherence to the traditional view of early motte origins, the difficulties of working out a chronology for mottes in France were already emerging in the 1960s. At that time, when the detailed excavation of such sites in France had hardly begun, it was recognized that the vocabulary of the chronicles and charters was inadequate for studying the form of early castles. Not only was a wide array of words employed (see above), but the specific word *mota* or *motta*, whose basic meaning was any mound of soil or turf, was unhelpfully rare in Latin texts until the twelfth century. But Latin texts are not a comprehensive guide to contemporary usage, and the vernacular *motte* was probably already in use, not simply for castle mounds but also for other natural and man-made features.

There must have been a common word for the castle mound shown under construction on the Bayeux Tapestry, which was described there in Latin as *castellum*. The word *motte* occurred in place-names during the eleventh century, and in the twelfth century, both in Latin and the vernacular, it could also mean a windmill mound.[49] The difficulty could be illustrated by any number of examples. Whereas around 1060 one of the lords of Amboise (Indre et Loire) possessed a stone tower, another had a house (*domus*) which was called, after him, the *mota* of Fulk.[50] This might well be a contrasting case of stone donjon and an implied timber building on a motte. But could the word here possibly mean an enclosure around the house? Or could it simply represent place-name formation with no particular archaeological significance? Equally difficult are the eleventh-century references to castles in which the word used is uninformative, and where there is now a motte. Even more difficult are cases where lordship of a particular property is known from the eleventh century, but where the first reference to its castle is in the twelfth century. Is the castle itself only of that date? Or had it existed silently for a generation or more? And if it now has a motte when did it appear on the site? Only very specific documentary evidence, or extensive excavation could hope to answer such questions.[51]

Excavation has certainly produced surprises, for example (though strictly speaking outside the field of timber castles) at Doué-la-Fontaine (Maine et Loire) in Anjou. Here an unfortified stone ground-floor hall of *c*.900 was converted into a two-storey defensible building with first-floor entry added later in the same century. Early in the eleventh century this building was 'enmotted' with a mound piled around its base. Whether this development is connected with the growth of mottes proper is a matter of speculation.[52]

The famous castles established by Fulk (Nerra), count of Anjou, at the turn of the tenth and eleventh centuries, are now notable for their surviving stone structures. These range in date from the eleventh century to the later Middle Ages. It has been argued, perfectly sensibly, that the sites may have been initially defended in timber. Whether this means that the mottes now surviving, in whole or in part, at some of these sites represent these primary defences, or whether they themselves are later additions, is an important but as yet unanswered question. The donjon at Langeais, now thought by some to date from *c*.1020 rather than from the castle's foundation in 994, stands on a mound which appears to be a shaped natural outcrop rather than a true motte (fig. 3.14). Whatever it is, it is obviously contemporary with or earlier than the building which it supports. It may indeed have carried a timber building earlier than the stone one. The latter, it should be noted, was a residence with no defensive quality of its own, though it was strengthened a century later. The earlier defence of the site must have depended upon its (presumed) outer timber palisades.[53]

3.14 View of the donjon at Langeais (photo: P.A. Barker).

It is appropriate to end a discussion of French matters with some remarks on Britanny and Normandy, the areas from which so many of the conquerors of England came in 1066 and its aftermath. Both have recently been the subject of fascinating research on early castles. The native Breton tradition of the early Middle Ages included the use of fortified camps for military purposes, as well as private fortified residences for the princes and the aristocracy.[54] The documented, but unidentified, tenth-century royal palace at *Morman* was well fortified. The Carolingians met Breton resistance from both types of site. But such places have rarely been revealed archaeologically. At Peran, near St Brieuc, an enclosure with a (vitrified) timber and stone rampart dates from the early tenth century. At

Trans, near Dol, two enclosures have been dated in excavation to the same period. Such places may well relate to the period of Viking incursion, and it has been suggested that the sites at Trans are actually the native and invader bases for a battle fought in the area in 939. In addition, there is the evidence of place-names, in which such elements as *motte*, *haie*, *guerche* (from Germanic *werki*, fortification) and *ferté* (from Latin *firmitas*) are found in great profusion, especially near the borders with Normandy, Maine and Anjou. Not all these, however, relate to existing sites, and their chronology remains very vague.

At Nantes, the ducal castle was established in the late tenth century, though its form is unknown, and the same period also saw the development of town defences at Rennes and Nantes, again documented but not known physically. An important, but unanswered, question is how long the enclosures persisted, and whether they overlapped with the use of mottes. At Camp des Rouets, Bodieu (Morbihan) a motte was built in an earlier enclosure thought to have belonged to the Breton princes, but actual continuity of occupation as opposed to long-term use of the site has not been proved. It would, however, be surprising if all the earlier works went out of use with the advent of mottes. There was undoubtedly an important tradition of timber castles in Britanny. When the castle of Josselin (Morbihan) was established early in the eleventh century, its owner started off the building operations, in the presence of monks from Redon who recorded the event, by setting the first timber.

Thanks to a renewed interest in the subject, the listing and mapping of mottes has now revealed how numerous and widespread they were,[55] for example their distribution in Finistère (fig. 3.15). The Breton sites are diverse in shape and size, and the baileys have in many cases been destroyed, though they are known to have existed from early maps. Some published profiles suggest ringwork forms rather than mottes. The sites were somewhat less numerous in the south, where the dukes had most of their own lands and wielded most power. The earliest archaeological evidence comes from carbon 14 estimates from buried soils sealed by mottes, for example La Garnach in the south-east. These, given their inherent vagueness, suggest a *terminus post quem* of *c.*1000. At other sites, for example Ploumoguer (Finistère) and Kernec (Morbihan) occupation in the eleventh century is attested by pottery or coin evidence. The earliest documentary references to sites with mottes, either specific or by the association of seignuries, are also eleventh

century. Whatever their exact significance, the representations of Dol, Dinan and Rennes on the Bayeux Tapestry were also of mottes. The chronology is bedevilled, as always, by a general absence of information on whether mottes were primary or secondary features of the sites in question. The building of mottes went on through the twelfth century, when they emerge more clearly as the centres of estates. Some were probably only of thirteenth-century origin, since they had no social context before a seignurie of that date was created.

Mottes were also receiving stone structures by this time, and at Montbran (Côtes du Nord) a twelfth-century stone tower had an enmotted ground floor. At Leskellen en Plabennec (Finistère) excavation has revealed a fascinating sequence of events.[56] In the tenth century, promontory-sited defences, whose earthworks defined a more or less rectangular enclosure, provided protection for the inhabitants of the adjacent village and also formed the seat (Breton *lis*) of a local lord. In the eleventh century, the enclosure became

3.15 Detailed fieldwork and documentary study suggests there were about 120 mottes in Finistère, Britanny, many of which have been destroyed in the last hundred years (after R. Sanquer, in *Bull. Soc. Arch. Finistère* 105, 1977).

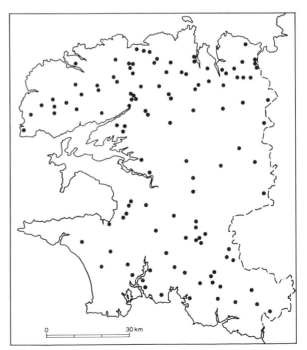

the bailey to a newly erected motte, with a timber tower or house of which only the burnt debris was discovered. In the twelfth century a stone tower was built on top of the motte, whose sloping sides were now encased in stonework. The motte was abandoned c.1400 in favour of a new house in the bailey, where the chapel was already situated. It seems very likely that many other Breton mottes continued in use to the later Middle Ages. Recent fieldwork has revealed how often the later manor houses stand near to mottes, but with no evidence of a residence of intermediate date. In this particular respect, the situation is not unlike that in Scotland, described earlier.[57]

Normandy has always been a centre of attention in early castle studies, and particularly so for British historians and archaeologists. This attention has been matched in recent years by researches in Normandy which have considerably altered the traditional picture. There is documentary reference to some castles here from the tenth century (see below, p. 121), but sorting out exactly what they were like is no easy matter. Some documentation is of help, for example the twelfth-century account by Robert of Torigny of duke Robert's stone tower at Rouen, to which Henry I of England added further fortifications. William of Poitiers noted the stone hall (aula) at the castle of Brionne which duke William besieged in 1047, and recently an attempt has been made to analyse the castle descriptions and terminology of the earliest Norman chronicler, Dudo of Saint-Quentin. Many references are however, unhelpful. What are we to make of the aggeres and munitiones which, according to William of Jumièges, the Norman rebels built against their duke in the years 1035 to 1047, and indeed of the castella which William demolished after his victory in that year? These have often been interpreted as mottes, but these general words could also indicate any sort of castle, though the circumstances of their erection

and destruction suggest strongly they were of timber. A century later, the poet Wace thought these works had had ditches and palisades. He also said that in 1047 the Norman lord Hubert de Ryes had a castle which he described as a mote. These may have been specific and informed statements, but they may also have been influenced by castle design of Wace's own twelfth-century age.[58]

Equally difficult can be the task of relating surviving castles to their general, or even their specific, historical context. Excavation is certainly no guarantee of a solution. Bonneville-sur-Touques was the site of a ducal residence in the time of duke William, but the excavations there produced stone-built remains only of the mid-twelfth century and later. The earlier phases, presumably of timber, must have been totally destroyed or were on a different site.[59] A recent survey of mottes in the Cotentin recorded 18 surviving mottes and two enclosures, together with documentation for another 19 destroyed earthwork sites. Apart from three sites referred to in a ducal charter of 1026, none had references earlier than the twelfth century. The form of one of the three is not known, another is now a motte and the third is an enclosure.[60] On such evidence, how could, for instance, the mid-eleventh-century landscape of castles of this area be reconstructed?

An important development from the 1960s onwards has been the attention given to forms of castle other than mottes, and the demonstration of something of their date range. This is of interest in three slightly separate contexts. First, at Fécamp and Caen excavations have shown the ducal castles of the early eleventh century comprised ramparts, with stone curtain walls, enclosing domestic buildings. At these and other ducal castles which seem to have been enclosures, and which sometimes had tenth-century origins, it has been suggested that what is apparent is a reflection of the Normans' Viking background and an adherence to a traditional form.[61] Second, some other castles of the same period were also enclosures. At Plessis-Grimoult, the late tenth-century enclosure containing timber buildings was fortified with a stone wall not long before its probable abandonment in 1047. At Arques-la-Bataille, which figured in the revolt of 1053–4, there was also an enclosure (fig. 3.16), now surmounted by stonework of largely later date.[62] A general survey of Norman castles whose existence is documented, directly or indirectly, before 1066 had also pointed out (fig. 3.17), allowing for the survival of only half the total, how many of the sites may have been enclosures or promontory sites rather than mottes.[63] Third, excavations have revealed relatively late dates for the building

of some other enclosures. Urville was not established until c.1100, Bretteville-sur-Laize and Audrieu in the twelfth century and La-Chappelle-Colbert in the thirteenth.[64] All these sites are in Calvados, an area to which attention was drawn when enclosures were first discussed, and where a study of the densely distributed mottes and enclosures in the region known as Le Cinglais had suggested an origin for most of the castle sites much earlier in the eleventh century.[65] It is clear that enclosure forms were important in Norman castle-building over a very long period, and Urville and Bretteville demonstrate that this form was also applied to lesser works with minimal defence and relatively humble buildings (fig. 3.18a–c).

Finally, the traditional view of mottes as

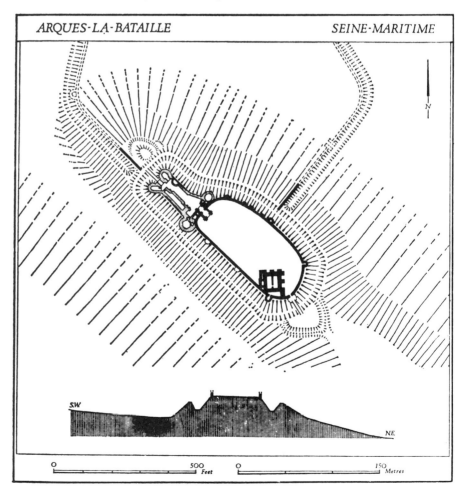

3.16 Plan and section of Arques-la-Bataille, Seine Maritime, Normandy (B.K. Davison in *J. Brit. Archaeol. Ass.* 36, 1973).

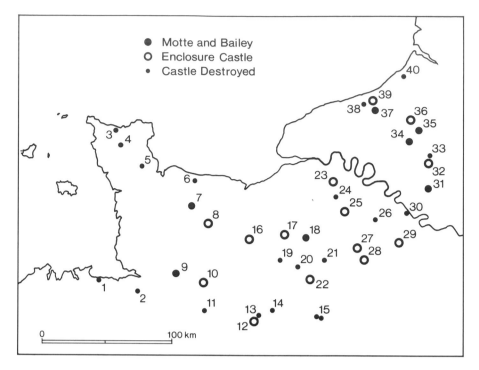

3.17 Castles in Normandy with documentary evidence for foundation before 1066 (B.K. Davison in *Ch.G.* III, 1969). 1 Cherrueix. 2 St James de Beuvron. 3 Cherbourg. 4 Brix. 5 Le Homme. 6 Bayeux. 7 Briquessard. 8 Le Plessis-Grimoult. 9 Mortain. 10 Domfront. 11 Ambrières. 12 Montaigu. 13 St Cénéri. 14 Alençon. 15 Bellême. 16 Falaise. 17 Montgommeri. 18 Montreuil l'Argillé. 19 Exmes. 20 Echauffour. 21 L'Aigle. 22 Moulins la Marche. 23 Montfort-sur-Risle. 24 Brionne. 25 Beaumont le Roger. 26 Evreux. 27 Breteuil. 28 Tillières-sur-l'Avre. 29 Ivry la Bataille. 30 Vernon. 31 Neauffles. 32 Neufmarché. 33 Gournay. 34 La Ferté en Bray. 35 Gaillefontaine. 36 Mortemer. 37 Manéhouville. 38 St Aubin. 39 Arques. 40 Eu.

early features of Norman castles, first questioned by Brian Davison in the 1960s, has continued to be eroded. At Sebecourt (Eure), for example, the development of the complex earthworks (fig. 3.19) began only c.1100 and owed much to later medieval changes.[66] At Mirville and Gravenchon (Seine-Maritime) excavations have produced very important results.[67] At Mirville (fig. 3.20) the motte was simply the final phase of the site, which had undergone several major developments in the eleventh century. It was only after 1100 that the motte was created by filling in and raising an enclosure of the sort described above. At Gravenchon excavation showed

that the timber-built manor of the eleventh and early twelfth centuries was undefended. Only in the middle of the latter period was it enclosed with a palisaded ring-work and baileys (fig. 3.21, see also chapter 8).

In contrast, at Grimbosq in the Cinglais region (Calvados), excavation of the motte with its two baileys (fig. 3.22) has revealed a layout in which the motte appears to be a primary feature of the site, being raised only 3–4 m (10–13 ft) above the rock outcrop of which the builders took advantage. A date just before the middle of the eleventh century has been proposed, but this rests not on archaeological evidence but on the known rivalries within the Taisson family, its owners, which appear to create a castle-building situation at this time. Pottery associated with the excavated timber buildings – hall, chapel and kitchen in the northern bailey, and fragmentary tower on the motte – conforms with this suggested mid-eleventh-century date.[68] Assuming this date to be correct, however, Grimbosq is well into the eleventh century, and a Norman motte with a very early origin remains elusive. Current opinion accepts that many surviving mottes may not be primary features of their sites. None are likely to be earlier than the mid-eleventh century, the date suggested not only by Grimbosq but also by Gaillefontaine (Seine-Maritime) where the motte of the documented *castrum* of *c*.1050 seems also to be original.[69] When the

Normans eventually built mottes in England their experience of them may only have been twenty years old.

Overall, the evidence points later rather than earlier for the proliferation of Norman castles in general. If this is in any way true for France as a whole, it helps explain the apparent paradox between the historical view of early castle-building restricted to the elite on the one hand, and a landscape now full of earthworks, on the other: that landscape may have been a long time developing. Just as historical research reveals the growth of a castle-building society, so also excavations such as Mirville and Gravenchon (see pp. 264–7) reveal the growth of castles out of earlier residences.

The accumulated research on Norman

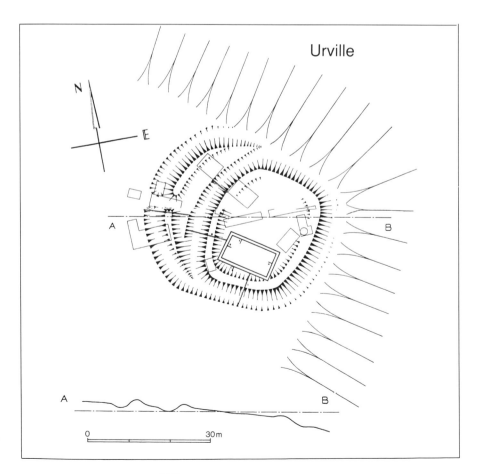

3.18 (a) Urville
(J. Decaens in *Annales de Normandie* 18, 1968).

society shows clearly that up to the second quarter of the eleventh century castle-building had been largely restricted to the dukes, or to a few most powerful Normans, as at Ivry. The most recent survey of early Norman history shows clearly how it was not until *c.*1020–50 that powerful Normans concentrated their landholding interests, created lineage and inheritance in the direct male line, and began to take their family names from the place-name of their point of origin or favoured residence. In the same period, their establishment of monasteries reflected a growing interest in local patronage. It was also now that they were assuming the title and office of *vîcomte* in the developing framework of ducal government. It is no coincidence that only now do we find regular references to non-ducal castles, as well as William of Jumièges' statement about the building of

unnamed *aggeres* and *munitiones*. It was apparently only in these years that the Norman nobility acquired its castle-building habit which was to flourish later in England as well as in Normandy.[70]

For example, at St Germain de Montgomery and St Foy de Montgomery (Calvados) there are two earthworks, the sites of timber castles built by the family which took its name from this place, which now comprises two communes. Their relative date and function is not known for certain, but the strong enclosure (fig. 3.23b) on higher ground may pre-date the weaker, but more accessible site below (fig. 3.23a). Neither pre-dates the 1030s: in *c.*1030 Montgomery was described (in a charter which also referred to the family's Viking origin) simply as a *vicus*, but by 1040 it must have been fortified, since it resisted a siege mounted by count Alan of Britanny, one

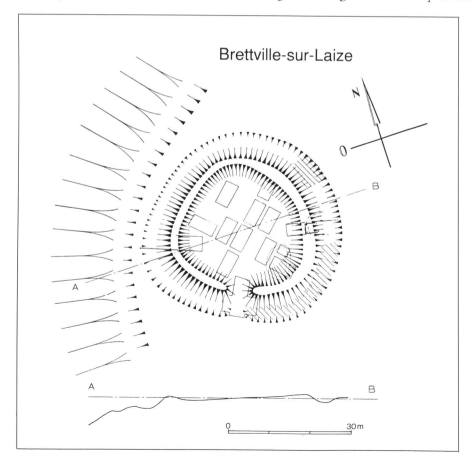

Brettville-sur-Laize

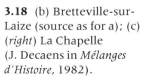

3.18 (b) Bretteville-sur-Laize (source as for a); (c) (*right*) La Chapelle (J. Decaens in *Mélanges d'Histoire*, 1982).

of the guardians of the young duke William. In the twelfth century the family could not accurately remember their ancestry beyond Roger I and his son Roger II, who was born about 1030. These two men were *vîcomtes* of the Hiémois, founded monasteries and markets, and the younger increased his fortunes by marrying into another powerful family, that of Bellême in southern Normandy. Custodian of the duchy during the invasion of England in 1066, Roger II later became lord of Arundel in Sussex and earl of Shrewsbury. He

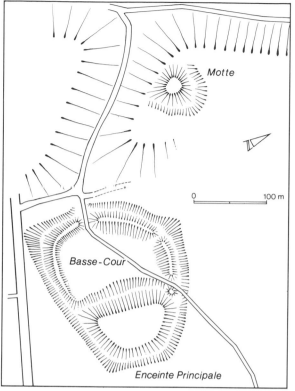

3.19 Plan of earthworks at Sebecourt, Normandy (J. Decaens in *Ch.G.* VII, 1975).

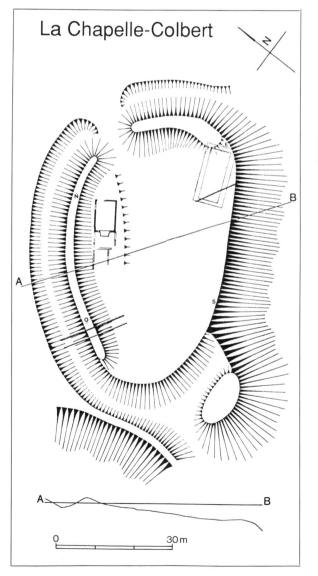

built a castle in Arundel, inherited a royal one at Shrewsbury, and built another on the Welsh border to which he gave his own family name.[71] For such a man the Norman Conquest did not involve a simple transference of a fully-developed castle-building tradition from Normandy to England. It involved rather an opportunity to develop a recently acquired habit in a land of opportunity (fig. 3.24). Inevitably, both the numbers and designs of castles expanded in this period. In Normandy itself, the number of castles continued to increase as the practice of castle-dwelling became entrenched. The civil war which broke out between the sons of the Conqueror at the end of the century also encouraged the building of castles. Some of the archaeological evidence quoted above

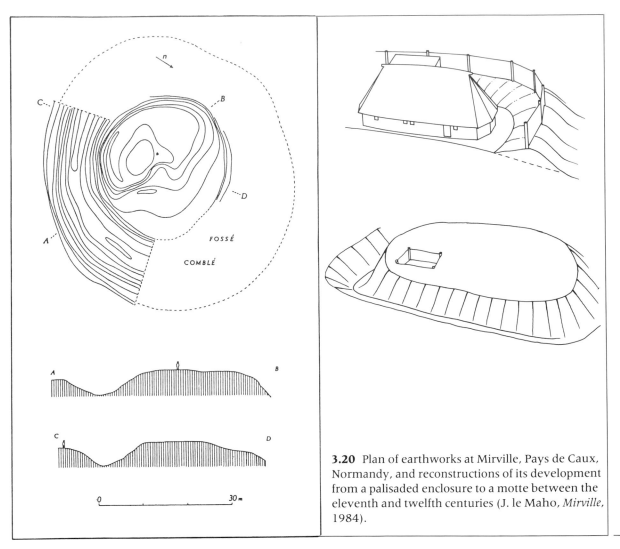

3.20 Plan of earthworks at Mirville, Pays de Caux, Normandy, and reconstructions of its development from a palisaded enclosure to a motte between the eleventh and twelfth centuries (J. le Maho, *Mirville*, 1984).

belongs to that period, and it was also now that ducal control of all castles was enshrined in a famous written statement (below, chapter 4). To a considerable degree, castle-building in England and Normandy is better seen in parallel than in tandem. Looking back from a century later, the Norman experience of it was not a great deal longer than the English.

Conclusion

Neither the documentary nor the archaeological evidence reveals when, where and in what form timber castles were first built. Developments were occurring, in various parts of Europe, in the tenth and eleventh centuries. These eventually produced the castles we can study more fully, both in their social context and in their physical form, in the late eleventh and twelfth centuries. But in the earlier periods, our sources allow us to see the particular, in a number of fascinating instances, but prevent us from seeing the general at all satisfactorily. The tradition of fortification through enclosure was inherited from earlier times, and continued to be adapted

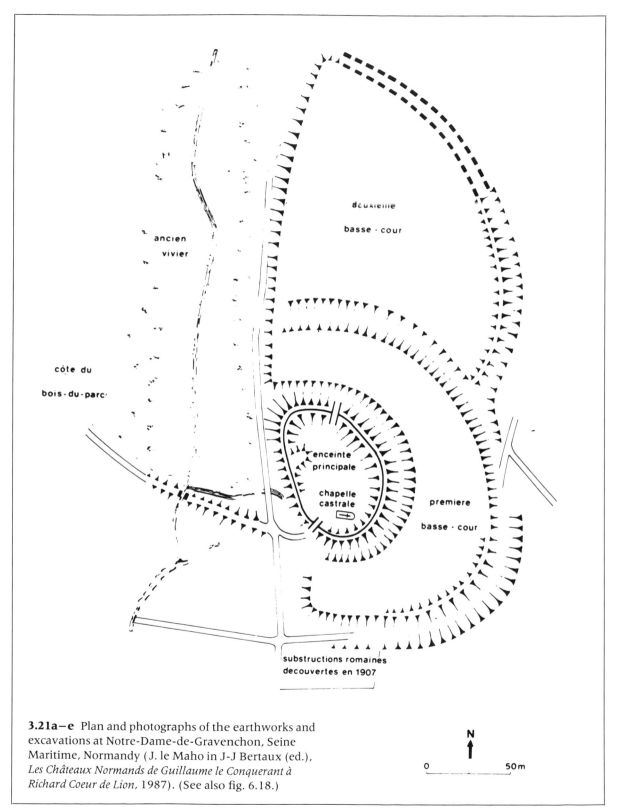

deuxieme

basse - cour

ancien

vivier

côte du

bois - du - parc

enceinte
principale

chapelle
castrale

premiere

basse - cour

substructions romaines
decouvertes en 1907

3.21a–e Plan and photographs of the earthworks and
excavations at Notre-Dame-de-Gravenchon, Seine
Maritime, Normandy (J. le Maho in J-J Bertaux (ed.),
*Les Châteaux Normands de Guillaume le Conquerant à
Richard Coeur de Lion*, 1987). (See also fig. 6.18.)

N

0   50m

for centuries. The specifically medieval contribution was the motte. This seems to have
emerged, in different ways and in different
places, during the eleventh century. It does
not seem to have been widespread until late
in that century, more notably in the following century.

Archaeologically, mottes are elusive before
the middle of the eleventh century. The
handful of documentary references which
some have seen as indicating mottes before
that date are all in some way difficult to
interpret. Moreover, they virtually all come
from twelfth-century writers who may have

been influenced by the conditions and terminology of their own day (below, chapter 4).
Since excavation has revealed an almost endless variety of structural evidence on and
within mottes, we might in any case question
whether 'the motte' as a category is as useful
to us as normally supposed. Contemporary
writers more often picked out buildings, or at
least a combination of mound and building,
and we might be better advised to follow their
priorities.

In considering castle origins, the net has
been cast here more widely than is common.
Too often the continental view has been

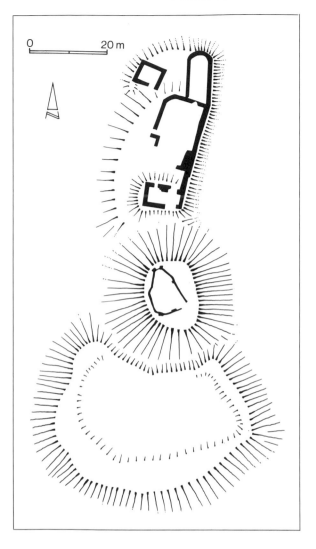

3.22 Plan of earthworks at Grimbosq (J. Decaens in *Archéologie Médiévale* 11, 1981).

dominated by the development of feudal society in northern France, and the British view by the Norman Conquest.[72] A broader geographical treatment, and due regard for the long-term traditions of timber fortification, puts castle origins, including those of timber castles, in a broader cultural perspective. In all regions the ancient practice of defence through enclosure continued. In Ireland, the tradition of mound occupation was already developing in the early Middle Ages. In Denmark and Poland the building of mottes was a particularly late medieval phenomenon. In other areas, the twelfth century saw their most extensive use. Regardless of these regional variations, there was a long period when social conditions – and we might here relieve ourselves of the burden of deciding whether 'feudal' is the only, or best way to describe them – encouraged the embodiment of power and status in residences which were not only expressions of wealth but also of the need for protection. When such conditions prevailed, timber technology and earthwork fortification provided a ready means of building which was available generally, and not simply to the richest rulers.

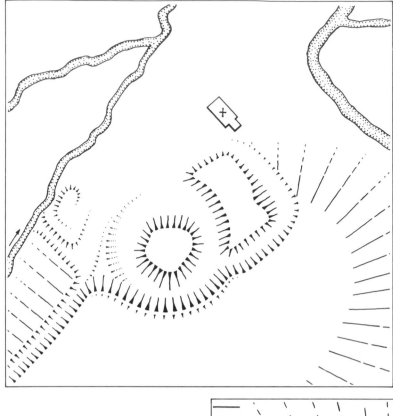

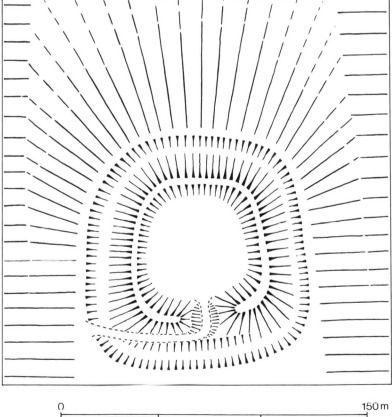

3.23 Plans of earthworks at (*above*) St Foy de Montgomery and (*below*) St Germain de Montgomery (courtesy of B.K. Davison, unpublished surveys).

0   150 m

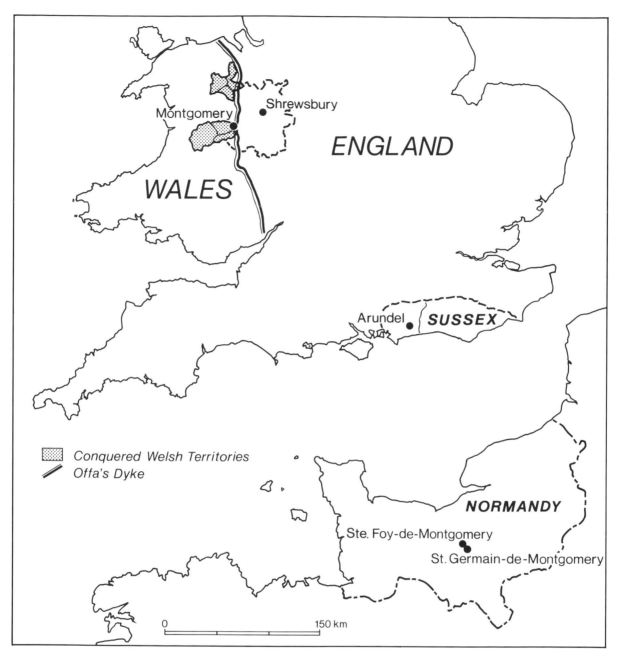

3.24 The lands of Roger de Montgomery in 1086 (Barker and Higham 1982).

— 4 —

The documentary contribution

In this chapter various categories of documentary sources are discussed to illustrate their contribution to our understanding of timber castles, particularly their physical form and date range. No attempt is made to reproduce every documentary reference to be found in these sources. The examples have been chosen to illustrate the geographical and chronological spread of the evidence, as well as to illustrate those points which are less well revealed by archaeology. While there is inevitably some overlap in the categories quoted, they are dealt with generally in the order: chronicles; administrative sources; and literary materials.

Chronicles

The importance of medieval chroniclers (in the wider sense of narrative authors) emerged in the last chapter, and some crucial references to early castles occur in their accounts of contemporary or recent events. Their value to our subject continues, since the eleventh, twelfth and thirteenth centuries were a period both of prolific castle-building and of prolific chronicle writing. Political life was dominated by the possession and control of castles, and sieges were the most common means of pursuing warfare. It is hardly surprising that chroniclers frequently included reference to castles, sometimes only by name but sometimes with more descriptive detail. As the

period progressed warfare was increasingly conducted around the stronger forms of stone castle whose defences were developed to withstand sophisticated siege methods. Accordingly, the majority of detailed chronicle references are to these castles rather than to their timber counterparts. Nevertheless, chronicles are of great interest to the study of timber castles.

An important qualification must immediately be made, however, in evaluating this evidence, since chroniclers who included descriptions of castles were never concerned with commentary for its own sake; they were not 'recording' physical detail in the manner of topographical writers of later centuries. The general purpose of the author has to be considered and any effect that this had upon the way descriptive passages were treated taken into account. A castle might be described in varying terms depending on whom it belonged to, the author's patron, one of his allies or alternatively one of his enemies. Its strength or weakness might be stressed depending upon who was attacking and who was defending, or upon what the outcome of the attack was. Moreover, the information provided might be wholly factual or interspersed with imaginative detail. It might be based on personal knowledge or on the indirectly acquired oral witness of someone else who knew the place. It might also be based on some earlier written narrative. These varying circumstances could all affect the truthfulness and comprehensiveness of what was recorded.

Above all, most medieval writers aimed to produce elegant prose, to display their education in the classical Latin authors, and fulfil their broad purpose which could vary from pleasing a secular patron to producing a general history from the standpoint of a monastic house.[1] It follows that the inclusion of descriptive passages about buildings played a limited role in the work of most chroniclers. Timber castles, which were such a common feature of the contemporary landscape, did not figure very often in much detail, though there are a few famous exceptions. On the other hand, there are more numerous passing references to the subject, where the absence of detail reduces the problem of bias, and which are of considerable general interest.

In illustration of this point may be quoted Alexander Neckham (1157–1217), the eminent English monk-scholar whose writings included *A Treatise on Vocabulary*. In this work, designed to illustrate the range and meaning of words, he gave a description of a castle in which he brought together elements of contemporary design as well as advising how a castle should be provisioned, armed and garrisoned. His castle had a double ditch (*duplex fossa*), a motte (*mota*) set upon the native rock and formidable outer defences consisting of a palisade of squared timbers and prickly thornbushes (*sepes horrida, pali quadrangulati et vepres pungentes*). But it was also a castle with many stone components, walls with buttresses, mural towers and crenellations surrounding a central tower or keep. What is described is not a particular castle at all, but a composite made up of many parts, in effect an ideal castle possessing features which were normal in the later twelfth century.[2] The passages discussed below differ from Neckham's in relating to specific places, but the tendency of chroniclers to simplify and to idealize their descriptions remains. It is unlikely that any chronicle description provides a comprehensive and objective account of its subject.

Discussion of a few well-known passages is inevitable. The sources were examined by Ella Armitage and others and have been quoted frequently ever since. The fullest examples concern Ardres (near Calais in northern France), Merchem (Merckem, near Dixmüde in Belgium, or Merckeghem near Dunkirk) and Durham in England. Each presents difficulties of interpretation and each gives a different picture in detail. They do not therefore provide the basis of a generalization about the form of timber castles. They do however emphasize the motte as a type of castle construction and they are all of twelfth-century date.

Lambert of Ardres relates how about 1060 a very high motte or towering donjon (*mota altissima sive dunjo eminens*) was built at Ardres by Arnold I, seneschal of Eustace, count of Boulogne. Its buildings, presumably of timber, were brought from another castle and re-erected here. About 1120, a later lord of Ardres, Arnold II, reconstructed the castle after its damage in a war with the count of Guisnes, his overlord. He built upon the motte (*dunjo*) a timber house (*domus lignea*) whose details were described at length:

Later, when peace had been established between Manasses count of Guisnes and Arnold lord of Ardres, Arnold built upon the motte [*super dunjonem*] at Ardres a timber house [*domus lignea*] which was a marvellous example of the carpenter's craft and excelled materials used in all contemporary houses in Flanders. It was designed and built by a carpenter from Bourbourg called Louis, who fell little short of Daedalus in his skill; for he created an almost impenetrable labyrinth, piling storeroom upon storeroom, chamber upon chamber, room upon room, extending the larders and granaries into the cellars, and building the chapel in a convenient place overlooking all else from high up on the eastern side. He made it of three floors, the topmost storey supported by the second as though suspended in the air. The first storey was at ground level, and here were the cellars and granaries, the great chests, casks, butts and other domestic utensils. On the second floor were the residential apartments and common living quarters, and there were the larders, the rooms of the bakers and the butlers, and the great chamber of the lord and his lady, where they slept, on to which adjoined a small room which provided the sleeping quarters of the maidservants and children. Here in the inner part of the great chamber there was a small private room where at early dawn or in the evening, or in sickness, or for warming the maids and weaned children, they used to light a fire. On this floor also was the kitchen, which was on two levels. On the lower level pigs were fattened, geese tended, chickens and other fowls killed and prepared. On the upper level the cooks and stewards worked and prepared the delicate dishes for the lords, which entailed much hard work on the part of the cooks, and here also the meals for the household and servants were prepared each day.

On the top floor of the house there were small rooms in which, on one side, the sons of the lord slept when they wished to do so, and, on the other side, his daughters as they were obliged. There too the watchmen, the servants appointed to keep the household, and the ever-ready guards, took their sleep when they could. There were stairs and corridors from floor to floor, from the residential quarters to the kitchen, from chamber to chamber, and from the main building to the loggia [*logium*], where they used to sit for conversation and recreation (and which is well named, for the word is derived from *logos* meaning speech), as also from the loggia to the oratory or chapel, which was like the temple of Solomon in its ceiling and its decoration.

The passage is of enormous interest in revealing the details of a timber building whose ground plan, if recovered in the most meticulous of excavations, would never suggest the complex superstructure described here. Nevertheless, the account must not be viewed uncritically. Lambert, a priest of Ardres, wrote his *History of the Counts of Guisnes and of the Lords of Ardres* from 1194 to 1203 at the request of Arnold, son of Baldwin, count of Guisnes. His work therefore had a panegyric quality and it would be natural for him to describe the castle in splendid terms, just as he described Arnold's career in chivalric society in glowing terms. He certainly gave emphasis to domestic rather than defensive matters. His account may have been influenced by the vocabulary current in his own time (perhaps *mota* in relation to 1060), as well as by buildings with which he was familar, seventy years later than the one he described, which may or may not still have been standing. Nevertheless, he must be regarded as a well-informed family chronicler, unlikely to invent anything which an aristocratic audience would find unconvincing, although it may not be a complete description of the castle (no bailey or other buildings elsewhere are mentioned, for example). Although it would be impossible to draw a plan of each floor from the information given, a clear impression emerges of a three-storey tower whose uppermost level was jettied out from the one below. The account is an invaluable corrective to one-dimensional excavated ground plans, even more to the countless bare earthworks about which nothing at all is known. The site of the castle at Ardres was levelled in 1855 together with the town's other defences. A survey made in the 1540s by an Italian engineer, Giovanni Rosetti, for Henry VIII of England shows an apparently thirteenth-century plan with later angled bastions (fig. 4.1). The great round keep is shown on a mound which may be the motte of the twelfth century. The town defences originated in 1060, with the enclosure of the market established with the original castle. They were enlarged with enormous earthworks about 1200 by Arnold V, son of the count of Guisnes, and these works impressed Lambert greatly.[3]

4.1 A sixteenth-century survey of the castle at Ardres (Cott. Aug. I, ii, 74; by permission of the British Library).

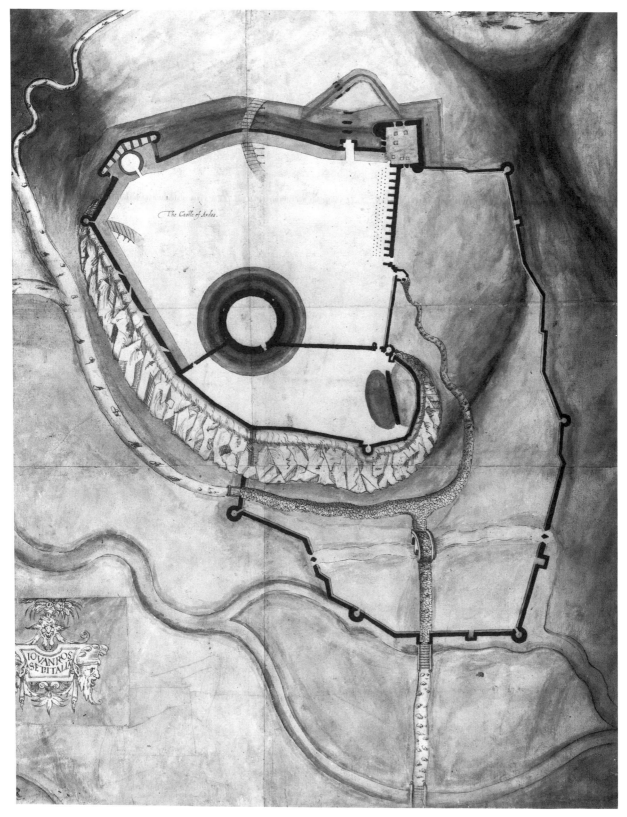

The Castle of Ardes.

IOVANROS
SE TIT ALIA

The second passage comes not, strictly speaking, from a chronicle, but from a biography, the *Life* of John Commines, bishop of Terouenne from 1099, written by Walter the Archdeacon within a decade of his death in 1130:

It happened that in the town [*villa*] called Merchem the bishop had a residence [*mansio*]. There was, near the atrium of the church, a fortress [*munitio*], which we may call a castle [*castrum*, or *municipium*], exceedingly high, built after the custom of that land by the lord of the town many years before. For it is the habit of the magnates and nobles of those parts, who spend most of their time fighting and slaughtering their enemies, in order thus to be safer from their opponents and with greater powers either to vanquish their equals or suppress their inferiors, to raise a mound [*agger*] of earth as high as they can and surround it with a ditch [*fossa*] as broad and deep as possible. The top of this mound they completely enclose with a palisade [*vallum*] of hewn logs bound close together like a wall [*murus*], with towers set in its circuit so far as the site permits. In the middle of the space within the palisade they build a residence [*domus*], or, dominating everything, a keep [*arx*], so that the entrance to this enclosure [*villa*] can be reached only by a bridge, rising from the outer edge of the ditch supported by columns, double or even triple, fixed underneath at suitable intervals.

The narrative continues with a description of a visit from the bishop in which the bridge collapsed under the weight of the crowd following him down from his lodging (*hospicium*). Bishop and followers noisily fell 35 ft into the ditch, surrounded by broken timbers and a great cloud of dust. But, with God's mercy, the gloom was dispelled and all were safely led from danger.

Although the *agger* here could conceivably be a ringwork rampart, defended by a palisade and towers and enclosing the *domus/arx*, the references to the great height of the castle and to the steep bridge make it more likely that a motte is intended. The first part of the description seems devoid of any exaggeration, but the episode of the collapsing bridge may have

served a biographical purpose, since despite the disaster God intervened and saved the bishop's entourage. As at Ardres, the omission of reference to any bailey buildings suggests the account is selective: the motte was the prominent feature and its description nicely introduced the story of the bridge. Two possible locations for the site have been suggested, Merchem near Dixmüde (Belgium) and (less probably) Merckeghem near Dunkirk. The existing Belgian site known as Merkem is not that described by Walter, but a short-lived thirteenth-century motte associated with land reclamation. Earthworks do survive at Merckeghem but are not necessarily identifiable with the castle described.[4]

The description of Durham castle given by Laurence, monk of Durham (prior from 1149–54 and former chaplain to the bishop), in his *Dialogues* (composed before 1149) presents a fascinating but enigmatic image:

Not far hence [from the road into the city] a mound [*tumulus*] of rising earth explains the flatness of the excavated summit, explains the narrow field on the flattened vertex, which the apex of the castle [*arx*] occupies with very pleasing art. On this open space the castle is seated like a queen; from its threatening height, it holds all that it sees as its own. From its gate, the stubborn wall rises with the rising mound, and rising still further, makes towards the comfort of the keep. But the keep, compacted together, rises again into thin air, strong within and without, well fitted for its work, for within the ground rises higher by three cubits than without – ground made sound by solid earth. Above this, a stalwart house [*domus*] springs yet higher than the keep, glittering with splendid beauty in every part; four posts [*postes*] are visible, on which it rests, one post at each strong corner. Each face is girded by a beautiful gallery, which is fixed into the warlike wall. A bridge gives a ready ascent to the ramparts, easy to climb; starting from them, a broad way makes the round of the top of the wall, and this is the usual way to the top of the castle. The keep holds out the charm of a round appearance, pleasing in its craft, its elegance, its posture. Hence into the castle [*castellum*] the bridge looks down, bringing also an easy return. The

bridge is divided into easy steps, no headlong drop, but an easy slope from the top to the bottom. Near the [head of the] bridge, a wall descends from the citadel, turning its face westward towards the river. From the river's lofty bank it turns away in a broad curve to meet the field [i.e. Palace Green]. It is no bare plot empty of buildings that this high wall surrounds with its sweep, but one containing goodly habitations. There you will find two vast palaces built with porches, the skill of whose builders the building well reveals. There, too the chapel stands out supported on six pillars, not too large but fair enough to view. Here chambers are joined to chambers, house to house, each suited to the purpose that it serves. Here are fine costumes, there shining vessels and flashing arms, here money, meat and bread. Here is fruit, there wine, here beer, there a place for fine flour. Since house joins to house, building to building, no part lies empty. There is a building in the courtyard of the castle which has a deep well of abundant water . . . the haughty and powerful gate faces out to the south, easily held by the hand of weakling or woman. The bridge of the gate is extended as a way out, and thus the way goes across the broad ditch. It goes to the plain which is protected on all sides by a wall, where the youth often held their joyous games. Thus the castle wall keeps off the northern winds, and the castle is skilfully placed on a lofty ridge. And from this castle a strong wall goes down southwards, continued to the end of the church.

Literal translation is made difficult by the work's composition in verse and by the obscurity of some individual phrases – 'written

in such flowery Latin as almost to defy precise translation', as one recent commentator remarked. Nevertheless, this inevitably clumsy rendering conveys a sense of structural detail which would be lost in a more elegant paraphrase. The castle description is part of a broader treatment of Durham city and cathedral, and the castle itself seems at this date to have been partly stone- and partly timber-built, a phenomenon which was widespread throughout the Middle Ages. The chapel is the major structure mentioned still to survive, though early fragments are also preserved of the domestic ranges and the south gate. There was a serious fire in the mid-twelfth century with much rebuilding by Bishop Hugh Pudsey (du Puiset, 1153–95), as well as extensive later medieval work.

The main point of interest concerns the motte, which had an ascending wall (of timber or stone?) and carried the keep. Its site is now occupied by the enlarged motte and polygonal shell keep of Bishop Thomas Hatfield (1345–81), entirely rebuilt in 1840 (fig. 4.2). In the twelfth century the motte apparently carried a circular enclosing wall, though whether this was of timber or was already a stone shell-keep is not clear. This wall also revetted the motte-top, since the internal ground surface was higher by 1.5 to 2 m (5 to 6 ft) than the external. Within it (and connected by the bridge?) stood a rectangular (square?) building certainly built of timber, since its corner-posts are mentioned. Yet it was no mere stronghold, though the galleries mentioned may have been projecting hourdes. Allowing for the author's enthusiasm for his subject, we are still left with a clear impression of the beauty of this structure, probably one of the site's major residences.

Durham cathedral is one of western Europe's most impressive churches. Its patrons are unlikely to have tolerated anything less than the highest standards of domestic architecture in their castle. The fine castle chapel of the period which still survives is a reminder of contemporary standards, and the splendid stone tower keep built at Rochester from 1127 for the archbishop of Canterbury is a parallel structure which reinforces the point. The keep at Durham may have exhibited numerous features of decorative carpentry in Romanesque style, its timbers displayed to good effect (the corner posts were certainly visible). Alternatively, much of the timber-work may have been rendered, so that the contrast with the adjacent stone buildings would have been less marked. In this case, some of its beauty may have been achieved with decorative plasterwork, perhaps painted. All in all, this account of Durham, despite the difficulties it presents, is a forceful reminder of the rich achievement of timber building, as well as of the crowded character of a major twelfth-century castle. The structures described cannot be closely dated. They may have been original features of the castle (from 1072 onwards) or alternatively the work of Ranulf Flambard (bishop 1099–1128) whose building works were mentioned by Simeon, another Durham chronicler. Though it is impossible to be certain, the timber tower on the motte may still have been standing when

the stone shell keep was begun in the fourteenth century.[5]

The remaining chronicle evidence for timber castles is less spectacular but contains some very interesting examples. There are undoubtedly large numbers of brief references and those which are included here (also including some charter evidence) are not offered as a comprehensive catalogue. They are chosen to illustrate interesting structural details and to illuminate the circumstances of timber castle building.

The references to early castles introduced above (chapters 2 and 3) include some in which the major structures are specifically mentioned. Large numbers of general references to what are presumed to have been timber castles are, however, totally uninformative about structural matters. This is not the case with the early references alone. Wherever we read of castles being built in some numbers over a short period, and perhaps suffering equally rapid destruction, there is a strong presumption that the sites were mainly of timber. The unnamed *aggeres* mentioned by William of Jumièges, thrown up in the revolt against duke William of Normandy (1046–7) and destroyed when he resumed power, are most likely to have been of timber, whether or not they had mottes. The *Anglo-Saxon Chronicle* refers to widespread castle-building in England both in the Conqueror's reign and again during the civil war of Stephen's reign (1135–54). The 'adulterine', or unlicensed castles of the latter period were also emphasized by the major Latin chronicles of the time. The destruction of these 'new castles' in 1154–5, on Henry II's accession, was extensive. One writer, the Norman chronicler Robert of Torigny, mentioned a (presumably exaggerated) figure of over one thousand. Some of this demolition is reflected in expenditure recorded at the time (see below).

Although it cannot be demonstrated in detail, there is no doubt that large numbers, perhaps a majority, of the castles referred to by chroniclers, directly or obliquely, up to the twelfth century, were built of timber and earth. Occasionally, the actual process of creating the earthworks is mentioned, though it was more often the resulting structures which were noticed. In the early eleventh century Count Wichman of Vreden built a castle, near the river Meuse, on rising ground in marshy surroundings. The description of its building says the site was raised higher by the digging of a surrounding ditch and the addition of towers: perhaps the creation of a motte, or perhaps that of a defended enclosure.[6]

That so few were described briefly, let alone in detail, reflects their mainly unexceptional nature. There are, however, passing references to timber structures where a chronicler decided to mention them, perhaps because he had seen the place, or was informed by someone who had, or perhaps because it was a particularly strong or fine building which had some reputation among contemporaries. In some references the building material is not specified, as at Ivry (Eure, Normandy) of which Orderic Vitalis wrote in the twelfth century, describing the huge and powerful tower which was the citadel (arx) of the castle (turris famosa, ingens et munitissima) built in the tenth century by Aubrey, wife of Raoul, count of Bayeux and Ivry. On Orderic's evidence this could equally have been of stone or timber. He mentions the architectus who built it, one Lanfredus, which might imply it was a stone construction, though at least one medieval definition of architectus was 'master carpenter'. Ivry is a promontory enclosure, with fragmentary remains of a stone tower. These do not necessarily represent the building to which Orderic referred, though if, as has often been assumed, this is the case, it is a very early building to have survived.[7]

Elsewhere references to timber structures are more specific, though they require careful interpretation.[8] At Montereau-fault-Yonne (Seine et Marne) a timber donjon or turris was built in 1015 and not replaced in stone until after 1190.[9] At Montboyau, near Tours (Indre et Loire) a timber structure was built which has attracted much comment. Fulk, count of Anjou, established a castellum in a campaign against the city of Tours in 1016, and in 1026 Eudes II, count of Blois laid siege to it, building a wooden tower of amazing height (turris lignea mire altitudinis). This has often been interpreted as a tower on a motte, because the twelfth-century Angevin chronicler who described the episode (but was he actually describing the practices of his own day?) said the tower was super dongionem. But such a tower could hardly have been built on the motte of the castle being besieged. It was either part of a siege castle which had its own motte, or it was a moveable siege tower and contra would make more sense than super. Whatever it was, the besieged later burnt it down.[10] The nature of the castle built at Mont-Glonne (Maine et Loire) in the Loire valley has also given rise to varying interpretations. We are told that in c.1030 the same Fulk, count of Anjou, and his son Geoffrey started a castle (castellum) on the western side of a hill near the monastery of St Florent-le-Vieil. This venture was abandoned in favour of a fortification within sight of the monastery itself, and which included an agger with a timber-built courtyard (curtis lignea). The agger was perhaps a motte and the courtyard a bailey: a charter of 1061 referred to a mound of earth of great height. Yet there is also the strong possibility that the original earthwork was the enclosure for the courtyard itself.[11] At La Cour-Marigny, near Montargis (Loiret), the residence in the mid-eleventh century was a tower house of timber (domus lignea turris). The tower had an upper storey (solarium) where the lord, Seguin, lived, ate and slept with his household. Beneath it, the lower floor (cellarium) was used for the storage of vital necessities. The floor (pavimentum) of the upper storey was fixed together with hewn timbers 'of scarcely any thickness but of considerable width and even greater length'.[12]

The references to timber buildings discussed here provide only the sketchiest coverage of what must have been a common feature of the European landscape. There is a tendency for the great towers, often on mottes, to be picked out, presumably because they were the most prominent feature as well as the most novel. But they may not have existed in isolation. The timber courtyard referred to at Mont-Glonne is one reminder of this. Another is the castle at Rumigny near Rocroi (Ardennes) which in the late twelfth century was surrounded by ditches and timber towers.[13] An apparent bias in the references quoted is their concentration in the Pas de Calais and adjacent areas of modern Belgium as well as in the region of the Loire. This merely reflects the coverage of the available chronicles. While both areas were undoubtedly important in the development of castles, other important developments were also taking place elsewhere. Sites in Normandy have also been mentioned, and evidence from further afield may also be quoted. A charter of duke Hugh III of Burgundy, c.1190, refers to an unnamed castle (municipium) with ditches, timber palisades and towers.[14] At Savigny, near Lyons, a tenant of the abbey built a castle c.1121 in defiance of the abbot, fortifying an existing house with earthworks, ditches, timber palisades and towers.[15]

The evidence from the British Isles is equally patchy, though as elsewhere the general implication is clear enough: timber castles were numerous and widespread. In addition to the indirect evidence of the *Anglo Saxon Chronicle* and other sources already discussed, more detailed references also occur, though not in great numbers. A greater quantity of information will occur in the discussion of administrative records (see below, pp. 126ff.). At Hastings (Sussex), whose foundation took place soon after duke William's landing at Pevensey, the castle was said in the late twelfth-century Chronicle of Battle Abbey specifically to have been of timber (*ligneum agiliter castellum munivit*). In the context of a pressurized military campaign in a hostile country, this is hardly surprising. A source of similar date states this work to have been of prefabricated timber construction, brought across the Channel with the duke's fleet. Though this may not necessarily have occurred it must at least represent a possibility (see below, pp. 144 and 155). The tradition of the Norman campaign at Hastings was long-lived, and in the twelfth and thirteenth centuries some writers omitted all mention of Pevensey, the first land-fall. In his Anglo-Norman *Life* of Edward the Confessor, Matthew Paris, the famous historian of St Albans Abbey, wrote of the 'tower' which the Normans built at Hastings. The passage contains an example of a contemporary pun about a castle: not only was the tower called *Hastings* but it was also built *hastivement* (speedily).[16] Another English example is Great Torrington (Devon), where in 1139 Henry de Tracy captured the castle from its lord, William fitzOdo, by attacking at night and throwing torches through the windows of the tower (*turris*) and setting the rooms inside (*domus*) alight. At Brough (Westmorland), attacked by William the Lion of Scotland in 1174, there is a similar implication of timber defences. First the bailey palisade (*le baile*) was captured, then the tower to which the defenders had retreated (*la tur*) was attacked and burned. At both, the 'towers' were presumably of timber, either tower or shell keeps. Later still, the timber keep on the motte at York was burned down in 1190. Even at this date it was rebuilt in timber (see below, p. 138).[17]

From Wales, the examples of Pembroke, Rhuddlan, Llandovery and Cardigan may be quoted. Arnulf of Montgomery, a son of Roger, earl of Shrewsbury, established Pembroke in 1091. Gerald of Wales, in his account of his journey through Wales a century later, recounts that the castle (*castrum*) was not very strong, being made of wooden stakes and turf (*ex virgis et cespite*). Gerald relates how the constable of Pembroke, Gerald of Windsor, valiantly held out with a small garrison against a long Welsh siege in 1094. There is no reason to doubt that Arnulf's castle was of timber, but this account of it is heavily coloured by its author's desire to praise its constable, from whom he was descended. Gerald's itinerary in 1188 took him to Rhuddlan, then in Welsh control, which he described as 'a fine castle'. The documentary and archaeological evidence points strongly to this being a timber castle, which it remained until replaced by Edward I's new foundation (see below, p. 138 and fig. 7.33).[18] At Llandovery, besieged by the Welsh in 1113, the outer defences, though not the inner, were set on fire in the attack. Here again is strong presumptive evidence of a castle with major timber works.[19] At Cardigan, the castle was demolished in 1171 by Rhys ap Gruffyold who rebuilt it 'with stone and mortar'. The implication is that the site had remained timber from its foundation in 1093.[20]

Finally, four episodes from chronicle sources may be used to illustrate the circumstantial detail which occasionally accompanies references to timber castles. The first concerns two sieges of the castle of Le Puiset, near Chartres (Eure-et-Loir), by Louis VI of France in 1111 and 1112. These episodes were described by Suger, abbot of St Denis, in his *Life* of Louis VI, king of France.[21] Interesting features of the castle are mentioned, as well as details of the siege methods, which pre-date the more sophisticated techniques of the later twelfth century. The campaign consisted of attacks on horse and on foot, with attempts to burn the gates with cart-loads of combustibles. The defenders threw stones as well as stakes and timbers at the attackers, and made mounted sorties against them. Both sides employed archers and the attackers protected them-

selves with doors and boards when their shields broke. This simple warfare, seen also on the Bayeux Tapestry, is what timber castles were originally designed to cope with. In the first siege the attackers progressively took control of the castle's outer defences (*castrum*), its inner defences (*castellum*) and its motte and timber keep (*mota scilicet turris lignea*), finally destroying the site. There is nothing in the account to suggest any part of the defences being stone-built. Its outer ramparts had crenellated palisades and steep slopes into the ditches and the attackers eventually forced a way through with axes.

After the subsequent repair of the inner defences it was again attacked by the king. The initial encounter having taken place around the abandoned outer ditches, he now occupied an old motte (*mota*) nearby and built a siege castle (*castrum*) with jointed timbers. The site was again destroyed after its capture. As well as a graphic description of timber castle warfare of the period, we have also here a reminder of the importance of such sites in contemporary politics. The conflict between Louis VI and Hugh du Puiset represented the struggle between royal overlordship and the independent ambitions of castellans in Capetian France. The castle was besieged by the French kings on a total of five occasions between 1031 and 1118. In our enthusiasm for exploring the chronicle evidence for what it tells us about the physical details of castles we should not forget that the reason for their inclusion in these sources was their political and social importance. The broad outlines of the site at Le Puiset were mentioned by Abbot Suger because they were relevant to his theme of royal victory. In the early nineteenth century, when the castle was mapped, it comprised an inner motte and bailey (2) and outer earthworks with their own motte. Other parts of the plan (fig. 4.3) have been reconstructed from further survey work and from aerial photographs. The broad outlines conform well with the written account, and the outer motte

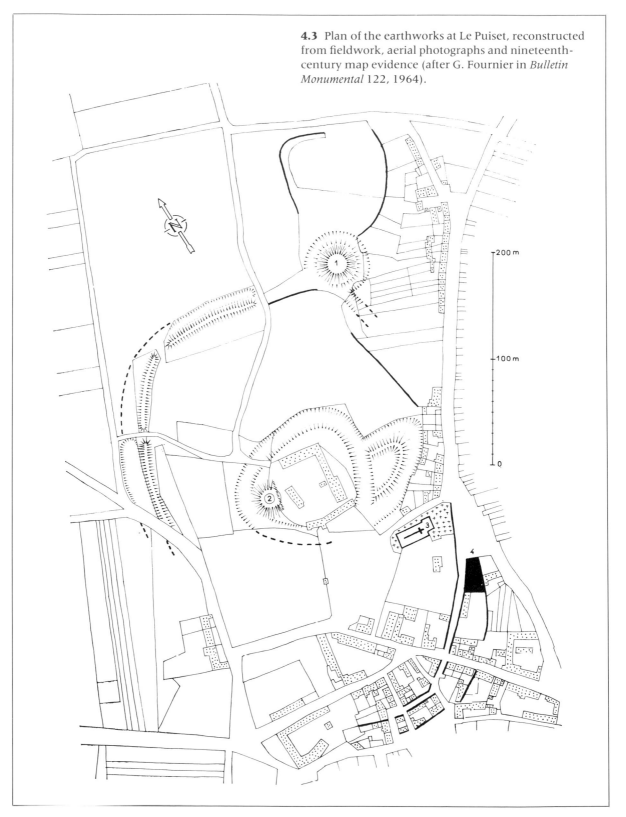

4.3 Plan of the earthworks at Le Puiset, reconstructed from fieldwork, aerial photographs and nineteenth-century map evidence (after G. Fournier in *Bulletin Monumental* 122, 1964).

(1) was presumably the site of the king's siege castle built in the second attack.[22]

Another fascinating episode comes from Lambert of Ardres' Chronicle, quoted earlier in this chapter, concerning the castle of Aumerval (Flanders) about 1139, in a war between Henry of Bourbourg (a castellan of the count of Flanders) and Arnold of Ghent (count of Guines from 1137). Henry abandoned his castle at Audruicq, which was subsequently occupied by Arnold. Nearby stood an old motte (*agger et dunjo*) called Aumerval after its builder, one Almarus, who had erected it in defiance of an earlier count of Guisnes. Its defences had long since been destroyed, but the earthwork remained. To this site Henry sent his carpenters to make a survey in secret. They then made prefabricated defences (*bellica propugnacula*) of timber, including a great tower (*turris*), and brought them in the cover of darkness to Aumerval, where they re-fortified the old motte. Waking to find himself confronted with this new castle, Arnold called on his allies and prepared to attack. Finding that Henry had already withdrawn from Aumerval, Arnold dismantled the tower and other timber defences and subsequently took them back with him to Audruicq.

Particularly in campaign, the practice of prefabrication may have played a greater role than is apparent from most written accounts. The siege castle built by Louis VI at Le Puiset, for example, probably took this form. Another detail of interest is that Henry called his new castle at Aumerval *La Fleur*, because he installed there the flower of his knights and archers. How many other timber castles might have had pet-names? In 1095 William II besieged earl Robert of Northumbria in Bamburgh castle. He built a siege castle here, which in French was ironically called *Malveisin*, in English 'Bad Neighbour'.[23] At least one other instance is known, from the career of the great crusading warrior Richard I of England. On his way to the Holy Land he spent the winter of 1190–1 in Sicily. His occupation of the town of Messina included the building of a *castellum ligneum* nearby to overawe its inhabitants. He celebrated Christmas 1190 in this castle together with king Philip of France. Leaving Sicily for Palestine he had it dismantled and transported by boat. It was later re-erected and used as a siege tower at Acre in 1191. That it struck contemporaries at all suggests it was a formidable structure, and the account of it was provided by Roger of Howden, a royal clerk who was present on the expedition. It also had a name. In mockery of the Greek inhabitants of Sicily, the *Grifones*, (as the westerners called them) Richard called his timber castle 'Mategrifon' – or 'Kill the Greeks'.[24]

Finally, an English example from the twelfth century provides a reminder of the human side of events surrounding medieval castles. Between 1150 and 1160 a knight called William Fossard seduced the sister of William, earl of Aumâle and made her pregnant. In a war of revenge, the earl destroyed Fossard's timber castle at Mount Ferrant, near Birdsall (Yorkshire) (fig. 4.4). The materials from this *castellum ligneum* were transported by Robert de Stuteville to the Cistercian house at Meaux, whose monks constructed several buildings with them. This incident (as at Aumerval) is another reminder of the movement of timbers from one place to another.

Just as in the sixteenth and seventeenth centuries the fabric of stone castles was disposed of by sale, gift or theft, in earlier centuries the sites of many timber castles would have been similarly vulnerable whether through demolition or abandonment and decay. Always a valuable commodity, timber in good condition was easily reusable. At Magny-les-Villiers (Burgundy) a manor house was built in 1295 out of the materials from on top of a neighbouring motte. These examples might be typical of the eventual fate of many timber castles.[25]

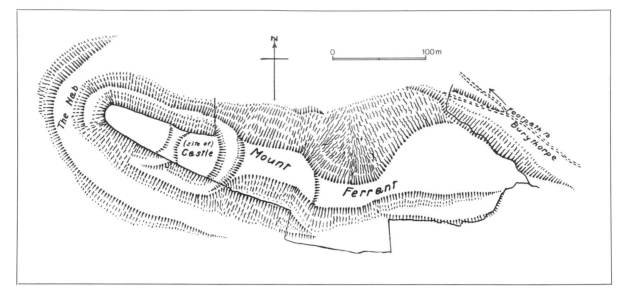

4.4 Earthworks at Mount Ferrant, Birdsall, Yorkshire (after *VCH York*, vol. II, 1912).

Administrative sources

A second major category of written evidence for timber castles comes from what can be called administrative sources. These are very varied in character and include legal records, financial records and the records of everyday government. Different though they are from the narrative chronicle sources, they share with them a major limitation. The information about castles which they contain is normally included because it has some legal or financial implication. None of the sources had as their primary function the recording of castles as such, and they are very uneven in their coverage of the subject. First, the sources are fuller from the twelfth century (and certainly from the thirteenth) than for earlier periods. Thus they do little to illuminate much of the heyday of the timber castle, and are of much greater use to the student of stone castles. Second, there is a very strong bias in favour of royal castles, or those that came into a ruler's hands, since it is royal administration, rather than baronial, that is reflected in most of the sources. Again, this limits their use in

the study of timber castles, since so many of these were built by lesser members of society and since the rulers, having the greatest resources at their disposal, turned frequently to stone castle technology, particularly from the twelfth century. Nevertheless, much useful information may be gleaned from these records, in which timber castles figure more commonly than is often supposed.

A group of sources recording contemporary laws and customs throws some light on attitudes to fortification. Most famous among these are the *Consuetudines et Iusticie*, a record made in Normandy in 1091, by William II, king of England and Robert, duke of Normandy, of the customs of the duchy as they had applied in the time of their father, William the Conqueror. Among these customs was a clear statement of the duke's rights over castles: no one could refuse to hand over their castles to the duke if he wished to occupy them, and no one could build a castle (*castellum*) without his permission.[26] This general principle, applied by rulers in all parts of western Europe, had its origins in the late Carolingian period. It was of long-lasting influence, though employed in different ways by different rulers. The political importance of castles stemmed as much from the frequent violation of this principle as from its observance. The theory of overlordship of castles made, naturally, no distinction between stone and timber castles in principle, though occasionally in practice (see below, p. 128). But the details of the Norman 'customs' are of particular interest because the physical features specified indicate simple defended enclosures of timber rather than stone castles, or even more elaborate timber ones. Ditches were not to be dug so deep that the spoil could not be thrown out by a single shovel's throw. A palisade (*palicium*) could only be built in single form and without battlements and wall-walks (*sine propugnaculis et alatoriis*). That such relatively weak timber defences *were* permissible may indicate that stone ones, as well as stronger timber ones, were totally forbidden.

Notably absent is specific mention of any of the features which were certainly important in castle-building by *c.*1090: mottes, towers and gatehouses. The text may have reproduced phrases from existing written (or oral) records and consequently tell us more about earlier castles and administration than about contemporary practice. The growth of Norman castle-building from the 1020s (above, chapter 3) may well have provided the need for the development of these ducal customs, which seem to have catered for a simple style of castle-building. It is interesting to speculate how the growth of castle-building in Normandy, described in the previous chapter, was reconciled with this theory of ducal power.

Another enigmatic passage comes from the so-called *Laws of Henry I*, a statement of English laws current in the early twelfth century. Among the rights which the king of England exercised was control of 'fortifications consisting of three walls' (*castellatio trium scannorum*), as well as building castles without permission (*castellatio sine licentia*). Since these 'laws' were a compilation of traditions stretching back several generations, the detailed relevance of the first passage to the twelfth century is questionable. But it has been interpreted as meaning three earth embankments (*scannum* is an obscure word), which could possibly indicate a site with two ramparts and ditches and an outer counterscarp. Or perhaps the third element was a motte?[27] The earlier restriction of the *Consuetudines* to building single palisades, as well as Alexander Neckham's later inclusion of a motte and double ditches in his ideal castle, may all be pointing in one general direction: single lines of defence were domestic and permissible, whereas mutliple ones were military and controlled. In an English context it is also interesting to consider the relationships of English and Norman tradition. Given the royal character of late Saxon urban *burhs*, as well as the highly-developed character of royal administration generally, it would be surprising if English kings had not kept control over whatever development of private defences is represented by the evidence from Goltho, Sulgrave etc. That no written expression of this survives may, perhaps, indicate that such places were not a threat to royal authority. Simple domestic defence may have been a thegn's right regardless of royal authority. Alternatively, was the level of defence involved here the equivalent of those private defences which the Norman dukes *had* tolerated in their duchy? In controlling castle-building in England, the Norman kings may simply have transferred their existing ducal powers from Normandy. But, given their insistence on legitimate assumption of power from Edward the Confessor, they may also have felt it was appropriate to their royal inheritance.

It is also interesting that in the *Consuetudines* the defence of the palisade tops was specified, since it was the crenellation of walls which eventually became the criterion for royal licensing in England. The numerous 'licences to crenellate' of the thirteenth and later centuries were a reflection of a very long tradition of castle control, though by this date they were more of social than military significance. Although the castles built as a result of these licences were primarily of stone (walls of stone and lime, with towers and crenellations, are often specified), simpler examples may also be found.

In 1261, Robert of St John was licensed to fortify his house at Basing (Hants) with a palisade upon a bank. In 1294, John de Cokefield received licence to enclose his house at Melton (Suffolk) with an earth and timber wall and to crenellate it. In France, too, timber fortifications had a role to play at this date. In Nevers the French king Louis IX decreed in 1268 that earthworks with palisades constituted castles. Licences granted in Gascony in the later thirteenth century sometimes mentioned timber defences. At Ahetze (near Ustaritz, between the rivers Nive and Nivelle) in 1289, the ditches, palisades, drawbridge and wall-walks were specified. In the records of thirteenth-century Champagne 'strong houses' surrounded by ditches and with timber structures are commonly referred to. At Gurcy-le-Châtel (Seine-et-Marne) a licence was received in 1242 for the building of 'a house with ditches fifty feet wide and a wooden palisade with a gate of stone or timber...' An account which is unusual both in its fullness and its late date describes the building of an earth and timber fortification in 1324–5 at Gironville, Ambronay (Ain) by Edward count of Savoy. It included four timber towers and other buildings, as well as a timber gateway and drawbridge. The three-storey towers were built of oak frames with clay-clad wickerwork panels.

The *maisons fortes* of later medieval France were a common feature of the landscape. Though some occur in the context of licensing, their weaker brethren may have fallen below the level of defensibility to which the tradition of licensing attached. They must have had earlier equivalents, perhaps to be found among the simple earthwork enclosures of northern France. In an English context

there may be a parallel in the 'defensible houses' sometimes mentioned in Domesday Book. At a later date the numerous 'moated sites' found on both sides of the Channel represent a class of dwelling whose low level of defensibility merges gradually into the stronger sites which contemporaries would have regarded as castles.[28]

The tradition of control of castles was not confined to France and England. In Germany there were similar limitations on the depth of ditches, height of walls and palisades, height of entrances above ground level, number of storeys in buildings and embattlement of wall-tops.[29] In the Low Countries a distinction was sometimes made between stone castles which were forbidden and timber ones which were not. In 1265, for example, the Count of Guelders permitted the building of a wooden castle (*munitio lignea*) at Waardenburg (Guelderland). Elsewhere, as at Ter Horst, near Rhenen, the documented division into an upper part of the castle (built in stone) and a lower part (built in timber) in the twelfth century may also have reflected a social distinction as well as one of defensibility. The two parts were in separate occupation and presumably comprised a motte and bailey.[30] Other examples where the stone-timber distinction is reflected in the practice of control of castle-building have been noted. In 1223, Gautier d'Avesnes, builder of the castle at Etreux, near Guise (Aisne), was limited by the lord of Coucy to revetting his motte in stone. The palisades and towers on the rest of the site were to be in timber only.[31] In 1214–15 count William II of Ponthieu, in an area of strong urban communities, agreed with the citizens of Rue en Marquenterre (Somme) that the castle he wished to build at his nearby residence of Gard would pose a minimal threat to them: it would have no stone defences or battlements, but only a palisade on a bank and ditch, together with a gatehouse and drawbridge of timber.[32]

As a final reflection of the legal aspects of

timber castle-building some evidence concerning services related to their erection and maintenance may be quoted. In pre-Conquest England the obligation to work on royal fortifications was well established. It produced labour for the defended towns (*burhs*) of the late Anglo-Saxon period, and for their earlier equivalents in eighth-century Mercia. The labour for other great undertakings such as the linear earthworks – the two Wansdykes, the East Anglian dykes and Offa's Dyke – must also have been raised in an organized way. Normally kings reserved this service (*burh-bot*), together with service in the army and work on bridges (closely connected with many riverine *burhs*), when making grants of land, this being specified in many charters of the period. Other labour for the maintenance of late Saxon burhs was raised on a shire basis and reflections of this system are still to be seen in Domesday Book. Its fullest description is in the document known as the 'Burghal Hidage', now known to reflect late ninth-century conditions, in which a territory within a shire was attached to each of about 30 defended towns to provide men for their maintenance.[33] In early Norman England, when military conquest also provided ample opportunity simply to press English labour into work-forces, these long-established obligations could easily be adapted by the new king to provide men for castle-building. There are several indications that labour for royal castle-work (literally, as it was known to the English as *castelwerke*) continued to be raised from the shires down to the thirteenth century.[34] This line of enquiry is, of course, of more than institutional significance. Although some late Saxon *burhs* are known (from excavated evidence) eventually to have had stone defences (or, indeed, inherited them from the Roman period), the overwhelming tradition of defensive technology in pre-Conquest England was of earthwork and timber construction. It was this technology which produced the linear earth-

works, the original Mercian and West Saxon burhs and their counterparts built in the areas reconquered from the Danes.

There was, then, a solid English tradition in the technology which produced timber castles. And while the designs of timber castles were no doubt dictated by the conquering class, in detail they may have owed something to English workmanship. In an early stone building such as Exeter castle gatehouse (built after the siege of 1068) late Saxon architectural features are prominent (fig. 4.5), and Orderic Vitalis mentioned the Englishmen serving with the Conqueror in this campaign.[35] The English contribution to Norman timber castles, in both earthwork and carpentry techniques, may not have been insignificant. In many other walks of life, native practices contributed to Anglo-Norman culture, not only in institutional matters but also in more tangible ones such as sculptural stonework.[36] The details of labour and its raising and organization, have, however, all but disappeared from view. Occasionally, later sources preserve traditions of early origin. At the Sussex castles of Arundel, Bramber, Lewes, Pevensey and Hastings a later money payment ('heckage') was a commutation of palisade (*haga*) maintenance, a duty which presumably had its origins when these sites were of timber construction. At other castles obligations to provide timber must have had the some origin. At Bamburgh (Northumberland) this service was finally commuted to money payment in the late thirteenth century, but probably had its origins two centuries earlier.

As well as defences, buildings within castles also needed maintenance. At some royal castles, such as Bamburgh, Dover and Newcastle upon Tyne, there is evidence that the king's barons had responsibility for their own residences. While again this was not recorded until the thirteenth or fourteenth centuries, its origin was undoubtedly early. Elsewhere, the practice might be different. At Old Montgomery (Hen Domen, Powys) the

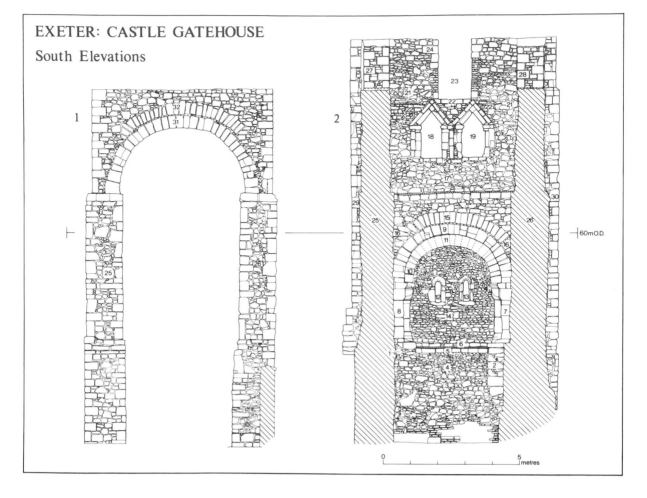

EXETER: CASTLE GATEHOUSE

South Elevations

4.5 Elevation of Exeter castle gatehouse (Devon), with mixture of Norman and Saxon architectural features (courtesy Exeter Museum Archaeological Field Unit).

twelfth-century lords provided a house at their own expense for the periodic use of their steward and his family. This is an unusual glimpse of such an arrangement in an early and non-royal castle, and one which (unlike others for which later evidence survives) was a timber castle throughout its life.[37] The late medieval date of so much of the evidence for castleguard and castle maintenance, recorded when these services were of more financial than military interest, has clouded our view of the period when timber castles flourished. Services recorded for the repair of battlements in stone castles, such as Launceston, Trematon

and Totnes in south-west England, may well have originated at a very early date when their defences were largely of timber. Occasionally details recorded at an earlier date hint at a timber, or partly timber castle. Between 1121 and 1130, Baldwin de Redvers, lord of Plympton castle (Devon) freed his local priory from the obligation of castle-work there. The service included maintenance of the (?) ditch (*puteus*), the bridge (*pons*), the timber-tower (*britesche*) and the palisade (*hériceon*), all of which sound like components of a wholly or largely timber castle (fig. 4.6). Similarly revealing references could probably be found in other private charters surviving from the twelfth century. The lay tenants of Plympton continued to owe maintenance service long after the site was rebuilt in stone and in the sixteenth century this was still remembered.[38]

Despite such glimpses of timber castle organization our documented view of this subject is wholly inadequate. Much that was written has not survived and many early arrangements may not have been written down at all. Solutions to the practical problems of mustering, feeding and controlling labour for castle-work would not, in any case, have been constrained by legal considerations. In campaign, or in emergency, a king or powerful lord would use political muscle rather than, or as well as, institutional rights to raise and direct manpower. From the time of Alfred, and probably long before, the English were accustomed to centrally-directed building and organization of fortifications. Responding to similar pressures from the Normans would not have constituted a major upheaval. What changed was the purpose to which some of the new installations were put – repression rather than defence – a fact which is reflected in the laments of the *Anglo-Saxon Chronicle* in the Conqueror's reign and again in the twelfth century.

Apart from sources concerned with the control of timber castles and the related obligations towards their construction, there are others which provide a different view. Most helpful are the records of Angevin government in England in the twelfth and thirteenth centuries, particularly the pipe rolls and other documents which either recorded or authorized expenditure. Much of this material relates to the normal processes of building and maintenance of castles, but sometimes it has more political overtones. As an example of the latter may be quoted the evidence of castle demolitions which followed the settlement of civil wars and rebellions. In the civil war of Stephen's reign (1135–54) there is evidence both specific and general of royal destructions: in south-west England, for example, in 1136 Stephen razed Plympton castle (an existing legitimate castle in Devon) after the rebellion of its lord, Baldwin de Redvers; in 1140 he

4.6 Plympton castle, Devon, where documentary evidence suggests the earliest phase was of timber (R.A. Higham *et al.* in *Proc. Devon Archaeol. Soc.* 43, 1985).

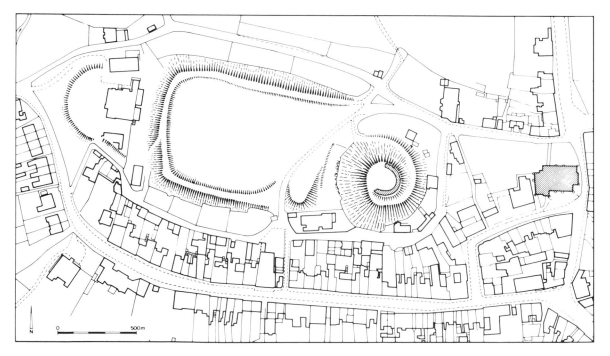

destroyed other (unnamed) castles in Devon and Cornwall which were unlicensed. At Plympton the documentary evidence (see above) suggests a timber castle at this date and many other south-western castles of the period now remain only as earthworks.[39] In the Treaty of Winchester (1153) which arranged for the succession of Henry of Anjou to the English throne, it was agreed that all 'new' or adulterine castles would be destroyed, meaning those established or illegally fortified since the beginning of Stephen's reign.

The chroniclers noted some confiscations, such as Stamford, where the *turris* of 1153 may have been a timber keep; they also noted general destructions without specifying actual places. The Norman chronicler Robert of Torigny, thought that over a thousand were

demolished, presumably an exaggerated figure. There is relatively little reflection of these episodes in the pipe rolls, perhaps because most of the destruction had taken place before 1155 (the first surviving roll being for 1155–6). Best known is the demolition of the castles of Henry of Blois, bishop of Winchester, which were already built in stone by this date. There is also reference to structures being demolished slightly later, as in 1158 at Pleshey and Saffron Walden, the Essex castles of Geoffrey de Mandeville. Given the insistence of the chroniclers on the rapid building and destruction of adulterine castles throughout the period there is a strong presumption that a great many of the sites in question were of timber. This would also apply to siegeworks built in the previous twenty years, which

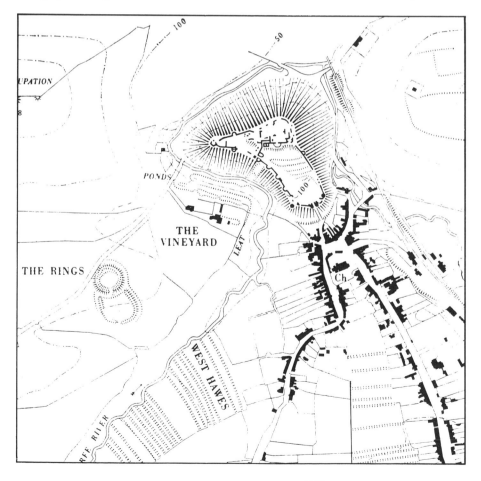

4.7 The Rings, Corfe, a twelfth-century siegework against Corfe Castle (*RCHM Dorset* vol. II, 1970; copyright RCHM England).

would have been timber-built for reasons of speed. The chroniclers imply the building of large numbers, some of which are known by name. The site known as 'The Rings' was probably built by king Stephen in opposition to Corfe Castle (Dorset) in 1139 (fig. 4.7). The earthworks in Hampshire known as Powderham and Bentley probably represent siegeworks built in 1147 aginst nearby Barley Pound (fig. 4.8). Stephen was a notable builder of siegeworks, and we may assume timber construction for those known to have been built by him, at Dunster, Castle Cary, Harptree, Ludlow, Wallingford, Worcester and Lincoln, as well as Corfe.[40]

In the later twelfth and thirteenth centuries, when both the techniques of siege warfare and of stone castle-building became much improved, there is a greater likelihood of politically troublesome castles being sizeable stone buildings rather than timber ones. Nevertheless, the latter do not disappear from view. The question of rebellious castles emerged again in the aftermath of the insurrection against Henry II (1173–4). The chroniclers laid more emphasis upon the king's arrangement (the Council of Windsor, 1176) for baronial castles receiving royal constables, but again the pipe rolls provide evidence of the destruction of castles upon which the Assize of Northampton (1176) insisted. There were demolitions at over 20 sites, some of which were of stone. But some were still substantially timber castles and such places could pose a significant threat to political authority. At Framlingham (Suffolk), where the demolition was recorded on the pipe rolls for 1174–5 and 1175–6, the relatively low costs of the work, together with the very extensive surviving earthworks, suggest the site was still timber: all its stonework dates from the Bigods' rebuilding of c.1190. At Tutbury (Staffs), the Ferrers' castle may also have still been of timber. The rebellion also saw ancient sites refortified, as at Kinardferry (Isle of Axholme) and siegeworks built, as at Huntingdon. The demolitions at Huntingdon reveal the timber character of both the castle and the siegework, hooks, crooks and axes being purchased to pull down the palisades (fig. 4.9).[41]

A final reflection of royal demolitions can

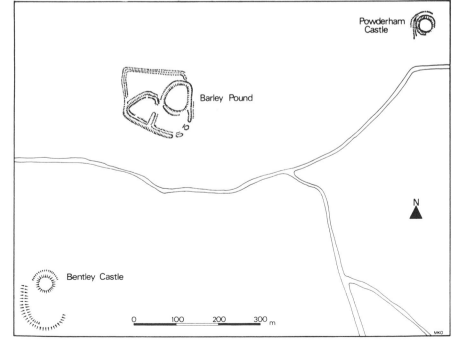

4.8 Bentley and Powderham, siege castles of 1147 built against Barley Pound, a castle of the bishop of Winchester (P. Stamper in *Proc. Hants. Field Club Archaeol. Soc.* 40, 1984).

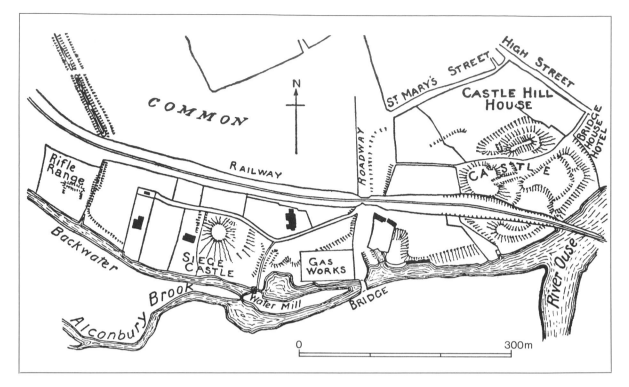

4.9 Earthworks of Huntingdon castle and a siege castle dating probably from the 1170s (after *VCH Huntingdonshire*, vol. I, 1926).

be seen in the aftermath of the civil war at the end of John's reign. John had employed an active policy of occupying established baronial castles since 1208, and in 1212 had actually demolished some. But in the war itself, from 1214, new fortifications sprang up. As individual sites however, they are largely obscure, though one chronicler referred to the building of *munitunculae* by the rebels in 1215. The 1217 reissue of Magna Carta (clause 47) insisted on the destruction of adulterine castles built or rebuilt since the onset of war. The resulting works cannot be followed in any numbers, but the instruction of 1218 to demolish the castle at Anstey (Herts) to the form it had taken before the war is an interesting example. The recorded events of the 1220s were more concerned with recovering control of long-established castles such as Bedford. Some tardy reductions

of defences, for example at Barnstaple and Great Torrington (Devon), were still occurring a decade later.[42] Though the evidence discussed below reveals the continuing importance of timber fortification, the early thirteenth century saw (at least in England) the end of one aspect of its history. Never again did civil war or rebellion produce widespread building or occupation of such works.

In reviewing the evidence for the processes of timber castle-building the underlying problem of managing timber resources should not be forgotten. On their frontiers with France the dukes of Normandy forbade the sale of timber without ducal permission. In Poitou customary tenants owed a variety of services at castles, including the provision and transport of palisading.[43] The apparent simplicity of building in timber in comparison with stone perhaps disguises the organization of resources which major timberworks required. For building, in both defensive and domestic contexts, for charcoal for burning, for withies for wickerwork, for the production of a wide range of tools and implements — woodland management had developed from the Neolithic period onwards.[44] The frequent use of prefabricated timber in castle-building is another reflection of resource management: particularly in campaign a builder could not necessarily rely on the instant availability of suitable timber in new, possibly hostile, territory. Even on home territory resources were precious, though sometimes exploited on a massive scale: between 1250 and 1300 large quantities of timber from King's Wood near Colchester (Essex) were used in the works at Dover. The value of timber is also reflected in its frequent reuse, for which some European evidence was quoted above (see pp. 115 and 125). In 1174 bretasches were made at Dover castle with timbers taken from houses in the town. In 1278–80 timbers at New Montgomery were taken from the palisade around the town and reused on the castle. At Tintagel (Cornwall) timber from the ruinous great hall was kept in storage in the early fourteenth century, and in the sixteenth century timbers were reused in one part of the castle taken from another at Kenilworth (Warks).

If timber was so highly regarded in an age of predominantly stone castles it must certainly have been equally valued in earlier times. The demands of military building could deplete local supplies of building timber. Abbot Suger recorded how difficult it was to find suitable timbers for the work at St Denis from the region around Paris. The forests had been reduced by the felling of trees for constructing three-storey defensive towers, though whether these were permanent parts of castles or transportable siege-towers is not stated. How far this can be taken as a wholly objective statement is not clear, since Suger's writings generally displayed antipathy towards seignurial castle-building. Nevertheless, it is a reminder that timber supplies could not always be taken for granted. The distance over which timber was sometimes transported

is another reflection of this. In the later fourteenth and fifteenth centuries supplies of timber (as well as of stone), were transported from England for the works around Calais. There was simply not enough local material suitable for timber roofs, bridges and bretasches. In earlier times, when timber castles were at their peak, there is sadly insufficient direct evidence for this crucial topic of timber management. At Hen Domen (Montgomery), there is evidence for use of massive timbers (some prefabricated and one, at least, reused) in the early Norman period, when Roger de Montgomery, earl of Shrewsbury, built the castle. There is evidence for similar use of good timbers in the thirteenth century, when the castle was in royal hands. But in the intervening period, when it was the centre of a much smaller marcher lordship, the buildings were constructed of poorer quality timber clad in clay. These changes may well indicate that the twelfth-century lords did not have access to such good materials. In the thirteenth century, the Shropshire forests of Snead and Shirlet, outside the lordship, supplied crucial timber for bretasches and palisades at the royal castle of New Montgomery. Other later evidence may occasionally throw indirect light on earlier periods. When the English acquired the County of Guines in 1360 they were able to exploit the Forest of Guines for their works in the area around Calais, which was otherwise devoid of good timber. It is tempting to see this forest as the source of building supplies for the timber castles which are known to have been built in the eleventh and twelfth centuries in this region: at Ardres, Guines, Audruicq and elsewhere.[45]

The evidence of routine maintenance in the twelfth and thirteenth centuries illuminates timber castles in various ways. First, some conclusions about the organization of building operations may be gleaned. Second, the references to works at certain sites imply they were still largely if not completely timber-built.

Third, references elsewhere indicate sites where the process of rebuilding in stone was slow and there were consequently major timber components at a relatively late date.[46] The most specific information on timber construction comes, naturally, from the evidence recovered in excavation, to be discussed later. In addition, some of the chronicle evidence already described contains evidence of construction practices, but such information is unusual. At Aumerval, the surveyors measured the earthworks for the preparation of new timber defences, perhaps using the measuring rod which figures in the account (from the same chronicler, Lambert of Ardres) of the building of defences around the town of Ardres c.1200. Here, 'pacing with rod in hand', Master Simon the ditcher laid out the work to be done. At Aumerval, some of the work was carried out at night, a practice not unknown in later building operations on stone castles. At this site and elsewhere, prefabricated timber was used, a common practice, especially in campaign, which would assist speed of operations.[47]

Speed is a requirement also mentioned in some of the chronicles. Aumerval, prefabricated, was put up during a single night. Between the first and second sieges of Le Puiset (see above p. 123), Hugh du Puiset rebuilt the inner part of his destroyed castle in a week of unbroken work. At neither site did this speedy work involve construction of earthworks, which already existed. It is the undoubtedly slow process of digging extensive ditches and building consolidated mottes and ramparts which casts suspicion on the precise meaning of some contemporary statements. When William of Poitiers wrote that William the Conqueror spent eight days in 1066 building Dover castle and Orderic Vitalis gave the same length of time for the building of the second castle at York in 1069, what exactly did they mean? Surely the entire sites could not have been completed? The most probable explanation is that a defensible perimeter,

quite possibly prefabricated, could be created in such a time, together with a minimum of accommodation. The other building operations no doubt dragged on and on. Nevertheless, timber castles must have been quicker to build than stone ones, but the processes of their construction have disappeared almost without record.[48] Rarely did chroniclers provide such details and by the time English administrative records begin in the mid-twelfth century the majority of timber castles already existed. Some, indeed, had already gone out of use. Behind the occasional glimpses in such records lay a building industry working not only in structural timber, but in wattle and daub, clay-clad timbers, wooden shingles and thatch. An early reflection of this industry may be seen in Domesday Book, where several royal carpenters, for example, Stefan, Durand, Rayner and Landric, held land directly of the king. Later references to tenure of land by service as carpenter at royal castles may also indicate arrangements with an early origin.[49]

The single pipe roll surviving from the reign of Henry I (1129–30) is sadly uninformative on castle matters, but from 1155 information is regularly recorded. Much, however, is imprecise: expenditure *in operatione castelli* being totalled and not itemized. The building works themselves were largely the result of efforts by local craftsmen supervised by the royal sheriff or constable. Viewers of works ensured the king's money was properly spent. Most famous among the individuals known by name are the 'engineers' (*ingeniatores*), such as Ailnoth, Richard and Maurice, all of whom were influential in castle works under Henry II. These, however, were primarily concerned with the stone building industry, though they were not ignorant of other matters.[50] Of more direct relevance to work in timber were the carpenters who worked on the timber aspects of stone castles as well as upon siege engines. In the early thirteenth century Master Nicholas de Andeli, a Norman, and William the Englishman figure promi- nently in royal service. Presumably men like these were active on the timber castle works which are sometimes recorded at this date. They were the inheritors of skills which at an earlier date had dominated castle-building. The specialist craftsmen (*hurdatores*) who made timber hourdes or galleries for stone wall-tops must also have been adapting tech- niques developed by previous generations in timber castle construction. And the master diggers (*fossatores*) who made banks and ditches were practising skills with much earlier origins.[51]

The works carried out by such craftsmen for the Angevin kings were for the most part on castles built of stone. But in the records of these works timber castles also appear. This applies commonly to long-established sites, but not always. In his expedition into north Wales in 1211, King John undertook works on existing castles as well as establishing new ones. The low costs of the operations, as well as the statement by contemporary chroniclers that his new works were soon destroyed by the Welsh, suggests these were largely of earth and timber. John, in fact, was not scornful of timber fortification. In 1204 he had ordered the repair 'of our timber castles' (*castrorum nostrorum ligneorum*) in Shropshire, and in 1212 he built a wooden tower at Chirk (Denbighshire). In 1211 he built a motte and bailey at Sauvey (Leics) as a hunting lodge. Its palisades and buildings were repaired in the 1220s and a wooden chapel built in 1244, though other parts of the site were of stone.[52]

In the previous decades there are revealing references concerning castles which were already old. There was expenditure on a bretasche at Southampton in 1155–6, and on bretasches and palisades at Eye (Suffolk) in 1173–86. At Warwick in 1175 work was carried out on a building on the motte (*in mota*) and on a bretasche.[53] At Newcastle under Lyme (Staffs), the castle seems to have been substantially of timber until rebuilt in

stone in the early thirteenth century. A bridge, palisade and seven bretasches were men- tioned in 1190. A similar chronology can be suggested for Wallingford (Berks), Skenfrith (Monmouth), and the lower bailey at Windsor (Berks). At Worcester a useful series of references reveals a timber castle eventually rebuilt in stone from the later twelfth century. A great fire had destroyed the site in 1113, and its reconstruction was also in timber. In the reigns of Henry II and Richard I main- tenance is referred to on the motte and its tower, the palisades, the gate and bridge. The motte was repaired at the beginning of John's reign, but in 1204 the timber gate was replaced in stone, part of a process of reconstruction soon cut short by the partition of the castle with the monks of the adjacent abbey in 1216.[54]

Despite the sophistication of thirteenth- century stone castles, references to timber works in the reign of Henry III are by no means absent. At Nafferton (Northumberland) a timber castle was built, apparently without royal permission, in 1218. In May 1221 the king insisted on its demolition, the larger timbers, including those from the bretasches, to be taken for use at Bamburgh castle, the smaller ones to be taken to Newcastle upon Tyne for the building of a gaol. The order was quickly amended, however, and the larger timbers were also sent to Newcastle, one of the bretasches being erected at the gate to the bridge to replace a tower which had collapsed. Here, as in instances discussed earlier, the mobility of timber defences is clearly indicated, presumably dismantled and reassembled in their new home.[55] Henry III himself, patron of great works at Dover and other castles as well as Westminster Abbey, sometimes employed timber defences. In 1223 bretasches were prepared for the campaign leading to the recovery of Montgomery from the Welsh, either to refortify the existing castle (Hen Domen) or for the initial works on the new site of Montgomery castle. In the following two years the tenants of the lordship of

4.10 Clifford's Tower, York (mid-thirteenth century), whose motte carried a succession of timber towers to the early thirteenth century (photo: R.A. Higham).

Montgomery were twice instructed to see that their castles (*forteliciae* and *motae*) were defended with bretasches. These were a series of small mottes, whose origins lay probably in the late eleventh century (e.g. figs 7.16 and 7.18). In 1244, Henry had Coleshill, near Flint (Denbighshire), fortified in timber, and in 1241–2 repairs had been carried out on the timber defences and buildings (including a new timber chapel) at Rhuddlan. This motte and bailey had been established by the Normans in the 1070s. It was often in Welsh control, but had been refortified by Henry II and John. It had a long history down to its replacement in 1277 by Edward I's new stone castle. In 1242, while at Bordeaux, Henry had built a new motte (*mota*) and timber castle (*castrum ligneum*) on the Isle of Ré, off the western coast of France, with money from a captured French vessel.[56]

In the thirteenth century several dramatic events were recorded involving timber defences at ancient royal castles. At York, expenditure on the great tower was recorded in 1172–3, a structure dating from perhaps a century earlier. It was destroyed in 1190 when the persecuted Jews of York burned themselves to death there, but rebuilt, again in timber. It was then blown down in a gale in 1228 and the motte-top remained delapidated until the building of Clifford's tower was undertaken in 1245 (fig. 4.10). Clifford's Tower itself was surrounded by a palisade. The bailey remained palisaded in timber (having been repaired as recently as 1225) until replacement by stone walls began c.1250, but excavation has shown the new wall was never completed and part of the palisade must have remained. At Shrewsbury, the repairs to the motte and tower in 1164–5 and 1172–3 may also have been on the original, almost century-old, structure. In 1228–9 a palisade was built round the tower and was still standing in 1266. But in 1255 a survey showed the motte to have suffered damage from river erosion during the previous 30 years and the

4.11 An eighteenth-century view of the motte at Shrewsbury, which carried a timber tower up until the later thirteenth century (courtesy of Shropshire Records and Research Unit and Dr P. Stamper).

process of decay was soon hastened. Between 1269 and 1271 the great wooden tower (*unus magnus turris ligneus*) finally fell to the ground, 'a belated survival of Norman methods of fortification' (fig. 4.11). The twelfth-century timber tower on the motte at Durham, discussed earlier, may also have survived to at least this date.[57]

This discussion has been dominated by evidence relating largely to royal building activity. It is a reasonable conclusion that if timber building continued to be important to kings then it was also of importance to less powerful castle-builders in the thirteenth century. Unfortunately the surviving documentary material does not reveal this so readily, but we may be sure that the landscape of this period was liberally scattered with wholly or partly timber-built castles.[58] As a final illustration of this, the evidence from Scotland and Ireland reveals contrasting situations in which timber had a continuing importance. In Scotland, the Edwardian campaigns displayed not, as in Wales, a grand scheme of massive castle-building in stone, but a dependence upon timber fortifications. Their tradition was already well established from the twelfth century and earthworks survive in quantity. The relative sparsity of early chronicle evidence, compared with that available for England, hampers their interpretation, though charter evidence has been used to good effect in linking the spread of motte-building with the Anglo-Norman settlement (see chapter 2). The castles (*munitiones et castella*), whose destruction is recorded in Scottish revolts in 1174 and 1185, presumably included such timber sites, and in similar uprisings up to the early thirteenth century the burning of specifically timber castles (*munitiones ligneae*) is referred to. It has been suggested by more than one commentator that many Scottish castles remained essentially timber-built until they underwent replacement or rebuilding in stone in the fourteenth and fifteenth centuries. For example, the motte and bailey at Strathbogie (Grampian) probably retained its timber defences until its destruction in 1452, after which it was replaced in stone by Huntly Castle.[59]

Recent evidence suggests some new mottes were built by the Scots c.1300 (above, chapter 2). Edward I himself made consistent use of timber-defended enclosures, usually known as 'peels' or 'peles', a word derived from the Latin *palus* (stake, pale). Eventually the word was applied to other types of Scottish castle, where a stone tower house was also surrounded by a timber peel. This word, although found primarily in a Scottish context, was also used elsewhere. The timber defences at Haywra (Yorks) were referred to as a peel in the fourteenth century, and at Emlyn (South Wales) and St Briavels (Glos) there were peels around the entrances in the same period. At

Liddell (Cumberland) the earthworks of an early motte and bailey were reused for a peel c.1300. The temporary outer defences of timber (which in some cases were long-lived) at the Edwardian castles in Wales were sometimes referred to as peels. The English also built a peel at Frétun near Calais in 1351–2.

In his campaigns in Scotland, Edward I used peels from the outset. In 1298 a peel was added to the newly captured castle of Lochmaben (Dumfries and Galloway). Carpenters, sawyers and other workmen were sent from Carlisle to carry out the work, which successfully withstood a prolonged attack the following year. In 1300, Dumfries castle was strengthened with an outer peel, the timber being brought by sea from Cumberland and up to 200 diggers and 80 carpenters being employed. The ditches were water-filled, the palisades had wall-walks and towers and the timber gatehouse had its own outer peel. For the siege of Bothwell on the river Clyde, in 1301, Edward had a wooden siege tower made at Glasgow. It took 30 wagons two days to transport its prefabricated parts the 13 km (8 miles) to Bothwell. The English king and his army spent the winter of 1301–2 at Linlithgow, 27 km (17 miles) away, adding a timber peel to the existing castle. The works carried out later that year by the famous engineer of the Welsh campaigns, Master James of St George, were also largely in timber, presumably because of financial constraint. These included water-filled ditches, palisades, towers and gates. Over £900 was expended by November and in 1303 the site held out against a siege (fig. 4.12).

Similar developments took place at a number of other castles, including the old motte and bailey at Selkirk where over £1300 was spent in 1302, though the works had to be rebuilt in 1304 after their destruction by the Scots (fig. 4.13). In the campaign of 1303

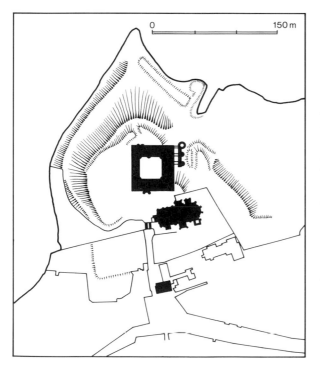

4.12 Linlithgow Palace, whose earthworks represent the timber peel of 1301–2 (after the *Official Guide*, 1934).

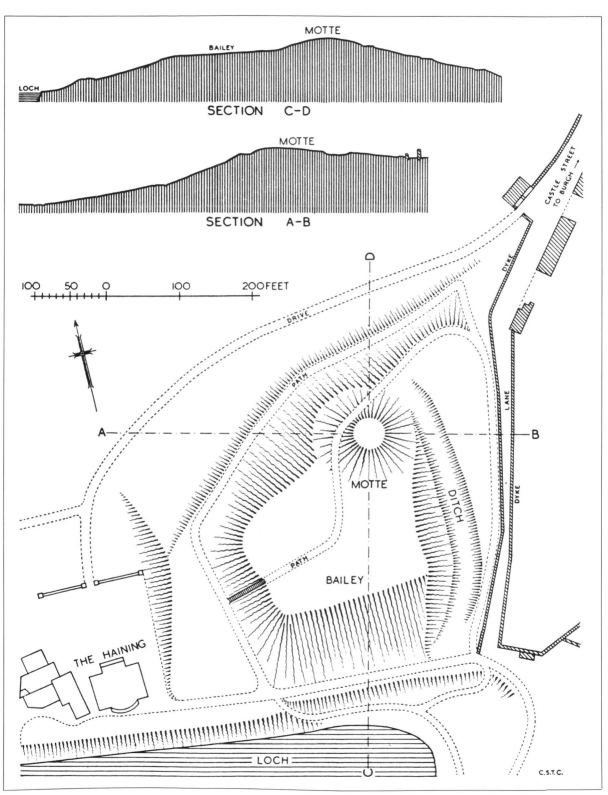

4.13 Selkirk, a motte and bailey rebuilt as a peel in 1302 (*RCAHM Selkirkshire*, 1957; copyright RCAHM Scotland).

Edward made use of prefabricated floating timber bridges for his crossing of the Forth. There were three, of differing sizes, built at Lynn (Norfolk) and transported by sea to Scotland. They each had a timber tower housing a drawbridge. Despite his efforts, the contrast between Edward's achievements in Wales and in Scotland is strong. Where he conquered permanently in Wales his gains were soon lost to the Scots. Moreover, the demands made on his finances by the Welsh campaigns left him unable to undertake a comparable series of new stone castles in Scotland. Instead he utilized traditional forms of timber defence, though sometimes (as in the case of the gatehouse at Linlithgow) there had been an original intention to build in stone. Just as the strength of contemporary stone castles was in their perimeter, so also he concentrated on outer works, and the timber defences which he developed left their mark on Scottish castle traditions. In the Scottish wars of his grandson, Edward III, timber was again used alongside stone, and the works carried out in 1375 at Lochmaben included an earthen rampart, a timber bridge and tower, and large quantities of boards and thatch for roofing.[60] A statute passed by the Estates of Scotland in 1535 concerned the ranks of border society and the levels of domestic defence attributed to those ranks. As well as the stone towers and surrounding stone walls, or barmkins, built by the well-off, the timber peel was still recognized as suitable protection for lesser folk.[61]

The native antecedents for castle-building in Ireland were discussed above (chapter 2), providing more relevant evidence of pre-Norman date than is available elsewhere in the British Isles. Castle-building in the Irish Sea zone more generally was established in the late eleventh century when the Normans extended their conquests along the coasts of Wales, building castles at Rhuddlan and Caernarfon, for example. In 1098, Magnus Olafson, King of Norway subdued the Orkney Islands and sailed into the Irish Sea. Impressed with the Isle of Man, he established a base there, building fortifications with timber which he had sent from Galloway, whose population he had subdued. What these were is not known, though they are likely to have been in the earlier tradition of Viking works on Man, within Iron Age promontory forts.[62]

The Norman invasion of Ireland itself was reminiscent of that of England and Wales a century before: timber castles were widely and effectively employed, and the occupation of some mottes and baileys continued through the thirteenth and fourteenth centuries. The pipe roll of 1171–2 contains specific evidence for the construction of prefabricated timber castles to be sent to Ireland. The cost of two castella lignea was £14 11s 0d. What this covered was not, of course, the complex variety of structures, developed over many years, which excavation sometimes reveals. Nor did it cover the cost of building the earthworks upon which the timberworks might be erected. It covered the bretasches and palisades for the perimeter, the components which made a site quickly defensible. The Irish Pipe Roll of 1211–12 contains numerous items of expenditure on castles. In some the nature of the work is not specified; in others carpenters were employed, sometimes on domestic or ancillary buildings (for instance granaries at Trim and Carrickfergus or halls at Waterford, Dromore and Seafin), sometimes on defensive structures. Construction of the motte at Clones (Co. Monaghan) was referred to, gates and bretasches at Waterford and Dromore (Co. Down). It is sometimes difficult to distinguish works in timber from those in stone, as in the case of Dundrum where the bridge and palisade were presumably timber but the large tower (magna turris) and small turret (parva turella) could have been of stone.[63] The evidence of 1171 and 1211 is a useful reminder of what is lacking in our view of the Norman Conquest of England because comparable administrative records have not survived. The episode of two workmen fighting with shovels at Hastings, depicted on the Bayeux Tapestry, may be mirrored in Irish incidents of the period. Gerald of Wales relates how in 1186 Hugh de Lacy was killed by a young Irishman with an axe while inspecting a newly finished castle at Durrow and his body fell unceremoniously into the castle ditch. In 1200, William le Brun was attacked at Dublin castle and the same fate befell him.

In 1200, King John threatened (probably with little force) to replace the tenants of the march of Ireland unless they defended their lands with *castella* – perhaps timber castles in this context. In Ireland, later evidence has also been used to illuminate the period of timber castle foundation. An inquisition of 1245 reveals the building of a motte and wooden tower at Roscrea (Co. Tipperary) in 1213–15. Work on the castle, started on King John's orders, had been halted by the bishop of Killaloe because it was on his land. A compromise was reached and the project completed.[64]

Evidence of a similar date reveals the continuing transport of timber structures from one place to another. In 1245 eight bretasches were constructed in Ireland and shipped to Wales, where they were destined for Deganwy (*Gannoc*). There Henry III was establishing a castle, and the shipments from Ireland were paralleled by movements of provisions, and in one or two cases of bretasches, from various parts of England.[65] Details of the topography and buildings of Irish timber castles are also revealed in some written sources. At Kells (Co. Kilkenny), established in 1192–3, a charter reveals that the motte was originally built on an island in the King's River. The lord's mill in front of the castle gate and the castle chapel are mentioned in other charters.[66] Late thirteenth-century accounts refer to expenditure on ditches, bridges, gates, palisades and timber domestic buildings on Irish moated sites.

Manorial records also refer to the buildings standing in Irish timber castles in the thirteenth and fourteenth centuries. At Inch (Thurles, Co. Tipperary) an unusually full early fourteenth-century survey described the *castrum* on the motte with its delapidated palisade. The domestic buildings included a hall, an old wooden chapel, a kitchen, larder, stables, barns, granaries, sheepcote, bull-pen, byre, grange, dovecote and mill.[67] This sort of evidence is a healthy corrective to the available field evidence of earthworks which represents timber castles all over different parts of Europe.

Literary evidence

Finally, in this survey of the documentary sources, occurrences of timber castles in medieval literature may be considered. These are not numerous, though castles in general figure quite commonly. A much-quoted passage of *c*.1180–90 from a song of the troubadour Bertran de Born, *Vicomte* of Hautefort (Périgord), reflects the contemporary aristocratic ethos of military life.[68] The castles to which he alluded were clearly of earthwork and timber: 'and my heart is filled with gladness when I see strong castles besieged, and the stockades broken and overwhelmed, and the warriors on the bank, girt about by fosses, with a line of strong stakes, interlaced . . .' An incident of about the same date, recorded 40 years later in the *History* of William the Marshall, concerned a struggle of the hero of the piece with a group of Frenchmen after a tournament in France. The fugitives took refuge on an old motte (*une viez mote*) surrounded by a palisade (*heriçon*) and ditch (*fossé*), where William pursued them relentlessly.[69] By this date the landscape may have contained considerable numbers of timber castles in decline, even though at other places they still had a long future.

From twelfth-century France there is also the evidence from the poetic history of the dukes of Normandy, the *Roman de Rou* (i.e. Rollo). Its author, Wace, was born on Jersey *c.*1110 and spent most of his life in Caen. He started work on the piece, for Henry II, in 1160, consulting a wide range of Norman and Anglo-Norman sources. Though the value of his own contribution to the narrative has recently been pointed out, he has been much criticized for introducing anachronisms, and his work remains literature rather than history. He tells us that several of the castles which figured in the wars of duke William's early years were timber castles, with ditch, earthwork, palisade and in one case a motte. In his account of Geoffrey of Anjou's seizure of Alençon and Domfront in *c.*1050 he relates that the town and castle of Alençon were defended by ditches and palisade with well-boarded and crenellated bretasches (perhaps an anachronistic use of the word if not of the idea it conveys). These defences were successfully set on fire by duke William's army. He also tells us that a prefabricated castle was brought to England with William's fleet by the Count of Eu. Robert of Eu, whose territory was near the embarkation point of St Valéry-sur-Somme, is certainly known to have been granted Hastings within a few years of 1066, though Wace is alone in placing him in the original landing:

When the carpenters had joined the archers
And assembled with the knights
They held a council and chose
A good place where they could establish a castle
Then they threw timber out of the ships,
And dragged it ashore
– Timber brought by the Count of Eu,
Already drilled and properly trimmed with adzes;
The pegs, all ready-trimmed,
Had been carried in big barrels.
Before it was completely dark
They had built a castle
And made a ditch around it.
And so they built a great stronghold there.

The episode occurs in the context of the Norman landing and Wace tells us that earl Harold soon heard news of their arrival and of the erection of a castle at Hastings enclosed with ditch and bretasches. The castle transported may very well have been the same as the one whose erection is seen also in the Bayeux Tapestry (below, chapter 5). In view of the accumulated documentary evidence for the movement of timber defences as well as the excavated evidence of eleventh-century prefabrication at Hen Domen, there is nothing implausible in this idea. But since the source is a century later than the event, by which time transport of defences was well known, there may be an element of anachronism here.[70]

In Scotland there are controversial implications for timber and clay castle building from a thirteenth-century Icelandic saga. The attack on Rothesay by king Hakon of Norway in 1230 included the Norsemen hacking successfully at 'the soft stone' of the castle walls with their axes. This may indicate a construction technique of clay-clad timber-work, although the interpretation has been questioned and the alternative, literal, meaning of the phrase is equally likely. Perhaps related to the issue is the description of a castle near the Solway Firth in the work of Guillaume le clerc, an early thirteenth-century *trouvère*: 'upon the summit [of a great rock] was a tower that was not made of stone and lime. Of earth the wall was built high and crenellated, battlemented'. The use of clay daub on the timberwork of the peel built in 1336–7 round the stone castle at Stirling is known from more mundane source material. The technique is known from a number of excavations and will be discussed later.[71]

A most enigmatic description is a fitting one with which to end this discussion. It will be obvious from all the material so far discussed that the surviving documentary evidence cannot be used as a general guide to the detailed character of timber castles. No source makes this point more forcefully than the *Ode to Sycharth*, written by Iolo Goch, court poet to the Welsh prince Owain Glyn Dŵr, about 1390:

4.14 Aerial view of Sycharth, the castle described by Iolo Goch (courtesy of C. Musson).

To his court I hurry ahead,
Most splendid of two hundred,
Court of a baron, courteous home,
Where many a poet's welcome.
Lo, the form of it – a gold cirque
Of water held by earthwork;
A court with one gate and bridge
Where a hundred packs have passage.
There are rafters coupled there,
Joined two and two together.
It's French, this Patrick's belfry,
Westminster cloister, easy of key.
Corners match, are bound together,
A gold chancel, all entire.
There are joists upon the hillside

As in a vault, side by side,
And each one, in a tightknit
Pattern, to the next is knit,
Twice nine dwellings to look up
To a wood fort on a hilltop.
Next to heaven his court towers
On four marvellous pillars,
A loft tops all, built with care,
With all four lofts for friendship
Joined as one, where minstrels sleep.
These four well-lighted lofts,

Fine nestful, make eight cocklofts.
The roof's tiled on each gable,
There's a chimney that draws well.
Nine halls in true proportion
And nine wardrobes in each one.
Elegant shops, comely inside,
And stocked as full as Cheapside.

There is an overwhelming tone of eulogy in which the poet describes his lord's residence (*Llys*) (formerly in Denbighshire, now Powys) and the poem goes on to describe its surroundings in the same manner (fig. 4.14). Further, the elements of the site being described are to some extent subordinated to the poetic form, particularly in the device by which the buildings and their interiors are enumerated. It has been suggested that the poem describes a timber-framed hall, a gatehouse, a bridge and possibly a tower or other taller building, but translating it into physical terms is very difficult. The excavated evidence was far less elaborate, consisting of foundation remains of two buildings (see chapter 8). The motte at Sycharth was probably built in the late eleventh century as a result of Norman incursions across the border (it lies barely a mile within Wales). It is not clear whether it remained in continuous use to the late fourteenth century or whether Owain Glyn Dŵr's use of it marked the reoccupation of an abandoned site. His *Llys* was burned by the English in 1403 and there is no evidence of later use. Apart from the interest of the poetic form in which it is described it is also valuable as an example of a motte occupied at a late date.[72]

— 5 —

The pictorial evidence

This chapter examines the evidence for timber castles found in a variety of pictorial sources. Far more evidence of this sort survives from the later Middle Ages than from earlier times and consequently provides better coverage for stone castles. Similarly the efforts of artists and engravers, who in later centuries made an important contribution to the recording of stone castles and other buildings, came generally too late to be of assistance to the study of timber castles. Some of the evidence here discussed depicts castles which were a mixture of timber and stone, for which other evidence, documentary, structural and excavated, is discussed below (chapter 6).

The Bayeux Tapestry

The Bayeux Tapestry is one of the most famous relics of medieval Europe, on public display more or less continuously since the early nineteenth century and rehung in a new museum in Bayeux in 1983. It is actually an embroidery, in coloured wools on a linen background, surviving to a length of almost 70 m (230 ft) and averaging 0.5 m (1½ ft) in depth. Its original end is lost. The precise date of its production and the intended manner of its display have long been subject to argument, but there is general consent on at least the major issues.

It provides a visual narrative of the Norman Conquest of England, portraying the Norman interpretation of events leading up to the Conquest and vindicating duke William's invasion. It was associated with Bayeux Cathedral by at least the fifteenth century and perhaps had always been so, though the case for its original display in a secular context – perhaps the great hall of a castle – has also been made. Odo, bishop of Bayeux and earl of Kent, was probably associated with its production, which took place beyond reasonable doubt in southern England, and perhaps at Canterbury: the language and epigraphy of the inscription make this clear, and the depiction of English arms and armour is more reliable than that of their Norman counterparts. Though relating a secular political narrative the Tapestry also has an ecclesiastical content, since Harold's oath on the relics at Bayeux – which he later broke – is a central episode. It is generally agreed that the tapestry was made in the 1070s, about the same time that William of Poitiers wrote his biography of William the Conqueror. But whereas the latter placed Harold's oath at Bonneville-sur-Touques, the Tapestry designer's insistance on Bayeux may indicate its future home was already known.[1]

The interest of the Tapestry to castle studies lies firstly in its depiction of four sites in the campaign which duke William conducted in Britanny in 1064 (figs 5.1–4). Attacks on the Breton castles of Dol and Dinan are shown, with Rennes in between

5.1 The Bayeux Tapestry: Dol (5.1–6: Special permission of Centre Guillaume le Conquérant, Bayeux).

5.2 The Bayeux Tapestry: Dinan

148

5.3 The Bayeux Tapestry: Rennes

5.4 The Bayeux Tapestry: Bayeux

by-passed by the Norman army (a very cir-cuitous route). Returning from campaign William proceeded to Bayeux in Normandy, where Harold's famous oath took place. The depiction of the four sites as mottes provides not only interesting detail about this type of castle, but also evidence for the debate about motte origins. The four depictions give a broadly similar impression: of a mound surmounted by a palisaded building reached via a bridge. The timber character of these structures has normally been assumed. Upright members are shown in the palisades at Rennes and Dinan, as well as in the superstructure of the building at Bayeux. At Dinan the building has a convex roof line, a feature which is the result of the bow-sided plan common in many early medieval timber houses. Dol is less obviously a timber site, and here and at Bayeux the internal evi-dence could easily be interpreted as a mixture of timber and stone. At Dol a tower (turris), probably of stone, was referred to in the mid-twelfth century.

Many details are shown at these sites but to understand their significance very basic problems must be addressed. Are the rep-resentations faithful to the individual places? Are they broadly faithful but modified by the physical constraints of the Tapestry? Are they, in contrast, imaginary? Aspects of the second problem are certainly apparent. For example, the absence of baileys alongside these mottes may well result from lack of space, or at least show that they were not considered important enough to warrant the use of that space. The documented attacks on Le Puiset in 1111 and 1112 involved a gradual progression from the outer defences to the inner (above, chapter 4). What the Tapestry depicts at Dol and Dinan may be only the final, more spectacular stage of events. Another aspect of physical constraint is the relationship between the scenes and the upper borders. At Dinan and Bayeux the buildings were allowed to intrude, whereas at Dol and Rennes they were not. Did the designer feel the former to be more im-portant for some reason? Or did the end result stem from design decisions lower down in the main scenes? At Dinan the incor-poration of soldiers standing against the motte may have increased its height, in turn pushing the superstructure into the border. At Bayeux the size of the approaching horsemen may have made a taller site nec-essary, with the same result.

The problem of individual authenticity is a more difficult one to resolve, and different commentators have expressed divergent views. At the turn of the century these de-pictions were seen as reliable evidence for the form of castles in northern France in the years before the Norman Conquest of England. The opposite view, expressed in recent years, is that the depictions were so far removed in time and space from the events which they described that they are all but valueless. The truth lies probably somewhere between these extremes. A basic difficulty lies in the lack of independent evidence for the nature of the sites in the period in question. The value of the depictions must therefore be judged from general consider-ations rather than from direct comparison with the places concerned. It seems reason-able to suggest that since they are shown as different from each other in detail, the designer knew that they had, or ought to have, some individuality. If we are to believe the depictions represent an accurate view of these places, then we have to assume either that the English designer had been with earl Harold in Normandy in 1064, which seems unlikely, or that an accurately transmitted oral description was available to him or her a decade later from someone who had been there in 1064 or at some other time. The second possibility cannot be discounted, and there is reason to believe that mottes were known in northern France by this date (above, chapter 3).

Alternatively, the designer may simply have represented these places by a type of castle which was visible in England in the 1070s and which was also believed to be typical of France. The Tapestry's mottes may even have symbolized the whole settlement, not just the castle. At Bayeux the mound lacks the ditches which are clearly shown elsewhere, and perhaps here it is a defended town which is depicted rather than a motte. The same could be true of Rennes, shown in the background of the Norman army on the move. The other places may also have been defended towns at this time (they certainly were later), whether or not they also had mottes. Their present lack of mottes is not in itself evidence of the Tapestry's unreliability, since these could easily have been destroyed during the extensive later medieval works which they all experienced. There is some evidence for this at Dol, and at Dinan the old castle site lay just outside the town's eventual walled circuit. At Rennes the remains of the early motte were incorporated in the north side of the city's defences from the twelfth century. Known as 'la motte du vieil chastel' by the later Middle Ages, the site was destroyed in the fifteenth century. Its exact origins remain obscure. It may have existed in the eleventh century, but there was a rebuilding following a siege in 1182 which could have transformed the site.

As a statement about real places in 1064, the Tapestry must obviously be used with extreme caution. But as a statement about mottes in general at the time of its production it must be taken very seriously indeed. Intended for the gaze of an aristocratic audience, it had to be convincing within its physical limitations. The medium of embroidery did, however, provide acceptable licence for mixing realism with decoration and not every feature depicted necessarily had structural significance. In the non-naturalistic use of colours, browns, greens and reds of varying shades were used to create castles which were pleasing to look at, even though the events depicted were very violent. What, then, can we learn from the Tapestry about motte castles in the third quarter of the eleventh century?

Whatever the difficulties of interpreting structural details, we are given a vivid portrayal at Dol and Dinan of the warfare which early castles might face. The attackers operate partly on horseback, partly on foot. The shield-bearing cavalry seem mainly concerned with rushing the motte bridges and hurling javelins at the defenders. At Dinan, those on foot, who also carry swords, have laid aside their shields and are attempting to set the defences alight, a reminder that fire was always a basic threat to the timber castle. Dol is shown curiously undefended. It is known to have been held against Conan of Britanny before William arrived to raise the siege (so Conan's flight from within the castle is a mistake – a reminder that the Tapestry could also contain other mistakes). The defenders of Dinan are concentrated within the palisade and at the top of the motte bridge. Their chief weapons in action are the shield and javelin. This is a convincing view of castle warfare in the age before massive stone castles and sophisticated siege techniques were developed. It is entirely consistent with the description of the attacks on the motte and bailey castle at Le Puiset in the early twelfth century.

The depiction of Dol (fig. 5.1) itself is somewhat enigmatic. Its motte, ditches, counterscarps and bridge with steps and gate are clear enough, but the structure on top of the motte is very curious. A surrounding defence with two ground-floor entrances seems to enclose a taller structure with a crenellated top. From its left hangs a very odd feature, perhaps a fire-protective screen (of hides?), perhaps flames issuing forth from the building, or perhaps again a collection of oval shields, carried by all the soldiers in these scenes, hanging over the defences. The building itself appears to be triangular in plan, though this hardly seems possible, and perhaps two sides of a rectangle are in view. If the building is of timber, which is by no means certain, it is either very tall or, as sometimes suggested, raised on stilts. Since the base of the building is invisible, however, the suggestion cannot be verified. The treatment of much of the building's surface with small squares has prompted some to suggest protective plates, of hide or metal, perhaps analogous with the hanging of shields, a practice deriving from ancient times. The use of such devices is certainly known from documentary sources. At Le Puiset, a crucial breakthrough was achieved in 1111 by the brave effort of a priest who, covering himself with a plank, reached the foot of the palisade and, hidden by the coverings (*operturae*) which were attached to it, hacked away at the timbers. The hanging of shields continued into the thirteenth and fourteenth centuries, when 'targes' were used either for defence or for purposes of display.

Next in sequence is Rennes (fig. 5.3), which is rather simpler. The motte has walls or palisades round its base, and instead of a flying bridge there are steps ascending the motte. The motte-sides are apparently covered, perhaps with vegetation since animals seem to be grazing there. But it has also been suggested that what is depicted here is the sort of drystone revetment excavated around the motte at Leskelen (Finistère) (see pp. 99–100). The motte-top is crowned with a crenellated palisade from within which a tall tower with two windows emerges. Its plan is not clear. Its roof appears to be conical, perhaps implying a circular building, or we may be looking at two sides of a rectangle with its corner posts exposed.

At Dinan (fig. 5.2) some of the features depicted are similar to those at Dol, notably the motte ditch and counterscarps and the flying bridge with steps at which the attack is directed. The gateway which at Dol stood at the bridge-top is here situated at its foot. At the top we find not only a palisade but also a breastwork on the edge of the motte. The true proportions of this are difficult to assess. Since it has its own windows, either it has been shortened by the designer or it descends out of view into the body of the motte. The building which the palisade encloses is of great interest. Much has been made of the fact that the right arm of one of the defenders passes behind the left-hand structural member. Upon this observation rests the argument that the building is supported on timber pillars or stilts, perhaps to increase the space available to the defenders. This argument has been of widespread influence and is commonly used in conjunction with the late-eleventh-century capital from Westminster which depicts a raised tower (see below pp. 156–8). The published interpretation of the excavated plan of the motte-top at Abinger (Surrey) rested heavily upon these considerations (see below, chapter 8).

A possible origin for this type of construction has been suggested in the design of watch-towers, as excavated and as seen on Trajan's column, from Roman times. The long period separating the latter from the eleventh century, and the lack of any evidence to connect the two, makes this particular aspect of the argument unconvincing. Moreover, there are features of the Tapestry's portrayal of Dinan itself which render even the basic assumption questionable. First, too much reliance should not be placed on the position of the defender's arm in relation to the structure. There are sufficient liberties taken with realistic detail in the Tapestry as a whole for this to be an acceptable artistic slip. Second, the superstructure of the building does not appear to be of the sort which would easily adapt to stilted construction. It looks very much more like a normal house with ground-floor entrance. It was argued above that its convex roof-line indicates the bow-sided building technique known from excavation, as well as from hog-back tomb-stones and from those reliquaries which are clearly modelled on houses – the first re-liquary of Harold's oath at Bayeux itself is an example. If this is true it is difficult to imagine in stilted form: a square or rec-tangular plan would be far easier to adapt. There is a very simple alternative explanation to the problem, which is that the designer wished to show as much as possible of the site. To achieve this he raised up in the air a building which in reality was on the ground. The decision also had implications for the use of the border at this point.

Finally, at Bayeux (fig. 5.4) a very strange building indeed is depicted. Is it a massive single structure with projecting parapets or hourdes? Or is it a crenellated palisade, with its own windows, surrounding a structure whose domed roof rises above? And if this roof really was domed then what sort of build-ing was it – presumably not a timber one? The stepped flying bridge which ascends the mound here reaches a more elaborate en-trance than is shown at Dol or Dinan. It has a large doorway and its overall scale is evocative of the fore-buildings of later stone keeps. Its ornamentation, too, suggests it is more than simply a defensive feature and reminds us that eleventh-century castles were products of domestic as well as of military architecture. Timber castles may have been far more ornate than we can possibly ever understand. Of all these depictions Bayeux is certainly the grandest, perhaps containing more symbolism than reality. Since it is the location of the Tapestry's central event, Harold's oath, the designer may have exercised considerable licence here.

In addition to these depictions of northern French castles, the Tapestry also provides a view of the construction of the castle at Hastings (Sussex). The works which duke William carried out at Pevensey, his first landfall, are not illustrated, but within two weeks he had built the castle at Hastings

whose erection is shown in progress.[2] The scene has a number of points of interest (figs 5.5 and 5.6). It is introduced by a man giving instructions for the castle to be built (literally 'dug'). Could this be count Robert of Eu to whom Hastings was granted within a few years and with whom the twelfth-century Norman poet Wace associated its building? The organization of the operation was clearly not without its difficulties, since two of the workmen are fighting with their tools. The single-shouldered spade, the splayed shovel and pick or mattock are all shown in use. The men actually working, who might be Nor-mans, or perhaps English prisoners pressed into labour, are supervised by a different over-seer from the one who introduced the scene. Could this be Robert of Mortain, the duke's half-brother, who figured in the council of war shown immediately before the episode at Hastings? Or could it be Humphrey of Tilleul, whom Orderic Vitalis described as the first castellan of Hastings in the period before the grant to Robert of Eu?

The castle is being constructed immediately next to a tall tower, shown on its right. It has been suggested that this represents a pre-Conquest church belonging to a Saxon community living within the the Iron Age defences which excavation has revealed on the site. This community, wherever it was situated, is referred to in the Burghal Hidage list and in the *Anglo-Saxon Chronicle*. The present remains of the church are indeed very close to the remains of the motte. The parallel with Dover, which William subsequently fortifed, is close. Here also the prehistoric earthworks contained a Saxon church and settlement. A similar situation may also have existed at Pevensey, though there the en-closure was of Roman origin.

The Tapestry's depiction of Hastings has been much discussed in the argument about English castle origins. Whether it represents what was actually built in 1066 or what the designer was familiar with a decade later, its

ISTE·IVSSIT:VT FO DERETVR·CASTELLVM:AT·H

5.5 The Bayeux Tapestry: Hastings – the (dis)organization of labour

details are nevertheless of great interest. Unlike the Tapestry's northern French castles, which were in occupation, Hastings is still under construction. The workmen are digging a (presumed) ditch and throwing the spoil upwards to form a mound whose layering is revealed together with a surface capping. Here at least two constructional stages are telescoped together, since the surface could hardly have been consolidated while the layers were being deposited. It has been argued that the horizontal stratigraphy shown here must be the theoretical invention of a designer who did not understand how to build a motte. Layers are more likely to tip inwards to the centre since the spoil thrown up first forms a ring-bank which is gradually filled up and then heightened. But the designer was obviously not ignorant of building

and constructional matters, which figure regularly throughout the Tapestry. Moreover, the excavation of some mottes has revealed horizontal stratigraphy, at least in part. At Okehampton (Devon) the upper part of one end of the motte was laid in this way in preparation for the building to be erected. At Baile Hill, York, clay layers containing turves were laid horizontally at the base of the motte. At Carisbrooke, Isle of Wight, a bedding of stones carried alternating layers of loose and rammed chalk. At Norwich (Norfolk) excavation of an extension of the motte revealed a similar pattern of loam and chalk deposits on top of the old ground surface. Excavation has also revealed consolidating layers on motte surfaces, as at Oxford and Urr (Kirkudbright-shire) where there were cappings of clay. This would certainly help prevent erosion of new or newly-enlarged mottes.

In addition to the mound there is also shown at Hastings a structure rising from its

5.6 The Bayeux Tapestry: Hastings

summit. This touches, and appears to be cut by, the border, so that we may not have a complete view of it. It appears to be a timber palisade some of whose members are higher and more massive than others. It can be interpreted in two ways. Either it was built on top of the motte and the designer has depicted the end result as well as the building process, or its construction preceded that of the motte which is therefore shown being thrown up around its base. In the latter case the horizontal layering might be very appropriate, since the mound would lack a centre into which the spoil would tip.

The practicalities of building a motte in hostile territory, under pressure of campaign, might well dictate this method of construction, since the weight of a structure upon a newly-built mound would not pose a problem. A century later the Norman poet Wace (who was a canon of Bayeux at some time and may well have seen the Tapestry) thought this castle had been brought prefabricated from Normandy (above, chapter 4). His account of the carpenters, trimming and drilling the timbers, though not shown on the Tapestry, is entirely consistent with the details of the scenes depicting ship-building prior to the invasion. If the castle at Hastings was prefabricated, then the piling of a mound around a structure standing directly on the ground surface is exactly what we would expect. It was perhaps why the castle was 'dug' at Hastings: in a sense its timber structure already existed. The only problem with this interpretation is that the obvious thing to bury in a motte would be a tower, whereas this is not what the Tapestry seems to show. Neither did the excavation of the site illuminate the matter. The Norman motte, constructed largely of sand, was buried in a fourteenth-century enlargement and its summit had suffered much destruction. No traces of timberwork were identified and no obvious pattern of stratigraphy observed, the mound consisting of dumps of unstable sand.

It has been suggested that what the workmen are throwing up are bags of sand which were then consolidated with layers of turf represented by the horizontal bands of colour. This might be one way of reconciling the nature of the site with the depiction. In addition, although the argument about the pre-Conquest origin of the church adjacent to the motte (above) may suggest the excavated motte is the same as that shown on the Tapestry, this cannot be proved. In any case the apparent use of a motte here contrasts strongly with the enclosure forms used elsewhere early in the Conquest, within earlier defences, at Pevensey and London etc. The Norman mound excavated at Hastings was dated by a single sherd of pottery and could have been built at any time after the Con-

quest. It is not even certain that it occupies the site chosen by William in 1066, since the seaward edge of the promontory on which it stands has suffered a long history of erosion (fig. 5.7). The castle shown on the Tapestry may have disappeared centuries ago. The excavated curtain wall was not built before the fourteenth century, though the debris of an earlier one was observed. Some of the expenditure in Henry II's reign was upon a keep, which has apparently disappeared into the sea. Some of this work (in 1181–3) was said to be upon the castle of 'New Hastings', perhaps indicating that the earlier site was already collapsing.

A capital from Westminster

Much quoted in connection with some of the buildings discussed above is the capital now in the Jewel Tower, Westminster (figs 5.8a and b). This is one of a group of Romanesque pieces which were built into the fourteenth-century

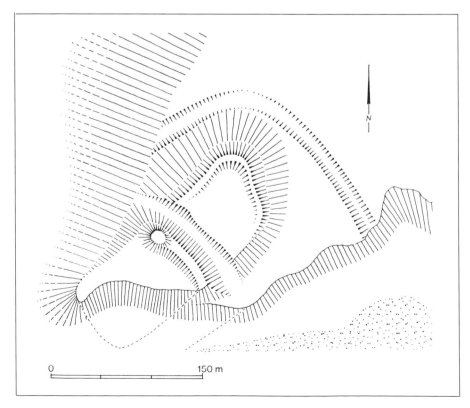

5.7 Hastings castle earthworks (B.K. Davison in *Archaeol. J.*, 124, 1967).

5.8 (a and b) Capital from Westminster, London. (Courtesy of the Conway Library, Courtauld Institute of Art.)

work at Westminster Hall and discovered during restoration in 1834.[3] It is normally assumed that the nine capitals which still survive were originally part of the structure built between 1091 and 1099 by William Rufus. This is almost certainly the case, though they could perhaps have been part of another building in the palace complex in the late eleventh or early twelfth century. They are small respond capitals, probably from interior blind-arcading, are made of limestone and have an average height of 25 cm (10 in). They are of great interest in the history of English and Norman sculpture, since they include early examples of capitals with secular narrative subjects. In their general style and in the fables which some of them portray they are reminiscent of the borders of the Bayeux Tapestry. They include scenes of a warrior, stag-hunting, and Aesop's fables of the ass and the wolf and lamb. The piece in question shows a crenellated structure raised on four uprights and reached by a sloping bridge or flight of steps.

In the most recent publication of these capitals, it is described as follows: 'The heads of two defenders appear between the crenellations. On the left face is a kneeling soldier in a short tunic, an axe in one hand and a round shield in the other ... In front of the soldier, steps lead up to the castle gate which swings back behind a third defender whose long sword pierces the attacker's shield and enters his mouth. This explains his kneeling, collapsing position.' Though recognized as some sort of castle at the time of discovery, it was drawn further into the discussion of timber castles when stilted construction was offered as a possible interpretation for Dol and Dinan as well as for the excavated remains at Abinger (see above pp. 147ff.). It is often regarded as the only visual evidence, apart from the Tapestry, of a motte tower of timber, though this is only an assumption and there is no indication of a motte on the capital itself. The small rectangular divisions which extend

across the upper part of the structure have been interpreted as protective plates of the sort discussed above in relation to Dol. But it has also been pointed out that they look suspiciously like ashlar masonry, neatly bonded together.

We have, then, two alternatives. On the one hand, a timber building supported on wooden posts could be the sort of structure hinted at by Laurence of Durham in the twelfth century (above, chapter 4) and sometimes argued for the Bayeux Tapestry. On the other hand, we may have a stone building supported by pillars of the sort found in contemporary church crypts such as Wulstan's cathedral at Worcester. Against this interpretation is the very straight shape of the pillars, which show no sign of arches at their tops, and on balance a timber building is probably preferable.

Modena cathedral and the Abbaye-aux-Dames, Caen

A stone carving of a quite different sort is the archivolt above the north door at Modena cathedral, in northern Italy (figs 5.9a and b). Building operations began in 1099 and the carving, which shows a rescue of Guinevere by Arthur and his knights, dates from sometime in the first half of the twelfth century.[4] The fortification which is under attack is clearly not a motte of any sort. It is a walled and crenellated stone enclosure whose central stone tower has a shield hanging from it. The patterns of wavy lines in the foreground are presumably a water-filled moat. On each side of the enclosure stands a timber tower, perhaps protecting an entrance, built in two storeys whose main structural elements are clearly visible. Though not identical in detail, they are constructed of uprights and horizontals framed with 'X' braces, and are filled in with vertical planking. The towers also have projecting and crenellated wall-heads supported by further braces.

These towers may have been of the sort for which there is some surviving evidence in medieval belfries, discussed later (chapter 8), and they perhaps indicate the character of bretasches referred to in written sources. Projecting upper stories are also suggested in some of the literary descriptions (chapter 4), and they were probably the antecedents of the timber hourdes which later crowned the walls of stone castles.

A slightly earlier carving, from the late eleventh century, reveals that the main features of the Modena towers – 'X' braces and projecting wall-heads – were already well established. Here, on a capital from the choir in the Abbaye-aux-Dames at Caen in Normandy, an armoured elephant carries a timber castle of exactly this sort (fig. 5.9c).

It is impossible to say whether the architectural details of the Modena carving represent contemporary north Italian buildings or whether they are based upon some other depiction. But it has been argued that the Bretonized personal names on the border of the sculpture (Guinevere is called Winlogee) reveal its origin in the story-tellings of the Bretons who passed through Italy in 1096 *en route* for the First Crusade. Sculptors from Bari, in southern Italy, are known to have worked at Modena and it was at Bari that these crusaders, including Alan Fergant, Duke of Brittany and his followers, spent four months of the winter 1096–7 waiting to sail to Greece. The church of San Nicola at Bari also has an archivolt with a castle (quite unlike that at Modena) under attack from both sides. This may have had some influence on the Modena scene. Whatever the inspiration of the scene's architectural content, as opposed to its narrative content, it was presumably acceptable to a contemporary audience and did not contain anything too fantastic. Its flanking towers are an important source for the study of timber castles. They

may indicate the character of buildings which stood on countless mottes and earthwork perimeters and, in comparison with the depictions on the Bayeux Tapestry, they seem quite comprehensible structurally.

A French romance

The remaining sources are all late medieval in date, though the first, like the Modena carving, depicts an Arthurian theme. Three early fourteenth-century manuscripts contain beautifully illustrated French texts of the romances of Merlin, of Lancelot and of the death of King Arthur. One manuscript bears the date 1316 and all three are thought to have been produced in northern France between 1316 and 1320.[5] Castles figure frequently in the illustrations, normally stone-built but often with timber galleries and parapets on their wall-tops. Two depictions, however, show more extensive use of timber. In the first (fig. 5.10a), a moat is crossed by a planked timber bridge with handrails leading to a single-tower gatehouse. Its crenellated and projecting parapet, made of boards pegged together, is supported by diagonal braces. The gatehouse itself, though not obviously boarded, is clearly of timber since it lacks the ashlar joints shown on the inner buildings. The site is defended by a palisade of pegged boards whose crenellations are closed by swinging shutters. Gatehouse and palisade alike are pierced by slits. The parapets of the twin-towered inner (stone) gatehouse may also be of timber since they seem to have pegs, and the parapet of the upper tower is supported by diagonal braces. The roofs of all the inner structures are covered in shingles. This scene, measuring 6 sq.cm (1 sq.in) is coloured in green, brown, blue, purple and orange. Its attractiveness is enhanced by details such as the fish in the moat and the various trees. Nevertheless, there is nothing here which is incongruous with a castle of c.1300 whose central components were of stone but whose

Phot. L. K. Porter

160

outer defences were still of timber. In the accompanying text, the timber gatehouse, or perhaps these outer defences as a whole, are referred to as a bretasche. Numerous documentary references for such sites are quoted below (chapter 6).

Elsewhere in the same manuscript is a comparable depiction of a castle with outer timber works, bridge, gatehouse and palisade (again called a bretasche), as well as timber parapets on its stone buildings (fig. 5.10b). That such sites were chosen for illustration among a predominantly stone landscape of castles is itself evidence of their significance for contemporaries. There may be many more manuscript sources with similar de-

pictions of the period and a more extensive search might reveal further evidence. The *Armorial* produced in the mid-fifteenth century by the herald of arms William Revel for Charles, duc de Bourbon, is one example.[6] It also shows stone castles, with timber components, in the Auvergne region of France.

A woodcarving from New Buckenham

Also from the later Middle Ages there survives a wood-carving (measuring 2.02 m (6½ ft) long at the base, 1.71 m (5½ ft) long at the top and 0.4 m (1⅓ ft) high) of an enclosed site, built in both stone and timber, from New Buckenham (Norfolk) (fig. 5.11a). Its published fourteenth-century date may have been suggested by an interpretation of the animals which flank the carving. These

5.9 (a) and (b) general view and detail of the twelfth-century carving from Modena cathedral, Italy (Photo: L.K. Porter in R.S. Loomis, *Arthurian Legends in Medieval Art*, New York: MLA 1938); (c) (*below*) Late-eleventh-century capital from the Abbaye aux Dames, Caen, Normandy (courtesy of André Heintz).

162

closely resemble the chained hart which was the badge of Richard II (1377—99) and which appeared in contemporary sculpture and painting as well as in the livery of his retainers. Since its first publication, little attention has been given to this piece.[7] It shows an enclosure with a palisade of upright timbers joined by internal and external horizontals, with larger uprights set at intervals. At the rear are two towers (? — they hardly project above the palisade), though it is not clear whether they are of stone or of timber. Between them stands a stone building of some size, in front of which a stone gatehouse sits astride the palisade.

The carving has usually been interpreted as depicting a timber-defended castle with some stone components. If this is the case then either it shows an unknown castle elsewhere or it is a stylized view of an imaginary site. It seems irreconcilable with the plan of New Buckenham castle (fig. 5.11c) which was a ringwork and bailey with a circular stone keep. It can hardly be a depiction of Old Buckenham castle since this was destroyed c.1146 when William de Albini II, lord of Buckenham and Castle Rising and earl of Sussex, founded on its site a priory of Augustinian canons. The foundation charter of the priory specifically made provision for the castle to be destroyed (*castellum diruendum*). Though the monastic plan is known from aerial photographs nothing is known of the castle defences and buildings which preceded them. The general outline of the site is shown only by the surviving moats (fig. 5.11b).

More recent consideration of the carving

5.10 (a) and (b) timber and stone castles in a fourteenth-century French manuscript (by permission of the British Library; Add.Ms. 10293).

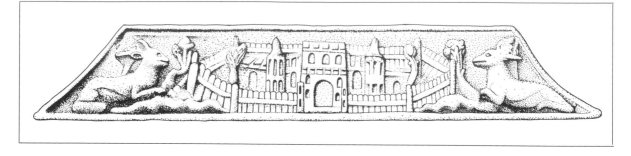

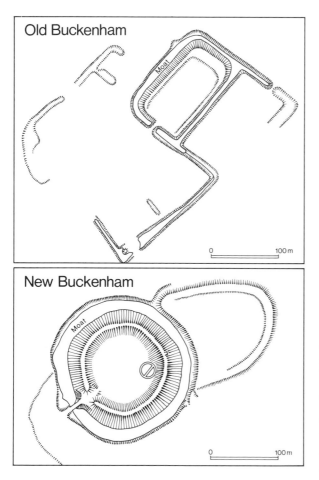

Old Buckenham

New Buckenham

5.11 (a) wood carving from New Buckenham, Norfolk (after H. Braun, *The English castle*, 1936); and (b) and (c) plans of Old and New Buckenham castles.

*Buck*enham, and partly a reference to the hart included in the arms of the Knyvett family, lords of the castle and borough. From the Crown Inn the carvings were taken to the Market House where they remained until 1983 when they were removed for restoration. They are now housed in the parish church.

Simone Martini

A much published piece is the fresco, attributed to Simone Martini, on the wall of the council chamber in the Palazzo Pubblico, Siena (detail in fig. 5.12a). It dates from 1328 and was a celebration of Guidoriccio da Fogliano's liberation of the towns of Montemasso and Sassoforte (between Rome and Florence). While not in any sense a depiction of timber castles, it is a helpful reminder of the use of timber in late medieval warfare. Some of the stone defences have timber parapets (not illustrated) and there are extensive, if temporary, timber palisades among the siegeworks.[8] Immediately below, and only recently revealed, is a further depiction of a stone castle surrounded by timber outworks (fig. 5.12b).

Guilio Campagnola

Of later date, an engraving of *c*.1500 in the Ashmolean Museum, Oxford, may provide an

suggests it dates from the late fifteenth century. It was originally one of three carved oriel sills in the Crown Inn, New Buckenham, a building of *c*.1500 which stood on the south side of the market place until the nineteenth century. The local significance of the depiction lies not in the form of the castle, which is generalized, but in the deer which flank the piece. These are partly a pun on the name

a

b

5.12 (a) and (b) timber outworks of stone castles, from paintings by Simone Martini.

5.13 *The Old Shepherd*, by Guilio Campagnola (courtesy of the Ashmolean Museum, Oxford).

unembellished view of a somewhat decayed timber castle (fig. 5.13). Entitled *The Old Shepherd*, it is a work of the north Italian artist Guilio Campagnola, and has already been discussed in the context of interpreting excavated remains.[9] The shepherd reclines on what appears to be the outer edge of a ditch whose inner slope represents either a natural mound or an artificial motte. Upon this stands a collection of two-storey buildings constructed of vertical timbers and sometimes with jettied upper floors. There is no surrounding palisade on the near side, though on the right the jettied structure projecting over the slope may be defensive. In the background a tower (and perhaps a second) rises above the domestic ranges, and on the left stands a gatehouse from which a bridge ascends to the nearest building. The central complex may surround a courtyard which is out of view, and the larger building to the right may be a hall.

Details such as windows, chimneys and louvred smoke outlets are included. Though the artist was probably not familiar with structural carpentry his depiction does not appear to be fanciful. It may well represent a real place known to him. It would be dangerous to extrapolate too much from an individual example. Nevertheless, the gatehouse, bridge, and jettied construction on buildings and defences are all features for which there is much earlier evidence of other sorts. Its crowded character may be a helpful guide to timber castles of any period or place, and certainly confirms the impression given by the excavated evidence from Hen Domen (below, chapter 9). The late date of the source is a further reminder that timber castles continued in use alongside stone ones for many centuries.

Dampierre le Château

By the sixteenth century, however, the majority of timber castles were represented in the landscape only by their earthworks. The engraving by Claude de Chastillon (1547–1616) of the motte at Dampierre le Château (Marne) is an early view of a site whose earthworks were not at that date obscured by later stone buildings (fig. 5.14a). The function of the buildings shown occupying the site and its surroundings are not clear. Apart from structure C, which could be a gatehouse surviving from the middle ages, they may not be related even to the site's late medieval occupation. The proportions of structure B, on top of the motte A, may indicate a small chapel though this is not certain. Unfortunately no text exists to explain the artist's labelling of the various buildings and other features (A–K). The main lines of the earthworks shown on the modern survey (fig. 5.14b) do not conflict with the depiction, though there are some points of variation. There was a castle here by the mid-twelfth century, though not necessarily including the motte in its present form.[10]

Castlemilk

Of similar interest is the depiction of Castlemilk (Dumfries and Galloway), in one of many sketches and maps made during the Anglo-Scottish wars of the sixteenth century. It was by this date becoming common English practice to make a plan or 'platte' of places attacked, captured or fortified. Engineers and surveyors with wide experience not only in Scotland and England but also in Calais were employed for this purpose. Castlemilk fell to the English in the aftermath of their victory at the battle of Pinkie in September 1547. The 'platte' in question was drawn up probably by Thomas Petit, well known for his work in Calais. It measures approximately 58 by 66 cm (23 by 26 in) and was executed in pen and ink with areas of brown, green and yellow. In addition to depicting Castlemilk in detail (fig. 5.15) it also shows castles and towns in the surrounding area, with distances in miles shown to neighbouring places.

Castlemilk was a rectangular tower with first-floor entry. Its dimensions as given on the 'platte' were 33 ft (10 m) in length, 18 ft (5 m) in width, 33 ft (10 m) in height and its walls were 7½ ft (2 m) thick. It stood on a flat-topped motte with a parapet around its summit. The top of the building may have been crenellated, and it had one large first-floor window. Three other openings were narrower, and may have been gunports. It has been argued that the tower was an example of clay and timber construction, for which there is possible documentary evidence in Scotland: peles built of earth, and castles which could not be burned down but could be attacked with axes (above, chapter 4). Other castles shown, for example Lochmaben (not illustrated here) were more obviously stone-built. Though the suggested clay construction cannot be proved, Castlemilk had a timber stair and very thick walls, was situated on a motte, and was apparently of different construction from the other buildings shown. The piece is also of interest in being the earliest depiction of a motte in Scotland. The site, though not necessarily what is shown here, was in existence by 1174 when there is a documentary reference to it.[11]

A drawing of timber and cannon

Timber and earth continued into the age of artillery, earthworks proving effective in absorbing the impact of cannon. A mid-sixteenth century drawing (measuring some 20 cm (8 in) across) of an unnamed circular gun emplacement, perhaps a field battery rather than a permanent fortification, illustrates this well (fig. 5.16). It consists of an

~ LA . BVTTE . DE . DAMPIERRE LE CHASTEAV AVLTREFOIS, VILLE , ET , ANTIANNE , CONTE .

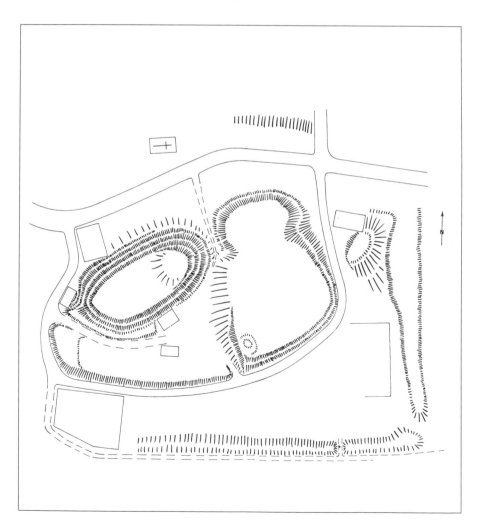

5.14 (a) engraving of Dampierre le Château by Claude de Chastillon, and (b) plan of same (M. de Bur, *Vestiges d'habitat seignurial fortifié du Bas-Pays Argonnais*, 1972).

5.15 Detail of Castlemilk, redrawn from a sixteenth-century map (after M. Merriman in *Trans. Dumfries. Galloway Nat. Hist. Antiq. Soc.* 44–5, 1967–8).

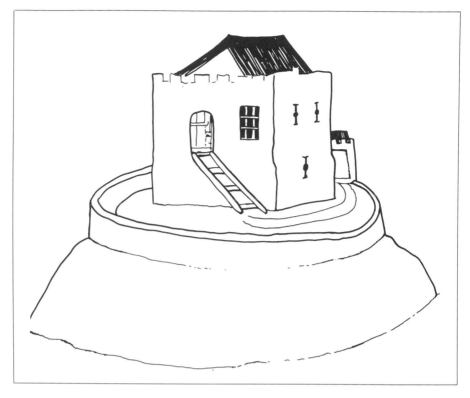

5.16 A sixteenth-century artillery fort of earth and timber (by permission of the British Library; Cott. Aug. I, ii, 106).

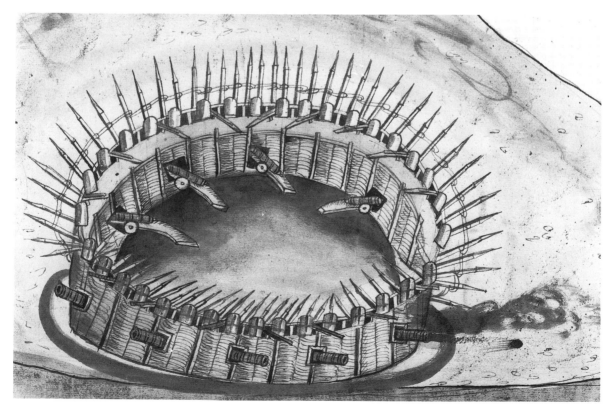

earth-filled wall with timber and wickerwork revetting, pierced with square cannon-ports and with a paling of sharp stakes. Handguns are laid out between the timber crenellations which project from the wall.[12]

Conclusion

These illustrations will not bear any generalizations. They represent not so much a body of evidence as a small collection of isolated phenomena. The closest relationship between any of them is the possible parallel between the style of the Bayeux Tapestry and of the Westminster capitals which include the example discussed. Nevertheless, despite their limitations, they make a valuable contribution to the study of a subject for which the evidence above ground has all but disappeared. The examples gathered here are unlikely to cover all the relevant material to have survived. Late medieval and early Renaissance art, in its various forms, may well contain further evidence.

— 6 —

Stone and timber

Passing reference has already been made to the mixture of stone and timber found in large numbers of castles. Indeed there was never a so-called stone castle that did not make some use of timber. Even if there were no actual timber buildings on the site, timber would be employed in roofs, joists and floors, bridges, gateways, and in numerous minor uses. Equally common was the use of timber for shoring and other temporary works asociated with ditch digging, as well as the scaffolding, centring for arches, cranes and staging used in the construction of stone buildings. References to expenditure on such works are widespread and are not enumerated here. In this chapter the evidence for the mixed character of the main elements of castles is brought together, except for the pictorial evidence which has already been discussed. The evidence takes three forms: documentary, structural and excavated.

Documentary evidence

The obscurity surrounding the earliest castles makes it impossible to separate the contributions of stone and timber technology to their origins. It seems likely that both were in use from the beginning. Timber was obviously important in early castles. Early stone buildings are also known, such as that excavated at Doué-la-Fontaine or the famous standing keep at Langeais (above, chapter 3).

Documentary evidence also indicates the importance of major stone structures. In the twelfth century the Norman chronicler Robert of Torigni described the improvements made by Henry I to the ducal castle at Rouen. As first built by duke Richard I in the second half of the tenth century this had a great stone tower as its focal point.[1] William of Poitiers mentioned a stone hall or keep (*aula lapidea*) in existence at the castle of Brionne in 1047. This site was later replaced by another nearby which has the remains of an imposing stone keep. Orderic Vitalis referred to the great hall (*principalis aula*) of the latter having a roof of timber shingles in 1090 when it was successfully attacked with fire during a siege by duke Robert of Normandy. The attackers heated the tips of their arrows and javelins in a smith's furnace, made especially for the occasion, and set the dry roof alight.[2] About 1060 Supplicius, one of the lords of Amboise (Indre et Loire) built a stone keep (*arx, turris lapidea*) where formerly his brother had a timber house (*domus lignea*), and at la Bussière (near Cluny) the wooden *donjon* built around 1153 was replaced by its lord with a stone version as soon as he was able to undertake it. This close association of different building traditions already had a long history: a tower built in 885 for the defence of Paris against the Vikings had a ground floor of tile and brick and an upper storey of timber.[3]

At Ghent (Belgium) the counts of Flanders in the later twelfth century had not only a major stone residence in their castle but also a timber one (*domus lapidea, domus lignea*), an element surviving from the earlier timber castle whose gradual transformation into stone from the eleventh century onwards has been revealed by excavation.[4] In the same period the rivalry of the Angevin kings of England with the kings of France made the security of Normandy one of their major concerns. Robert of Torigny related how Henry II built earthworks along part of the Norman-French frontier and undertook improvements to his properties including those built by his grandfather, Henry I. The rolls of the Norman exchequer recorded much work, particularly in the years 1180–4, mainly in stone but including timber construction. Timber was brought from the forests of Caux for palisades at his dwellings in the Cotentin, and a thousand oaks were used on a residence at Bur. At Gisors, as well as building in stone there was also expenditure on the bridges, gates and a wooden house within the bailey. In the following decade, when Richard I established his great stone castle at Les Andelys known as Château Gaillard, there was a significant timber contribution. The record of works at the castle and in its immediate surrounds included the purchase of stakes and palisading, the payment of woodmen and carpenters and the building of héricons, bridges and bretasches.[5]

Another documentary view of the simultaneous use of stone and timber comes from the administrative records of Angevin government in England. These provide evidence of timber works, both minor and major, in royal castles whose defensive and residential standards were increasingly dominated by stone technology. And if royal castles still made use of timber it is certain that others would also have done so. For roofing, the use of shingles and (surprisingly, since it was so combustible) thatch is referred to recurrently in the twelfth and thirteenth centuries.[6] Timberworks in stone keeps of various sorts were recorded, as at Gloucester, Arundel (Sussex) and Carlisle

in Henry II's reign.[7] The following list of stone castles at which timber palisades, bretasches and hourdes were maintained is a long one and is by no means exhaustive.[8] At the dates mentioned such features were being built, repaired or replaced in stone for the first time, at: Orford (Suffolk), 1172–3; Norwich (Norfolk), 1173; Neath and Kengfig (Glamorgan), 1184–5; Kington (Hereford.), 1187; London ('the Tower'), 1192–3 and 1238; Marlborough (Wilts), 1211; Old Sarum (Wilts), 1215; Gloucester, 1222; Rochester (Kent), 1226; Odiham (Hants), 1225; the church and pharos site at Dover (Kent), 1227; Corfe (Dorset), 1235; Colchester (Essex), 1237; Guildford (Surrey), 1239. A further group have such references dating to the middle years of the thirteenth century: Carlisle, Montgomery (Powys), Hereford, Pevensey (Sussex), Northampton and Nottingham. A final group continues this evidence well into the fourteenth century: Beeston (Cheshire), Pickering and Knaresborough (Yorks), Portchester (Hants), St Briavel's (Glos), Hadleigh (Essex), Hanley (Worcs) and Haywra (Yorks).

References at Carisbrooke (Isle of Wight) in the thirteenth and fourteenth centuries reveal in some detail the defensive timber accoutrements of a large stone castle. There was expenditure on drawbridges, portcullises, gates, bretasches, walkways or galleries (*alures*) on the keep, shutters (*wickets, loupes*) to fit between the merlons of the crenellations, and small lookout turrets (*garetta*). The use of timberworks on wall-tops was normal and some references to these are graphic. Among the improvements to the White Tower in London made in 1240 by Henry III was the erection of *alures* to enable the defenders to see directly to the bottom of the walls. In 1248 a strong gale damaged the galleries on the wall-tops at Nottingham.

Some of the early fortifications built by the English around Calais after its capture in 1347 were of timber. At Marck the original timber palisade and bretasche were replaced ten years later with stone defences. Timber defences could be used at even later dates: emergency works at Kidwelly in South Wales undertaken during Owain Glyn Dŵr's revolt in 1404–5 included timber towers. The conclusion is inescapable that timber continued to play a role in defence as long as castles were being built.[9]

The very full records of Edward I's operations in north Wales at the end of the thirteenth century make the timber contribution to stone castle-building very clear. It is interesting to note also that two of the king's sons, Alphonso and Edward, had toy castles of painted wooden construction among their possessions, presumably imitations of contemporary stone castles. On the construction of such castles, as well as numerous masons, large numbers of diggers, carpenters and sawyers were employed in the building of temporary palisades and accommodation as well as in constructing the floors, roofs and other timber components of the permanent sites. In addition, great quantities of timber were used for scaffolding, ladders, cranes, shuttering and other equipment. Much was transported from the forests of Lancashire and Cheshire in the early stages of the work, later supplies being drawn increasingly from within Wales. Temporary palisades were constructed at Builth, Conway, Caernarfon and Beaumaris. At Flint and Rhuddlan the outer timber defences, sometimes referred to as 'peels', were still being maintained in 1337. An interesting defensive detail found here (as well as in other castles of the period) was the hanging of wooden shields or targes on the battlements. Two hundred of these were sent from Bordeaux in 1287–8 for use on the castles in Wales. One hundred were displayed at Rhuddlan alone in 1304.

At Builth, Flint, Rhuddlan, Hope, Harlech and Conway there is evidence of timber domestic buildings among the initial works. Some ancillary buildings were always timber, such as the granary at Aberystwyth and the bakehouse at Harlech referred to in 1286 and 1306 respectively. At Conway a Welsh royal residence (as well as a Cistercian abbey) already occupied the site chosen by Edward for his castle. Referred to as 'Lywelyn's Hall' in the English sources, it had probably been established by Llywelyn the Great (died 1240), whose burial place lay in the adjacent abbey. Its chief component, from which it took its name, was a substantial timber hall. This was retained (unlike the abbey, which was moved elsewhere) within the defences of the Edwardian town, and works on its maintenance and improvement were carried out down to the early fourteenth century. Together with other buildings it provided a residence for the Prince of Wales during the king's lifetime. It remained standing until 1316, when it was dismantled and taken to Caernarfon where it was re-erected for use as a storehouse. A comparable example of a mobile building was the timber hall which stood at Harlech castle from 1307. This was brought from a former Welsh royal residence a few miles away at Ystumgwern. Its dismantling, transport and re-erection with improvements cost £9 6s 8d.[10] It probably stood on the stone footings still visible on the south side of the inner ward (fig. 6.1).

The continuing use of timber residential buildings alongside other buildings and defences of stone was more widespread than generally recognized. The following examples (which are by no means an exhaustive list) are known because they occur in documented contexts at royal castles, or at least at castles in royal hands. There must have been many more lower down the social scale for which the record is less accessible or even non-existent.[11] In 1236–7 a timber chapel was built in front of the king's chamber at St Briavel's (Glos). It was rebuilt in stone in the fourteenth century. In 1244 Henry III also had a timber chapel built at Rochester as an extension to his apartments in the bailey. Originally reached via his own chamber, it was given its own external staircase in 1254. In the same period, Ludgershall (Wilts) had a number of timber buildings. In 1244–5 a new stone hall was built whose timber aisle posts were coloured in imitation of marble. A timber-framed almonry stood nearby, and in 1285 a timber chapel and chamber were also erected.

6.1 Harlech castle, showing the position of Ystumgwern hall (Crown copyright; after *Harlech Castle*, Cadw 1985).

Work on the new castle at Montgomery started in September 1223, but by November its chapel was already in use. This suggests a primary phase of timber domestic buildings, as found later at some Edwardian castles in north Wales. A survey of 1592–3 at Montgomery, which revealed a castle in a state of considerable disrepair, mentioned several buildings which were still of timber, though they are unlikely to have been thirteenth-century survivals. These included two-storey lodgings and chambers in both the

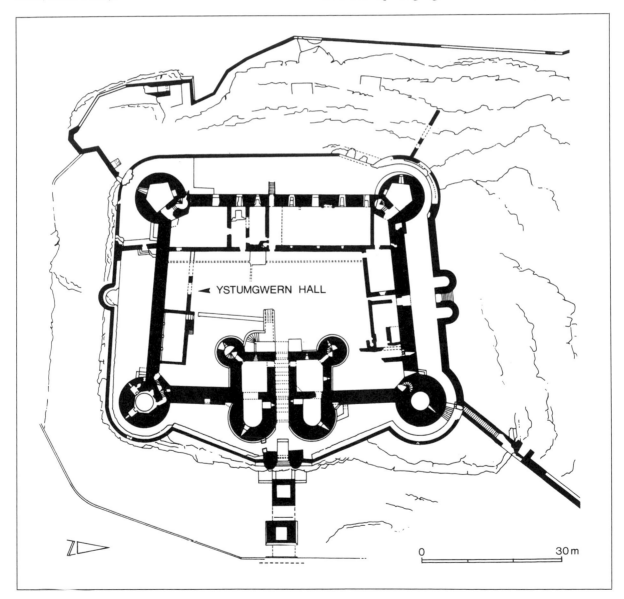

YSTUMGWERN HALL

0　　　　　　　30 m

6.2 Timber-framed lodgings in the lower ward at Windsor castle (R.A. Higham).

outer and inner wards. Behind the entrance to the inner ward stood a timber chapel supported on two posts. Together with the upper rooms of the adjacent stone-built range it was reached via a timber staircase. Established by 1301, Haywra (Yorks) was a mixture of stone and timber from the start. Its timber-framed chapel above the gateway was rebuilt, again in timber, in 1333. At Launceston (Cornwall) the 'little chapel' of timber and plaster mentioned in 1337 presumably dated from the extensive works of the previous century. At Somerton (Lincs) a high wind caused the weak timbers of the stables to collapse in 1372, and when they were later rebuilt it was again in timber.

It was not only chapels, chambers and ancillary buildings which were built in timber. The survival of some timber motte-towers well into the thirteenth century, as at York and Shrewsbury, was discussed earlier (chapter 4). At Windsor (Berks), where there had already been some timber chambers in the thirteenth century, the extensive works by Edward III included not only timber lodgings of *c.* 1355 (fig. 6.2) in the lower ward, but also timber apartments (now dated by dendrochronology to 1354–61) built within the renovated twelfth-century shell-keep. These were of two

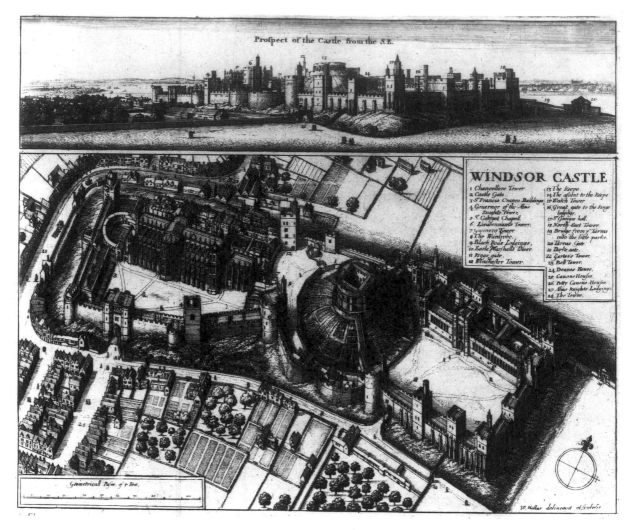

Prospect of the Castle from the S.E.

WINDSOR CASTLE

1 Chancellors Tower
2 Castle Gate
3 S.r Francis Cranes Buildings
4 Gouernor of the Alms Knights Tower
5 S.t Gabriel Chappell
6 Lieutenants Tower
7 Yuniers Tower
8 The Wardrobe
9 Black Rods Lodgings
10 Earle Marshalls Tower
11 Posne gate
12 Winchester Tower

13 The Keepe
14 The ascent to the Keepe
15 Watch Tower
16 Great gate to the kings Lodgings
17 S.t Georges hall
18 North East Tower
19 Bridge from y.e Tarras into the little parke
20 Tarras Gate
21 Darke gate
22 Garters Tower
23 Bell Tower
24 Deanes House
25 Canons House
26 Petty Canons House
27 Alms knights Lodgings
28 The Towne.

Geometricall Paser of 5 Feet.

W. Hollar delineavit et sculpsit

6.3 Hollar's seventeenth-century view of Windsor, showing apartments within the Round Tower (courtesy of the Royal Library, Windsor).

storeys, except where an open hall occupied one range, built around a small square courtyard. The many subsequent alterations to the Round Tower have disguised its original character but some early views are quite informative (fig. 6.3). The apartments were probably intended to provide short-term accommodation while the more lavish building programme in the upper bailey was pursued. Thorough examination, conducted during the recent underpinning of the Great Tower, has revealed more of their structure

surviving within the later fabric than was supposed, and a part reconstruction is shown (fig. 6.4).

As well as their main sites, castles also had peripheral sites for the leisure pursuits of their occupants. Henry V built a pavilion to the west of the castle at Kenilworth. Its buildings were of timber on stone footings, and Leland described one as a 'praty banketynge house of tymbre'. At Leeds (Kent) there was a timber-framed hunting lodge of c.1370 in nearby Langley Park and such structures must have been common elsewhere. An enclosed garden was added to the park at Odiham (Hants) c.1335. It had a timber fence with five doorways, seats with turf roofs and a garderobe

6.4 A recent survey of part of the surviving Windsor Round Tower timber structure (courtesy of J. Pidgeon and English Heritage).

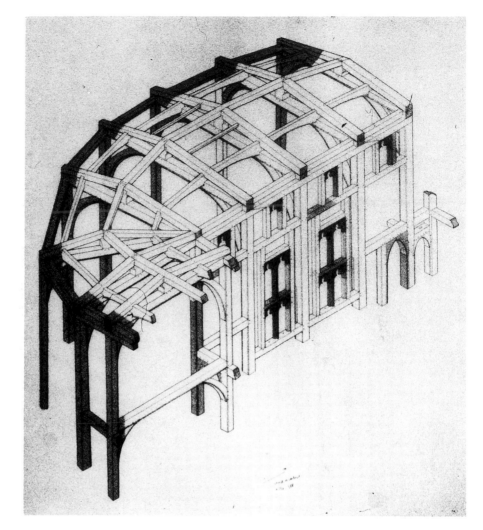

out of view behind a hedge. Such references are reminiscent of 'the fairest castle that ever a knight owned' which figures in the late fourteenth-century English Arthurian romance *Sir Gawain and the Green Knight*. This stone-built castle, with its moat and drawbridge, had a timber palisade around its adjoining park. In its literary context it is no mere incidental physical detail, but a forceful symbol of refuge and an answer to Gawain's prayer for shelter.[12]

Structural evidence

The second major category of evidence comes from stone castles within which timber build-ings, or parts of them, survive, though without precise documentary dates attached to them. These are few in number though they are a valuable reminder of the character of the timberwork which is seen normally only in ghost outline through excavation. Other forms of standing timber building are discussed below (chapter 8) as an aid to understanding the excavated evidence.

The first example is a fragmentary but interesting survival.[13] Farnham castle (Surrey) was established c.1138 by Henry of Blois, bishop of Winchester. From the twelfth century date the motte, the tower base within it and the massive revetment around it (see below, p. 187). The domestic buildings in the bailey, which included a hall and chapel, dated also from around the middle of the twelfth century and together comprised an episcopal palace of high quality. Extensive alterations between the thirteenth and eighteenth centuries have destroyed or masked much of the earlier work. But the hall was evidently a sizeable structure with aisle posts of timber. One arcade was apparently destroyed in the seventeenth century, the other being buried in masonry. From the latter there is still visible a pier with a carved scalloped capital (fig. 6.5).

Also of mid-twelfth-century date was the original hall at Leicester castle.[14] This too was

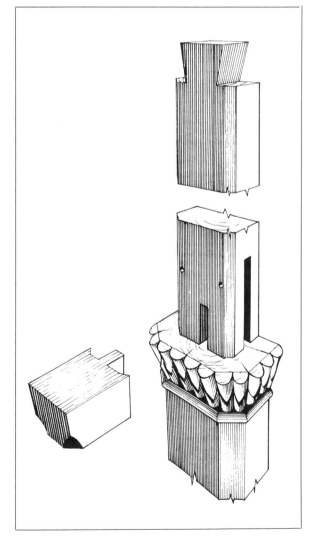

a stone building with timber aisles. The precise dates of the surviving timber were formerly controversial, owing to a confusing pattern of radiocarbon dates ranging from the tenth to the fifteenth centuries. Dendrochronological dates now available provide a reliable basis for dating the roof to the early sixteenth century and the aisle posts beneath to the middle of the twelfth. The probable builder was Robert de Beaumont (1104–68), Earl of Leicester. A truncated capital survives *in situ* on an aisle post and another (scalloped) example survives as a detached piece. This hall was a very substantial structure, as befitted a builder of Robert's status. It comprised six bays and measured 24 m (79 ft) by 17.5 m (57 ft) overall, supported with timber arches in Romanesque semicircular fashion. The details of the timbers suggests there were clerestories above the aisle roofs, and the style of the preserved capital suggests the interior of the building was ornate. The present form of the building and a reconstruction of its twelfth-century form are shown in section (fig. 6.6).

A close parallel to Leicester, not in a castle but in a socially comparable context, is the hall of the bishop's palace at Hereford. Also built with timber aisles (clerestories above) and on a similar scale, the building has been reconstructed from original fragments surviving within the eighteenth- to nineteenth-century rebuilding (fig. 6.7). The Romanesque details carved in the timbers suggest a date in the later twelfth century. This building also had a porch and a three-storey chamber block. Leicester and Hereford represent a specific choice of timber construction to produce halls of equal quality to contemporary structures built entirely of stone. They were not archaic survivals of an earlier tradition but represent 'the contemporary fashion of the Angevin court translated from stone into

6.5 Surviving twelfth-century timber detail from Farnham castle (Surrey) (C. Hewett, *English Historic Carpentry*, 1980).

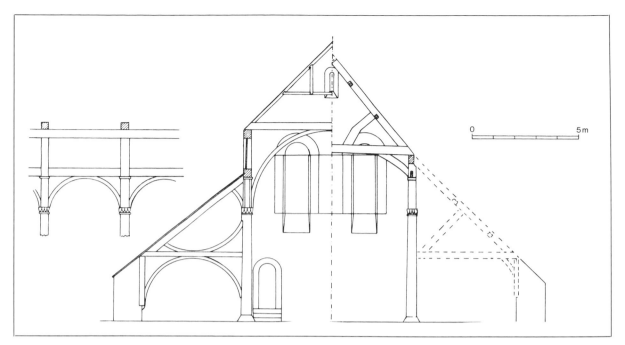

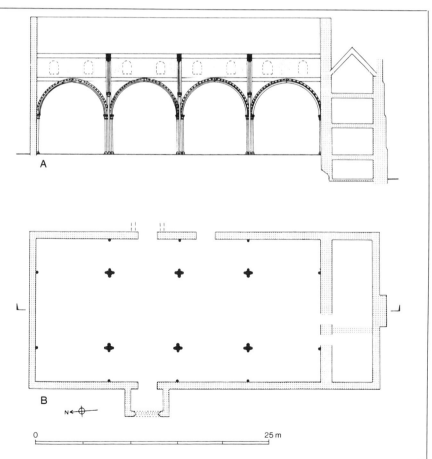

6.6 Section and reconstruction of Leicester castle great hall (N.W. Alcock in *Med. Archaeol.* 31, 1987).

6.7 Plan and section of Hereford bishop's palace hall (J. Blair in *Med. Archaeol.* 31, 1987).

timber'.[15] In scale and appearance they were probably not typical of the majority of timber castle halls in the eleventh and twelfth centuries, which were of more modest proportions.

An example of a later style of timber building within a stone castle may be cited at Tamworth (Staffs). Here the twelfth-century polygonal shell-keep contains on its north side a thirteenth-century stone building, probably a first-floor hall in its original form, and on its south side a seventeenth-century residence in brick. Situated between them – in all respects, physically, chronologically and functionally –

stands an open hall dating from the later fourteenth or early fifteenth century.[16] This was a sophisticated, fully-framed structure with no aisle posts, representing an up-to-date late medieval adaptation of the space enclosed (fig. 6.8). Though none survive of earlier date (for another late medieval adaptation see Windsor, above, pp. 175–7), timber buildings had probably been common within shell-keeps in the twelfth and thirteenth centuries.

The examples so far described were domestic buildings of timber within sites having other components of stone. The documentary evidence discussed earlier also demonstrated

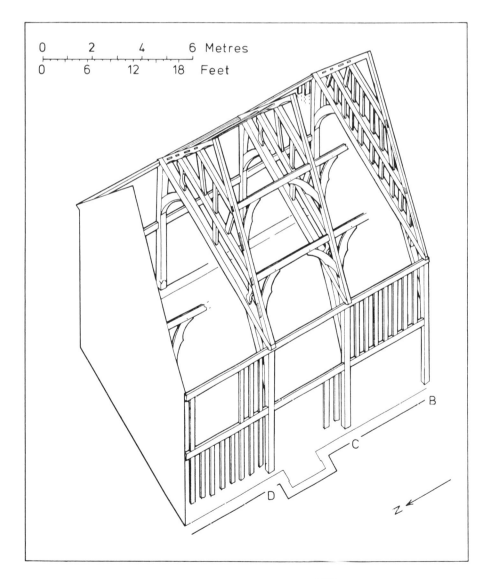

6.8 Axonometric view of timber-framed hall at Tamworth Castle (R. Meeson in *Archaeol. J.* 140, 1983).

the importance of timber defences. These took two forms: outer palisades and towers built entirely of timber; and timber hourdes or galleries on the tops of stone walls and towers. From neither category are there any surviving western examples, but some aspects of their appearance are suggested by pictorial evidence (above, chapter 5). The sockets (sometimes with corbels) which mark the positions of timbers near wall-tops often survive, and such evidence is visible at Kidwelly, Warkworth, Caldicot, Longtown, Restormel, Rochester, Conway and no doubt many other places (fig. 6.9). It is not clear whether these timberworks were permanent fixtures or whether they were only erected in time of war. Nevertheless, they are clearly analogous with, and partly ancestral to machicolations of solid stone.[17] A few timber galleries have

survived in castles and fortified churches and towns in eastern Europe though their relevance to western evidence is unclear. An example nearer home is the church at Woël (Meuse), whose tower is surmounted by a continuous timber hourding.[18]

The unique timber storey on top of the north tower at Stokesay castle (Shropshire), a fortified house of mainly late thirteenth-century date, combines domestic and defensive needs.[19] The site comprised a walled and moated enclosure with an entrance whose stone foundations are visible beneath the existing half-timbered gatehouse, built c.1620–5. The main residential range, with its famous hall, solar and detached southern

6.9 Reconstruction of timber hourde on stone curtain wall (B.K. Davison, *Observer Book of Castles*, 1979).

tower, lies opposite the gatehouse. Other domestic buildings have disappeared from the courtyard. A substantial timber-framed kitchen block of thirteenth-century origin stood adjacent to the north tower. This was improved in the late seventeenth century, when a similar building was erected next to the solar. Both were demolished c.1850. Unlike many castles, Stokesay saw an increasing employment of timber construction over the centuries, rather than a decline (figs 6.10 and 11).

The lower two storeys of the north tower contain masonry dating from the middle of

the thirteenth century, but the third floor (which contains a fireplace datable to c.1300) is contemporary with the hall and other works of c.1285–1305. Unlike the southern tower this structure, which has an irregular plan, was built integrally with the hall itself. In 1291 Lawrence of Ludlow, a rich merchant, received a licence to crenellate his house at Stokesay. In 1290 he had already accommodated the bishop of Hereford and his retinue here, so some of the buildings must have been well advanced by that date. On the sides facing away from the hall, and towards the exterior of the site, the walls of the tower's

6.10 Timberwork on north tower at Stokesay (R. Cordingley in *The Art Bulletin* 45, 1963).

6.11 View of north tower at Stokesay (photo: R.A. Higham).

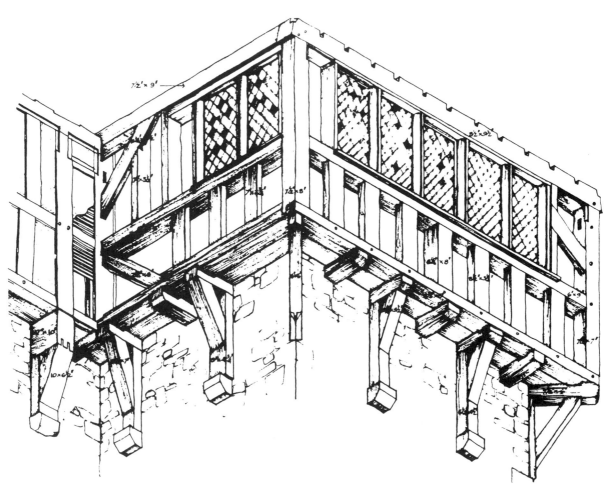

third floor consist of a jettied timber framework projecting over the masonry beneath and supported by a row of timber braces on stone corbels. This construction was closely examined during repairs in 1959, when it was argued that it was largely contemporary with the late thirteenth-century phase of construction. Clearly, some of its present details, such as its windows, date from the late seventeenth century, and most of the roof timbers are modern. Even if less survives from the original timberwork than has sometimes been argued, the medieval building must have carried something very similar.

The jettied construction may have been made necessary by the decision to incorporate the existing irregular shaped tower in the roof-line of the new hall. At the time of writing further restoration by English Heritage is in progress and examination of the structure has supported the idea of a late thirteenth-century origin. Occupying a complete storey of the tower, and possessing a fireplace, this timber room was clearly part of the castle's accommodation. But its general character, and its absence from the side of the tower facing into the courtyard, are a reminder of the parallel with timber hourdes. Indeed, it has also been suggested that in its mid-thirteenth-century phase the tower had carried a simple timber hourde and that some of the stone corbels date from that period.

A further aspect of the use of timber with stone was the practice of reinforcing masonry with timbers which were not visible in the finished structure. This was an ancient European practice, used for centuries in both secular and church building. In Britain it is known in both Roman and Anglo-Saxon contexts. In its application it varied from the crude to the very sophisticated, and it was generally intended to redress some weakness. This might be in the choice of a sloping building site, in the nature of the subsoil or underlying man-made stratigraphy, in the quality of the masonry itself, or introduced by hasty construction.[20] A simple use of timber was for the strengthening of foundations, which in some buildings (for example churches) might take the form of timbers laid in chases in the stonework. Chases for such foundation timbers are known at some castles, for example at Clifford and Goodrich (Hereford and Worcester) and Corfe (Dorset).

In other castles the available evidence suggests a raft of (normally oak) beams was laid beneath the new foundations, particularly where these were to overlie and oversail earlier masonry. These have been observed in various forms under twelfth-century keeps at Brough (Westmorland) and Chilham (Kent), and beneath a probably twelfth-century building at Sheffield (Yorks). The late eleventh-century east curtain and mural towers at Richmond (Yorks) were laid on timber piles, though here of birch. The technique of laying down timber platforms for buildings could be applied, not surprisingly, to timber structures themselves. At York examination of the motte revealed a platform of thick oak beams, laid on forked tree-trunks more than 2.4 m (8 ft) long. This was sealed by the material with which the motte was later heightened and which now carries Clifford's Tower. The platform was probably associated with either the twelfth- or early thirteenth-century timber keep for which the documentary evidence was discussed above (p. 138), or possibly with the earliest Norman keep of the late eleventh century.

The masonry at Richmond was reinforced with two levels of timbers running longitudinally through the walls, and it is for this use of intra-mural timbers that good evidence is provided by empty chases at a number of sites. In England it has been noted in the curtain walls at Castle Acre (Norfolk), Lincoln, Old Sarum (Wilts), Eynsford (Kent) and in Wales at Hay-on-Wye (Powys). The technique was used in shell-keeps at Lewes (Sussex) and Plympton (Devon), in circular keeps at New Buckenham (Norfolk) and

Tretower (Powys), and in other towers or keeps at Ludgershall (Wilts), Rochester (Kent), Castle Rising (Norfolk), Bridgnorth (Shropshire) (fig 6.12) and Threave (Kirkcudbrightshire). The technique was also well known in France and has been observed at Brionne (Eure, Normandy) in the late eleventh-century keep which succeeded the earlier castle, and in other twelfth-century keeps at Malesmains (Vieuxborg, Calvados) and St Verain (Nièvre, Caumont). In curtain walls and mural towers it is known at Châtillon-sur-Seine (Cote d'Or), Gisors (Eure), Moncontour (Vienne) and Château Gaillard (Eure). The thirteenth-century circular keep at Coucy-le-Château (Laon, Aisne) was a splendid example whose basement and three floors were bound by a complete system of intra-mural timbers. It was unfortunately destroyed during the First World War.

In the more sophisticated examples such as Coucy and Rochester the intra-mural timbers were joined to the ends of floor joists extending into the adjacent rooms, so that the whole building was strengthened by an interlocking timber framework. This was also the case at Bridgnorth where there were double timbers on the three levels of the building. Sometimes intra-mural timbers were laid in conjunction with the putlogs of the constructional scaffolding, so that the putlog holes and the chases now open into each other. This was observed at the twelfth-century shell-keep at Plympton (Devon) where some of the putlogs ran through the wall thickness but others terminated at the intra-mural timbers. The latter provided a system of ring-beams, made of timbers some 4 m (13 ft) in length, one at foundation level, another 2.5 m (8 ft) above and perhaps others higher up again (fig. 6.13). Recent examination of this site suggests the softness of the motte top, and perhaps speed of construction, dictated the use of timber reinforcement in its masonry.

Finally, a tantalizing European example may be quoted. At Nollich, near Lorch in the middle Rhineland, in a stone keep of c.1300 impressions of timberwork were still visible until covered by new internal plaster in a

6.12 Timber reinforcement at New Buckenham, Ludgershall and Bridgnorth castles (after R. Wilcox, *Timber and Iron Reinforcement in Early Buildings*, 1981).

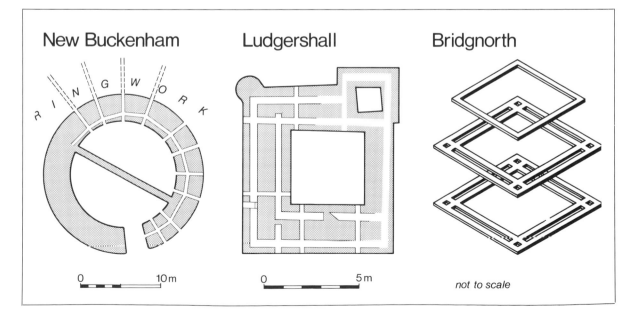

New Buckenham

RINGWORK

Ludgershall

Bridgnorth

0   10 m

0   5 m

not to scale

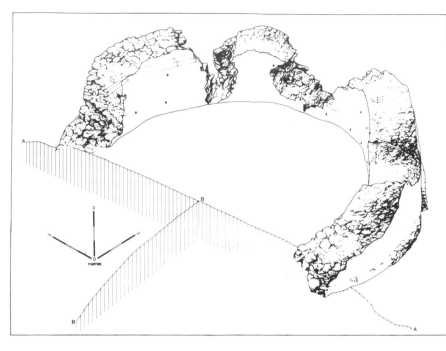

6.13 Timber reinforcement in shell keep at Plympton (Devon) (R.A. Higham *et al.*, in *Proc. Devon Archaeol. Soc.* 43, 1985).

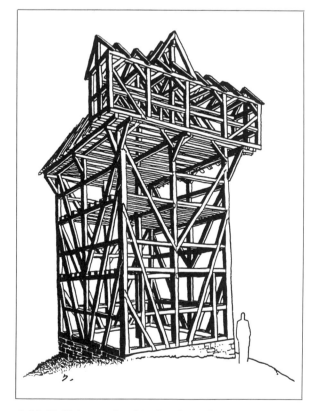

6.14 Nollich, Lorch, Rhineland. Timber tower encased in stone keep (after W. Hermann, *Le Château Préfabrique*, 1989).

renovation of 1939. It has been suggested that the evidence represented not combined timber and stone construction, but an earlier timber tower around which the stone building had been erected. The tentative reconstruction (fig. 6.14) is based on records made in 1939. The date of this timber tower, other than being earlier than 1300, is not known.[21]

Excavated evidence

From some excavations a mixture of stone and timber evidence has emerged, and some of this is discussed more fully below (chapter 8). This might be of purely chronological significance, as at Sandal (Yorks) for example, where a completely timber castle was rebuilt as a stone one. Alternatively the contemporary use of stone and timber could take two forms. Firstly there were sites with buildings obviously of timber, with evidence of post-holes and other features, alongside ones of stone. Secondly there were sites with buildings whose stone foundations suggest they carried timber rather than stone super-structures. In such cases framed construction must often have been employed since there were no ground-fast timbers to provide support. For less sophisticated buildings rafters could have sprung direct from low stone walls. At Penmaen, Lismahon and Clough, drystone footings were used for such timber superstructures alongside other timber buildings. At South Mimms, in contrast, an important site the evidence from which has not yet been fully published, a timber-framed tower stood on flint footings within a motte. The motte was itself revetted in timber, so that no earthwork was visible.

Other excavations have also produced evidence of mixed building technique. At Rathmullan (Co. Down) a rectangular stone footing for a timber-framed building was associated with the raising of an Irish rath into an Anglo-Norman motte c.1200.[22] The entrance to the motte top was also revetted with drystone walls, presumably to take a timber gateway (fig. 6.15). At Sycharth, whose fascinating though enigmatic description was discussed above (pp. 144–6 and see also pp. 300–3, below), excavations on the motte top revealed the incomplete plan of a rectangular (hall?) building with drystone foundations together with the plan of an adjacent structure built entirely of timber.[23] Any number of stone footings excavated in castles could actually represent timber structures, whether domestic buildings or defensive towers,[24] and other examples of this type of construction presumably await examination, such as the flint foundations set in boulder clay observed in 1902 on top of the motte at Anstey (Herts), perhaps the base of a timber tower.[25] Excavation of the motte at Totnes (Devon) (fig. 6.16) revealed a rectangular rubble foundation bonded in clay.[26] Although at least 2.4 m (8 ft) deep, these foundations were very narrow (0.8 m (2½ ft)) and more suited to a timber superstructure than a stone one. They were contemporary with the motte which had been built up around them, almost certainly in the late eleventh century. The

relationship, contrasts and similarities between stone and timber towers and their mottes deserve further attention.[27]

At Abinger and elsewhere timber towers were built on top of (though at South Mimms, within), the mound. A stone tower was built on the (mostly rock rather than earth) motte at Okehampton (Devon) and within that at Ascot Doilly (Oxon). At Farnham (Surrey) the massive stone basement buried within the motte, but supporting a broader building platform of stone on its summit, probably carried a square stone keep of some sort (fig. 6.17). It has been suggested that its design may reflect a well-established tradition of building motte substructures in timber which was here adopted for a different building material.[28] The lower part of this basement also contained a well, which was another reason for its construction. Whether in a building of stone or timber a well in this position was in the most secure part of the entire site and the provision of a water supply may have influenced the design of any number of unexplored motte interiors.

The mixture of stone and timber technology as revealed by excavation is not confined to mottes, but also includes other forms of defences and their domestic buildings. At some sites a major stone building was enclosed by timber defences. The earliest castle, dating to 1067, on the site of the Tower of London was an earthwork enclosure in an angle of the Roman city walls.[29] The White Tower was soon built within it, resulting in a keep and bailey plan. At Castle Acre (Norfolk), the late eleventh-century stone hall was defended by a rampart with timber palisade and gatehouse.[30] At Penard (Glamorgan), a stone hall was also enclosed by timber defences, here in the late twelfth century.[31] In contrast, at Pontesbury (Shropshire) the ringwork had internal buildings of timber and a stone (gatehouse?) tower with massive foundations of mortared rubble.[32] This was probably a twelfth-century addition

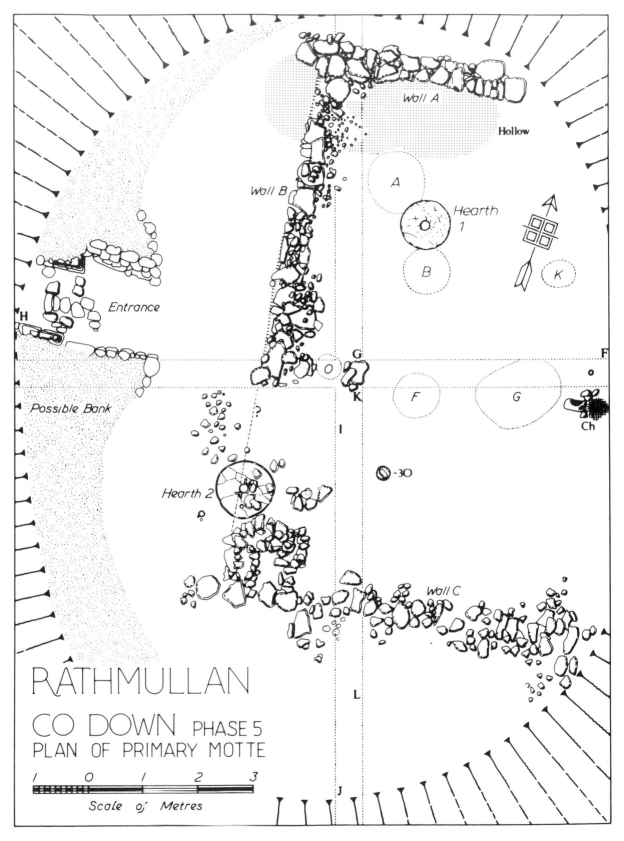

Wall A

Hollow

A

Wall B

Hearth 1

B

K

Entrance

H

G

O

F

K

F

G

Ch

Possible Bank

I

-30

Hearth 2

?

Wall C

RÁTHMULLAN

L

CO DOWN PHASE 5
PLAN OF PRIMARY MOTTE

J

1   0   1   2   3

Scale oʃ Metres

to a rampart whose primary defences had been exclusively of timber. At Barnard Castle (Durham) the ringwork of *c*.1100[33] had a timber domestic range but a stone gate-house, itself perhaps the successor to a timber one (see p. 279).

Recent excavation has suggested that the stone gatehouse at Exeter (Devon), which was begun perhaps as early as 1068 (see p. 129), originally stood astride timber defences, though these had been replaced by stone walls when the castle was besieged in

6.15 (*Left*) Stone footings for timber building on motte at Rathmullan (Co. Down) (C. Lynn in *Ulster J. Archaeol.* 44–5, 1981–2; Crown copyright).

6.16 (*Below*) Stone foundation for timber tower on motte at Totnes (Devon) (S. Rigold in *Trans. Devon. Ass.* 86, 1954).

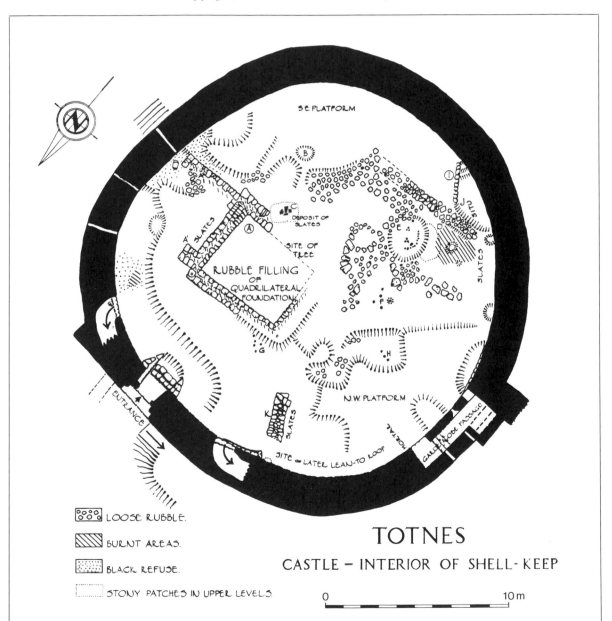

TOTNES
CASTLE – INTERIOR OF SHELL-KEEP

LOOSE RUBBLE.
BURNT AREAS.
BLACK REFUSE.
STONY PATCHES IN UPPER LEVELS.

0   10 m

1136.[34] At the motte and bailey at Pleshey (Essex), some of the twelfth- and thirteenth-century domestic buildings were of timber and clay, but the bailey defences incorporated a circular stone foundation for a tower of either stone or timber.[35] At Cae Castell, Rumney (Glamorgan), the twelfth-century ringwork had a timber gatehouse and domestic buildings as well as a timber-revetted rampart.[36] A mixture of stone and timber structures replaced these in the replanning of the following century. A stone-revetted earth rampart enclosing timber buildings is also known from Llanstephan (Carmarthen).[37] At Ludgershall (Wilts) excavations have revealed a sequence of defensive and domestic developments from the eleventh to the thirteenth centuries.[38] A stone hall and kitchen with other buildings of timber were contemporary with the first defences. The latter comprised earthworks revetted in timber and included a massive timber tower around which the rampart was piled. The concurrent use of stone and timber was a regular feature of the site's history despite much replanning over the next two centuries. Some aspects of the work are well documented and were discussed, together with the site's timber-reinforced stone keep, earlier (see pp. 174, 185).

Finally, it is interesting that some of the sites which have produced evidence of late Saxon defended residences beneath Norman castles reveal the combined use of timber and stone technology at an early date. Although the tradition of pre-Conquest secular building seems to have been overwhelmingly of timber, a small number of stone structures are known (see chapter 2). At Sulgrave (Northants) the defences enclosed a timber hall with a detached stone building, apparently a tower.[39] The situation was not unlike that at Portchester (Hants) where the same combination occurred in a late Saxon aristocratic context within the *burh* created out of the late Roman fort of the Saxon Shore.[40] At Sulgrave the timber hall was replaced by a stone one in the Norman period when the site was enclosed with a massive rampart. The stone hall was in turn accompanied by other timber structures added at a later date, so that although the site was made more defensible by its Norman owners its building technology showed considerable continuity.

In many of the cases cited, contrasting building materials and methods were used side by side in various types of structure. Sometimes, however, the use of stone was preserved for a building of particular importance. Gatehouses are a good illustration of this in the defensive context. In the domestic, chapels could be a suitable choice. At Durham, a stone chapel stood near the

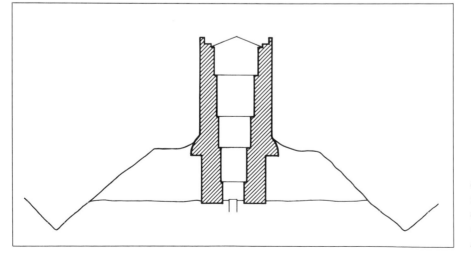

6.17 Conjectural reconstruction of motte at Farnham (Surrey) (M.W. Thompson in *Med. Archaeol.* 4, 1960).

motte with its timber tower which was described in the twelfth century (see pp. 118–20). At Winchester (Hants), a stone chapel was built for the king between 1067 and 1072 when the adjacent defences (and perhaps other buildings) were of timber. At Dover, the Anglo-Saxon church of St Mary was enclosed in the twelfth and thirteenth centuries by a succession of earthworks which carried first a timber palisade and later a stone wall.[41] At Sébecourt (Eure, Normandy), excavations revealed the remains of timber buildings beneath the defences, together with a stone structure partly buried in the same way. This building, associated with several burials and orientated east-west, was almost certainly a chapel.[42] The site was established c.1100 but underwent major changes two centuries later (see p. 105). Indeed, the evidence for mixed building technology extends far beyond the mainly British examples cited here. Timber and clay super-structures on rubble footings have been found at Bretteville-sur-Laize and Urville (Calvados, Normandy) in twelfth-century sites which were enclosed but not heavily defensible.[43] A mixture of stone and timber buildings and defences has also been recovered in the eleventh century at le Plessis-Grimoult.[44] At Gravenchon (Seine-Maritime) (see also pp. 107ff. above and pp. 267ff.) several large timber buildings were erected within the twelfth-century ramparts, but in the thirteenth century a chapel and other buildings were built in stone (fig. 6.18), the defences were rebuilt in mortared flint and timber was retained for only minor structures.[45] At Kontich (Belgium), the low motte erected in the twelfth century carried a timber building which was later accompanied by a small stone tower.[46]

Three themes should be emphasized in concluding the discussion of this topic. First, builders of castles, whether working in stone or timber, or in a mixture of both, were trying to achieve the same ends: to provide domestic accommodation within a defensible lay-out. The broad issues of choice of design and materials were discussed at the start of this volume, but the point is also evident at a more detailed level. Some of the documentation given above reveals a desire to make timber-work look like masonry, presumably because some people thought it superior. The aisle posts of the thirteenth-century hall at Ludgershall were disguised as stone, and at Windsor in 1243 the roof timbers of the new chapel were similarly treated.[47] Some of the excavations discussed below (chapter 8) produced evidence of clay-clad timbers in which a smooth and possibly rendered face would look more like stone than timber. The plaster-work in some stone castles bears traces of imitation ashlar joints painted on to compensate for a lack of high-quality masonry: the interior of the chapel at Okehampton is a good example. The rendering of timber could also have been treated in the same way.

Other excavations produced evidence of the earthworks themselves being revetted in timber, and then possibly plastered over. Here too the general impression would be more like stone. Sloping surfaces of surviving earthworks may once have been very different, the earth simply providing the bulk of a structure which was vertically faced, so that in both stone and timber construction a 'wall' was achieved regardless of building material.[48] This feature of earth and timber construction is a reminder of the potentially misleading appearance of some of the field evidence (fig. 6.19 and p. 279).

Second, the relationship of stone and timber is further complicated by the fact that the twelfth and thirteenth centuries saw an increasing use of stone in many contexts: not only in castles, but also in high-quality houses in town and country as well as in the houses of the peasantry, revealed by the excavation of deserted settlements. Various influences may have been at work. For the nobility the desire to produce castles as splendid and defensible as possible was crucial, and as the methods of siege warfare became increasingly formidable in the later twelfth century the advantages of stone became more and more obvious. Nevertheless, as is clear from evidence quoted throughout this book, the usefulness of old (and sometimes new) timber castles was still appreciated for a long period. Moreover, it was impossible to build even a 'stone' castle without extensive recourse to timber, as this chapter has shown. The high-

quality timber halls at Leicester and Hereford also illustrate a deliberate decision to exploit timber to the full when comparable structures of stone were available to their builders. In the lower social classes a desire to imitate the standards of the wealthy in their increasing use of stone may have been important. It has also been argued that the twelfth–thirteenth century expansion of the rural population and of agriculture generally may have depleted the resources of building timber available

6.18 Notre-Dame-de-Gravenchon. Twelfth-century timber buildings with stone chapel of the thirteenth century (P. Halbout, J. le Maho, *Aspects de la Construction de Bois en Normandie,* Caen 1984). (See also pp. 107–9.)

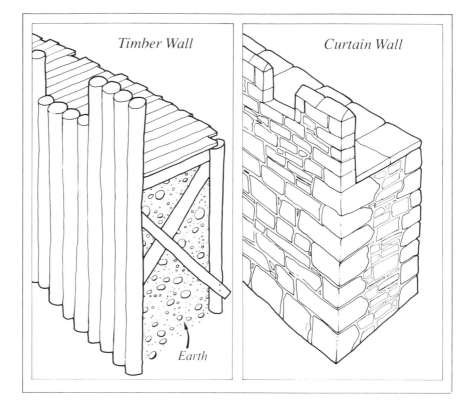

6.19 Schematic comparison of timber and stone wall construction and appearance (B.K. Davison, *Observer Book of Castles*, 1979).

Timber Wall

Curtain Wall

Earth

to the peasantry.[49] Timber castle-building may also have contributed to the considerable pressure on timber resources.

Third, there is the undoubtedly important, but nevertheless obscure, relationship between the design of timber and stone castles. The disappearance of the former above ground makes direct comparison impossible, but it seems unlikely that either escaped the structural influence of the other. It has been argued that the popularity of rectangular stone keeps was the direct result of a timber model, since building in this plan would have been normal in timber. This may have been true generally, though the exception of bow-sided timber domestic buildings, common in northern Europe in the early Middle Ages,

should not be forgotten. Details of stone buildings may also have had timber origins. Pilaster buttresses, common on stone churches as well as castles, may have been a skeuomorph of the principal (and visible) structural members of their timber counterparts. The description of the timber tower at Ardres, with its vertically stacked storage and domestic chambers, can be viewed against the surviving stone keeps, and, tentatively, against later medieval tower houses. Since by the early twelfth century, however, the use of both materials was common in castle-building it is impossible to identify an obvious source of inspiration. Nevertheless, the example reinforces the basic point: the achievement of the same end by different routes.[50]

—— 7 ——

The earthworks of timber castles

The landscape is full of earthworks of all kinds, from the defences of large prehistoric hilltop towns to the ridge-and-furrow of a once-ploughed field. While it is notoriously difficult to date earthworks simply by looking at them, some are less ambiguous than others. The best-known and most characteristic medieval earthwork is the classic motte and bailey, a mound with one or more attached courtyards, defended with ditches and ramparts (e.g. figs 7.12–15 show some typical examples). However, not all mounds were mottes nor were all timber castles motte and baileys.

As Gertrude Stein might well have said, 'a mound is a mound is a mound' and there is often confusion between prehistoric burial mounds and mottes – a good example is the mound at Tenbury (Worcs) (fig. 7.8) which could be either. Others could have been both – for example, there is some evidence that the mound next to the church at Clungunford (Shropshire), was a prehistoric barrow before it was turned into a motte many centuries later. Some isolated mottes have lost their baileys through ploughing and so look very barrow-like (e.g. figs 7.10 and 11), though in some cases and in the right conditions, the bailey(s) may be revealed as crop or soil marks (fig. 7.6). It will be noticed that on many of their maps the Ordnance Survey hedges its bets by using the equivocal terms 'tump', 'mound' or simply 'earthwork'.

On the one hand, therefore, mottes may be confused with burial mounds; on the other, the distinctions between the classic motte and bailey and what are actually called 'moated sites' is often blurred, especially where the motte is low and flat-topped or the moated site circular and raised. There is, in fact, a whole range of earthwork forms transitional between the motte and bailey and the fully developed square or rectangular moated site. There is even more difficulty where the 'motte' is a ringwork, shaped like an empty flan-case (see figs 7.1–4). This is perhaps the simplest and one of the earliest forms of defensive earthwork, a ditch and rampart which can, if necessary, be thrown up round an already existing building. It is the type known as the 'ring-fort' in Ireland, where there are many thousands of examples, the earliest dating from the Iron Age but continuing in occupation as late as the seventeenth century (see chapter 2). In Britain, such sites have sometimes been called 'ring mottes' but it is not a term to be recommended as it known or presumes the site to be medieval, which it may not be. The more neutral term 'ringwork' is to be preferred. 'Castle ringwork' is favoured by some writers, where a medieval date is known or presumed, while very large examples, such as that at Exeter, become simply 'enclosure castles', whereby any analogy with mottes is totally lost.

It is not at all clear why some chose to build ringworks rather than mottes. For example, Roger de Montgomery, one of William the

Conqueror's chief vassals, almost certainly came from St Germain de Montgomery in the Calvados region of Normandy and was very probably born there. The village is now very shrunken but includes a massive but over-grown ring-work , as yet unexcavated. When Roger was made Earl of Shrewsbury he built a castle just inside the Welsh border which he called Montgomery, presumably after St Germain de Montgomery (see p. 104). But, instead of copying his (presumed) ancestral home, his new castle in Wales was a motte and bailey from the first (see below, chapter 9). Yet, a few miles down the road towards Shrewsbury, his vassal, Roger Corbet, built a small but formidable ringwork, Caus Castle (now called Hawcock's Mount, fig. 7.3), which he, also, named after his place of origin in Normandy, the Pays de Caux, though he must have known the first Montgomery castle and its motte, built only four or five years after the battle of Hastings (see also chapters 1 and 3).

The subject has been discussed at length in an English and Welsh context by King and Alcock, without them reaching any satisfactory explanation. They concluded that,

the human variable is the only explanation. The pattern of lordship gives us some slight assistance; in three cases, concentrations of ringworks correspond with compact baronial holdings: in Cornwall, Glamorgan and Gower. We are left, indeed, with little more than the accident of personal preference to account for any choice of ringwork as against motte, or vice versa. The evidently irrational grouping of our earthwork castles can hardly be explained on any other basis. Our compact groups of ringworks may be explained either by the local castle builders having imitated some conspicuously successful earthwork in the neighbourhood, or by the personal preference of the local overlord or his military advisers — who may well have aided and counselled his tenants in the building of their castles.

More recently, variations in geology have been suggested as an influence on the choice of the siting of mottes or ringworks in South Wales where, it has been suggested, ring-works were the preferred earthwork on subsoils of rock, and mottes the choice on glacial drift (see above, chapter 2).

Inevitably, in the absence of almost any large-scale detailed excavation of these hundreds of earthworks, schemes of classi-fication have been attempted in order to see if patterns emerge and also because it is in the nature of archaeologists to classify and to bring order where perhaps there was none. The results, in fact, show an unexpected degree of individuality in the castle builders. Just as, though we recognize the Early English, Decorated and Perpendicular styles, no two churches are the same, and our cathedrals, particularly, are all highly individ-ual, so, within the obvious parameters of castle earthworks, there is an astonishing variety, sometimes because the defences are skilfully adapted to the terrain but in other cases it appears to be nothing more than individual design or preference.

Because of the inevitable anonymity of much medieval building, the myth has arisen of a sort of collective design, with individuality only surfacing with the Renaissance. Nothing, it seems to me, could be further from the truth. Everywhere in medieval times we see the expression of intensely lively and creative individuals and this individual expression extends even to castles, culminating in the work of the greatest of castle builders, Master James of St George, each of whose castles is astonishingly different from all the others. If we had no documentary evidence for the castles of Master James it might well be that they would be attributed on stylistic grounds to individual builders, since they hardly form a coherent corpus such as the work of Rembrandt or Michelangelo — in this respect they are nearer to the unpredictability of a multi-stylist such as Picasso. If this is so in the case of the great stone castles how much more unlikely it is that we shall be able to categorize and pigeon-hole our timber castles and their earthworks on any evidence that we can now recover.

A series of castle earthworks is illustrated here, in figs 7.1–35; it would not be possible to provide a representative sample of plans and photographs to cover all the areas in which timber castles occur. The task of presenting a corpus from all over Europe in a uniform way which would permit useful comparisons to be made would be a mammoth task beyond the scope of this book.

So, purposely, we have here a sample deliberately chosen from primary sources rather than reproduced from other books and articles, which illustrates Wales and its border with England. It also provides a suitable context for the detailed study of Hen Domen (see chapter 9). Selection also owes much to the great generosity of Jack Spurgeon and Chris Musson, both of the Royal Commission on Ancient and Historical Monuments of Wales, who have provided examples of their work (the surveys from Jack Spurgeon and the aerial photographs from Chris Musson) which they have allowed to be reproduced in advance of their own publications. This selection, though geographically restricted, nevertheless shows something of the range of sizes and forms which may be encountered throughout the British Isles.

An important point must be made here – earthworks can be very deceptive and can conceal as much as they reveal. In a considerable number of cases castles of stone have disintegrated and been robbed of their masonry so effectively that no stonework is visible. It is then tempting to assume that what is left are the earthworks of timber castles, an assumption which excavation often disproves. At Richard's Castle (Hereford and Worcester), for example, the motte, which may be very early, or even pre-Conquest (see chapter 2), proved to contain

the foundations of a massive polygonal stone tower of late medieval date, while at Brockhurst Castle, Church Stretton (Shropshire), the earthworks completely disguised the remains of a stone curtain wall and no doubt of other, more massive, stone buildings.

Perhaps even more often, the major defences and buildings of castles were of stone, while their outer works were only ever of timber. Chapters 4 and 5 illustrate this from documentary and pictorial material and excavation has confirmed it where documentary evidence is lacking. At Brockhurst Castle, Church Stretton, it appears that the outer bailey had only timber defences while the same is true at Stafford Castle and very probably at nearby Chartley (fig. 7.32) though this has yet to be excavated. Other castles which appear superficially at least, to have stone keeps but timber outer works are Clun and Hopton both in Shropshire.

The outer defences of stone castles have, inevitably, received less attention than keeps, gatehouses and curtain walls, yet they were essential and integral parts of the buildings they defended and should, at least, be surveyed. A glaring example of this apparent lack of interest can be seen at Orford in Suffolk, where the fine twelfth-century polygonal stone keep is given full treatment in the official guide, while the extensive, indeed spectacular, earthworks surrounding it are ignored and unillustrated. Castles are part of the landscape in which they sit and while it is simply not possible to excavate all the defences and other earthworks which surround them, they should at least be planned, thereby integrating the castles with the countryside they were built to defend.

A further reason why earthworks can be misleading is that we have no way of knowing, before extensive excavation, how close the remaining earthworks are in size and shape to the original defences. It must always be kept in mind that the earthworks are merely the foundations for the castle proper, which was always either of timber or stone, or both. This is why the term 'earthwork castle' is quite misleading – earthworks, however impressive, can easily be scrambled over by the tolerably fit – witness the thousands of visitors to the most formidable of hillforts – Maiden Castle in Dorset or British Camp in Malvern (fig. 7.31) – who breach the defences every weekend. It was the vertical walls of wood or stone which crowned the ramparts and the interval towers and heavily-defended gateways which made these castles, however small, daunting to the attacker.

All earthworks will have suffered greater or lesser degrees of erosion – it will of course be greatest in those built of sand or gravel, and least in those hewn out of the solid rock. Between the two, some soils, such as chalk or boulder clay, retain their profiles remarkably well. Eventually, all the profiles of earthworks reach the angle of rest of the materials from which they are built, or into which they erode. It follows that the present appearance of all earthworks is less steep and less formidable than when they were first constructed. Even where ditches were cut into solid rock, they will have silted up to some extent over the centuries and the rocky mottes or ramparts will themselves have been weathered. In many more cases, however, considerable slumping will have taken place, filling the surrounding ditches, making the gradients less steep and reducing the height of mottes and ramparts – and, of course, reducing or removing the evidence for the structures on their summits.

The extent of erosion from the tops of mounds or ramparts can be estimated from the amount of silting found in excavated ditches, though this estimate will only ever be approximate and is usually complicated by the fact that most defensive ditches have been re-cut or cleared out in order to reinstate them. Some ditches are re-cut many times

and it is never clear whether the spoil has simply been carted away. Clearly, if a structure, such as a tower on a motte or a palisade on a rampart, was still viable, in spite of erosion from the sides of the mound, the material from the re-cut will probably have been taken elsewhere. Only if there is a complete rebuild is the motte or rampart likely to have been rebuilt and heightened.

The very act of demolishing a structure, a tower, a gate or a palisade, will cause disturbance of the earthworks which will tend to collapse down the sides. This can be seen particularly, of course, at the end of a timber castle's life when there may be large quarry holes in the top and sides of the motte with mounds of earth in the ditches below. Irregularities in the shape of the motte at Hen Domen, currently being excavated, may have this origin (fig. 7.15). However, the situation is more complicated than this, since there is increasing evidence and supposition that ramparts and even mottes were revetted with vertical timber walls (see also chapter 8). One of the earliest excavations to postulate this unexpected theory was that at South Mimms (now in Herts), dug by Dr J.P.C. Kent in the early 1960s. Here (as fig. 8.39 shows) the evidence points to a sloping timber tower, very much like bell towers of a similar, or later, period in England and clock towers in Denmark, surrounded by an earthen mound vertically revetted so that from the outside no earth would be seen, only a vertical wall of wood with a wooden tower rising above it, the earth playing much the same role as the mass of concrete in a modern bunker or gun emplacement. A very similar construction, though in stone, can be seen at Farnham Castle, Surrey, where the basement of the once massive keep has been excavated and the surrounding 'motte' revetted in stone still survives (see pp. 177–8).

It will be obvious that, once the vertical timbering of a structure like that at South Mimms has rotted and collapsed, or been removed, the earth behind will slump, eventually reaching its angle of rest. If the central tower was open down to ground level, as at South Mimms, when it rots the earth will slump inwards. The earthwork will eventually look very much like a ringwork – a rampart with a lower internal area. Without excavation, it would be easy to assume a palisade along the crest of the 'rampart' with some kind of unknown internal buildings, but this would be far from the truth. There are a number of mottes which have hollows in their summits and these may simply be basements to towers on sloping-sided mounds but it would clearly be misleading to assume so without further evidence.

In addition, mottes were often constructed by piling the material dug from the surrounding ditch on the perimeter of the intended mound; as the ditch was deepened the earth would be piled upwards and inwards, so that an unfinished motte would look like a ringwork. A likely example is the enigmatic Norman mound at one end of the earlier Irish fortification at Downpatrick (Co. Down). Here, the higher part of the mound corresponds with the larger profile of the ditch, the lower part with that of the less substantial ditch. The mound is a likely candidate for an unfinished motte, but only excavation would show if this were truly the case.

The earthworks which we see now, therefore, are mutilations of their original size and shape – flatter, with lower mottes and shallower ditches, damaged by deliberate demolition or by trees which have grown on them and been blown down, or, most drastic of all, by levelling for agriculture or the breaching of ramparts to enable cattle to reach water-filled ditches, or to take a plough into the more level interior. Perhaps for these reasons, the attempts to classify mottes and other earthworks, while valuable as a means of organizing the field monuments, do not take us very close to the important structural details of medieval times, though they do reveal interesting variations in the overall plans and sizes of sites.

The earthworks of timber castles fall into five broad categories:

1 Ringworks without baileys.
2 Ringworks with one or more baileys.
3 Mottes without baileys or with no apparent baileys
4 Mottes with one or more baileys
5 Ringworks or mottes (with or without baileys) within earlier earthworks.

1 *Ringworks without baileys* (figs 7.1 and 7.2) As has been pointed out, this is the simplest form of defensive earthwork, capable of being added, if necessary, to an already standing building and with a history going back long before medieval times into the Iron Age at least. In a sense, it is a bailey without a motte and has therefore the function of a bailey, to enclose residential and animal accommodation, storerooms, kitchens and so on. What it lacks, of course, is a raised strong point on which a tower can be mounted. There is little sign, in the ringworks known to the writer, of interval towers along the perimeter and it is possible that, as at Castle Tower, Penmaen (West Glamorgan) (fig. 8.67) the only tower was a gate-tower. However, since so few ringworks have been extensively excavated and since it is possible for a timber tower to leave little trace in the ground, it would be unwise to assume that ringworks never had interval towers.

Some defended enclosures which began life as ringworks eventually achieved mottes. Well-documented examples of this development include der Husterknupp, Goltho, Castle Neroche and others (see chapters 2 and 3). More, in Shropshire, (unpublished) is another example (B. Hope-Taylor, *pers.comm*) (fig. 7.26).

There may be many more of these transformations waiting to be discovered but it requires extensive excavation of what are often massive earthworks to provide proof beyond doubt and in the present economic circumstances such excavations are unlikely.

2 *Ringworks with baileys*
A number of ringworks have attached baileys (figs 7.3–8). Little is known about the function of these outer enclosures, just as little is known about the functions of second or outer baileys attached to mottes. It is usually assumed that they are for the enclosure of stock, perhaps horses in particular, since they were so valuable, though knights' horses, the supreme fighting animals, would almost certainly have been kept in the innermost enclosure.

3 *Mottes without apparent baileys* (figs 7.8–11)
Mottes themselves come in all sizes, from the smallest, such as Hockleton (fig. 7.16) to the largest such as Windsor and in many shapes – circular, oval, rectangular or subrectangular, almost square or simply irregular. All of these shapes are significant for whatever was on top of them, and it may be assumed that the shape of the top of the mound reflects in some way the structures built on or into it, though in each case this would have to be tested by excavation. These are the most difficult of earthworks to understand. The examples illustrated show mounds lying in isolation apparently surrounded only by fields. There is no sign of bailey earthworks, though these, being slighter, would be more vulnerable to ploughing. It is possible that they could have had surrounding palisades, built directly on the ground, without ramparts or ditches, which would leave little trace, though such defences would be comparatively weak. If we assume a residential tower of some kind crowning the motte, it is difficult to see how all the necessary accommodation and services such as kitchens (in a timber tower with the attendant danger), space for animals and storage for grain could be included, though the documentary evidence reminds us how

complex the buildings on the tops of mottes could be. It may be that we lack understanding of the functions of these isolated mottes, which may simply have been watch towers, serviced from elsewhere. Even so they seem to be very vulnerable.

4 *Mottes with one or more baileys* (figs 7.12–30)
These are the classic forms of the timber castle earthwork. Figs 7.12–16 are fine and typical examples of the motte and single bailey castle. It is clear, from the excavations at Hen Domen, that single baileys, however small, could be crowded with buildings. It is less certain what outer baileys were used for, and there is a real need for the complete excavation of a multi-baileyed site if these castles are to be fully understood since unlike some deserted village sites, the interiors of baileys tend not to be full of obvious building platforms from which deductions about their internal planning can be made.

Some quite small mottes have two or more attached baileys (figs 7.21–22) and Castell foel Allt, at Pilleth in Radnorshire (fig. 7.27) apparently has four. The most famous and spectacular, as well as the largest, motte with two baileys is, of course, Windsor, and it is difficult now to strip off the accretions of the centuries and imagine it as a huge timber castle, but presumably it was so at the beginning.

While castles such as Windsor, Arundel, Stafford were fortresses of the most powerful men in the society of their day, a little site such as Hockleton, a mini-motte (fig. 7.16) could have been little more than a fortified farmhouse with perhaps a watch-tower (akin to a machine-gun post) on its mound. It was one of the group of similarly small mottes in the Rea-Camlad valley, apparently built during the colonization of the area by the tenants of Roger of Montgomery. In fact, Lismahon (Co. Down) (figs 8.73–75, chapter 8) had a typical peasant hall on its mound, but with a small stilted tower in one corner and a palisade surrounding it. Yet Hockleton, Lismahon and Windsor share the same fundamental earthwork forms and stem from the same traditions.

5 *Ringworks and mottes within earlier earthworks* (figs 7.28–31)

Since, before the invention of the bulldozer, earthmoving was a major undertaking, requiring a massive labour force, if suitable earthworks survived in the landscape they were adapted in medieval times to the needs of the castle.

Iron Age forts and Roman camps were the most commonly reused earthworks, with mottes and inner baileys usually occupying one corner of the much larger enclosures, leaving the rest of the space as an outer bailey, perhaps in some cases the site of a village or other attached settlement.

Examples of castle earthworks built within prehistoric defences include Caus (Shropshire) (fig. 7.29) (which also used the pre-existing outer earthworks as the defences of a nascent borough); Elmley Castle (Hereford and Worcester); Caer Penrhos, Castell Cadwaladr, Ceredigion (fig. 7.28); British Camp, Malvern (Hereford and Worcester) (fig. 7.31) and, probably, Dudley (West Midlands). It has been suggested that the ringwork on British Camp, situated at the remote summit of the highest hill for miles around, was a hunting lodge, since it could not have effectively administered anything from its isolated position, nor does it control any obvious routes, though it has, of course, an unrivalled view of the landscape in all directions.

Timber castles which have turned Roman forts into baileys include Cardiff with its massive motte; Carisbrooke (Isle of Wight); Burgh Castle (Suffolk); Castell Collen (Powys) and Colwyn Castle, Glascwm (Powys) (fig. 7.30).

Similarly, though on an even larger scale, William the Conqueror built the earliest phase of the Tower of London (a ringwork?) in a corner of London's Roman walls, and again Norman earthworks have also used Roman town defences at Canterbury, York, Lincoln, Exeter, Worcester and elsewhere.

In urban contexts such as these, castles became permanently occupied features of the landscape. But in some rural contexts, existing enclosures would make valuable campaign bases, protecting large numbers of men and horses on the move – Neroche (Somerset), situated in the centre of the neck of the south-west peninsula (fig. 2.10) may have been important in the initial Norman impact on the south-west of England and Blackdown Rings, Loddiswell (Devon) may have been important in the campaign fought further west after the fall of Exeter in 1068 (fig. 1.6).

The siting of timber castles

It is worth pointing out that the siting of these early castles which we are here discussing seems to fall into two categories: those which are within settlements – towns or villages; and those which stand in isolation in the countryside.

The first category is easier to explain. The Normans used castles to dominate the people they had conquered, both as all too obvious symbols of conquest and as centres for the administration of justice and local government, as well as for residential needs. In many cases, therefore, they built castles within long established towns and cities, often with very destructive effect. The numerous wasted house sites listed in Domesday Book, and sometimes described there specifically in relation to castle-building, are clear evidence of this process.

In other cases, castle-boroughs were founded as part of the process of settlement, or villages grew up round castles founded in previously open countryside, for example Castle Pulverbatch (Shropshire).

On the other hand, as many of the illustrations here show, some timber castles were built in apparently isolated situations without any nearby settlement. There must be some cases, of course, where settlements around castles have been abandoned and obliterated by later agriculture, especially in areas where settlements remained small. The survival of thousands of deserted medieval village earthworks, however, suggests that the complete obliteration of large settlements is rare. It is probable that many isolated castles had a different function from those in towns or villages, in most cases being strong points strategically sited to control roads, ridgeways, river crossings or passes.

Hen Domen (Montgomery), is a classic example – it commands a major ford over the Severn as well as the ancient crossroads close by on the ridge on which the castle stands (pp. 326ff.). Hawcock's Mount, the first Caus Castle (fig. 7.3), controls the road from Shrewsbury westward into Wales (and, conversely, of course the road from Wales towards Shrewsbury) and Castell Crugerydd (New Radnor), controls the road westward over a low pass (seen in the background of the photograph in fig. 7.19a). In addition, this site has a superb view over the surrounding countryside. Isolated castles must also be seen in the context of the settlement pattern of which they form a part. Not all medieval landscapes were characterized by nucleated villages. In Wales and parts of England, such as the south-west, the settlement pattern remained dominated by hamlets and farm-steads, and such large nucleations as there were tended to be boroughs. In such areas, a castle might occupy its own discrete location chosen for topographical or tenurial reasons, in the same way that farms or churches might also occupy their own, separate sites.

We must presume that these isolated castles went out of use in the medieval period, though many of those built by the Normans may have been occupied until the end of the Welsh wars in the late thirteenth century.

Motte and bailey castles built by the Welsh may have had a much longer life, such as that at Sycharth castle, which was burnt by the English after the battle of Shrewsbury in 1403 (above, chapter 4).

Some short-lived castles are those known as 'adulterine', built during the second quarter of the twelfth century, during the civil war between Stephen and Matilda and at other times of disturbance (see chapter 4). Abinger and South Mimms are excavated examples but there is clearly no way in which these earthworks can be dated simply by inspection or distinguished from castles with a much longer life. Some mottes and ringworks have even shorter lives, as siegeworks – see figs 7.34–35 for a probable example – and others may have had unsuspected reuse – for example, it is probable that Pan Pudding Hill, Bridgnorth, sited opposite the stone castle, was a medieval ringwork, reused by Cromwell's troops as a siegework to bombard the stone castle, itself being reused at the time.

Very many timber castles were later rebuilt in stone and in most cases the evidence for the earlier, timber, castles has been destroyed in the rebuilding. Nevertheless, it is usually assumed that a stone castle on a motte and bailey foundation had a timber predecessor, even with sites as large as Windsor, Arundel, Warwick, Dudley or Stafford (fig. 1.2). Sometimes, as at Sandal in Yorkshire, the evidence for the early timber phase is extensive and unequivocal (see pp. 298ff.). Elsewhere, as for instance at Dudley, there is evidence for timber buildings in surviving islands of earlier stratigraphy. On the other hand, some mottes had stone structures from the start, particularly where, as at Okehampton (Devon), the motte was not so much an earthwork but an enormous pile of rock fragments quarried out of a surrounding ditch.

Re-sited castles

There are many cases where timber castles have, for various reasons, been replaced by stone castles, not on the same sites but close by. There may be a number of reasons for this. The shift from Hawcock's Mount to Caus Castle may have arisen from the destruction of the earlier site and perhaps the decision to develop a borough within an earlier, Iron Age enclosure (fig. 7.29 and chapter 1). In the case of Hen Domen, Montgomery (the first Montgomery castle) the new stone castle was built, appropriately, on a great rock, the stone from the ditches, cut by miners from the Forest of Dean, being used for the rubble walls. This new and impregnable site was chosen in spite of the fact that it had no view westward over the ford of the Severn known as Rhyd Whyman, which remained controlled by an outpost at Hen Domen (see chapter 9).

Bishop's Moat, on the Kerry Ridgeway running into Wales (fig. 7.12), was replaced by a stone castle further east, on the north-south route from Shrewsbury to Clun and beyond (but still retaining control of the ridgeway) and it was here that the new borough, called Bishop's Castle, with a large church, was established, probably in the later years of the twelfth century. At Rhuddlan, Robert of Rhuddlan's motte and bailey castle was replaced in 1277 by the new stone castle of Master James of St George (fig. 7.33). Here the reasons seem to be that Master James required a flat site and clearly it was easier to move than to level the motte and bailey.

The relationship between Powis Castle (fig. 7.34) and the diminutive motte nearby, known as Lady's Mount, is less clear, as is the origin of the motte's name. Could it have been nothing more than the foundation for a gazebo for the lady of the manor, or could it be a siege castle built in some unrecorded attack? This enigmatic example well illustrates the difficulties of interpreting the field evidence of timber castles. Nor is it certain that excavation would solve such a problem.

Note: References to the majority of the sites mentioned in this chapter will be found in D.J.C. King's *Castellarium Anglicanum*, 1983. Specific references to that work are given for those sites which are illustrated.

All the aerial photographs in this chapter are by C.R. Musson, to whom we are deeply indebted.

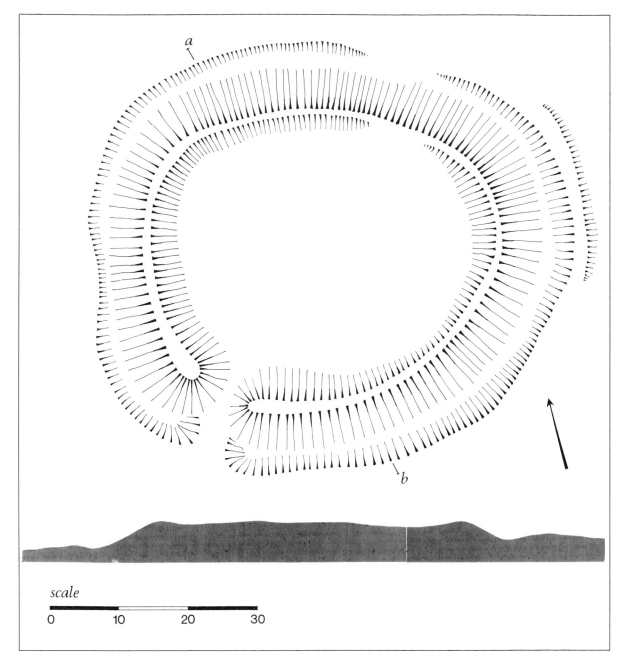

scale

| 0 | 10 | 20 | 30 |

7.1 Y Gaer, St Nicholas (Glamorgan)
This is a fine example of a large, simple ringwork, with, apparently, one heavily-defended entrance. As can be seen from the profile, the interior is built up above the surrounding land and, in such cases, there is always the possibility that this masks a series of developments, each buried beneath the next, as was demonstrated at der Husterknupp and Goltho, for example (King, I, 169).

7.2 Coed Caeau, Erwood (Powys)
A large ringwork with splendidly preserved
earthworks. The inner rampart is massive, enclosing a
slightly dished interior; a deep ditch separates it from a
crisply steep outer bank. This site would one day fully
repay highly detailed total excavation, since it
promises maximum information about sites of this
type. Until then, it should be jealously preserved. The
two small circles in the centre of the earthwork are
agricultural (not in King).

7.3 Hawcock's Mount, Westbury (Shropshire)
A small but massively defended ringwork and (?)
bailey. The name is a corruption of Old Caus Mound,
and derives from the Pays de Caux in Normandy,
whence Roger Corbet, a vassal of Roger de
Montgomery and the presumed builder of the castle,
came to England. The name was later transferred to
the much larger motte and bailey illustrated in fig.
7.29 (see chapter 1).

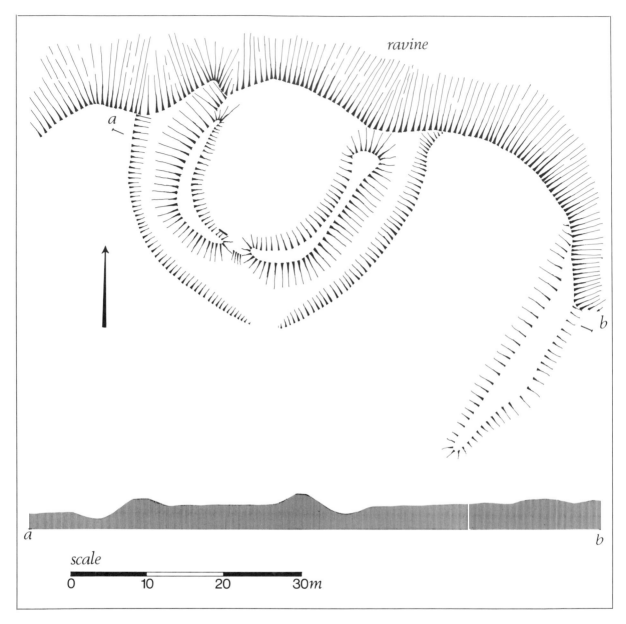

7.4 Bishopston Old Castle (Glamorgan)
Here a massive ringwork has been sited using a steep
ravine for the fourth side. A bulbous end to the
rampart on the north-eastern side suggests that there
was a tower here (such as that found in similar
circumstances at Hen Domen, see chapter 9) and part
of a bailey rampart is preserved to the east (King, I,
161, and see chapter 1).

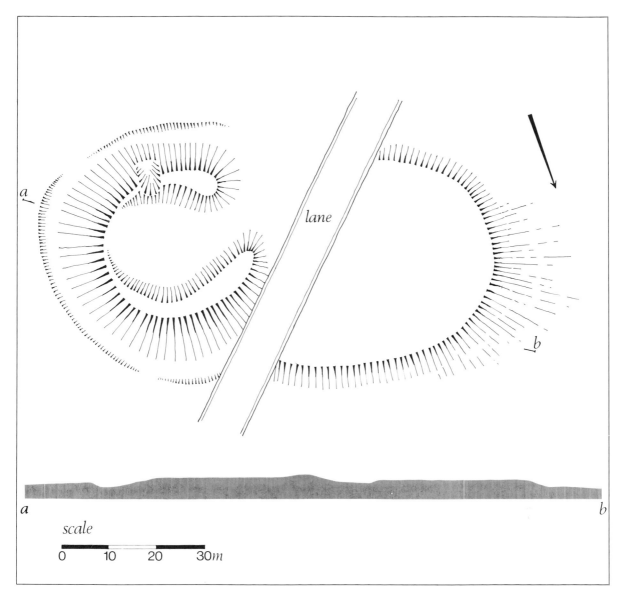

7.5 Amaston, Alberbury (Shropshire)
A small ringwork with a bailey. The entrance is now
very wide and has presumably been altered. The
bailey has no apparent rampart and was perhaps only
palisaded or fenced (King, II, 420).

207

7.6 Acton Bank, Lydbury North (Shropshire)
This crop-mark, which was formerly interpreted as
that of a round barrow, now appears to have a bailey
and another small enclosure attached to it, so that it is
more probably a ploughed-out motte and bailey or
baileys. It sits on a plateau, with natural defences on
two sides. If it is a castle, it is not clear why it was not
sited on the tip of the promontory. Here is a clear case
for excavation to solve the problem of date, especially
as the site is being eroded by ploughing (King, II, 426).

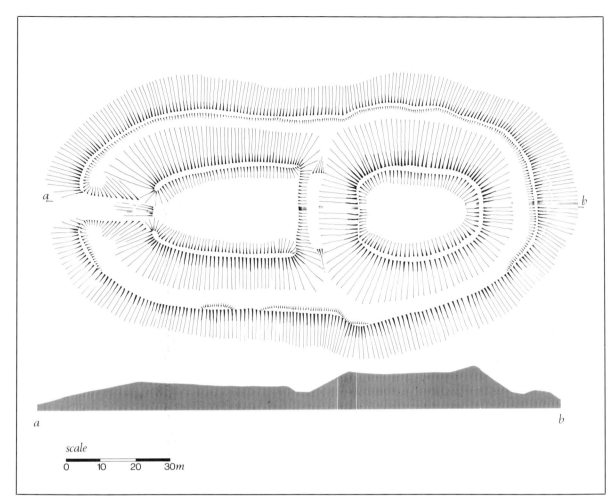

7.7 Cefn Bryntalch, Llandyssil (Powys)
This impressive site consists of an oval ringwork separated by a deep ditch from an oval bailey, the whole surrounded by a wide ditch and rampart. As can be seen from the profile, the ringwork dominates the bailey and is very strongly defended by a massive rampart.

Although the site has not been excavated, it is possible that the inner ringwork, at least, has stone defences (King, I, 297).

7.8 Tenbury Wells (Hereford and Worcester)
This mound, in a low-lying field near the river Teme,
has been variously described as a castle mound, a
'tump' and a barrow, and is a good example of the sort
of ambiguous earthwork which requires excavation to
elucidate it. The author's opinion, based on the slight
earthworks which surround it, is that it is probably a
motte. Aerial photography, under the right conditions,
might solve the problem (King, II, 507). (Photo:
Philip Barker.)

7.9 Cwm Camlais Castle, Trallerg (Powys)
This is a large motte with, probably, a later stone shell-
keep inserted into its summit. There is little sign of a
bailey (King, I, 170 – destroyed in 1265).

7.10 Eglwys Cross (or Mount Cop), Bronington
(Clwyd)
This is an extraordinary large low mound with the
possible remains of a small bailey to the left of the
large tree. It is difficult to envisage the sort of buildings
which would occupy such a mound, which looks more
like a barrow. Presumably, if it were a motte, there
was a palisade, whose line is not clear, at the slight
break of slope halfway up the mound. It is somewhat
similar to the large flat motte at Kingsland (Hereford)
(fig. 7.24) (not in King).

7.11 Tomen Castell, New Radnor (Powys)
A fine motte with a dished top, so that it is almost a
ringwork. It stands on the highest point of a ridge
overlooking a small, steep valley. Any bailey or
surrounding building sites may have been obliterated
by ploughing – compare with Moel Frochas (fig. 7.17)
(not in King).

7.12a and b Bishop's Moat, Castlewright (Powys)
A large and well-preserved motte and bailey lying
adjacent to the Kerry Ridgeway, a major prehistoric
and later route into Wales. There does not appear to
have been a settlement attached to the castle but it is
the presumed predecessor to the stone castle which
gives its name to the borough of Bishop's Castle in
Shropshire, some 5 km (3 miles) to the east and which
controls the north-south route (now the A49) as well
as the ridgeway (King, I, 296).

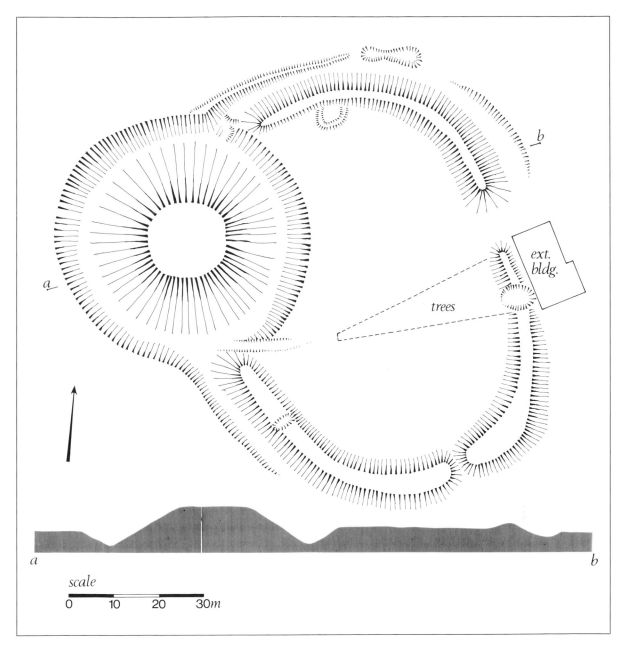

scale

0 10 20 30m

7.13 Pains Castle (Powys)
A motte and bailey of massive scale, where a small hill
has been sculpted into a defensive system. Note the
size of the rampart encircling the motte and the
terraced road heading into the bailey. It is probable
that this castle was eventually refortified in stone.
(King, II, 407 – early twelfth-century documentary
implications.)

7.14 Tomen Y Rhodwydd, Llandegla (Clywd)
A fine example of a 'classic' motte and bailey – the
motte with a wide flat top, the bailey with a
remarkably steep well-preserved rampart. Compare
Hen Domen, Montgomery (below) (King, I, 104 –
built by Owain Gwynedd in 1149, rebuilt by King
John in 1212).

7.15 Hen Domen, Montgomery (Powys)
This photograph was specially taken by C.R. Musson
at 2.15 p.m. on Boxing Day, 1984, in order to highlight
the ridge and furrow which has been shown to pre-
date the castle (Barker and Lawson, 1971) (see
chapter 9).

216

7.16a and b Hockleton, Chirbury (Shropshire)
Hockleton is one of the smallest of mottes, lying
within a diminutive bailey. It is sited close to a steep
ravine, Merrington Dingle, to the north-east, although
it does not take advantage of the natural defences of
the cliff edge. It sits within a slight platform bordered
on the south-west by a hollow way and on the south
by a slight bank, which may merely be a field
boundary, since the whole area further south is
covered with slight traces of ridge and furrow. It is
being eroded by sheep burrowing into its sides and the
bailey long ago had a road driven across it.

Whatever structure there was on the motte top can
only have been small – a look-out tower or the
equivalent of a machine gun post. Hockleton was
perhaps more like a defended farmstead than a castle,
in the usually accepted sense of the word. (Not in
King. The site was referred to, together with others in
the Vale of Montgomery, in 1224–5.)

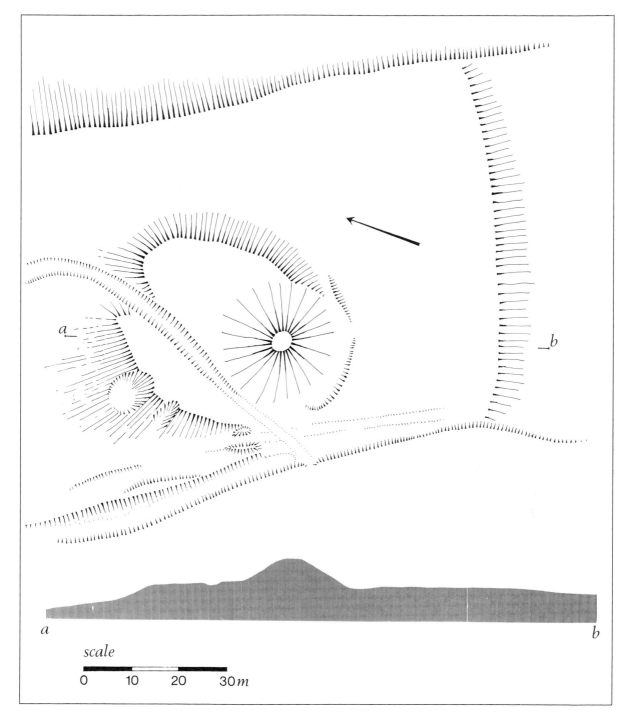

7.17 Moel Frochas, Llanrhaeadr-ym-Mochnant
(Powys)
This ridge-top motte has a small bailey which can only
be seen by glancing light and the snow cover – it is
barely visible on the ground (not in King).

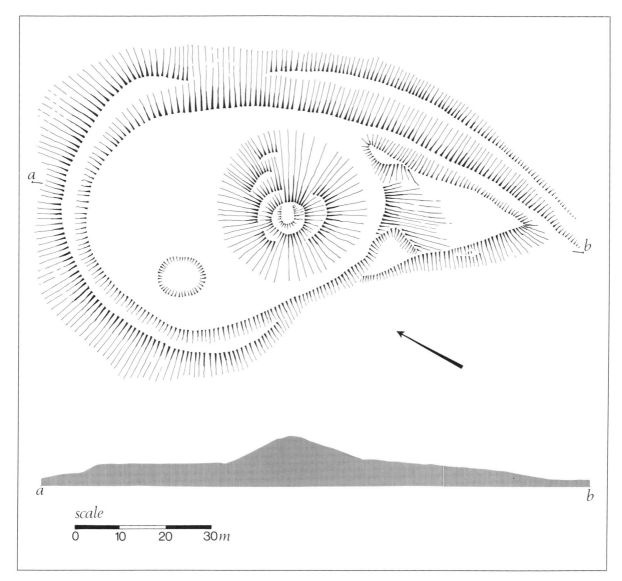

7.18 Wilmington, Chirbury (Shropshire)

The massive motte here appears to be a scarped and heightened hill, within an oval bailey, defended by terraces, themselves scarped out of the hillside. The rock here is extremely hard which may account for the lack of obvious ditches, though there is a suggestion of a filled-in ditch round the motte (see the section a–b). The southern tip of the site is cut off by the inner defences and may have functioned as a small outer bailey. (King, II, 422. The site was referred to, together with others in the Vale of Montgomery, in 1224–5.)

7.19a and b Castell Crugerydd, New Radnor
(Powys)
A motte with two (?) baileys, typically sited on the
highest point of a ridge controlling the main road
(now the A44) linking Kington and Rhayadr. Note
that the interior of the bailey has been ploughed. Fig.
19b is taken from the road at the top of fig. 19a (King,
II, 409 – a Welsh castle mentioned in 1188). (Photo:
Philip Barker.)

7.20 Tomen Bedd Ugre, Llandewi Ystradenny
(Powys)
A motte with two baileys, magnificently sited on a
remote hill top. Unlike many of the other sites
illustrated here, there is little sign of medieval
agriculture close to the castle, which seems always to
have stood on a bare hillside, away from its fields or
other settlements (King, II, 409).

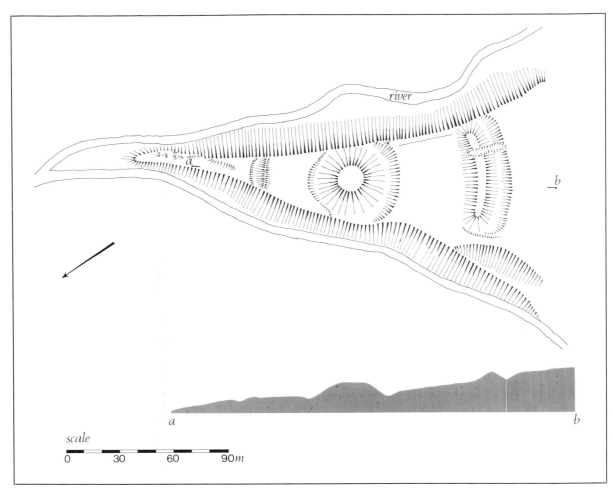

scale
0   30   60   90m

7.21 Rhyd Yr Onen, Llangurig (Powys)

The earthworks here are sited at the confluence of two streams on a sloping spit of land which is cut off on the south-west by a massive ditch and rampart, mirrored on the north-east by a smaller rampart which isolates the unusable end of the spit. The motte sits between them, separating the two baileys from one another so that the smaller northern one can only be reached via the motte, making it doubly secure. It would be most interesting to know which of the castle's buildings were sited here (King, I, 298).

7.22a and b Moat, Llandinam (Powys)
A fine motte with two baileys on the same side – the
modern farm buildings show the scale of the castle and
the number of buildings of similar size which could
have been accommodated within the inner bailey. The
outer bailey shows no sign of buildings but this may be
deceptive (King, I, 297).

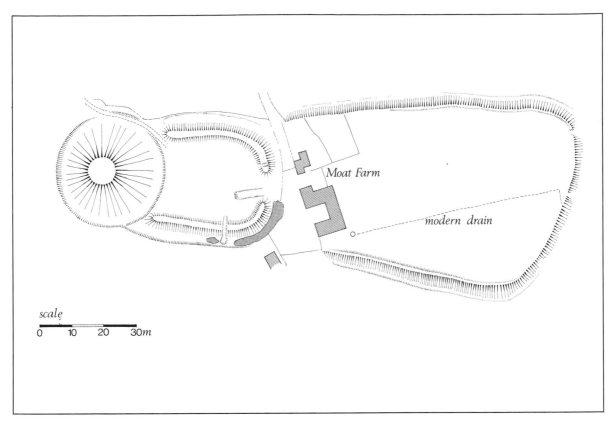

Moat Farm

modern drain

scale

0   10   20   30m

7.23 Aberllynfi Castle, Gwennyfed (Powys)
This photograph demonstrates the complexity of the
earthworks which may be encountered around mottes
– there could be one, two or three baileys here – only
excavation would provide conclusive evidence (King,
I, 16 – mentioned in 1233).

7.24 Kingsland (Hereford and Worcester)
The motte is a good example of the large, low, flat-topped variety very distinct from the high steep sort, of which that at Caus Castle (fig. 7.29) is a good example. The baileys at Kingsland are very large, with only slight ramparts, and appear to have been originally water-defended (King, I, 207). (Photo: Philip Barker.)

7.25a and b Lingen (Hereford and Worcester)
This fine motte and bailey is sited between the church
(among the trees) and the earthworks of an extensive
deserted village.

   The bailey is rectilinear, as is the churchyard, on the
east-west axis of the church, in contrast to the
curvilinear earthworks of the former settlement.
There is no obvious explanation for this, unless the
settlement is older than the castle and the church. As
can be seen, the present village has migrated
southwards (King, I, 208). (Photo. 7.25b: Philip
Barker.)

7.26 More, near Lydham (Shropshire) This splendid site is formed from a low spit of land surrounded by former marsh (the More or Mere of the name). It was detached from the nearby manor of Lydham in the twelfth century and the earthworks comprise a low motte at the tip of the promontory with two baileys beyond. A third enclosure contains the earthworks of a probable deserted village with house platforms on each side of the wide road which can be seen curving away to join the present road. The present village surrounds the church and the relationship between the medieval castle and village and the church is not clear – one would have expected the castle and the church (which is also of the twelfth century) to have been connected by a road, but there is no sign of one.

Excavations in 1959 (by Brian Hope-Taylor) showed that the now low, flat-topped motte began life as a ringwork which was later filled in and heightened (pers. comm.) (King, II, 427).

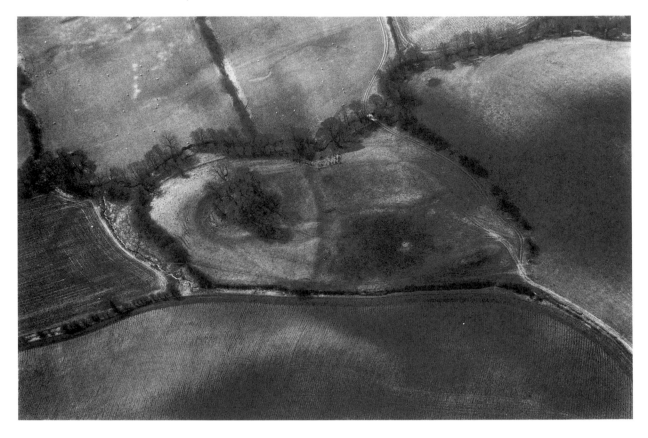

7.27a and b Castell foel Allt, Pilleth (Powys)
This interesting site lies on a low hill close to a stream.
It appears to have four baileys, formed by the
intersection of two ditches roughly at right angles to
one another. The larger of these cuts the site in two,
leaving only a small rectangular inner area close to
the motte. This cross ditch and rampart in some
respects resembles the defensive line (without a
ditch) that crosses the bailey at Hen Domen,
Montgomery (see chapter 9). It is possible that the
earthworks are of more than one period, and that the
large cross ditch is later (see the plan fig. 7.27b) (King,
II, 411).

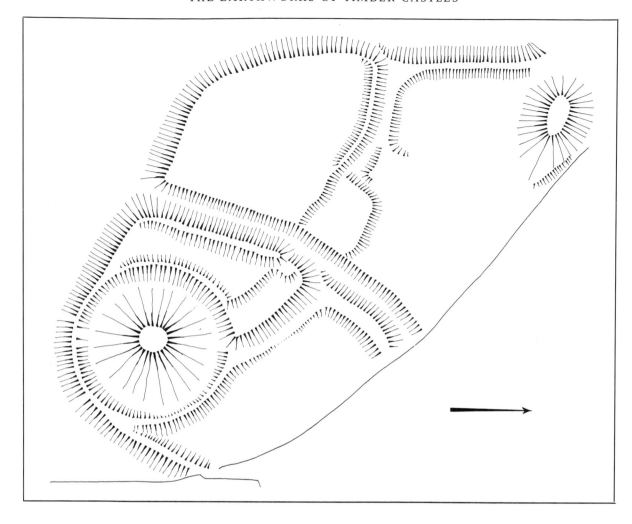

**7.28 Caer Penrhos, Castell Cadwaladr,
Llanrhystyd** (Ceredigion)
This is a ringwork within a presumed hillfort, which
has been used as a bailey. Another example of this sort
of adaptation is Caus Castle, Westbury, Shropshire
(fig. 7.29). (King, I, 47 – a Welsh castle, built in 1149
by Cadwaladr, son of Gruffyd ap Cynan.)

7.29 Caus Castle, Westbury (Shropshire)
It is probable, according to the late Miss Lily Chitty, that the outer earthworks of this site are those of an Iron Age fort, adapted in medieval times to form the outer bailey of this impressive castle. It consists of a high motte (at A) with a very small summit, crowned with the ruins of a small stone tower; and a massively defended inner bailey. This bailey contained a borough probably created by Roger Corbet in 1198 and it is recorded that by 1349 there were 58 burgesses living there. However, in 1521 the castle was described as being 'in grete ruyne and decay' (King, II, 421–2).

7.30 Colwyn Castle, Glascwm (Powys)
This is a ringwork, now occupied by farm buildings
which give some idea of the size and scale of the
probable castle buildings. It has an irregular bailey in
the foreground and a rectangular bailey beyond. This
has been shown to be a Roman fort whose defences
have been reused in the Norman period (King, II, 407
– mentioned in 1144).

7.31 British Camp, Malvern (Hereford and
Worcester)
This massive ringwork has been constructed at the
highest point within the great prehistoric earthwork
which crowns the Malvern Hills. Although isolated, it
commands the countryside in all directions. It was
perhaps a hunting lodge built in connection with
Malvern Chase (King, I, 204).

7.32 Chartley Castle (Stafford)

This castle presumably began its life as a timber castle with a motte and two baileys. The motte was eventually crowned with a stone tower and the bailey defences were rebuilt in stone, but there is no evidence that the outer bailey ever had anything but timber defences and buildings. The stone tower on the motte was rebuilt in the eighteenth or early nineteenth century in brick.

The photograph is taken from the east and it is worth noting that the ridge and furrow in the foreground overlies the earthworks of a former settlement attached to the castle. (King, II, 456 – mentioned in 1192). (Photo: Philip Barker.)

7.33 Twt Hill, Rhuddlan (Clwyd)

This motte and bailey is included because it is such a good example of a timber castle succeeded by a stone castle on a different, though adjacent site. The motte and bailey castle was built in 1073 by Robert of Rhuddlan on the traditional site of Gruffydd ap Llywlyn's palace and a small borough, mentioned in Domesday Book, was established beside it. In 1086 it had 18 burgesses, a church and a mint.

In 1241–2 the defences were recorded as being of wood, with timber-framed buildings occupying the bailey. There is a record in that year of payments for timber to repair the defects in the wooden works, and for carrying old wooden works back to Chester; orders are given at the same time for the construction of a wooden chapel in the castle where divine service may be celebrated, (A.J. Taylor, *Rhuddlan Castle, Official Guide*, 1960).

In 1227 as part of his strategy for the conquest of Wales, Edward I began a new, stone castle, designed by Master James of St George, a little to the north-west of the now obsolete motte and bailey.

In order to provide a deep water channel from the sea to the castle, a distance of over 3 km (2 miles), the river Clwyd was diverted and canalized. The new town of Rhuddlan lying beyond the new castle can be seen in the photograph (King, I, 154 – mentioned in 1086).

7.34 Powis Castle and Lady's Mount

The small mound at A, called Lady's Mount, appears
to be a motte, without an obvious bailey. It may be the
forerunner of the very much grander Powis Castle
beyond, or is perhaps a siege mound, or even a
gazebo? (King, I, 300 – Powis Castle mentioned in
1196.)

7.35 Castell Cwm-Aron, Llanddewi, Ystradenny
(Powys)
This impressive motte and rectilinear bailey uses the
natural topography to the greatest advantage. A
mysterious feature is the small mound (marked A) on
the slope above the site. Nothing seems to be known
about it, but it is possibly a siege mound (King, II,
407).

— 8 —

The structures of timber castles: the excavated evidence and its interpretation

Understanding the Evidence

The selection of excavated sites illustrated here and the comparable surviving examples are not only very small samples of what actually existed in the Norman and post-Norman period but are distorted samples due, in part, to the methods of excavation used under rescue or salvage conditions. Under those conditions, and also in many excavations carried out before the 1960s, the slight traces of what can be shown to be quite massive structures would not be recognized as significant or would be swept away by summary methods of digging. Nevertheless, we are beginning to understand the sort of structures which made up the quite formidable defences of these timber fortifications.

The development of timber buildings in northern Europe from prehistoric times, through the Roman period and the post-Roman centuries down to the medieval half-timber tradition is still not fully understood though it is now becoming clear that buildings founded on posts set in the ground – post-hole buildings – were constructed from Mesolithic times onward, but that in Roman Britain framed buildings, some of great size, with horizontal timbers simply resting on the ground or on dwarf walls, existed side by side with post-hole structures. In addition there was a great range of other building techniques – posts set on post-pads, or simply on the

ground, are well attested, as are walls of wattle and daub, turves or clay, or clay reinforced with wattle.

It seems likely that in post-Roman times the timber-framing tradition virtually disappeared not to reappear until the Norman Conquest. During these centuries the majority of all buildings seem to have been founded on posts set in the ground, since this is the type of construction most frequently discovered in excavation. However, more extensive and detailed excavation of post-Roman and Anglo-Saxon sites may yet prove this to be too simplistic a view. Certainly by the mid-eleventh century timber-framing was in use in England and Wales, as the excavations at Hen Domen, for example, show. The remarkable feature of many timber-built sites of the Norman and later medieval periods is the great variety of techniques used, often at the same time on the same site.

In attempting to understand and reconstruct the defences and internal buildings of timber castles it is illuminating to look at other timber structures which survive from the medieval period. Some are ecclesiastical – church and bell towers – others domestic – barns and the remains of great halls and lesser houses (see above pp. 178ff.).

For instance, it is quite clear from the surviving examples of timber towers that very tall and massive structures were possible. Now that it is recognized that a number of the surviving bell towers in this country date from the twelfth and thirteenth centuries it is more than probable that they reflect the sort of towers which crowned contemporary mottes.

Among the finest extant structures of these early towers are those at Brookland (Kent), Mamble, Pembridge and Yarpole (Hereford and Worcester), all illustrated here in figs 8.9–22. A diagnostic feature which they have in common is their tapering outline and diagonal braces. The tapering shape, is, of course, inherently more stable, especially when, as in these examples, the structure is framed and simply stands on the ground or on a low sleeper wall. Further examples of what our motte and gate towers may have looked like are provided by still existing bell towers in Denmark, such as that at Tandslet (fig. 8.1) or Birket. Though these are later in date than the English examples mentioned above they are clearly in the same tradition, a tradition which persisted in another form, the wind-mill, down into the nineteenth century.

Where the bell towers probably differ from defensive towers is in the form of the roof. While the high pyramid roofs of the bell towers could provide protection for the defenders, who could shoot from under the eaves, it is also probable that some timber towers had open flat roofs, as did many stone towers. The timber towers shown on a twelfth-century carving at Modena cathedral are of this form (chapter 5). In a variety of sizes, such towers were also used as siege towers, from the terminology of which the English word 'belfry' derived (see Appendix A).

The evidence from excavation cannot, of course, solve this problem. Towers based on uprights set into deep post-holes will be more likely to have vertical sides, since it is easier to set the timbers vertically than cant them all at the same angle, though the possibility should be borne in mind in excavating motte struc-tures. Although post-hole structures cannot strictly be framed, they could have braces

inset into the uprights after the main posts are raised, just as many towers have had later braces inserted into them using half-lap or other simple joints. Whether set in the ground, or framed and standing on the sur-face of the motte top, or as part of a defensive circuit, timber towers could have been very large and formidable. The tower at Pembridge is *c.* 27 m (90 ft) high, and if placed on a similarly high mound would dominate the surrounding countryside. In this respect, earlier reconstruction drawings, such as that of Abinger have done the timber castle a disservice, giving the impression that motte towers were often small and temporary.

Recent work at Windsor Castle, for example, has shown that the earliest structure on the very large mound, whatever its precise form, was of timber – presumably a round tower on a scale quite different from that at Abinger. The same scale of timber towers can surely be postulated as crowning the mottes at other major castles, such as Arundel, Sandal, Dudley or Stafford, as the recent recon-struction drawing of the latter, figs 8.48–51, attempts to show.

The range of towers on motte tops, and, equally, those defending gateways or the interval towers on encircling palisades must have extended from four posts holding up a structure no bigger than a machine-gun post (e.g. Lismahon (fig. 8.73–5) to the massive residential round or square towers of the great magnates of the time, of which Ardres is the best-known documented example.

Unfortunately, no great timber tower on the scale of Ardres or Windsor has been excavated, either because the mottes which carried them have gone or because the timber structures have been superseded by equally large stone structures which have all but obliterated the earlier evidence. Where massive towers were timber framed and simply placed on the ground surface, they will, of course, be particularly vulnerable to later rebuilding, but even where there has been no subsequent structure the traces left by a framed building may be so slight that they are difficult to detect and interpret. The excavation of the documented tower at Sycharth shows this clearly (pp. 301–2).

Among the most spectacular timber buildings of medieval date are the stave churches of Norway, many of which are, or were, contemporary with our timber castles. They demonstrate the size and complexity of

8.1 Tandslet, plan and section of tower.

8.2 Nes stave church (before 1864).

buildings which could be constructed on foundations consisting simply of spreads of boulders and cobbles giving little more than an indication of the plan of the building which stood on them.

One example which demonstrates this clearly, is the church at Nes in Hallingdel, which was demolished in 1864, though happily not before it had been recorded in some detail. A new church was built 0.5 km (⅓ mile) away, so that the site of the medieval church was available for excavation, which was carried out in 1965. In summary, there had been two successive churches on the site of a pre-existing cemetery.

The first church, whose date is not clear, but is almost certainly pre-thirteenth century, had been burnt down and replaced by a larger, apsidal building. Both had been founded on rough footings of boulders and cobbles (fig. 8.6) which can be shown to have stood here (fig. 8.4). The church demolished in 1864 consisted of a square nave with an eastern apse and with a central turret and spire 21 m (69 ft) high. This church had been enlarged, probably in the eighteenth century (fig. 8.2).

The medieval church (figs. 8.2–5) is dated by coins to 'somewhere in the middle or in the second half of the thirteenth century.' Figure 8.7 illustrates details of the building and show the sort of carpentry which might well have been found in the timber castles we are discussing in the examples that follow.[1]

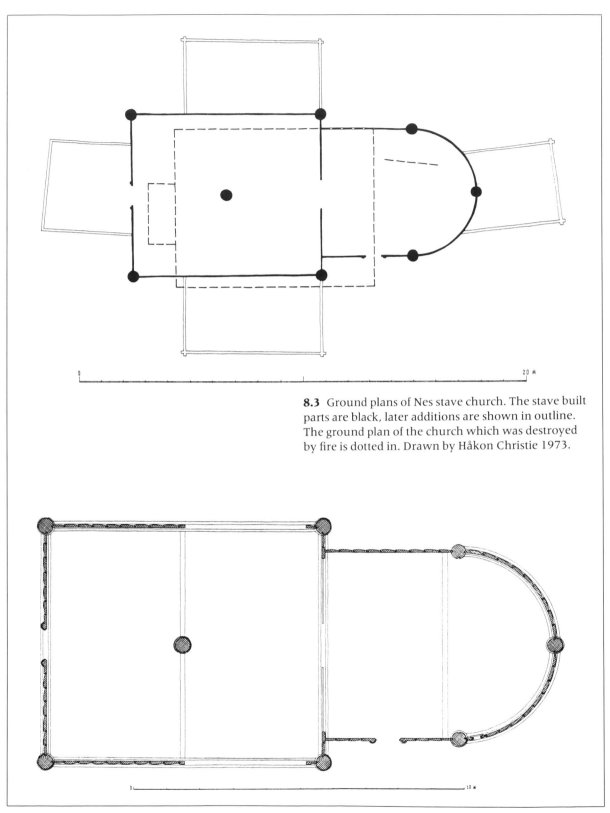

8.3 Ground plans of Nes stave church. The stave built parts are black, later additions are shown in outline. The ground plan of the church which was destroyed by fire is dotted in. Drawn by Håkon Christie 1973.

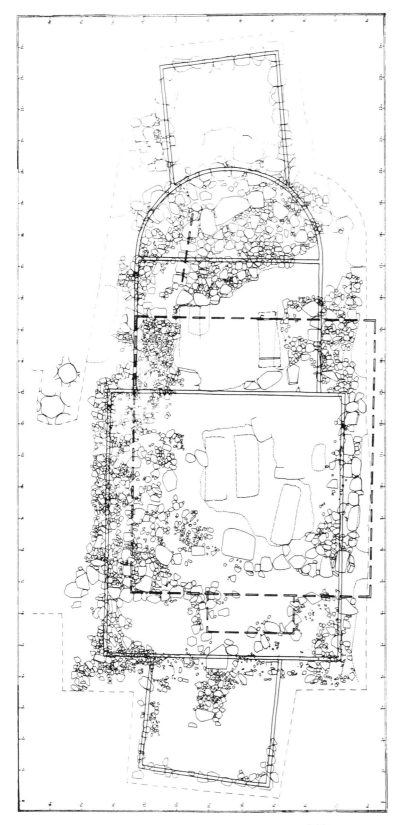

8.4 The site of Nes stave church, plan of the excavations.

8.5 Isometric reconstruction of the stave church at Nes.

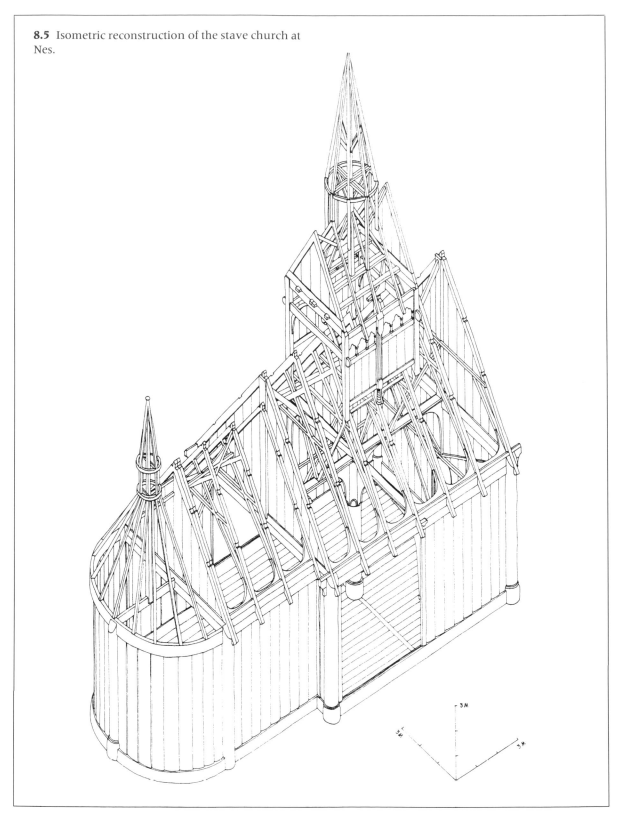

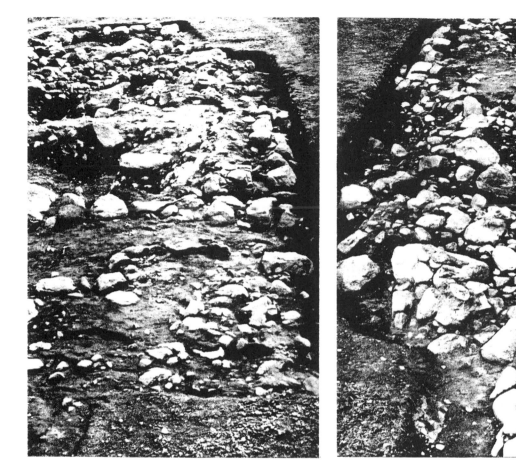

8.6 The excavated foundations of the church at Nes.

8.7 Wooden window openings of the church at Nes.

8.8 The tower of St Peter's Church, Pirton
(Hereford and Worcester)
Although this tower is at present undated (Pevsner,
Buildings of England: Worcestershire, 1968) suggests that
it is more likely to be fourteenth century than the
sixteenth century suggested by the *Victoria County
History* for Worcestershire.) it has 'double' scissor
braces of a formidable scantling between the nave and
the aisles, and with very massive cruck-form braces. In
all, it may well be early and it is hoped that it may
soon be dendrochronologically dated. Even if it is not
as early as some of the timber castles described here,
its construction would clearly have been possible in
the twelfth and thirteenth centuries, so that it may
serve as an alternative model to the tapering towers of
Yarpole and Pembridge. (With acknowledgements to
the architect, James Snell.)

252

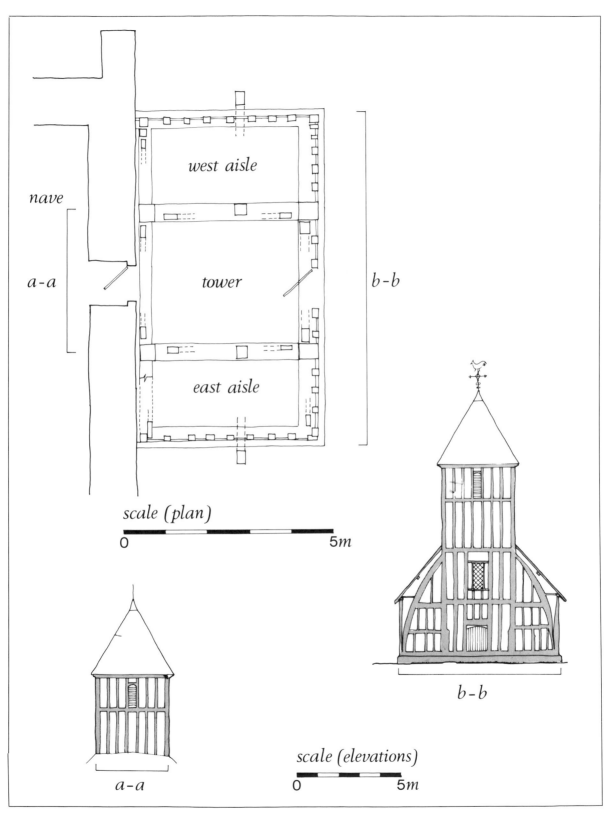

nave

a-a

west aisle

tower

east aisle

b-b

scale (plan)

0   5m

scale (elevations)

0   5m

a-a

b-b

8.9–11 Pembridge bell tower

The bell tower at Pembridge stands detached from the large church of St Mary which, though of Norman origin, is largely of the fourteenth century.

The bell tower now appears to be in three stages with a broad low first stage of stone with a high truncated pyramid roof, above which are two further, smaller stages, both weatherboarded. All this masks the core of the tower, a tapering structure of 'four mighty posts' (Pevsner's term) braced scissor-fashion and horizontally, rising to the height of the top of the second roof.

These primary timbers have been dated dendrochronologically to the period between 1115 and 1150, roughly contemporary with the phase of the castle at Hen Domen reconstructed in fig. 9.5. Figure 8.10 shows one of the four main raking posts with the rest of the timber work being later. Fig. 8.9 shows the mortices for two of the scissor braces now missing. The stone ambulatory is probably late medieval. (Photos: Philip Barker.)

8.12–14 The timber bell tower at Mamble
(Hereford and Worcester)
This bell tower, tapering with scissor bracing, was originally free-standing. This is shown by the weathering on what were the outer surfaces of the timbers, and the fact that the now enclosing stone tower is not aligned with the timber tower, and that the south-western brace is embedded in the stone work of the wall of the tower. When it was a free-standing wooden tower, the belfry appears to have been open, without cladding. Since the nave and the stone tower are datable to the early thirteenth century (*V.C.H. Worcs. iv, 288*) or even *c.*1200 (Pevsner, *ibid.*, 219) it follows that the tower is likely to be twelfth century in date. (With acknowledgements to the architect, John Wheatley). (Photos: Philip Barker.)

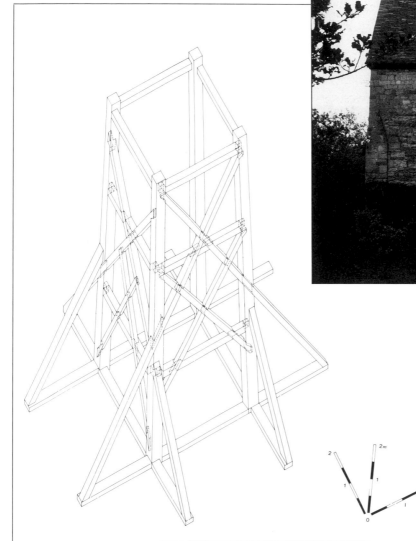

257

8.15 The bell tower at Navestock (Essex)
This tower, radiocarbon dated to the period 1133–
1253, is tapered and constructed with similar scissor
bracing to that at Brookland, Pembridge and Yarpole
(above). In addition, it is supported by very long thin
timbers buttressing the bottom half of the tower. The
joints are notched-lap of archaic profile. (Fig. 8.15
does not include the spire which crowns the tower.)
(After C. Hewett, *English Historic Carpentry*, 1980.)

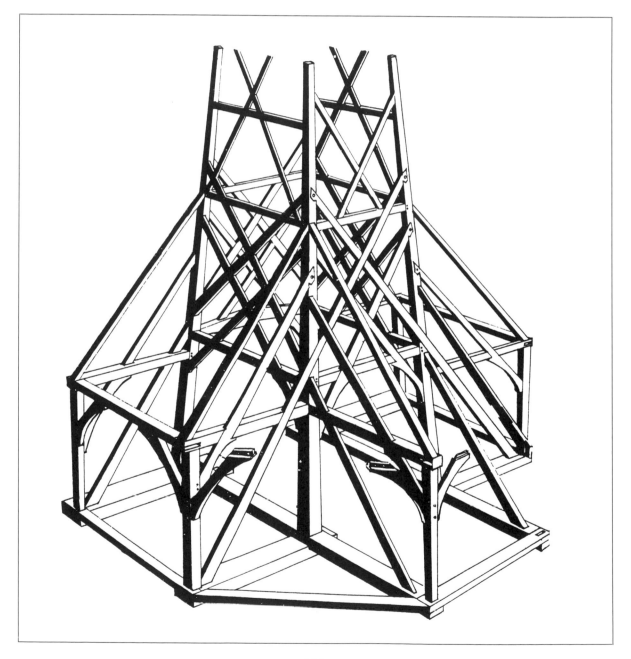

8.16 The timber bell tower at Brookland (Kent)
The attached bell tower at Brookland is similar to
those at Pembridge and Yarpole in being tapered and
with scissor-bracing. The notched lap joints date it to
some time in the eleventh or twelfth centuries. The
timbers are heavily weathered, suggesting that they
stood for many years in the open. The same
weathering has been noticed on the timbers of the
belfry at Yarpole, and it seems probable that some,

perhaps many, of these belfries stood at first in their
skeletal form with the bells exposed until they were
cased in the way we see today. The same may, of
course, have been true for some motte towers,
although cladding would protect the defenders in a
way not necessary for bell-ringers; and inserted floors,
even if not used residentially, would have been
valuable storage space. (Drawing reproduced by kind
permission of K.W. Gravett, Esq.)

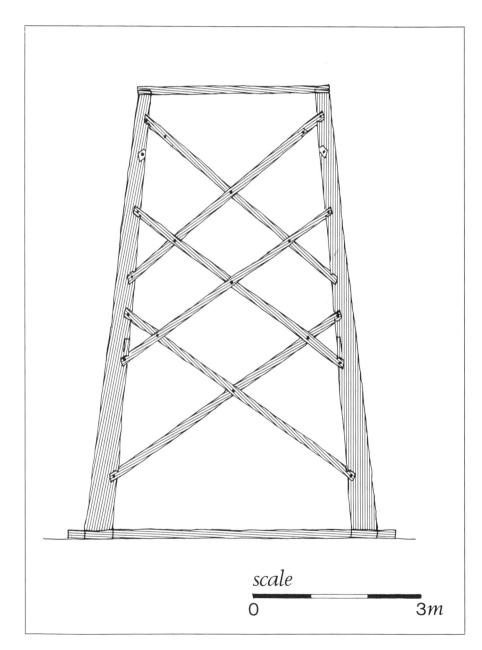

scale

0   3m

8.17–20 Yarpole bell tower (Hereford and Worcester)

The detached bell tower at Yarpole has only two stages in contrast to Pembridge's three. The tapering timber tower inside is closely scissor-braced as is the inside of the door, which may also be early (fig. 8.20). Though the date of neither the tower or the door is certain, both may be pre-1300. As can be seen on fig. 8.18 there are rows of quatrefoils above the weather boarding of the upper stage. Their relationship to the original timber tower is not known. It is hoped that dendrochronology will soon solve the problem of the dates of both. (Photos: Philip Barker.)

8.21–22 Pembridge market hall

The market hall at Pembridge, close to the church with its detached bell tower (fig. 8.11), demonstrates clearly why there has been (and is) difficulty in reconstructing timber buildings convincingly from the traces which may be left in the ground. The building, probably of the sixteenth century, formerly had an upper storey. It stands on eight massive and widely-spaced posts which themselves simply stand on post-pads. They are jointed into the horizontal beams which now hold the roof, but are only slightly braced laterally, and one cannot help feeling that if this building did not exist, a drawn reconstruction like this would be dismissed out of hand. Yet there are now many dozens of excavated building plans in which the evidence is very similar. It is quite clear that many substantial buildings and other structures, simply stood on the ground, without post-holes or elaborate framing. The structures of the last two phases at Hen Domen were among the first of these to be excavated, but similar evidence has now been found on Roman sites (see Barker *et al.*, *Excavations on the Baths Basilica at Wroxeter* (forthcoming)). (Photos: Philip Barker.)

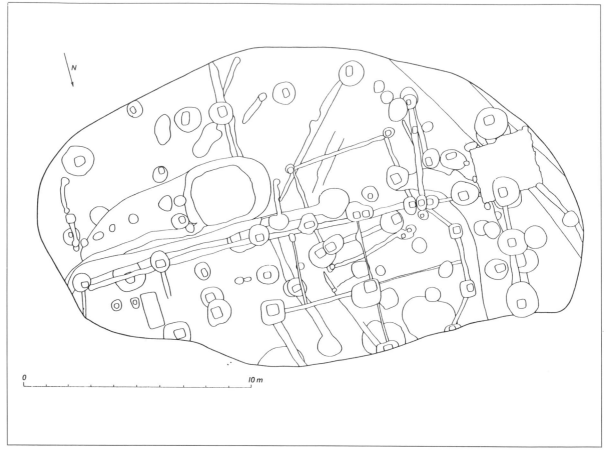

8.23 a) Mirville, plan showing intersection of ditches and structures, phases I to IX. (Reproduced by kind permission of Jacques le Maho.) b) Mirville, plan of house VII.

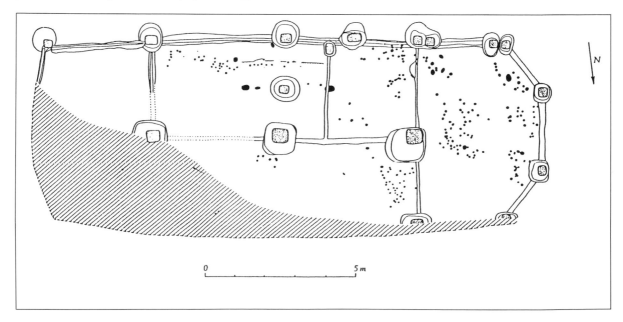

The excavated evidence – some examples
Mirville and Notre Dame-de-Gravenchon (Seine-Maritime; figs 8.23–27)

The timber castles of the Pays de Caux are of particular interest to those who study the castles of the central Welsh border, since Roger Corbet, one of William the Conqueror's Chief Lieutenants, came from the Pays de Caux and his principal castle, in Shropshire, now known as Caus Castle, derives its name from his Norman homeland.

Two of the timber castles of the Pays de Caux have been extensively excavated, both by Jacques le Maho, and have produced detailed plans of their buildings. At Mirville erosion of the top of the mound had removed all traces of buildings, but the mound itself sealed a remarkable sequence of structures, beginning with a ditch of the second to third centuries AD. Most of the structures, however, were datable to the eleventh century; the raising of the motte in the early twelfth century burying and obliterating the earlier buildings.

It will be seen, therefore, that the development of the site parallels remarkably the known development of such widely separated sites as Goltho and Weoley in England, Rathmullan in Northern Ireland and der Husterknupp in Germany, in each of which the periodic mounding up of earth to increase height and defensive effectiveness had buried, and thus preserved, evidence for the earlier phases of occupation. This can be presumed to have happened at hundreds of other sites, especially those which are low lying such as the *terpen* of the north European coast, where sections through the mounds have shown underlying occupation, though few have been excavated horizontally.

These long sequences of development contrast with that, for example, at Hen Domen, Montgomery, where, though there are traces of underlying occupation much earlier than that of the castle, the castle itself was built *de novo* on an abandoned field. The evidence of the structures at Mirville provides a typical palimpsest of intersecting post-holes and timber-slots the phases being separated by analysis of their intersection.

The sequence of phases is shown in figs 8.26 and 27. In phase III (eleventh century) the site was defended by a palisade and fighting platform with a tower 3 m (32 ft) square, of timber on a stone foundation (fig. 8.26). The buildings in the enclosure changed and

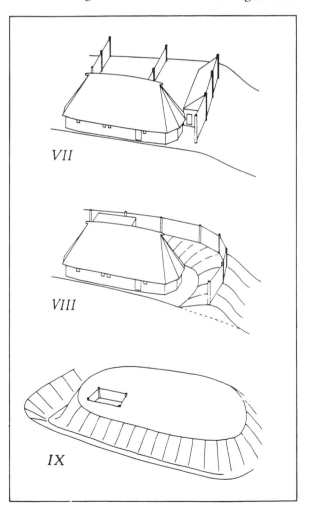

8.24 Mirville, reconstruction of phases VII, VIII and IX. See also fig. 3.24.

8.25 Mirville, reconstruction of house VII.

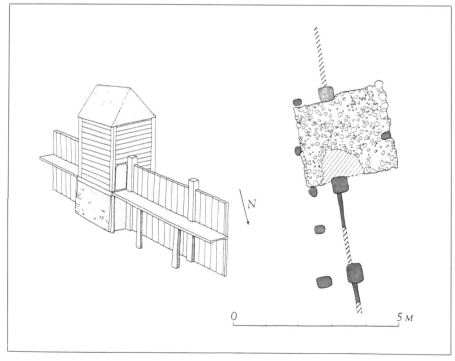

0   5 M

8.26 Mirville, wooden tower with stone foundations.

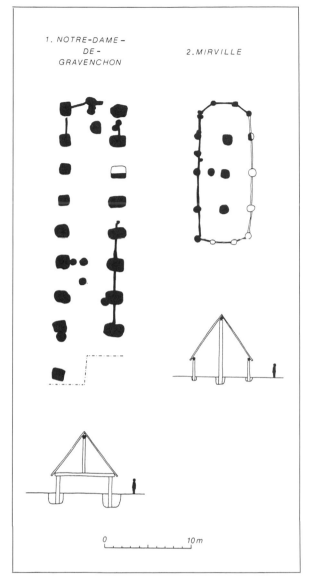

1. NOTRE-DAME-
DE-
GRAVENCHON

2. MIRVILLE

0   10 m

8.27 Comparative plans of buildings at Notre-Dame-de-Gravenchon (left) and Mirville (right).
(Reproduced by kind permission of Jacques le Maho.)

and palisade on a new alignment (fig. 8.24). Although it is not certain, since the northern part of the site has been badly eroded, it is probable that at this point it became a ring-work enclosing the building, a hall 17 m (56 ft) long and 8 m (26 ft) wide with a hipped roof and internal partitions. Its plan and con-jectural reconstructions are reproduced in fig. 8.23b and its remarkable resemblance to the houses depicted on the Bayeaux Tapestry is illustrated in fig. 8.25.

Two successive systems of drainage chan-nels and cisterns collected rain water from the roof of the building, presumably for animals and perhaps fire-fighting. Although there seems to be no trace of a hearth within the building, it is clearly divided into rooms and seems more likely to have been a house than, for example, a barn or stable. It may be that it was heated by braziers which leave only shallow traces on the ground.

At Notre-Dame-de-Gravenchon excava-tions on the site of a chateau known as 'La Fontaine Saint-Denis' uncovered three main phases of occupation: sunken floored huts of late Roman or early Frankish date, and two phases of castle building, one of wood and one of stone. The stone phase consists principally of the castle chapel of the thirteenth century which seals the timber buildings below it and gives them a *terminus ante quem*.

The principal buildings of the timber phase of the twelfth century are an elongated rec-tangular post-hole building surrounded, at its southern end, by a mass of post-holes which presumably represent attached structures but which are difficult to interpret (fig. 8.27 and see chapter 3). A plan of the rectangular building is illustrated in fig. 8.27 and com-pared with the much smaller building found at Mirville. The Notre Dame-de-Gravenchon building is somewhat narrower and has no central supports. Again, there is no evidence of a hearth but the excavator believes it to be a domestic hall, principally because of the numerous finds of food remains.

became more elaborate over the succeeding decades, until near the end of the eleventh century when the site was largely destroyed by fire. When it was rebuilt, it was entirely replanned without the tower and with a large bow-sided building replacing the earlier smaller buildings (fig. 8.24). This building was then encircled, at least in part by a rampart

Der Husterknupp (Germany; figs 8.28–33)

The excavation of der Husterknupp, was one of the earliest comprehensive excavations of a motte and bailey castle. It was carried out by A. Herrnbrodt and demonstrated the development of the site from a low-lying water defended ringwork to a fully fledged motte and bailey.

In period 1, dated to the late ninth or tenth century the site was enclosed by a water-filled ditch and a palisade, though no rampart. It contained five rectangular buildings lying on roughly the same axis near the perimeter of the enclosure. A bridge led across the ditch from the north-east.

In period II the earthworks were altered by the digging of a ditch across the centre of the site, dividing it into two. House 3 was retained; the others were demolished and a new building, House 6, was built (fig. 8.30). This converted the site into a figure-of-eight, though it was not yet a motte and bailey.

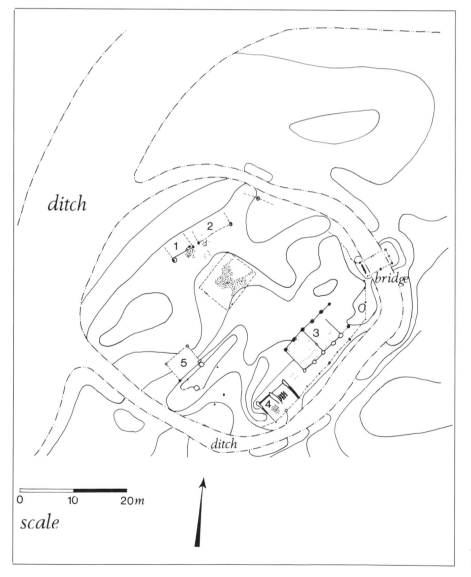

ditch

ditch

bridge

0   10   20m

scale

8.28 Der Husterknupp, period I.

8.29 Der Husterknupp, period II

8.30 Der Husterknupp, period IIIA.

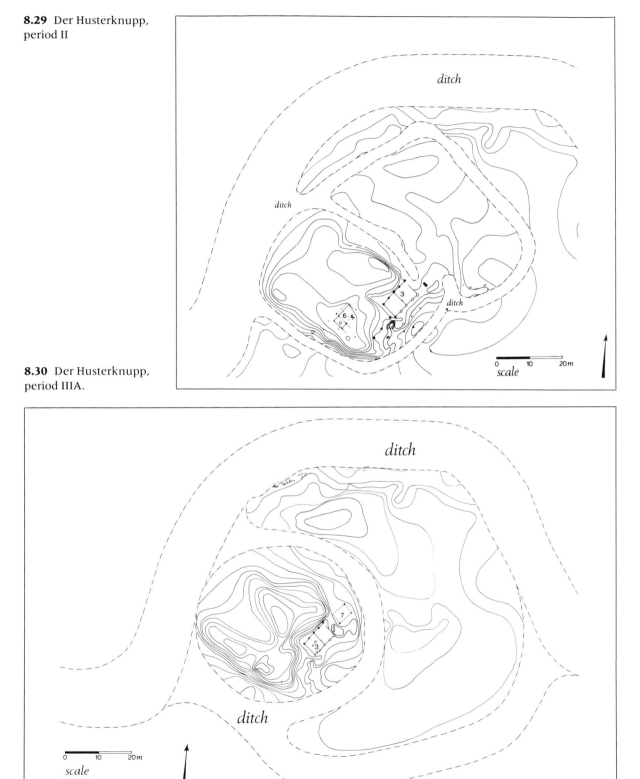

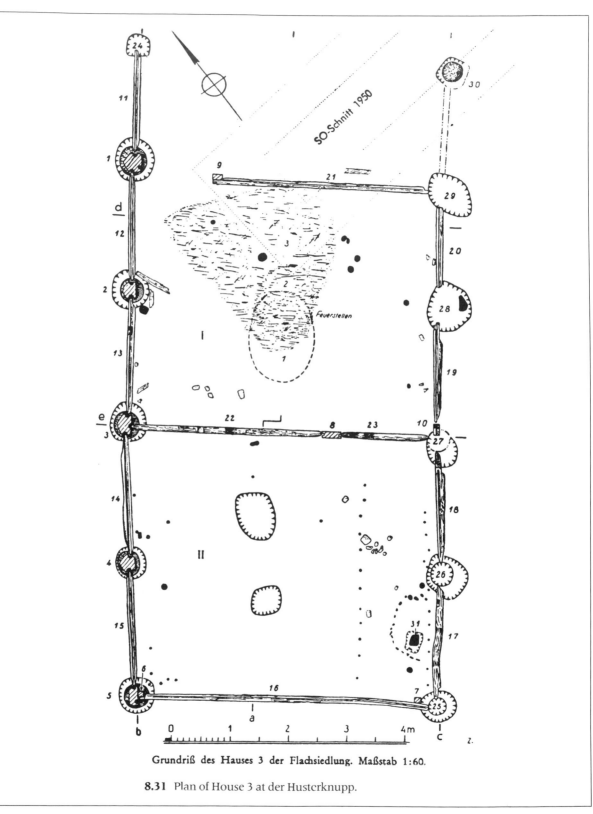

Grundriß des Hauses 3 der Flachsiedlung. Maßstab 1:60.

8.31 Plan of House 3 at der Husterknupp.

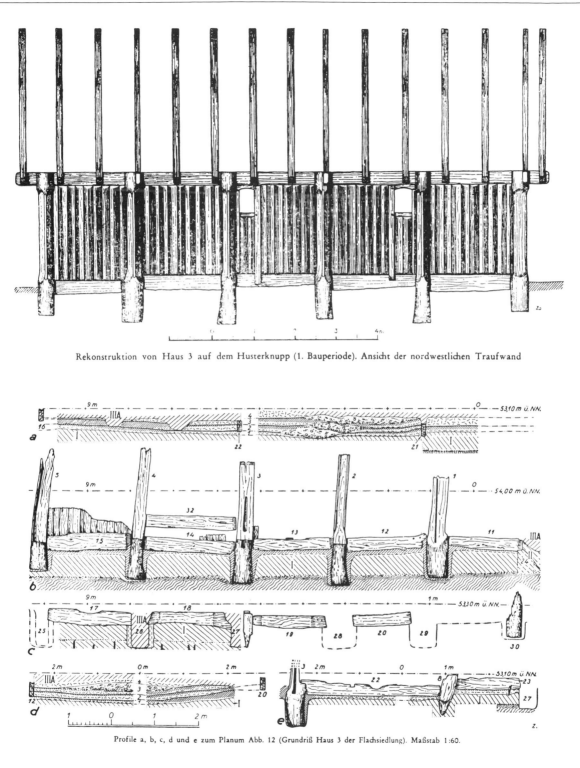

Rekonstruktion von Haus 3 auf dem Husterknupp (1. Bauperiode). Ansicht der nordwestlichen Traufwand

Profile a, b, c, d und e zum Planum Abb. 12 (Grundriß Haus 3 der Flachsiedlung). Maßstab 1:60.

8.32 House 3 at der Husterknupp.

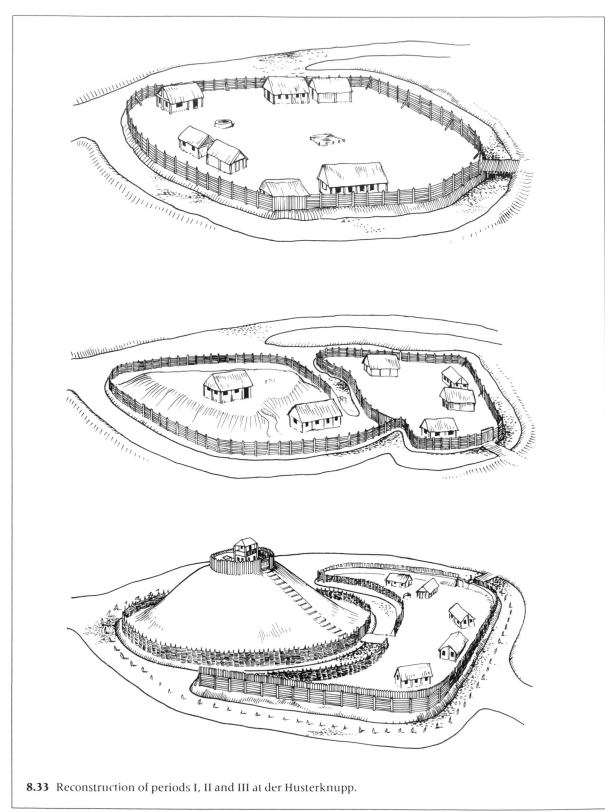

8.33 Reconstruction of periods I, II and III at der Husterknupp.

In period IIIa the earthworks were again altered, a motte being created by the digging of a complete circular ditch and the piling up of spoil in the interior. House 3 however, was still retained at the old ground level, the mounding-up avoiding it. House 6 was demolished and its site buried, and a new House, 7, was built close to 3. At the same time, a crescentic bailey was created to the north-east. No buildings were discovered here. In period IIIc, a fully developed motte was constructed, though there was no evidence of the form of the building which crowned it.

The importance of der Husterknupp is twofold. First, it demonstrated the development of a motte and bailey castle from what was initially a flat, comparatively weakly developed site into a proper timber castle, a development which is paralleled elsewhere, for example, at Goltho (Lincolnshire), at Rathmullan (Co. Down) and at Mirville (Normandy).

It is very probable that there are many more cases in which sites have grown in this way, though in all three examples mentioned the sequence could only be demonstrated because of the virtual total excavation of the sites, and it would be difficult to prove such a development from a small excavation.

The other important lesson to be learned from der Husterknupp stems from the fact that the earliest levels were waterlogged and the timbers of the buildings at ground level therefore preserved. As can be seen from fig. 8.31 the bottoms of the vertical posts, which were embedded in the ground, were simply unworked tree trunks, but above ground, where they became visible, they had been elegantly chamfered. Clearly if the site had not been waterlogged and the timbers had decayed it would have been impossible to ascertain this, and on the basis of the tree-trunk shaped post-holes any reconstruction would have been likely to have been a building constructed of crudely-worked timbers, a conjecture far from the truth.

Almost inevitably, in the absence of evidence to the contrary, we reconstruct on paper buildings which are likely to be cruder and simpler than they were in reality, and the excavation of der Husterknupp warns us of this danger.

Der Hoverberg, Birgelen (Germany; fig 8.34)

This motte, 50 km (31 miles) west of Düsseldorf and 35 km (22 miles) north-west of der Husterknupp (above) was dug by Adolf Herrnbrodt in 1953 and 1954. The excavation showed that there had been a timber building (House 1, fig. 8.34) at the centre of the mound. This had been founded on posts set in a continuous trench with traces of a wooden wall joining them. The building was almost square, measuring 5.60 m × 5.20 m (18 ft × 17 ft) and seems to have been a low tower. Close to this building and roughly aligned on it, were two sunken-floored buildings, *Grubenhaüser*, (houses 2 and 3) of a type familiar from Anglo-Saxon contexts both in Britain and on the continent. There was also a timber-lined well, 8 m (26 ft) deep, close to house 3.

The variety of buildings found on the motte is interesting, a corrective to the simplistic view of a mound crowned by a straightforward tower, a view reinforced by the excavation at Abinger, which became the type site, at least in Britain. The tower at the Hoverberg seems to have been of posts joined by a wooden wall set in a continuous trench. It is possible, however, that the woodwork was simply the skeleton of a clay wall of some thickness which would have enabled the tower to have been built much higher than if it had been solely of posts and timber cladding.

The purpose, or purposes, of *Grubenhaüser* has been the subject of much debate. Here they may have been store rooms with sunken

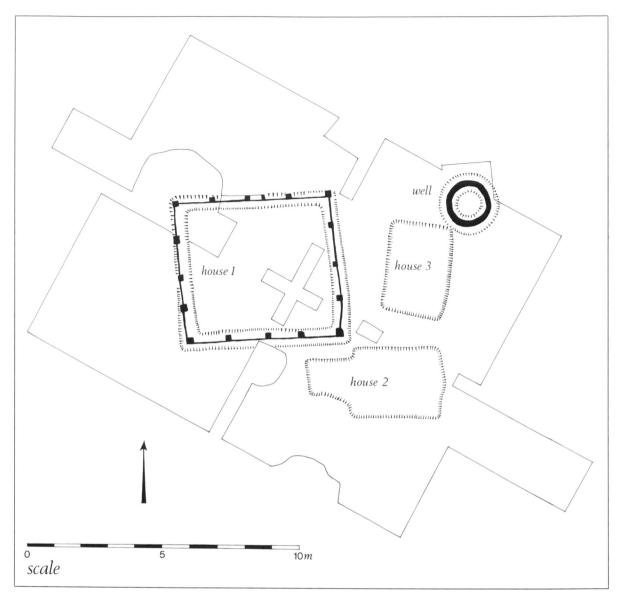

8.34 Plan of Hoverberg.

floors or cellars, cooler in summer for the storage of food, and, presumably, in Germany, beer. The well is of interest because, though motte towers are said to be refuges of last resort, to which the defenders would retire in the case of successful attack, few wells have been found on mottes, so the length of time they could hold out would be severely limited.

Launceston Castle (Cornwall,

figs 8.35–36; Gaz. 8)

The initial construction of the bailey enclosure probably took place shortly after the Norman Conquest following the siege and capture of Exeter in 1068. The defences in the south-west quarter appeared to be a timber revetted earth rampart though the front of the rampart had been cut away in the nineteenth century. Occupation within this part of the enclosure

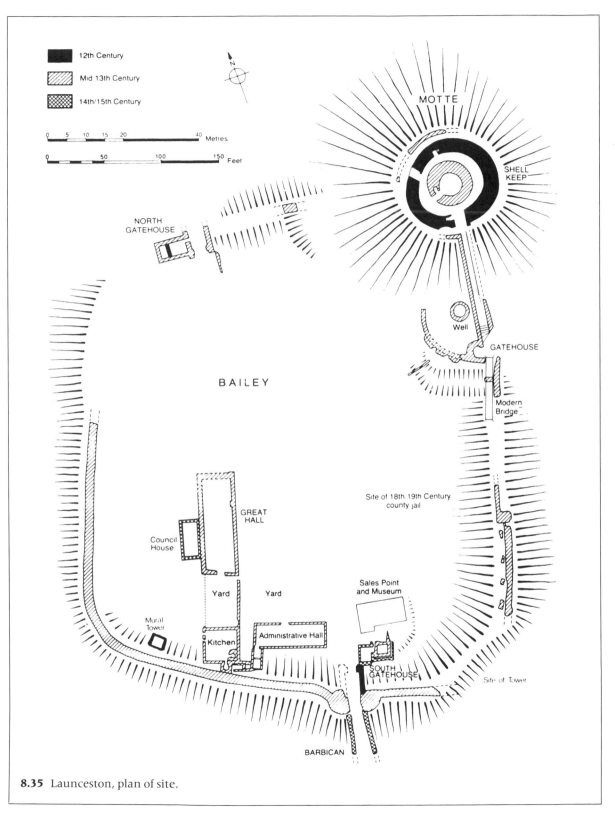

8.35 Launceston, plan of site.

Legend:
- 12th Century
- Mid 13th Century
- 14th/15th Century

Scale:
0 5 10 15 20 ... 40 Metres
0 50 100 150 Feet

N

MOTTE

SHELL KEEP

NORTH GATEHOUSE

Well

GATEHOUSE

BAILEY

Modern Bridge

Site of 18th/19th Century county jail

GREAT HALL

Council House

Yard   Yard

Sales Point and Museum

Mural Tower

Kitchen

Administrative Hall

SOUTH GATEHOUSE

Site of Tower

BARBICAN

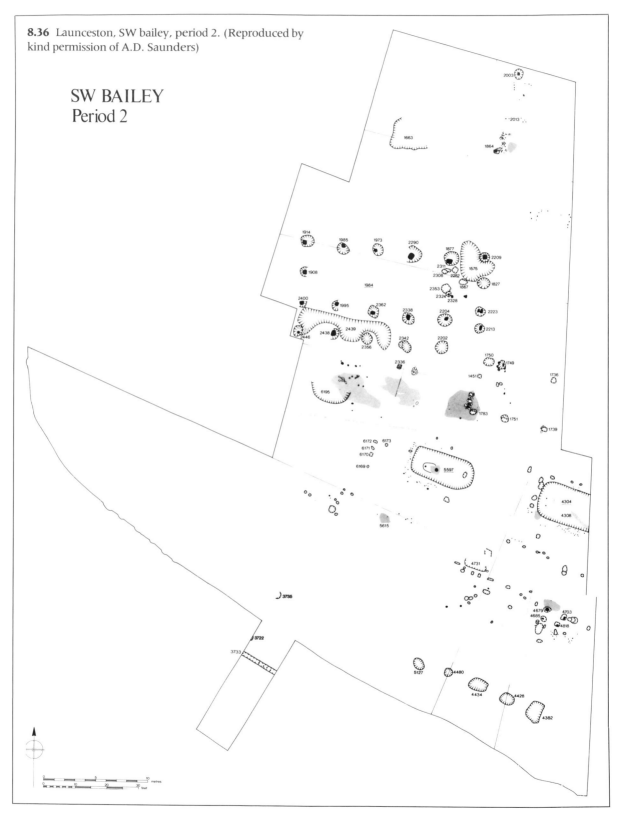

8.36 Launceston, SW bailey, period 2. (Reproduced by kind permission of A.D. Saunders)

SW BAILEY
Period 2

consisted of rows of sunken-floored structures and narrow sill-beam constructions. There was no major building in this part of the castle at this time.

Period 1 seems to have been of short duration. Period 2 was distinguished by the enlargement and re-ordering of the earth and timber rampart and by the widespread adoption of timber buildings constructed with earthfast posts. Some of the sunken-floored structures were reused but generally the buildings were larger and more substantial. Most significant was a timber hall (rebuilt to different proportions in a later phase). This site was successively rebuilt as the castle's great hall until eventual demolition early in

the seventeenth century, so it is likely that it was of similar significance in its first form.

The plan shows the two phases of hall to the north of the excavated area. Between this and the rampart to the south are parallel rows of timber buildings including two sunken-floored structures. The rampart retains evidence for timber structures on the crest and to the rear of the earthwork. (The timber hall lies at right angles under the later great hall.)

Lydford (Devon; fig. 8.37; Gaz. 12)

This is a small eleventh- to early-twelfth-century fort of half ringwork form. The burnt out remains of five timber and earth buildings

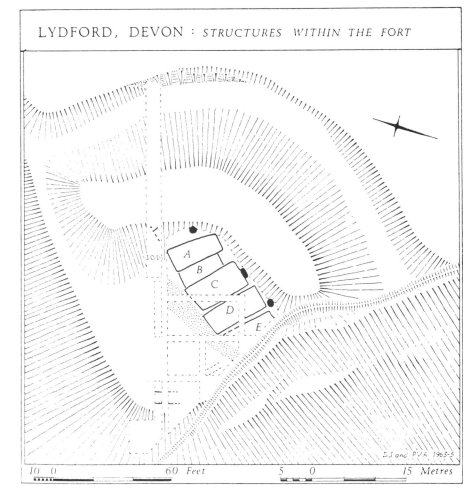

8.37 Lydford, structures within the fort. (Reproduced by kind permission of P.V. Addyman.)

LYDFORD, DEVON : *STRUCTURES WITHIN THE FORT*

A

B

C

D

E

D.S and P.V.A. 1963-5

10 0   60 Feet   5 0   15 Metres

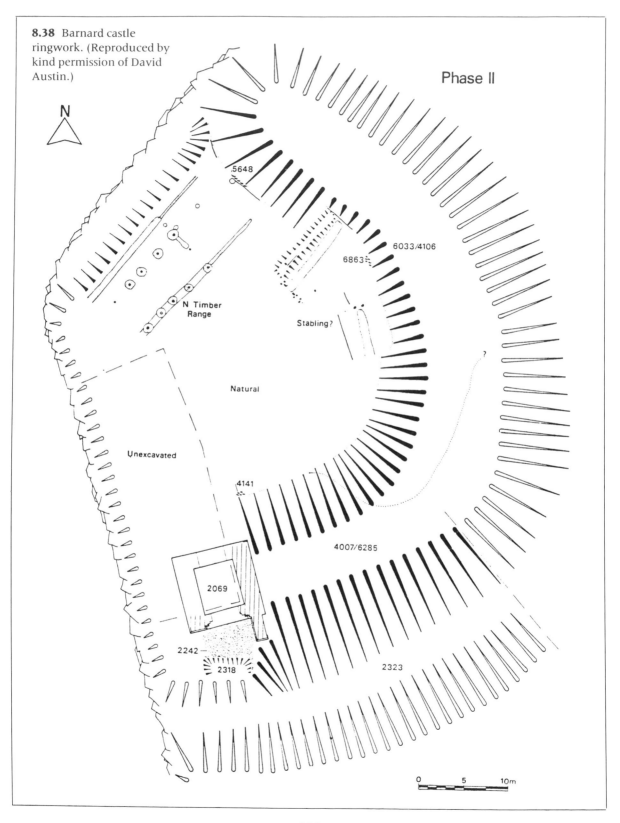

8.38 Barnard castle ringwork. (Reproduced by kind permission of David Austin.)

Phase II

N

.5648

6033/4106

6863

Stabling?

N Timber Range

Natural

Unexcavated

4141

4007/6285

2069

2242

2318

2323

0   5   10m

were revealed, set close together behind the rampart, their inward facing ends being flanked by deeply set, rough stone paving. Charred post settings remained where protected by the collapsed rampart, thus allowing an unexpectedly complete plan to be recovered of four of the five buildings. The buildings, more or less rectangular, were 2.5 m to 3.6 m (8 ft to 12 ft) wide and 7.3 m to 7.6 m (24 ft to 25 ft) long, with earth, clay or shillet walls about 0.5 m (1½ ft) wide, faced externally and internally with wattle woven round posts. The posts sometimes set only 15 cm (6 in) apart were usually 15 cm by 8 cm (6 in by 3 in) trunk-sectors. The buildings were subdivided internally. Over and around the burnt-out buildings was a mass of charred grain of which some 254 kg (5 cwt) (damp weight) was recovered.

The rampart was revetted internally with massive posts (with post-holes up to 1.4 m (4½ ft) deep), and though no external revetment-posts were located a box-rampart can be presumed.

Barnard castle (Co. Durham; fig. 8.38; Gaz. 15)

Excavation of the earliest levels at Barnard Castle, a ringwork founded c.1095, revealed a single-aisled hall approximately 14 m by 10.5 m (46 ft by 34 ft) with the aisle posts set in large pits, and with the walls set in trenches. Close by were traces of further timber buildings, perhaps stabling, and the stone gatehouse may have had a timber predecessor.

South Mimms (Hertfordshire; fig 8.39; Gaz. 31)

The diagrammatic section shows how the shape of the motte at South Mimms, probably an adulterine castle of Stephen's reign before excavation gave little hint of the extra-

8.39 South Mimms, reconstruction of the motte. (Reproduced by kind permission of Dr John Kent.)

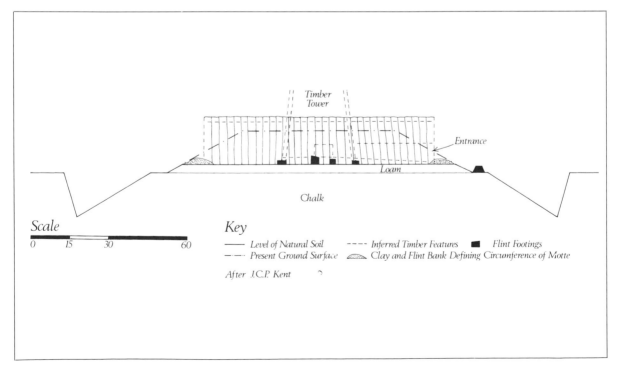

Timber Tower

Entrance

Loam

Chalk

Scale

0   15   30   60

Key

—— Level of Natural Soil   ---- Inferred Timber Features   ■ Flint Footings
–·–· Present Ground Surface   Clay and Flint Bank Defining Circumference of Motte

After J.C.P. Kent

ordinary form which the defences originally took. Excavation (by Dr J.P.C. Kent) showed that a tapering timber tower (rather like the twelfth-century church tower at Pembridge, Herefordshire, see fig. 8.11) rose above the vertical circular palisade which acted as a revetment to earth piled between it and the tower. Access to the tower was by means of a tunnel.

Therfield (Hertfordshire; fig. 8.40; Gaz. 32)

At Therfield a rescue excavation was undertaken by Martin Biddle in 1960, prior to bulldozing of the site. No structures were found on the top of the motte, which was partially sectioned, but the defences of the bailey were examined together with its entrance.

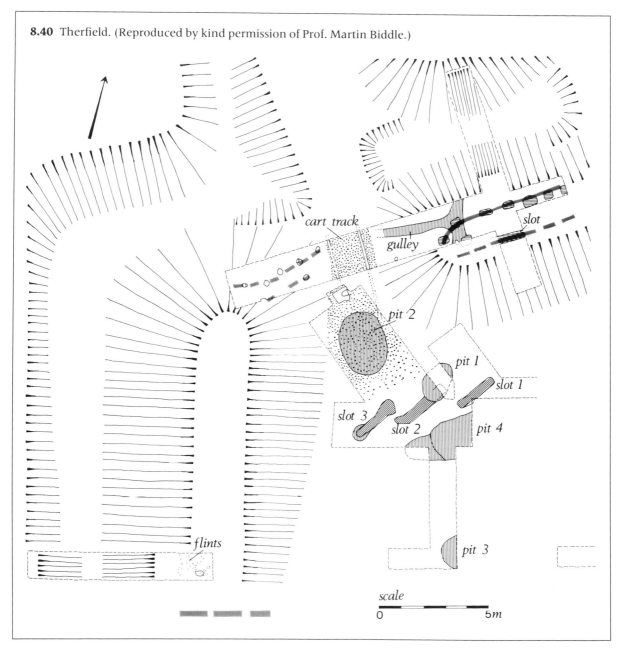

8.40 Therfield. (Reproduced by kind permission of Prof. Martin Biddle.)

The castle appears to have been occupied for only a short while during the mid-twelfth century anarchy and may even have remained unfinished. The evidence for the bailey defences consisted of a number of large post-holes lying parallel to a horizontal timber-slot. The evidence for the entrance to the bailey is slight due to the restricted area of the excavation, but it appears to have been inturned, rather like that of some Iron Age forts. There is no evidence of a bridge across the gateway, which is said to have been 4.3 m (14 ft) wide which seems unnecessarily wide and vulnerable. The two post-holes, 11 and 12, on the western side of the entrance were much slighter than those on the east, and lay on the slope of the rampart, rather than on its crest. No evidence for buildings was found in the interior of the bailey, but this may be due to the short life of the castle, its unfinished state, or the use of prefabricated, framed structures.

Two alternative reconstructions of the bailey defences are suggested by the excavator. In the absence of any firm evidence of timbers in front of the line of post-holes, of the two, his alternative A seems the more likely. It might also be suggested that the cladding would be more effective if the timbers had been vertical instead of horizontal, making them more difficult to climb. Vertical timbers would also eliminate the need for jointing along the whole length of the palisade.

Goltho (Lincolnshire; figs 8.41–46; Gaz. 39)

The excavation of the manor site at Goltho, Lincolnshire, was one of the most extensive and important investigations of the development of a fortified medieval site yet carried out in England and the published report is highly detailed. The chronology of the report is followed here, though this has been recently challenged (see chapter 2).

The site was occupied in Roman times, but the origins of the defensive site lie in the mid-ninth century and consist of a courtyard plan of domestic buildings, of clay with timber-lacing or of stone construction, surrounded by a ditch some 5.5 m (18 ft) wide and 2.5 m (8 ft) deep with a rampart at least 3.6 m (12 ft) wide. In the tenth century the defences continued in use but the domestic buildings were rebuilt. In the eleventh century the courtyard was extended with new defences enclosing the larger area. The rampart was now 7.5 m (25 ft) wide with a ditch similar in size to its predecessor. The new domestic buildings, which included a single-aisled hall, were again mainly stone built. We have here, therefore, a pre-Norman defended residential site of aristocratic status virtually indistinguishable from the ringworks of the post-conquest period; which raises the question of course, as to whether some of the ringworks which we have assumed to be Norman are in fact earlier. Only the serendipitous excavation of sites which prove to have such a history, will provide the necessary evidence.

In the late eleventh century the site was transformed into a motte and bailey, its motte revetted in timber, stone and turf (fig. 8.42) with a rampart 18 m (59 ft) wide. The small bailey contained two successive single-aisled halls. The position of the motte tower was marked by the remains of its 2.7 m (9 ft) square basement, which was lined with brick – among the earliest use of such material to be recorded in post-Roman contexts.

In c.1150 the bailey was filled in and the resulting broader mound became a platform for a large hall of timber with aisles on all four sides, reconstructed in the report as a clerestoried building. Because the site had been eroded before the excavation began and because the work was carried out mainly by machine, much of the finer detail and perhaps some slighter buildings were lost and little is known of the nature of the defences or the gateways or bridges. In addition, the soils, mostly heavy clays, made features very difficult to recognize or interpret. Nevertheless,

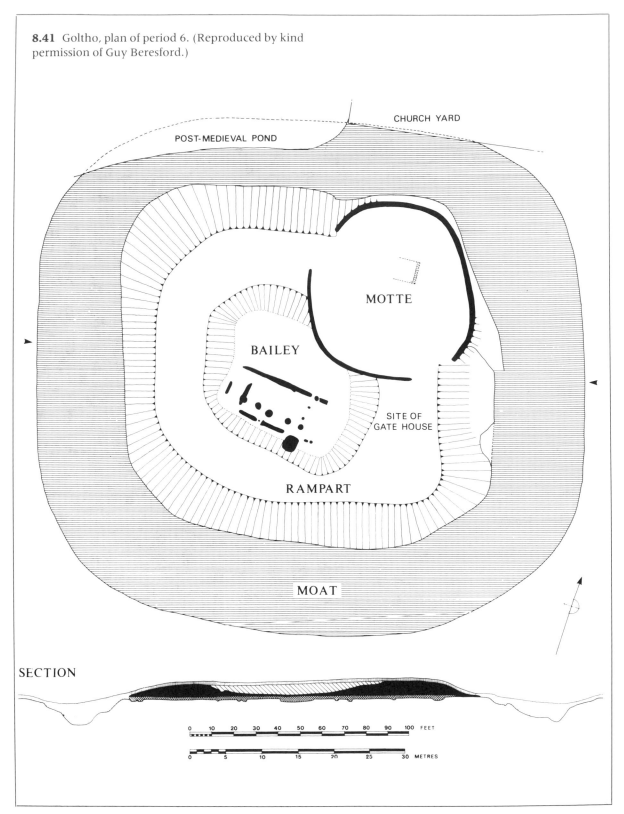

8.41 Goltho, plan of period 6. (Reproduced by kind permission of Guy Beresford.)

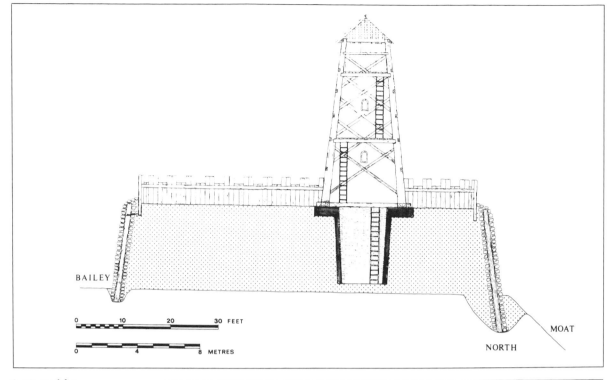

8.42 Goltho, reconstruction of the motte, *c.* 1080–1150.

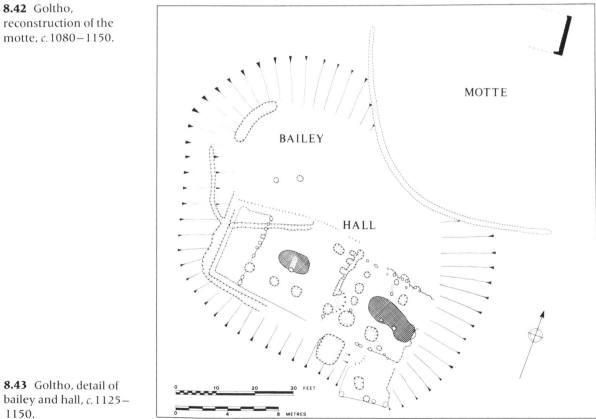

8.43 Goltho, detail of bailey and hall, *c.* 1125–1150.

the sequence of structures revealed under these less than optimum conditions shows the necessity for total horizontal excavation of such sites if even a broad outline of their development is to be understood.

8.44 Goltho, reconstruction of the motte and bailey castle, phase 2, *c*.1125–1150.

Prudhoe (Northumberland; fig. 8.47;

Gaz. 49)

The inner ward of this stone castle was almost entirely excavated before consolidation. The plans of a number of timber buildings in the first three phases of the site's occupation were found, dating (probably) from the mid-

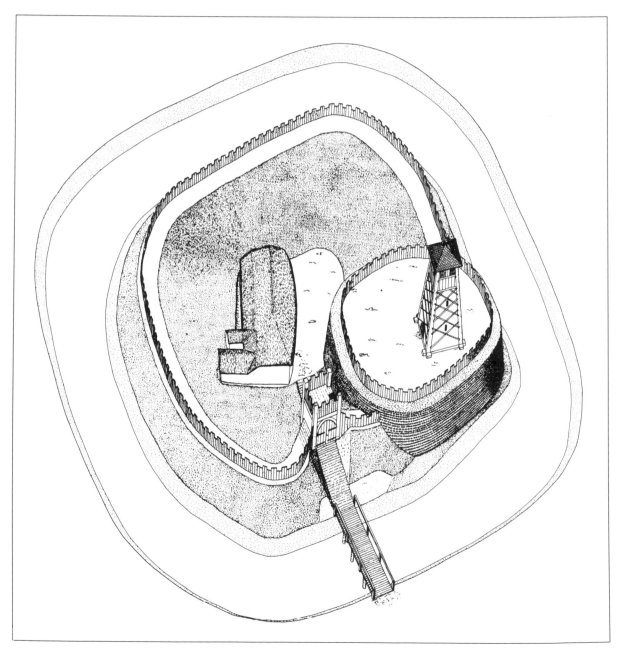

eleventh century to the end of the twelfth century.

The castle in its earliest phase, Phase One, was defended by a palisade founded on large posts set in deep post pits (fig. 8.47). The hearths (Nos. H1 and H2) precede the evidence for the buildings, of which there were two—one, Building 2, on the southern edge of the enclosure abutting the palisade; the other,

Building 1, on the northern edge opposite.

The evidence for Building 2 was incomplete but consisted of post-holes and a timber slot interpreted as the service end of an open hall, an interpretation difficult to follow on the published plan, which, however, does not include all the evidence in the text. Building 1

8.45 Goltho, period 7, castle mound c.1150.

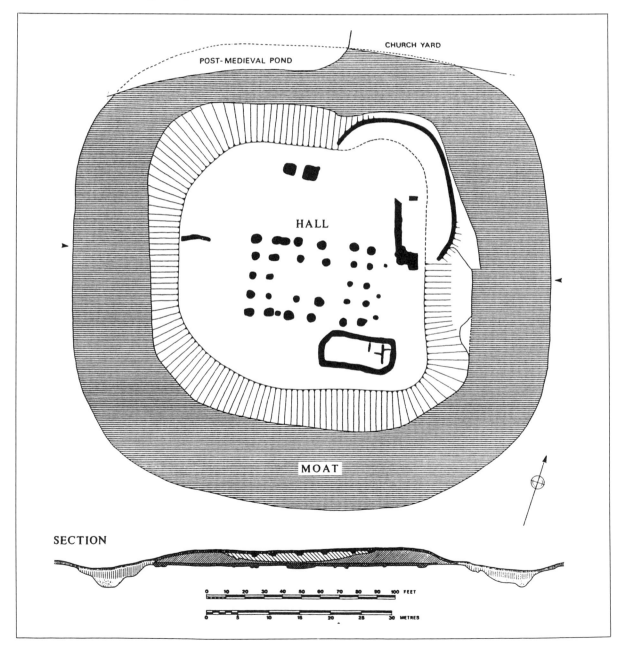

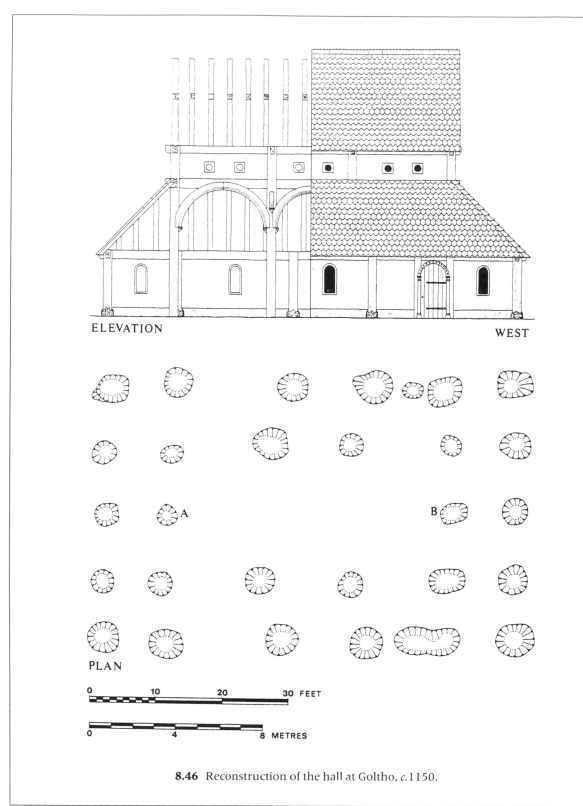

ELEVATION

WEST

A

B

PLAN

0   10   20   30 FEET

0   4   8 METRES

8.46 Reconstruction of the hall at Goltho, *c.*1150.

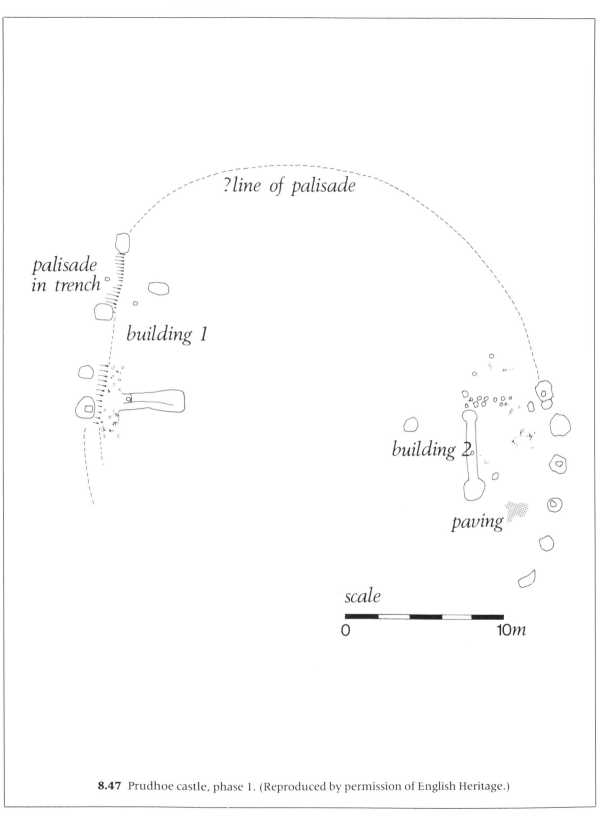

?line of palisade

palisade
in trench

building 1

building 2

paving

scale

0   10m

8.47 Prudhoe castle, phase 1. (Reproduced by permission of English Heritage.)

lay on the northern edge of the enclosure, close to more evidence of the palisade – four large post-pits and a 'substantial linear cut' presumably for a horizontal timber.

The evidence for Building 1 was also fragmentary, but sufficient to indicate a large post-hole and trench-built structure, apparently divided into two rooms, indicated by areas of mixed clay, cobbles and rough mortar. The published plan is itself too fragmentary to provide much evidence for comment.

In Phase Two 'a dramatic change took place. The palisade was replaced by a massive rampart of solid clay and stones, the remains of which were discovered in the southern part of the site. Elsewhere, later defences had removed it entirely.' On the northern side of the enclosure two of the palisade posts had been robbed out while two remained in use for some other purpose. There was also evidence, from the rampart tail, of supports for a parapet, though no evidence for the palisade itself. Building 2 of Phase One was retained in this phase and Building 1, with slight modifications, remained in use also. In the centre of the enclosure there were traces (beam slots and a few post-holes) of a third building, (Building 3) which was apparently not occupied for any long period of time. Along the south-eastern perimeter of the enclosure was a very large pit, some 5 m (54 ft) square and over 6 m (20 ft) deep, probably the site of a robbed-out tower or entrance tower set into the rampart behind the line of the rampart tail. It may have been of either timber or stone; if the latter, the structure is comparable to that found at Pontesbury, Shropshire. It is suggested by the excavators that this phase represents the first castle built by the Umfravilles who received the manor towards the end of the eleventh century.

In Phase Three the castle defences were completely remodelled in stone with a curtain wall and a gatehouse, though the internal buildings were still substantially of timber, occupying the sites of the earlier buildings. Later, probably after Scottish raids in 1173 and 1174, a stone keep was added in the western part of the castle. The site as a whole demonstrates the development of a small castle from its beginnings as a palisaded enclosure through a timber-defended ring-work with timber internal buildings, to its final transformation into a stone castle complete with keep and gatehouse.

This important excavation shows how essential almost complete excavation is for the understanding of the development of such a site, not withstanding the extensive destruction of the evidence which this entails. Trenching would hardly have produced the convincing sequence of phases here demonstrated. One reservation is worth making however, since it is fundamental to the origins of this small castle. The first phase, that of the palisaded enclosure, is dated by the excavators 'with some confidence' to 'the mid-eleventh century'. This date is based on archaeomagnetic and radiocarbon samples ranging from the ninth to the thirteenth centuries. The crucial question is whether the palisaded enclosure of Phase One is pre-Umfraville, that is, pre-Norman. It may be helful to quote the whole passage from the excavation report:

Phase One represents the earliest use of the site . . . A general clearance of the area is demonstrated in the southern part of the site, by areas of burning which are not hearths. Also associated with this activity are two hearths (H1 and H2) which were in use before any of the buildings, for which there is evidence, were erected. Archaeomagnetic samples give a date range from the eleventh to thirteenth century; C14 samples give a range from the ninth to twelfth century. The thirteenth century date is too late and the ninth to early. However, a central date of the mid-eleventh century may be suggested with some confidence. These primary deposits were sealed by three extensive build-ups of clay, compartmentalised into rectangular blocks, and apparently respecting the lines of the structural elements of Building 2, the main building in the south. These clay deposits may suggest the existence of a timber building earlier than Building 2, a post-built structure also of timber.

Stafford Castle (Staffordshire;

figs 8.48–51; Gaz. 57)

Stafford Castle now consists of a ruined nineteenth-century neo-Gothic keep on medieval foundations, standing on the summit of a very large oval motte. Attached to the motte are the earthworks of a massively defended inner bailey, and a very large, less heavily defended outer bailey. Beyond this lie the earthworks of a rectilinear settlement. A hollow way runs from the inner bailey through the settlement down to the present church of St Mary. (fig. 8.48). The earth-

works take the form of a very large motte and bailey castle with attached medieval settlement, a form which we have seen to be common to many timber castles of the immediate post-Conquest period.

Excavations on the motte top have not revealed any evidence of the timber precursor to the medieval building, which it is presumed has destroyed all traces of the earlier structure. Excavations in the inner bailey and in the settlement site have produced evidence of timber structures there and, although the excavations to date have only examined a small percentage of the whole site it seems safe to presume that it was occupied by timber buildings – there would be little point in constructing such massive and extensive earth-

8.48 Reconstruction of Stafford castle. (Reproduced by permission of Stafford Borough Council.)

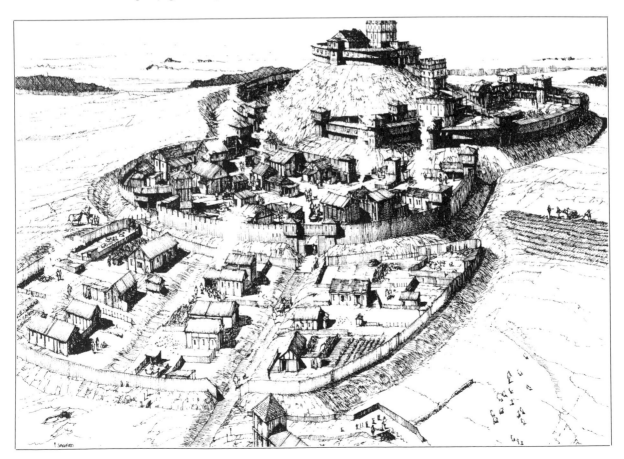

8.49 Stafford castle, approaching the outer bailey from the village.

8.50 Stafford castle, approaching the inner bailey from the outer.

8.51 Stafford castle, the gateway to the inner bailey.

works and massive earthworks must imply massive and formidable timber defences.

Working on this assumption and using the much firmer evidence from Hen Domen (Montgomery), as a motte, an attempt has been made to reconstruct on paper the timber phase of Stafford Castle. The arguments used for the reconstruction of Hen Domen (see pp. 329ff.) have been expanded and enlarged to produce drawings which are intended to form the basis for discussion, rather than anything approaching a definitive reconstruction. For while there is not direct excavated evidence for any of the structures, except the houses in the excavated part of the village, it seems inescapable that these huge and extensive earthworks would not have been constructed except as the basis for equally formidable timber defences, and that they

would hardly enclose empty spaces but would contain extensive ranges of buildings commensurate with the dignity and the size of the household of its owners, earlier the de Toeni family, later the Buckinghams.

The bailey at Hen Domen was packed with buildings and this concentration has been followed here, though it is possible that there was more open space in the outer bailey, which might have been used for corralling horses or exercising them, or for archery practice, and so on, for which, of course, there is no evidence. Fig. 8.48 attempts to show what the whole site may have looked like in its heyday as a timber castle. While, as has been stressed, the details of individual buildings may be wide of the mark, we believe that

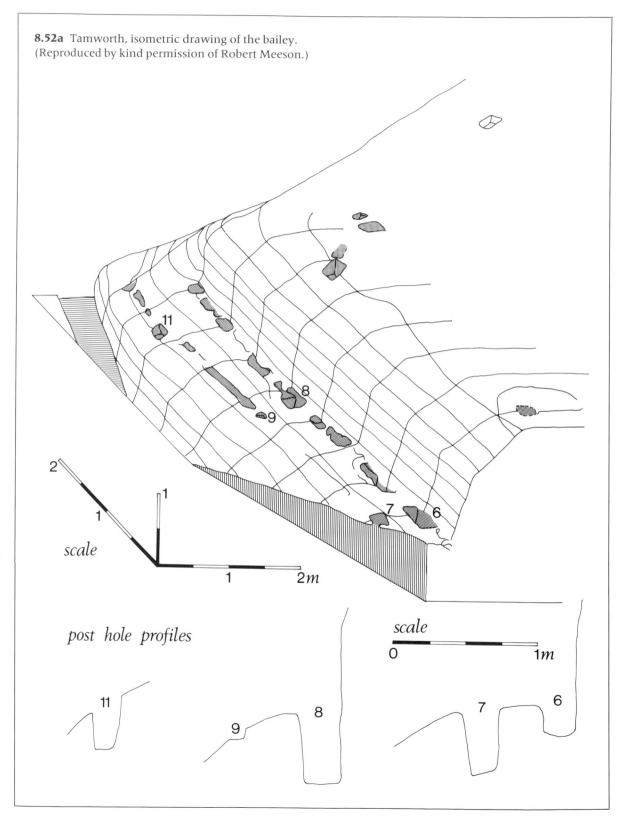

8.52a Tamworth, isometric drawing of the bailey.
(Reproduced by kind permission of Robert Meeson.)

scale

post hole profiles

scale

the general impression of a major castle like this must have been something like that of a small walled town, far removed from the half-empty weakly-defended sites shown in the majority of construction drawings which up to now have been common not only in school text books but in academic studies of early castles.

The three details in figs 8.49, 50 and 51 show what Stafford Castle may have looked like as one approached the outer bailey from the village (fig. 8.49); the approach to the inner bailey from the outer bailey, showing the keep and its defensive wall looming up in the background (fig. 8.50); and the gateway to the inner bailey with its inturned entrance flanked by defensive towers (fig. 8.51).

Stafford Castle and its earthworks are protected as an ancient monument, owned by the Local Authority. It would be possible, therefore, over the long term, for the site to be very extensively, if not fully, excavated, in which event the validity of these drawings could be tested. Certainly, there is no way in which the true nature of major timber castles will be understood without long-term excavation, and while the climate of opinion and the financial climate are both inimical to such research projects, it must be hoped that they will change at some time in the future.

Tamworth Castle Bailey

(Staffordshire; fig. 8.52; Gaz. 58)

An excavation in 1977 recovered remarkable evidence for the form of the timber defences of the bailey of Tamworth castle. A series of post-holes had been cut into the steep slope of the bailey bank which was terraced. The reconstruction drawing here reproduced as fig. 8.52b suggests the form of the palisade and its fighting platform, using the terracing in a highly efficient manner. The reconstruction is somewhat stylized, however, since, as can be seen from fig. 8.52a (below), the post-

holes are irregular in size and spacing and are not in matching pairs. Nevertheless, the principle is undoubtedly correct and it is probable that the irregularities were masked with clay or other cladding.

Abinger (Surrey; figs 8.53–54; Gaz. 59)

The excavation, in 1949, of the motte top of the small castle at Abinger in Surrey by Brian Hope-Taylor was one of the first to strip the entire top of a mound and recover a complete plan of its structures, and has therefore become a classic. It is nevertheless anomalous in that it appears to be a temporary, adulterine castle constructed during the civil war of Stephen and Matilda, and is therefore at one end of the spectrum which has at the other end the great residential motte at Ardres (see p. 115). So that, while Abinger was a fine pioneering excavation, it has been responsible for the implicit assumption in many history books, and even in specialist books on castles, that all timber castles were hurriedly erected, temporary structures, to be replaced in stone as soon as possible. This we now know to be far from the truth.

The motte was constructed of sand, which made features in its level top very hard to see (fig. 8.53a). As the excavator says, 'The layers were distinguished only by tonal variations and the presence in some of minute charcoal flecks'. A causeway of sandstone left undug across the motte ditch gave access to the motte. It had a curious profile with a central portion 'like an executioner's block'. It is suggested that the normal water-level was at the top of this causeway, the central hollow of which was bridged by a light (and presumably removable) bridge. There were no post-holes in or around the causeway so that any bridge must be presumed to have been framed or simply one or more squared tree trunks resting on the causeway's surface. No trace was found of palisading or revetment on the bottom of the mound.

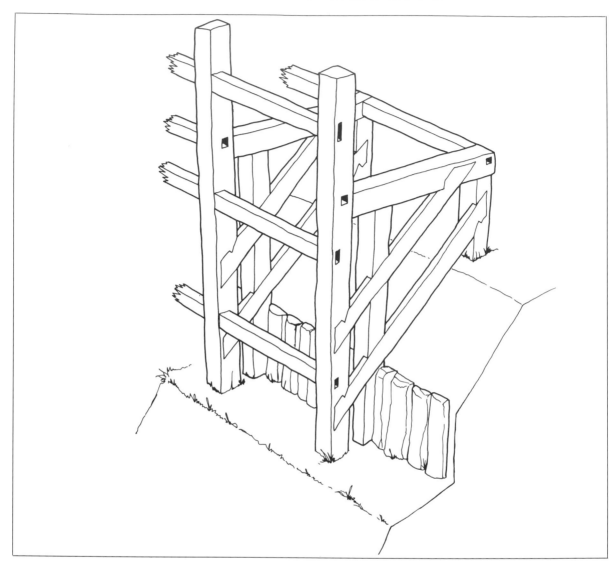

8.52b Hypothetical reconstruction of timber-faced rampart at Tamworth (source as 8.52a).

The top of the mound was de-turfed and trowelled down to the clean sand, in which there was evidence for post-holes (fig. 8.53b). It was assumed that the top of the mound had been lowered and levelled in modern times, thus truncating the features cut into the motte top perhaps by as much as a 30 cm (1 ft). These features consisted of post-holes outlining an encircling palisade and a square internal structure, presumably a tower. The palisade consisted of closely spaced posts, between 0.3 m (1 ft) and 0.6 m (2 ft) across, separated by a similar space. A ring of fewer, irregularly-spaced posts, 0.6 m (2 ft) inside the palisade, described by the excavator as bracing posts, though there is no clear evidence that they were sloping and the reconstructions shows a fighting platform behind the palisade. However, 0.6 m (2 ft) is very narrow for a fighting platform and leaves no room for passing behind a defender or avoiding a body. The posts of the palisade were set about 0.6 m (2 ft) apart and were filled with vertical tongued-and-grooved planks, a technique suggested by the reconstruction drawing

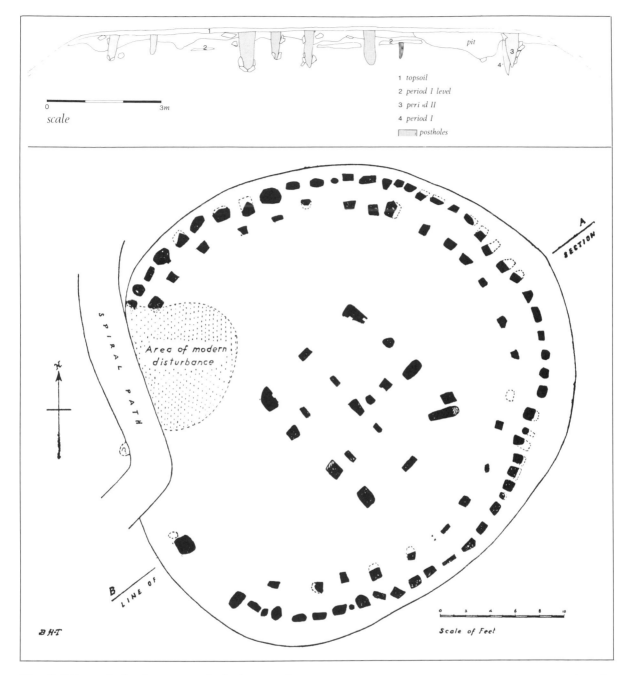

1 topsoil
2 period I level
3 peri d II
4 period I
posceholes

SPIRAL PATH

Area of modern disturbance

A SECTION

B LINE OF

BHT

Scale of Feet

scale

8.53 a) Abinger motte. b) Abinger motte top, plan of phase II.

(fig. 8.54), and also by a post-hole impression (illustrated on plate VIIIA of the report) which shows a slot cut in the post.

There is little doubt that the post-holes of the square structure within the palisade are evidence for a tower. It is argued by the excavator that the tower was stilted, that is, open in its bottom storey, but so much has probably been lost from the top of the mound that any evidence of wall lines will have been lost. It is argued that it would have been better to have had an open tower so that movement on top of the motte would not be hampered, but the internal posts shown on the plan

8.54 Reconstruction of structures on Abinger motte. (8.53 and 8.54 reproduced by kind permission of Dr Brian Hope-Taylor.)

would have made it difficult to run through the tower from one side to the other. In addition, two of the corner posts had slots or mortices cut in them, suggesting at least the possibility of infilled walls.

A curious feature of the palisade is that its plan is a series of six arcs (a possible seventh is on the site of the modern path and an area of modern disturbance). This suggests that the tower was erected before the palisade, otherwise it would have been a simple matter to have swung a piece of rope round a central part to form a circle as must have been done with the hundreds of ring-ditches whose circles are so accurate. If the tower was in the way, however, it would be necessary to describe the arcs from centres round the outside of the tower, which is what seems to have been done. There was an earlier tower on the motte of which only traces remained, too fragmentary to be reconstructed, perhaps because it had been dismantled, disturbing the evidence in the ground.

Castle Bromwich (West Midlands;

fig. 8.55; Gaz. 63)

This motte and bailey castle was dug in 1970 by Bill Ford in advance of road building. The motte ditch only encircled three quarters of the motte, ending in a steep escarpment on the northern side. The motte itself has been heavily disturbed but there were post-holes of a timber structure which yielded thirteenth-century material.

Trenches cut into the body of the motte showed a complex sequence of buried structures. A second large circular defensive ditch, containing medieval pottery, was found

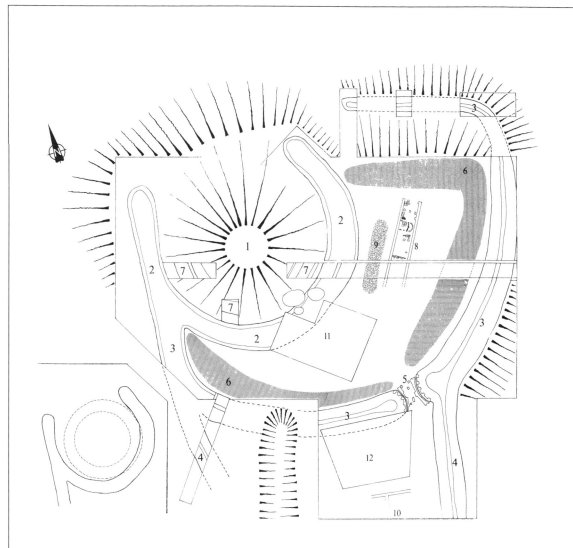

Key

Medieval features
1 Motte
2 Motte ditch
3 Inner bailey ditch
4 Outer bailey ditch
5 Causeway with timber structure
6 Extent of rampart base
7 Pre-motte ditch
8 Linear building

9 Cobbled area
10 Outer bailey building

Post-medieval features
11 Nineteenth-century house, garden and pits
12 Seventeenth-century house and garden

Inset
Relationship between pre-motte and motte
ditches

8.55 Castle Bromwich. (Reproduced by kind permission of Bill Ford.)

beneath the motte, associated with two separate stages of vertical timbering suggesting the construction and rebuilding of an earlier tower or revetted motte during the late eleventh century. These in turn had been preceded by a palisaded enclosure.

The bailey, which enclosed around 1 ha (2½ acres) in the twelfth century was considerably enlarged southward in the fourteenth century. In Phase I, of the twelfth century, an entrance causeway on the south had been surmounted by a timber structure and the butt ends of the ditches had been revetted in timber. The interior revealed the plan of a rectilinear building over 21 m (69 ft) long with partitions and evidence of a hearth, though it appears to have been industrial rather than domestic. A similar building (very disturbed and not shown on the plan) was found 5 m (16 ft) to the east. A heavily-worn cobbled pathway encircled the motte ditch and a well was discovered south of the motte. Below the eastern ramparts further excavation revealed a Romano-British timber and clay structure with associated pits.

In Phase II, datable to the fourteenth century, the bailey was increased in size by the continuation of the ditches southward. There was evidence of a medieval building but this had been extensively destroyed by the building of a post-medieval house. In this area also there was evidence of Romano-British occupation together with pits of the Bronze Age. The whole area is clearly one of long occupation and great complexity.

Sandal Castle, Wakefield (Yorkshire; figs 8.56—57; Gaz. 70)

The excavation of this castle was undertaken on behalf of Wakefield Metropolitan District Council in order to understand and conserve it as an ancient monument and to present it to the public. Although the castle remains are predominantly of stone, it was originally of timber, constructed probably between 1106

and 1130, and not rebuilt in stone until c.1240.

The castle had a circular motte separated by a ditch from a crescentic bailey (fig. 8.56). The bailey was defended by a substantial bank and surrounded by an outer moat. The whole was surrounded by a counter-scarp bank. The motte was 10.25 m (34 ft) above the old ground surface on a scarp slope overlooking the river Calder, and was 40 m (131 ft) wide at the base. Stone buildings had obliterated most of the structures on the motte, though there was evidence for timber buildings of the first phases elsewhere. The most conspicuous features of the bailey were a hall, with a kitchen beyond it to the north, and though there were earlier features stratified below the floor of the aisled hall, they made no coherent pattern. They may belong to the construction phase of the castle.

The aisled hall which was 14.5 m (48 ft) long by approximately 7 m (23 ft) wide had five bays, though only the north-west aisle survived complete. In the published reconstruction drawing the two end bays are shown with hipped roofs. The hall had an open central hearth, with a chamber and dais at the north-east end and a service room with chamber over at the south-west end. If, as is suggested, the south-western end of the building was of two storeys the sloping roof would have severely restricted the upper chamber.

Immediately north of the aisled hall lay a kitchen measuring 4.95 m (16 ft) by 4.1 m (13 ft) with a later extension (perhaps a lean-to) added on to the north-eastern side. It had a central, stone-built hearth though the charcoal lying on the hearth was thought to have come from a brazier rather than the hearth itself. This building presumably had a pyramidal roof with a central louvre or chimney.

Under the stone-built barbican was a stockade and a probable entrance was found. This appears to divide the original bailey into two unequal parts, the entrance leading

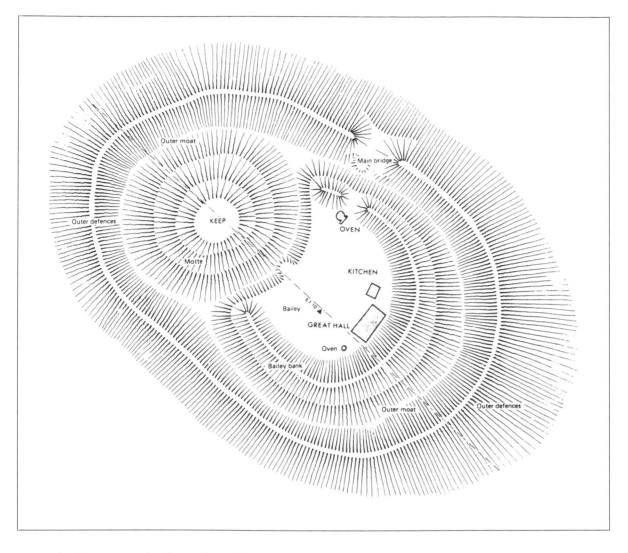

8.56 Sandal castle, earthworks of the timber phase. (Reproduced by kind permission of Philip Mayes.)

towards the motte bridge, though it seems not to be strongly defensive, with no evidence for a tower over the gate or a fighting platform behind the stockade. The arrangement may be compared with the much more powerful barrier across the bailey at Hen Domen.

There was evidence also for minor buildings of this phase along the southern perimeter of the bailey – a stone-built oven, a small four-part square structure close by, and a line of post-holes of a structure otherwise destroyed by later building.

Although a considerable area of the early bailey had been destroyed by the digging of the enormous barbican ditch the impression is

that the buildings of the bailey in the timber phase lay around the perimeter and that the central area was open. This contrasts sharply with the arrangement at Hen Domen where there was very little open space (see p. 336). This may, of course, simply be due to the fact that the bailey at Sandal was much larger, while the number of buildings to be accommodated was little more than at Hen Domen. This, in turn, has implications for the numbers of persons who could be accommodated. Could it be that the first Montgomery castle was not only packed with buildings but also with people? And that the size of a castle (unlike that of a town) does not directly reflect the size of its population?

Sycharth (Denbighshire; fig. 8.58; Gaz. 73)

The excavation, in 1962–3, of this beautifully preserved earthwork demonstrated graphically the gulf between what is known to have existed and what is there now, since, very exceptionally, we have a detailed, though highly poetic, description of the buildings which crowned the motte *c.*1400 (see pp. 144f. above). The excavated plan (fig. 8.58b), while only partial, revealed simply that there had been two rectangular buildings here, and it would hardly be possible to reconstruct Owain Glyn Dŵr's *Llys* from such meagre evidence. It is the same problem which has been illustrated in the section of the stone church at Nes, (p. 249, figs 8.2–8.7) where a similarly elaborate structure, perhaps in many ways not unlike Owain's house, proved to have been founded simply on lines of boulders. In both cases the limitations of excavated evidence are shown at their severest, and caution against interpretations which are unjustifiably simple or crude.

At first sight it is difficult to reconcile Iolo Goch's elaborate description of Owain's house (translated here in more literal terms than in the poetic version in chapter 2) with the church towers and belfries which we have suggested were parallels to our motte towers. On closer reading, however, and stripping away some of the hyperbole, the structure which Iolo describes might well have been similar in its essentials to the belfries illustrated in figs 8.8–8.20. For example, couplet 7 says specifically that 'it is of foreign [French] workmanship, like the bell tower [belfry] of St Patrick' (perhaps a misunderstanding for Westminster Abbey, dedicated to St Peter). In

8.57 Sandal castle, Great Hall and kitchen.

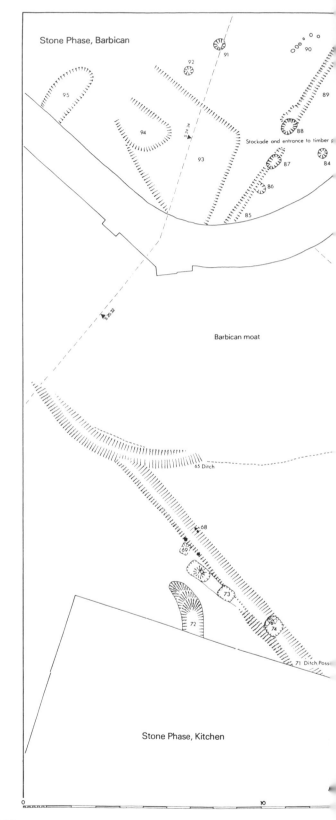

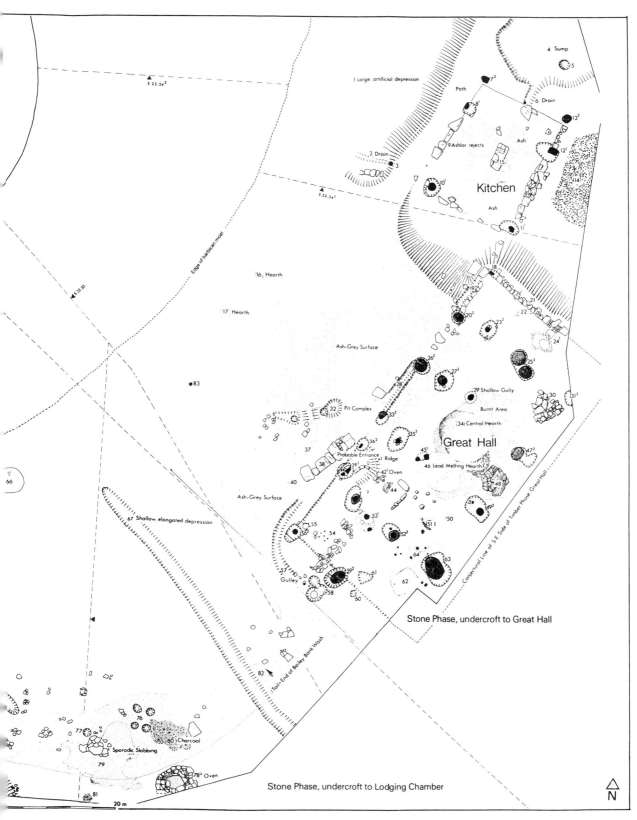

4 Sump
5

1 Large, artificial depression
Path
8¹
7²
6 Drain
13²
9 Ashlar rejects
Ash
15¹
12¹
14¹
2 Drain
3
10¹
Kitchen
Ash
11¹

S 23.34²

Edge of barbican moat

S 23.34¹

16, Hearth
18

17 Hearth
19¹
21
20²
22
Ash-Grey Surface
23¹
24¹

S 22.33
25²
83
26²
27²
29 Shallow Gully
30
31¹
28
32 Pit Complex
33²
Burnt Area
35¹
34¹ Central Hearth
Great Hall
36²
47²
37
45¹
39²
46 Lead Melting Hearth
38
Probable Entrance
Ridge
42¹ Oven
48
66
40
44
49²
Ash-Grey Surface
55
53¹
511
50
67 Shallow, elongated depression
54
52²
57
56²
64
63
Gulley
58
61
62
60
82
Tail-End of Bailey Bank Wash

Conjectural Line of S.E. Side of Timber Phase Great Hall

Stone Phase, undercroft to Great Hall

76
77
80 Charcoal
79
Sporadic Slabbing
78² Oven
81
20 m

Stone Phase, undercroft to Lodging Chamber

N

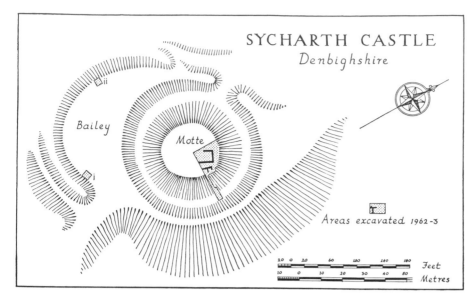

8.58 a) and b) Sycharth.
(Reproduced by kind
permission of the editor
of *Arch. Camb.*)

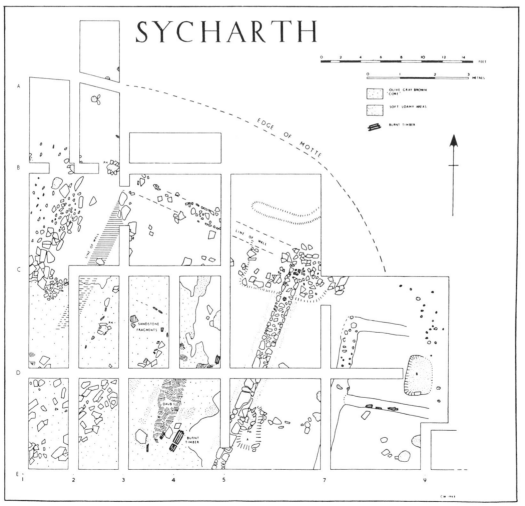

couplet 15, the translator says that she is certain that *plad* means 'the spaces between the pillars and the walls' — spaces which are clearly possible in structures such as those at Navestock or Yarpole or Pirton (figs 8.8, 8.15 and 8.18–20).

Couplet 17 describes specifically 'four wondrous pillars' and couplet 18 suggests that the upper part was subdivided into four lofts, the 'four beloved lofts coupled together where the bards sleep'. Certainly the four great timbers which form the main frame of the bell towers at Pembridge or Yarpole could be called 'wondrous' and it is not difficult to imagine the top of the tower sub-divided into four rooms.

It is more difficult to visualize 'nine halls, cut and shaped exactly alike' with their nine wardrobes, though the description of them as looking like 'fine shops with fair wares, a shop like Cheapside, London' warns us that we must not underestimate the sophistication of the furniture and contents of the timber castles of the wealthier lords (see chapter 2).

Llantrithyd Castle ringwork, Llantrithyd (Glamorgan; fig. 8.59; Gaz. 78)

About half of the interior of this ringwork was excavated. The earliest structure was a small square timber building (d on fig. 8.59) with six posts set in pits. Although it is referred to in the report as a house, it seems to this writer equally likely to be a granary or other kind of store-house (cf. the granary at Hen Domen, fig. 9.6 below).

A larger ten-post rectangular building, about 7 m by 5 m (23 ft by 16 ft) lay close to the rampart on the southern edge of the ringwork (b on fig. 8.59) with a small stone founded circular structure attached to one corner (a on fig. 8.59). This little building only 5 m (16 ft) in diameter was thought by the excavators to be a kitchen (though there was no hearth). Alternatively it could have been a defensive tower reached from the opening

in the corner of Building b (cf. Lismahon, pp. 322–3 below or a dovecot. The largest building discovered was an aisled hall some 16 m (52 ft) long and 10 m (33 ft) wide (c). It had a low drystone wall which curved outward on the western side, perhaps to form a sheltered entrance. Internally there were ten post-pits set quite close to the walls, and the siting of this building is curious in that the outer, eastern wall is built on the crest of the rampart (fig. 8.59). There could thus have been no palisade or fighting platform here, and if, as is presumed, the stone walls were low, less than 1 m (3¼ ft) high in the reconstruction in the report, there would be no room for arrow slits for archers within the building. Although the rampart was examined in two short lengths, no evidence for the palisade is recorded. It seems likely therefore, that the site was comparatively weakly defended, with little more than a surrounding fence. It should be noted also that since only about half of the interior was dug, there may have been more buildings than were discovered.

Cae Castell, Rumney Castle

(Cardiff; figs 8.60–8.66; Gaz. 80)

Excavation by the Glamorgan-Gwent Archaeological Trust has shown that the site began its life as a ringwork which was converted into a fortified manorial castle in the early thirteenth century when it was radically remodelled in stone. The ringwork had a timber gate-tower of two phases, a stone and timber revetment incorporated into the defensive bank near the entrance, several large timber buildings, one of which was single aisled, and a large area of metalling forming a central courtyard.

The earliest phases of the castle were not closely datable, but appear to be associated with the initial Norman advance into Glamorgan, as the castle is first mentioned in the Pipe Roll for 1184–5.

It was recorded as being in ruins by 1530.

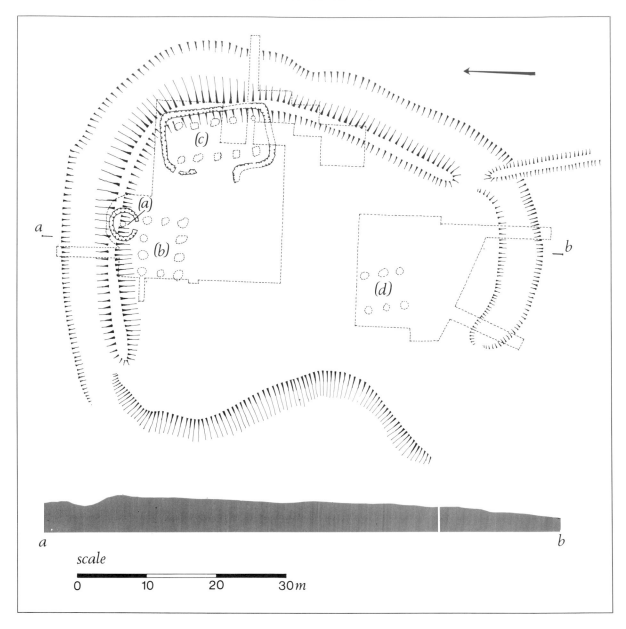

8.59 Llantrithyd castle ringwork. (Reproduced by kind permission of Cardiff Archaeological Society.)

Fig. 8.60 illustrates the sequence of posthole built timber halls on the north-west edge of the site.

These buildings belong to the ringwork phase of the castle before the defensive bank was cut down and the interior levelled. Contemporary with these halls was a series of inturned timber gateways (fig. 8.60) again founded on large posts sunk in the ground. It seems very likely that the gate was spanned by a bridge and it is suggested by the excavators that there was perhaps a portcullis, presumably of wood, which would imply a gate-tower tall enough to house the portcullis when it was raised. There was evidence of a timber palisade or revetment on either side of the gateway.

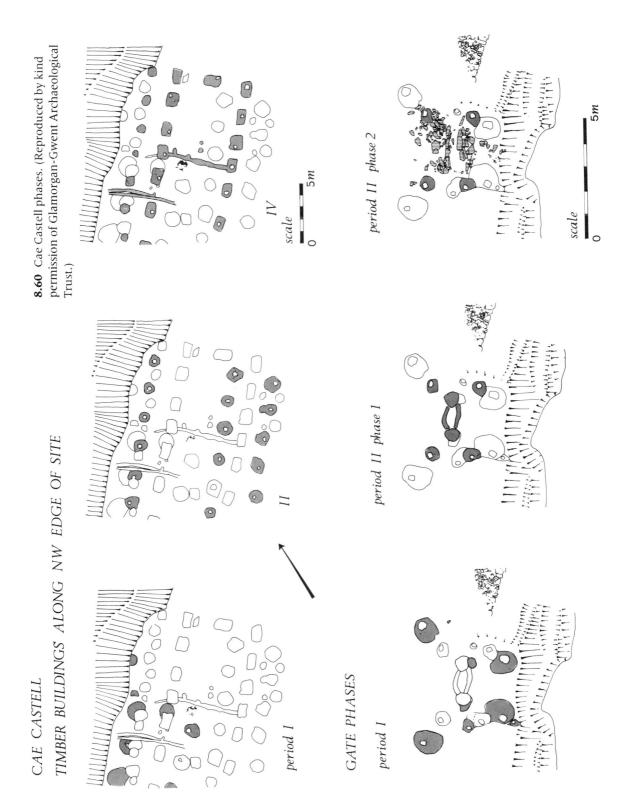

8.60 Cae Castell phases. (Reproduced by kind permission of Glamorgan-Gwent Archaeological Trust.)

CAE CASTELL
TIMBER BUILDINGS ALONG NW EDGE OF SITE

GATE PHASES

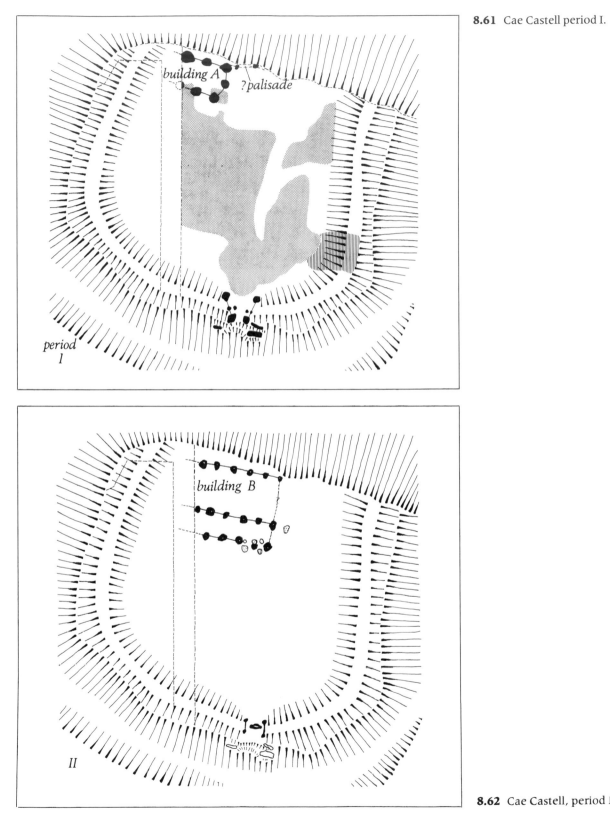

8.61 Cae Castell period I.

building A

?palisade

period I

building B

II

8.62 Cae Castell, period II.

8.63 Cae Castell, period III.

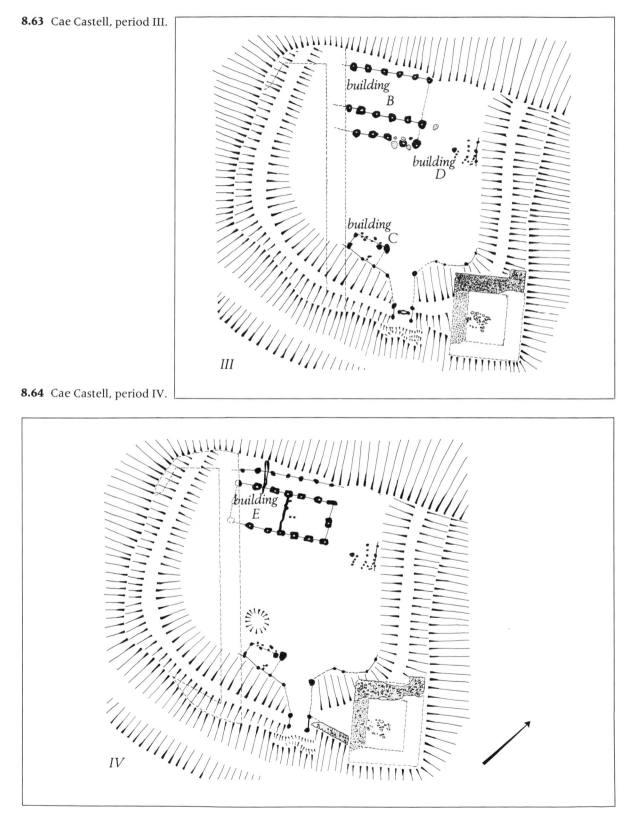

8.64 Cae Castell, period IV.

8.65 Cae Castell, period V.

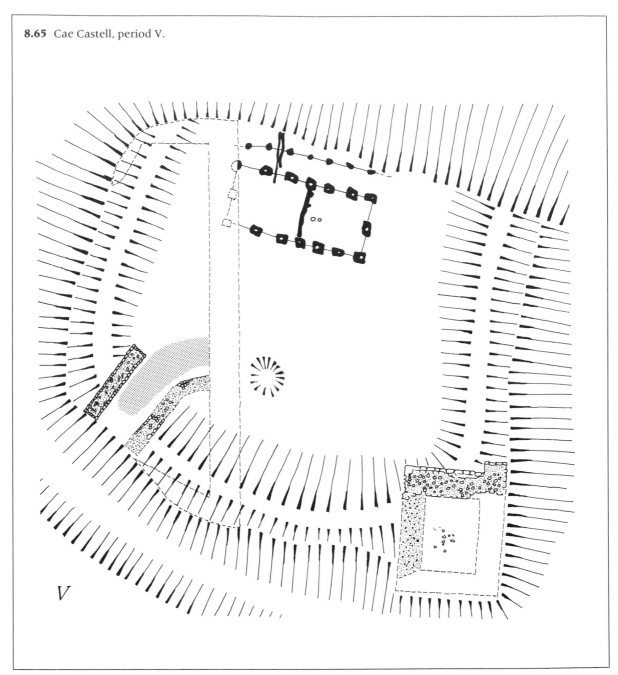

V

Castle Tower, Penmaen (Glamorgan;
fig. 8.67; Gaz. 85)

The ringwork at Castle Tower, Penmaen has a number of features in common with that at Llantrithyd (see p. 303). The first phase at Penmaen had a small hall and a gate-tower, both founded on rock-cut post-pits. These were succeeded by a gateway and a large hall with drystone walls, though only four of the postulated six post-holes were found, the other two being inferred. The form of the gateway and its antecedents have been fully discussed in the published report and there is

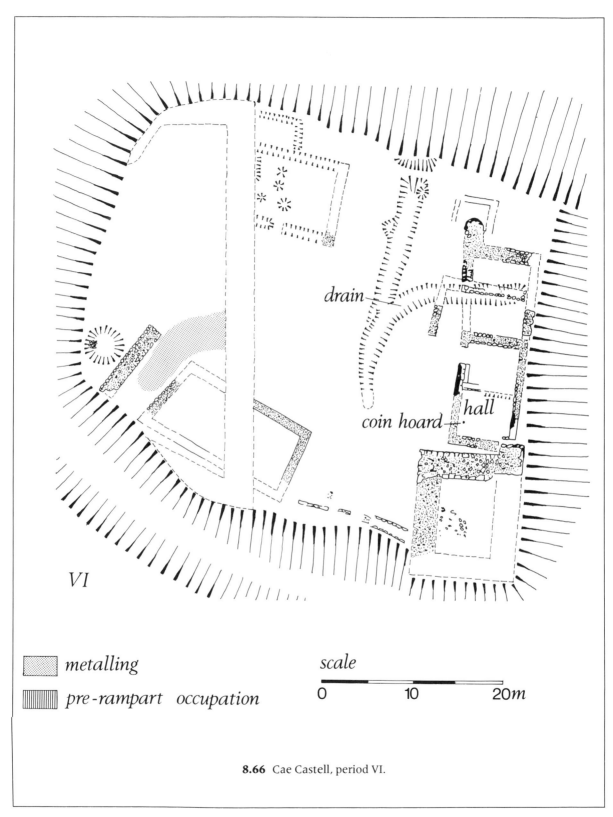

VI

metalling

pre-rampart occupation

scale

0   10   20m

8.66 Cae Castell, period VI.

little doubt that it was a gate-tower of at least two storeys with a fighting platform. However, the reconstruction proposed in the report (fig. 4) is of a fully-framed structure with horizontal ground-sills, a method of construction difficult, if not virtually incompatible, with posthole construction, especially on a rough and uneven surface such as that described at Penmaen. A normal post-hole building is much easier to envisage.

The small hall (T2) in the interior was, like building 2 at Llantrithyd, founded on deep rock-cut post-holes. It was about 5 m (16 ft) long and 3.6 m (12 ft) wide (thus smaller than the Llantrithyd example) and, as the excavator points out, with its central truss markedly skew. This may imply so called 'reverse assembly' the placing of the tie-beam below the wall plate.

Close to the south-western corner of Building T1, part of a further Building T2, was discovered. It was also founded in rock-cut post-holes. It had a horizontal slab which may mark a small hearth, and, with three smaller post-holes forming its north-western side, many have been open-fronted.

The second period structures consisted of the replacement of the timber gate with a narrower drystone walled entrance with four massive internal posts (two postulated) which presumably held a bridge across the gate, if not a small tower. The second period hall was also of drystone construction, with curved walls and corners, not unlike the stone-built hall at Llantrithyd, though without the aisle posts. As the excavator says, the walls were so crudely constructed that they could hardly have stood more than twice their present height, that is some 70 cm (28 in). There was no trace of internal posts so that it seems certain that the walls took the whole weight of the roof, with the feet of the rafters embedded in the tops of the walls. They must have been braced at some point, however, either just above head height, or occasionally at a lower level, forming crude bays.

The absence of floors in both the halls is difficult to understand. The site has not been eroded by ploughing or other cultivation – it is clear from the section of building S/1 that any original stone flagging would probably have survived, and that with the slab-like stones available it would have been easy enough to form a more or less flat surface. The internal surfaces revealed by the excavation would have been extremely uncomfortable to live on, even, if, as is suggested they were covered with straw. Plank floors (postulated at Hen Domen, Montgomery) seem unlikely here. The absence of hearths on this exposed site is also difficult to explain. Fire within the buildings would be impossible if they did have deep straw covered floors, and although, as has been suggested, charcoal left from fires might leach through the soil, one would expect at least a reddened area of rock where the sort of fire necessary to combat a winter spent here would have lain.

Professor Alcock is emphatic that Castle Tower is more likely to be Norman than Welsh. If this is so, it must surely represent the stronghold of the lowliest of Norman lords, cold, uncomfortable and primitive, a far remove from even a similarly small site like Hen Domen (whose bailey is about the same size) let alone the great timber castles implicit at Stafford or Dudley, Windsor or Arundel.

One would have thought that any Norman lord of however small a manor, would have had the energy and resources to enlist or enforce the services of the best craftsmen in the neighbourhood. Even without highly-skilled carpenters it would have been possible to level the interiors of the buildings, to build more effective drystone walling and to make the castle more comfortable and therefore more efficient, and the Normans were nothing if not efficient. The writer has pointed out elsewhere (chapter 9) that there is very little to distinguish life at Hen Domen from that of a site, say, of the Iron Age, and here the parallel seems to have even more force.

Cruggleton, Wigtown (Dumfries and Galloway; see fig. 2.25; Gaz. 91)

The motte at Cruggleton was developed from a stronghold dating to some time after the mid-eighth century, which had consisted of a timber hall surrounded by a palisade. In the late twelfth century the natural outcrop of shale was enlarged and excavation revealed a timber tower, measuring 4 sq.m (43 sq.ft), founded on four large posts. The hall (surviving from the first phase?) was enlarged and joined to the tower, which, the excavation suggests, may simply have been a solar. If this is so, the tower and the enlarged hall are very awkwardly joined especially if, as is implied,

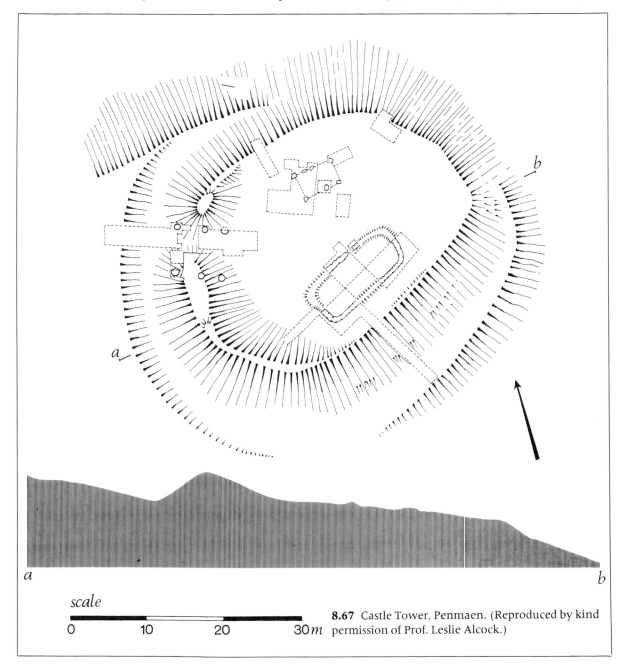

scale

0   10   20   30 m

8.67 Castle Tower, Penmaen. (Reproduced by kind permission of Prof. Leslie Alcock.)

the extension was built at the same time as the tower although, superficially at least, they look like two distinct phases. A parallel suggested by Kenyon is that of Lismahon (see pp. 322–3) with a small tower attached to the corner of a hall.

There are a number of unassigned post-holes in the suggested interpretation and one wonders whether the group at the south-western end of the original hall may not have been some form of attached tower (an upper chamber or solar?).

Keir Knowe of Drum

(Stirlingshire; fig. 8.68; Gaz. 90)

This motte, excavated by trenching in 1957 by the Royal Commission on Ancient and Historic Monuments of Scotland, is a promontory 'artificially modified to some extent'. The summit of the promontory is now oval in shape, 23 m (75 ft) on the long axis, and slopes down to the east (see section a–b on fig. 8.68). The excavations consisted of trenching across parts of the perimeter of the mound, together with a small area excavation in the interior, which revealed two large post-holes. Apparently on the basis of this evidence, seven more post-holes were predicted and holes dug to reveal them. They averaged 0.3 m (1 ft) to 0.5 m (1½ ft) in diameter, and 0.75 m (2½ ft) deep.

The western end of the site was occupied by several 'low irregular stony mounds covered with bracken and grass'. This stony area was examined by means of a trench which revealed a 'substantial dry stone wall measuring 2 feet 6 inches in thickness and standing to a height of 2 feet 10 inches'. Outside this was evidence of a single stockade (A1) and beyond it is a 'stone packed ditch, often only a shelf' (C).

As will be seen from the plan, the excavation explored only a very small proportion of the interior of the site. The post-holes of the central tower were found by highly selective

excavation and there is no evidence of other structures within the enclosure. The defences seem to have consisted of two parallel stockades on the north-eastern side with possibly another, though not necessarily contemporary, outside these. It seems possible that the dual stockades represent a palisade with an internal fighting platform. The relationship between the palisade trench and the stone wall inside it is not clear, unless, as seems to be hinted at in the report, the stone wall is the fighting platform, with the palisade rising in front of and above it. The report mentions a very few 'relics' and the nature of the occupation and its length and date are all very uncertain.

Castlehill of Strachan (Grampian;

fig. 8.69; Gaz. 96)

Excavation of this motte in 1980–1 revealed evidence for a timber hall on the summit surrounded by two phases of palisades. Although a large part of the mound had been eroded by rabbit burrowing and by the weathering of a quarry on its western side, enough of the summit was left for the excavators to recover evidence for a remarkable circular or oval building occupying the bulk of the top of the mound (fig. 8.69). In the first phase, datable to c.1250, a concentric palisade on the motte edge was founded on large widely-spaced posts. In Phase III, datable to c.1265–85 this palisade was replaced by one enclosing a larger area, and based on closely spaced, stone-packed posts.

Although the excavators suggest that the central circular/oval building might have been of two storeys, the reconstruction (by Hilary Murray) suggested in Appendix 1 of the report (p. 346) is much closer to that of a large Iron Age round house with a conical roof and walls, perhaps of clay, on a wooden skeleton with internal posts supporting the roof structure. The presence of a central hearth argues against an upper floor, which in addition would have required walls at least the height of the ground floor even if the upper floor were confined to the roof space. It is hard to envisage this building having walls two storeys high. On balance, this writer believes a single-storey round house to be more likely. In either case, the building is anomalous and

at present unique in castle structures (the circular building at Peebles, quoted as a parallel by the excavators, is not firmly medieval, see p. 315). The immediate antecedents for the Castlehill motte top are not clear, it having more in common with the Irish rath than the typical motte.

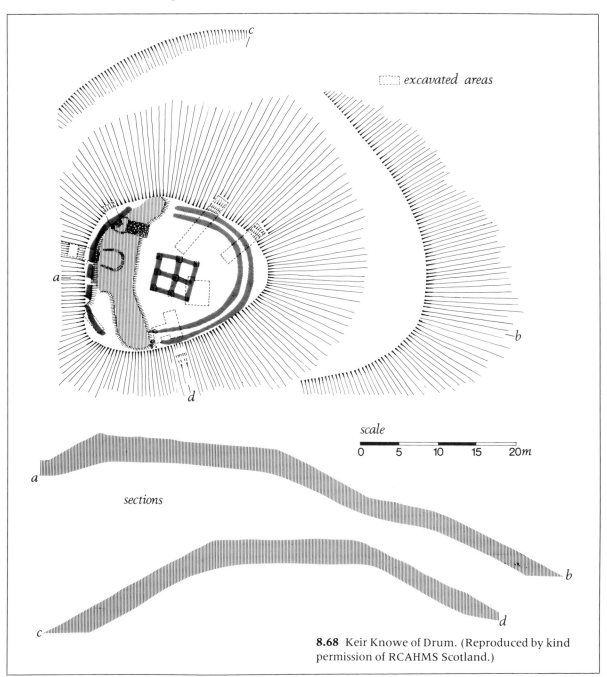

□□□ excavated areas

scale

0   5   10   15   20m

sections

8.68 Keir Knowe of Drum. (Reproduced by kind permission of RCAHMS Scotland.)

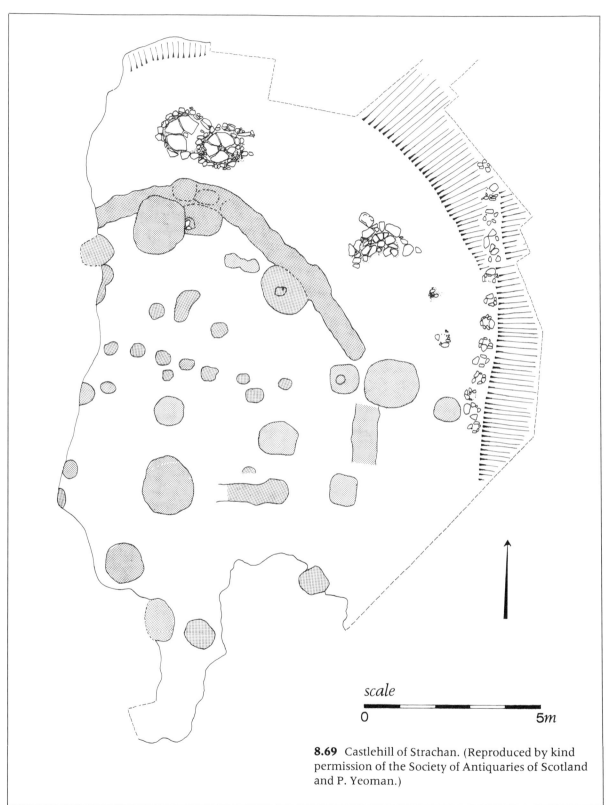

scale

0   5m

8.69 Castlehill of Strachan. (Reproduced by kind permission of the Society of Antiquaries of Scotland and P. Yeoman.)

Castle Hill, Peebles (Lothian; fig. 8.70; Gaz. 97)

The Castle at Peebles appears to have existed before 1152–3 and to have gone out of use and to have been destroyed by the middle of the fourteenth century. Excavations in 1977 before the projected building of a new church hall covered some 294 sq.m (3165 sq.ft), about half the total summit of the mound. The excavations defined three broad phases of occupation: evidence of a bowling green of the early eighteenth century, and two series of medieval deposits – one a fourteenth-century occupation sealing twelfth-century buildings. These timber buildings 'bear no apparent relationship to the features above them and so probably represent an entirely separate building plan.'

The circular building, A, on fig. 8.70 had a foundation trench 12.4 m (41 ft) in external diameter and 7.2–7.4 m (23–24 ft) internally, leaving a wall-gully c.2.6 m (8½ ft) wide with post-pits (96 and 77) abutting its outer edge at the north-east and south-east points of its circumference. The gully was deepest along its outer edge where it was 32–55 cm (13–22 in) deep with a nearly vertical side. The bottom of the gully gradually sloped up toward the interior of the structure where it had a maximum depth of 16–23 cm (6–9 in).

This was interpreted as a circular building, perhaps a tower, some 12 m (39 ft) in diameter and assumed to be medieval, though there was no dating evidence. The report contains an extensive discussion of the possible constructional variations which the evidence suggests.

The rectangular building B was approximately 5.5 m by 4.7 m (18 ft by 15 ft). The evidence consisted of wall gullies and 14 internal posts including 4 main posts. The report again included an extensive discussion of the possible form and construction of this building, with a hypothetical reconstruction. In addition a group of post-holes was found between buildings A and B and also within building A though the report stressed that 'it was not possible to relate these firmly to the circular building and they may belong to the structure represented by (the) series of post-holes between the two excavated buildings'.

There was also a group of graves which were believed to belong to the chapel which was granted ten shillings 'before 1327'. There was no evidence for the function of either of the buildings.

This excavation demonstrates the great difficulties encountered when excavating damaged or eroded sites, especially when there is virtually no pottery, nor other stratified datable artefacts. It is assumed in this report that the two structures are twelfth century, and contemporary, or more or less so, but it is interesting that the graves overlie building A but not building B. This, of course, might simply be fortuitous. It is also worth noting that the group of unassigned post-holes also appears to lie over, and both inside and outside, the gully of Building A, and that they are all south of the graves. The implications of this distribution are not clear but it is at least possible that Building A is earlier, and even much earlier, than the rest of the structures. Is it possible that the mound, now smaller than it was formerly, was originally prehistoric and that the circular building is prehistoric also?

The writers of the report stress that the bulk of the excavation records were not available at the time of writing. When they do become available, it is possible that these ambiguities will be resolved. Meanwhile, the timber structures of Peebles Castle remain somewhat enigmatic.

Barton Hill, Kinnaird (Perthshire; fig. 8.71; Gaz. 102)

This mound is a volcanic plug which has been modelled to form a motte with steep sides with a possible bailey to the west and south, now partly occupied by a church and churchyard. The summit of the mound has been artificially dished leaving the impression of a wall under the turf covering at the southern end. Excavations in the winter of 1971 revealed a pattern of large rock-cut pits on the southern half of the summit. They formed two squares, one inside the other. The excavators interpreted the inner group of four large pits averaging 1 m (3¼ ft) in diameter and the same in depth, and forming a quadrilateral measuring approximately 4.2 m (14 ft) on each side, as the sockets for the posts of a timber tower house, and the seven smaller pits forming a larger quadrilateral 6.2 × 6.8 m (20 × 22 ft) were seen as a 'post and log fencing' enclosing the tower (fig. 8.71).

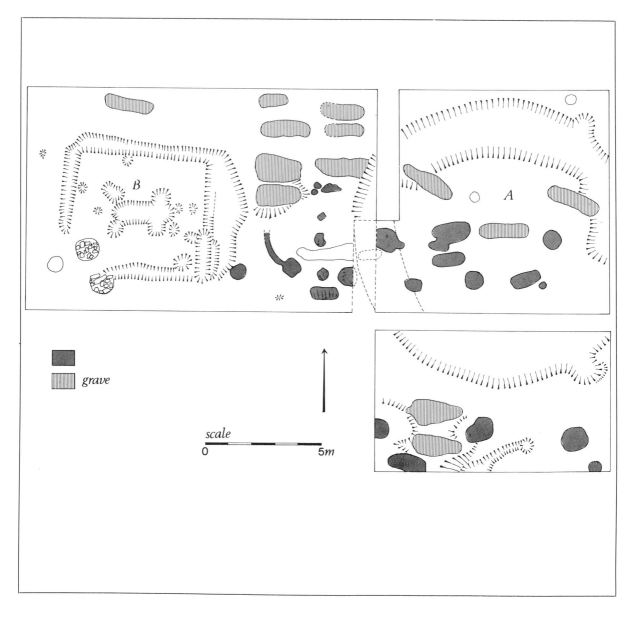

8.70 Peebles Castle Hill. (Reproduced by kind permission of the Society of Antiquaries of Scotland and Dr H. Murray.)

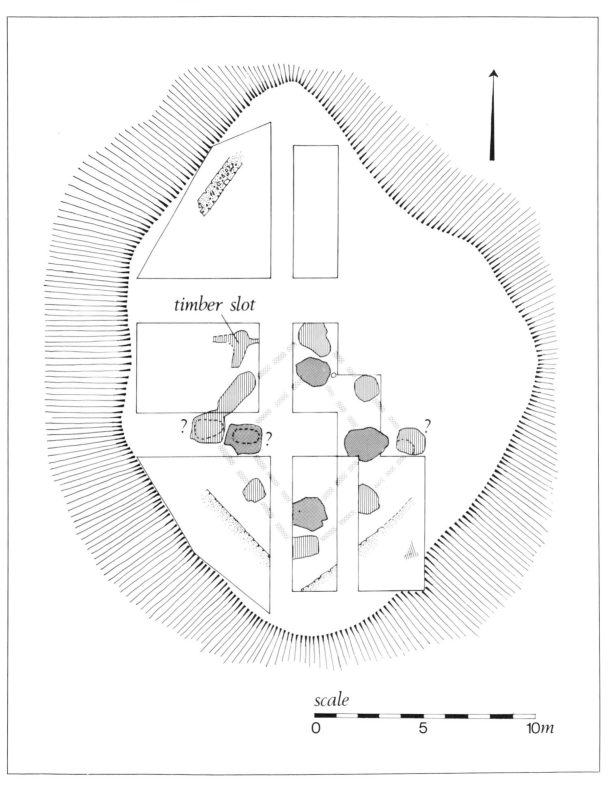

timber slot

scale

0   5   10*m*

8.71 Barton Hill, Kinnaird. (Reproduced by kind permission of Historic Scotland and Chris Tabraham.)

The excavators assume that these two quadrilateral arrangements of posts are contemporary, though no evidence is cited and it seems equally possible to this writer that there could have been two successive towers, one larger than the other. A timber slot to the north-west of the outer circuit is interpreted as the foundation of an external stair.

The southern end of the summit of the mound had been protected by a drystone wall built on to a specially cut rock ledge. Beyond this was an accumulation of soil containing much carbonized wood, interpreted as the decay of a wooden stockade, perhaps bedded in turves. The relationship of this stockade to the drystone wall was not clear and it seems possible that the wooden stockade was mounted on this wall in the form of a bretasche. The northern half of the summit contained much occupation debris with a hearth and rough paving though the southern half was virtually sterile, curious if the post-pits are evidence of an occupied tower or towers.

Clough Castle (Co. Down, Northern

Ireland; fig. 8.72; Gaz. 106)

The motte at Clough Castle was excavated under the direction of Dudley Waterman in 1951 and 1952. The motte top was almost completely excavated, with the exception of a number of baulks left to provide sections. In the first phase of occupation the perimeter of the motte was defended with a palisade founded on a fairly regular line of post-holes set about 75 cm (2–3 ft) back from the edge of the mound. The post-holes, which were circular or oval in shape averaged 7–10 cm (3–4 in) in diameter and penetrated between about 36 cm (15 in) and 60 cm (24 in) below the surface. The distance between the centres of the posts was usually 30 to 45 cm (12 to 18 in) but frequently less. The posts appear to have been driven into the soil (rather than set in pits) and the excavator mentions that some

of them encountered large stones which were included in the make-up of the mound and which 'must have offered undue resistance to the insertion of the timbers'.

At a number of places along the perimeter there were additional rows of posts set parallel to, or slightly diverging from, the main palisade. These were interpreted as palisading 'erected to fill gaps caused by the decay of the original structure'. Contemporary with this palisade were three pits, spaced at intervals round the perimeter of the mound, interpreted by the excavator as weapon pits designed to accommodate archers. No central wooden tower was identified, the mid-point of the mound being occupied by an irregular shallow hollow of large size (fig. 8.72).

Towards the middle of the thirteenth century, a stone building 'of normal medieval layout' was erected on the motte and appears to have been destroyed by fire almost at once. Later in the century a small rectangular keep of masonry was built and the original timber palisade was replaced by 'an earthen bank of small size'. Occupation of the motte continued into the early years of the fourteenth century, and the mound was reoccupied in the fifteenth or early sixteenth century, when the original stone keep was rebuilt and enlarged as a tower-house.

The additional rows of palisade posts mentioned above pose the question of the form of the original palisade. Timbers 7–10 cm (3–4 in) in diameter are not, in themselves, sufficient defence for a motte top – they are barely adequate for a fence to keep out animals. The spaces between the posts suggest strongly that they were supports for wattling – even so, such a fence would not be strong enough for defence against an enemy, and it is suggested that, since the mound was composed of stony yellow clay the wattling was the support for a clay wall thick enough to provide an adequate defence. Such walling has been postulated on the basis of a similar evidence from Hen Domen (Montgomery) (see below pp. 329ff.). The short additional rows of internal posts might then be explained as repairs to the inside faces of the clay walls rather than as replacement fences.

Some support for the suggested clay walls is given by the weapon pit 6. It was 1.44 m (5 ft) deep and about a 30 cm (12 in) behind the line of palisade posts, which were interrupted

here by two parallel settings of pairs of boulders, placed about 45 cm (18 in) apart at right angles to the lines of posts. The pit and the boulders were interpreted as 'a weapon pit, designed to accommodate an archer, with a stone built loop for the discharge of arrows'. A number of deductions follow from this assumption. First, the boulder settings would

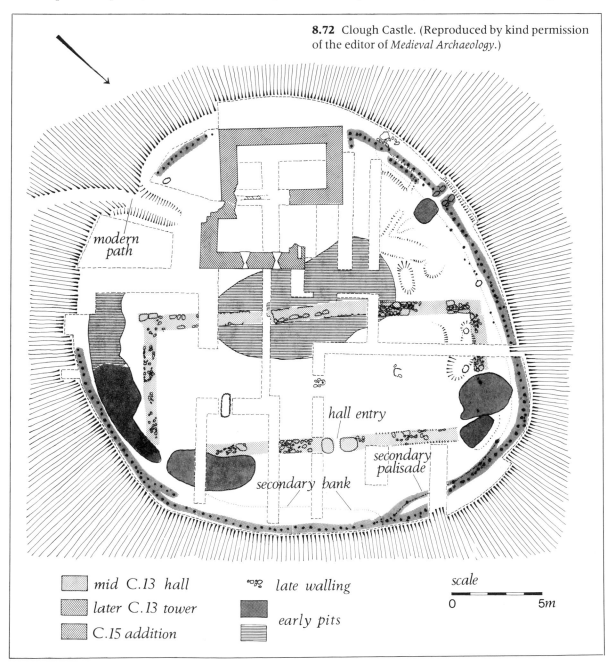

8.72 Clough Castle. (Reproduced by kind permission of the editor of *Medieval Archaeology*.)

modern path

hall entry

secondary palisade

secondary bank

mid C.13 hall

later C.13 tower

C.15 addition

late walling

early pits

scale

0   5m

hardly be necessary if the palisade were a free-standing fence – they support the suggestion that the defences here were as thick as the width of the two boulders, that is some 1.06 m (3½ ft). It should be added, however, that it is not clear from the excavated section if there was a gap in the 'bank' here, a gap which was revetted by the boulders, and it seems possible to the present writer that the 'bank' which does not appear to include stones might be the spread of the postulated clay wall after the rotting of the timbers. The presence of the weapon pit 6, and two others, 1 and 3, and the absence of any evidence for a wall-walk implies that the palisade/clay wall was only some 2 m (6–7 ft) high. This would be compatible with the fact that the timbers appear to have been driven into the ground – it would be impossible to do this with longer timbers.

The absence of any evidence for a central structure is surprising. It may be that whatever was there in the first phase was entirely clay walled. The function of the central pit is unknown. The only evidence for the gate was a single large post-hole on the west side of the modern path, which seems to have removed the rest of the evidence.

Lismahon (Co. Down, Northern Ireland;

figs 8.73–75; Gaz. 109)

This pioneering excavation, carried out in 1958 in 'constant rain' by the late Dudley Waterman showed that the motte here had been preceded by a dark-age occupation site which was occupied until the Norman Conquest of Down in 1177. The summit of the mound was enclosed by a palisade, with which was associated a defensive weapon pit. It also contained a residential building, with an attached tower adjacent to the palisade, and a second building probably used as a workshop. The palisade was subsequently rebuilt and in the later thirteenth century when the house was enlarged, part of the workshop was demolished in the process.

Figure 8.73 shows a plan and section of the motte and the extent of the excavations and fig. 8.74 shows two successive plans of the structures on the motte top. In the first phase, datable to c.1200, the house, measuring some 9 m by 8 m (30 ft by 26 ft), occupies only a small proportion of the space on the mound, with a small workshop on the opposite edge, though there may, of course have been other buildings in the undug area. The most interesting discovery was of a square tower or turret attached to one corner of the house, supported by two massive posts, access probably being by a central ladder (as in the reconstruction, fig. 8.75, though note that there is no direct evidence for this) or perhaps from a ladder represented by PH9 inside the house.

Close by on the edge of the mound was a double pit, interpreted by the excavator as a weapon pit, a form of defence common down to the present day, and now known as a fox-hole. Its implication here is that the palisade (for which there is no direct evidence) was not very high and did not have a wall walk. It is not clear why the turret and the weapon pit should be so close together, apparently doubling-up the defences here, though again there may, of course, have been other pits in the undug parts of the site.

The turret was retained when, in the second phase, the house was enlarged, but the weapon pit was filled in. The house now had a room attached to its western end, and with its opposed entrances and cross passage, its central hearth and division into what are perhaps a hall and bedroom, became very like the peasant houses familiar from the excavations of medieval villages in many parts of Britain.

The site is, therefore, much more like a defended farmhouse than a 'castle' with a keep crowning the motte, dominating a bailey full of domestic buildings. This excavation was an early warning, not always heeded, of the danger of making assumptions about the structures of mottes (and baileys) simply by studying their earthworks.

Weoley castle (Birmingham; figs 8.76–77; ex. Gaz.[2])

Weoley castle is a fortified manor house lying within the Birmingham City boundary. Its reason for inclusion here is the remarkable preservation of a wooden building buried deep below the surviving remains of the stone buildings which date from *c.*1264–80. While Weoley castle is properly speaking a 'moated site', the buildings within such sites must have been very similar to the domestic buildings within the baileys of timber castles, so that it is

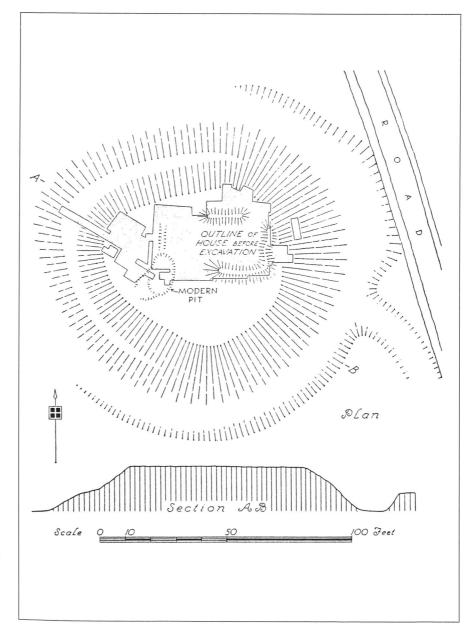

8.73 Lismahon, plan and section of the mound. (Reproduced by kind permission of the editor of *Medieval Archaeology*.)

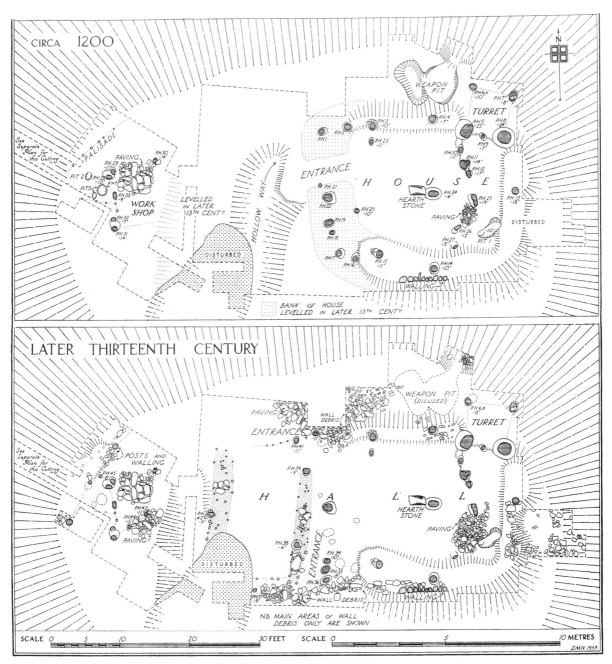

8.74 Lismahon, sequence of structures on the motte (source as 8.73).

8.75 Lismahon, conjectural restoration of house and tower (source as 8.73).

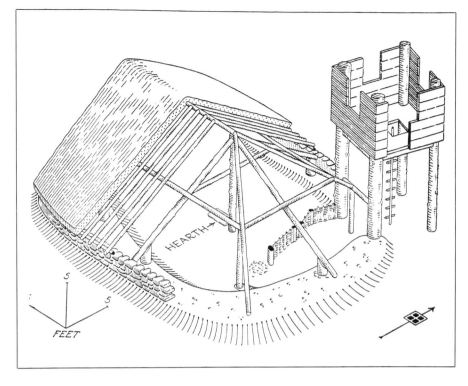

very probable that buildings similar to that excavated at Weoley, which at least in its early stages seems to have been a kitchen, could be paralleled in very many of the castles discussed here.

The building, whose woodwork was preserved to a height of as much as 1 m (3¼ ft) in places, was rectangular and of six discernible phases (fig. 8.76). It measured 12.5 m (41 ft 3 in) by 6.85 m (22 ft 6 in) and was constructed of oak with upright posts joined by sill-beams. The entrance was on the north side and connected the buildings to the nearby stone hall by means of a path. The building was divided into three rooms by partitions, the eastern room containing a very large hearth built of sandstone blocks. In Phase II the hearth was enlarged, perhaps, the excavator suggests, to provide a washing-up area.

In Phase III there is evidence that weatherboarding was used in repairs. The large hearth continued in use though reduced in size.

The interior partitions were removed and the whole converted into an aisled hall. As the aisle posts were set in post-holes it is likely that the roof was completely rebuilt at this time. One interesting detail was the addition of a small wooden drain leading to the outside of the building close to the door. It is suggested that this was a pissoir.

In Phase IV the large hearth went out of use and was perhaps replaced by one now overlain by the later fifteenth-century hearth which has been retained for display. In Phase V the entrance was reconstructed with a massive threshold beam, and the inner door of the chamber was provided with a wooden washer with a piece of leather in the hole to enable the door to swing.

In Phase VI the floor was raised and the door widened, and a long oak-boarded drain was put down outside the building, but ultimately the whole was buried in the upcast from the moat when the interior of the site was raised, and thus the timbers were pre-

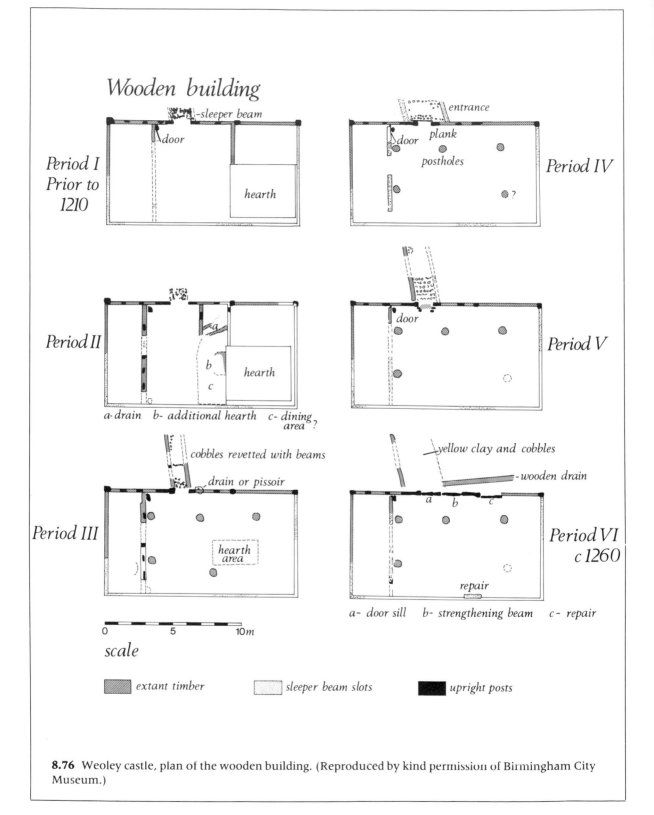

8.76 Weoley castle, plan of the wooden building. (Reproduced by kind permission of Birmingham City Museum.)

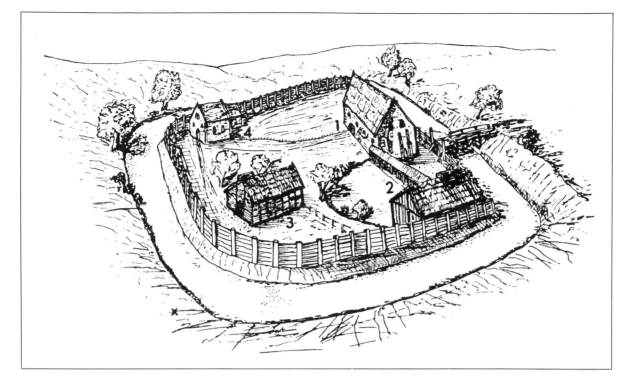

served. The enormous hearth, enlarged in Phase II, suggests that the building was a kitchen, catering for large numbers of people. It was connected to the nearby stone-built hall to the north by a covered corridor – necessary if food was to be kept hot and dry on its way

8.77 Weoley castle, *c.* 1260, looking north.

to the table. Unless there was a hearth under the later hearth, this building in its later phases was no longer used as a kitchen.

Hen Domen, Montgomery: a case study

Hen Domen, Montgomery (Powys — NGR SO214981) (see fig. 7.15) is the site of a medieval timber castle built by the Normans in the 1070s and occupied for approximately two centuries. It has been the subject of an extensive excavation spread over 30 years and still continuing. Much of this has been carried out for short periods and the total length of the various seasons' work is less than two years. Nevertheless it is the most fully explored site of its type in the British Isles, perhaps in Europe, and provides clear evidence of how structurally complex timber castles might be (see Barker and Higham 1982). The earth-works which are now the only surface remains of such sites conceal a history of development which only detailed excavation can illuminate.

Hen Domen (a Welsh name meaning 'the old mound') is a classic example of a motte and bailey castle; the motte at Hen Domen being 8 m (26 ft) high and 40 m (131 ft) in diameter at its base and 6.5 m (21 ft) in diameter at its summit (fig. 9.1). At Hen Domen the bailey is quite small, covering no more than a third of an acre, but it is heavily defended with double ramparts and ditches and excavation of the junction of the motte and the bailey rampart has shown that at Hen Domen the motte was a primary feature of the site's design.

The castle was built on a ridge of boulder clay overlying shale, and this boulder clay was an excellent material for the construction of the motte, the digging of the ditches and the piling up of the ramparts, as well as being used for the wall cladding of some of the timber structures. The pebbles and small boulders which the clay contained were separated out and used for pebble floors and the packing of post-holes and so on. There is no evidence that any part of Hen Domen was built in stone during its 200-year life.

The history of the castle

As is the case with many timber castles, there are few direct documentary references to Hen Domen which are contemporary with its occupation. Domesday Book (1086) provides the first clear statement of the castle's existence: Roger, earl of Shrewsbury since 1070, had built a castle and called it Montgomery after his home in Normandy. Whether he did this out of nostalgia, or as an aggressive act of defiance against the Welsh, is not clear. Perhaps he intended to establish a town and priory, classic features of Norman colonization in Britain, though he never did so. The castle (which, had it not, after its abandonment, acquired a Welsh name, would have been referred to as Old Montgomery) certainly became a base for conquest in central Wales: by 1086 considerable tracts of Powys were under Roger's control (see fig. 3.24), though, since he was an important figure in the Anglo-Norman world, he probably played little personal part in these attacks.

9.1 Hen Domen,
provisional site plan.

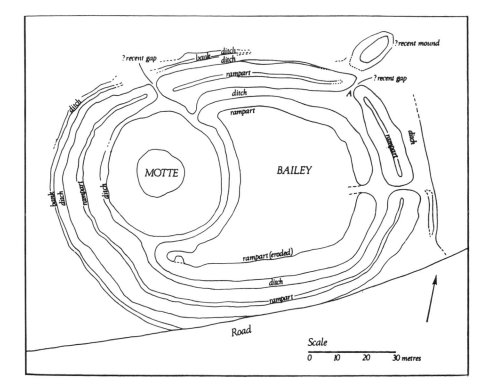

9.2 Hen Domen, the
context of the site.

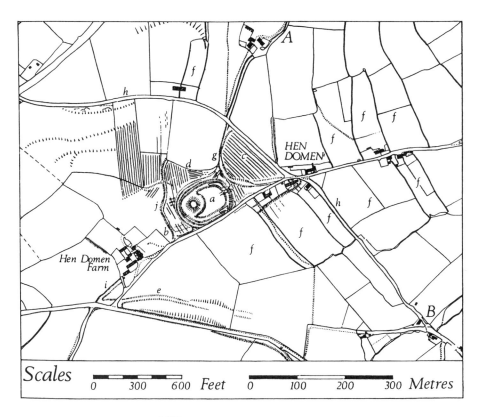

Many other small castles sprang up in the Vale of Montgomery (see fig. 2.1) and along the Severn Valley as a result of increasing Norman influence, but in 1095, the garrison of Hugh, Roger's son, was massacred in a Welsh attack, so the Norman conquest of the area did not go unchecked. This first phase of the castle's history came to an end with the fall of Robert of Bellême, Hugh's brother, in 1102. In rebellion against King Henry I Robert was expelled from England and his lands on the Welsh border and in Sussex and Yorkshire were confiscated. The earldom of Shrewsbury became a royal shire, the Welsh conquests were lost and Old Montgomery and the lands immediately around it became a new marcher lordship. In this first phase, the structural evidence, simple and massive, is a good reflection of the strongly military character of the occupation.

The family of de Boulers (Baldwin I, Stephen, Robert and Baldwin II) held Old Montgomery until 1207. They were far less rich and powerful than the earls of Shrewsbury had been and this was their only castle and its lordship the limit of their powers, though they acquired lands elsewhere through marriage into a Yorkshire family. In this second phase of its existence, however, the castle had important domestic and administrative functions as well as military ones. Sometimes the de Boulers were at war with the Welsh, but not always: one of them married a princess of Powys. Their local tenants provided a garrison

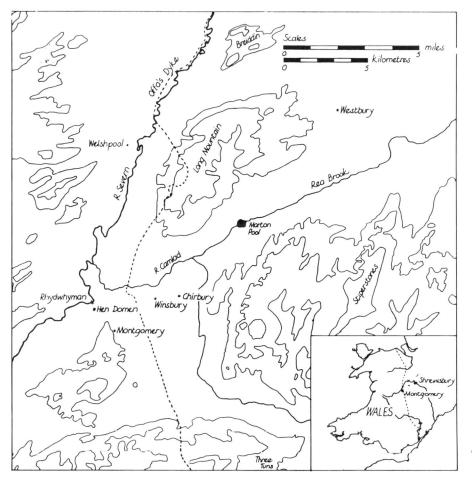

9.3 Location map of Hen Domen.

and hunting attendants, as well as provisions for the castle. The lord of Hodnet, an outlying manor in Shropshire, was their steward, periodically bringing his family to Old Montgomery and being provided with suitable lodgings to carry out his business. The de Boulers never rose to the highest ranks of Marcher society, but they were undisputed lords of their own territory, much of which would be visible from the tower which crowned the top of the motte at Hen Domen. It is from this phase that the fullest archaeological picture of the castle has been recovered (see below). Its defences and crowded courtyard of domestic buildings well reflect the mixture of military and domestic life that characterized the longest single period in the site's history.

By 1207 the family had died out and their lands passed to the king. The sheriffs of Shropshire maintained the castle, but in 1215 the area passed into Welsh control, and the archaeological evidence suggests that the castle was abandoned. In 1223, in renewed war against the Welsh, Henry III planned its refortification, but a new site nearby, the rock of Montgomery, was chosen for a much larger stone castle. All later references to Montgomery castle are to the new castle and Hen Domen disappears from history. The archaeological evidence, however, suggests that the site was reoccupied around 1223, and the explanation for this probably lies in the local topography (fig. 9.3). The crossing of the river Severn at Rhyd Whyman, not visible from New Montgomery, continued to be an important meeting place of Welsh and English down to the 1270s, when the end of the Welsh wars reduced the political importance of Montgomery. As a forward control point for the river crossing, the first castle probably had a final lease of life of fifty years' duration. In this period, however, it was a purely military outpost and had none of the social functions of the twelfth-century castle. The contraction of the occupied area in the latest

structural phase reflects this change of character very well (see fig. 9.8).

The structural evidence and its interpretation

The buildings which are described below in simplified terms were represented in the ground by very complex evidence which varied greatly in character. In addition, the problems of reconstructing and dating the site's structural development may be considered.

Four main construction techniques were used, and the builders seem to have chosen whatever method seemed most appropriate to the materials available and the function of the particular building. In the earliest castle (see fig. 9.4), the massive foundation trench of Building LIa, nearly 1 m (3¼ ft) wide and deep, held horizontally laid timbers with uprights morticed into them, either at intervals with other infilling or perhaps continuously as in stave-built churches. The massive character of such timbers is revealed by the survival at the foot of the motte ditch of the base plate of the adjoining bridge, which was some 0.3 m square (1 ft) and 4.5 m (15 ft) long (see fig. 9.4). Secondly, there were buildings with individual posts set in large post-pits. A twelve-post building (XXXVIII) of the earliest castle, which survived for many years, took this form (see figs 9.4, 9.5). Preserved fragments in the bottom of some of the post-pits of this structure showed the uprights to have been some 0.5 m (1¾ ft) in diameter. Thirdly, some buildings were represented by lines of much smaller posts which alone could not have provided support for the walls. Wattle and daub may sometimes have been employed, but in some places the remains of clay walling survived at foundation level, particularly for building XXII in the middle period (see fig. 9.5). Here the walls were some 0.75 m (2½ ft) thick and the timbers provided only a skeleton around which the clay was built up. Fourthly, some post-sockets were so shallow that they can only represent the setting of timbers belonging to buildings which were self-supporting, with framed timbers throughout their superstructures. Buildings of this type were found in the earliest phase (e.g. XXVI and XXVII) and almost exclusively in the latest phase of the site (see figs 9.4, 9.8). Although in most periods there was a mixture of building techniques, there was apparently no use of ground sills or fully framed buildings in the middle period when the de Boulers were in occupation. This could indicate that their supplies of good timber were more restricted than were those of the Montgomery family before them and the royal custodians who followed them.

It is hoped eventually to publish a reconstruction drawing for each phase of the site. The first of these is included here (fig. 9.6) and represents the middle period, X, for which the fullest plan is available. It is discussed below in detail, but may be introduced here briefly since it arises directly from consideration of the structural techniques outlined above. As with all archaeological reconstructions of timber buildings, it is reliable in ground plan and basic building technique for each structure, but choices of wall cladding, roofing materials, details of doorways, windows and many other aspects are more speculative. Sometimes the plan of a building reveals something of its superstructure. Building XLVIII, in the middle period, has opposing walls with different numbers of posts, so that its roof must have rested on wall plates: it cannot have been a building composed of bays. Very often, however, decisions about superstructure rest upon a general knowledge of medieval buildings and on common sense. Since there have been no finds of roof slates, and since thatch would present a fire hazard in a crowded site for which attack was always a threat, planking and shingles seem the logical choice of roofing material. Shingles are

also well attested in the documentary history of castles generally. For the most part decisions about reconstructional detail depend upon using the repertoire of techniques for which there is some evidence somewhere on the site. The use of clay-walling, for example, has been liberally suggested.

Finally, the difficulties of dating the structural development of the site should be emphasized. The overall dating rests heavily upon the documentary framework outlined above. It is assumed that the earliest castle dates from between 1070 and 1086, and that the latest castle dates from after 1223. There is also some archaeological evidence which corresponds with the two ends of the overall date range: Stamford ware (eleventh-century pottery from eastern England) was associated with the earliest castle, and late-thirteenth-century pottery with its decline. But between these two major horizons lay a multitude of structural events, both major and minor, whose dating is not assisted by the documentary, or any other evidence. It is tempting to relate the middle period plan (phase X) to the acquisition of the castle by the de Boulers in 1102. But the rebuilding may not have been embarked upon immediately. In any case, the north-western part of the bailey had a structural phase (not illustrated) between the earliest castle and phase X. The latter has therefore been cautiously labelled 'circa 1150' but this can be no more than an approximation. Equally it is impossible to decide whether phase Y, succeeding X, was within the de Boulers' occupation, or whether it reflects the period of Royal custody from 1207–15. If the former, then some major social change in the use of the site is indicated, as well as a significant change of building technique. Between phases Y and Z, a deep silt layer accumulated in the lowest part of the bailey, suggesting an abandonment. It is quite probable that this coincides with the period of Welsh control of the area from 1215 to 1223. On the whole, however, historical correlations are difficult, and the finds are not sufficiently diagnostic to help date the structural phases. In any case, with the exception of the first and last phases, the phases as presented are greatly over-simplified. The buildings here separated out into individual plans were probably the product of a more continuous process of repair and replacement. It cannot be proved that all the structures presented in one plan were erected at the same time, nor that they were demolished at the same time, but simply that at some stage in their use they were contemporary with each other.

The earliest castle (fig. 9.4)

The earliest structure of Roger of Montgomery's castle was a low marking-out bank of clay and turf piled up along the course of the rampart which was soon to be built over it. This bank, some 1.5 m (5 ft) wide, levelled up the downward slope at the point where the front timbers of the palisade were to be erected. It has not been traced throughout the northern defences of the castle, and it is interesting that it did not appear at precisely the point where some of the palisade timber positions were also elusive – perhaps there were details in the design of the defences which are now impossible to detect. At the extreme north-west corner the bank was higher and broader, although it was badly mutilated here by rabbit burrows. Perhaps this was the site of a tower, and a similar mound some 20 m (66 ft) further east may have carried an interval tower. These putative towers must have been heavily-framed structures, since they left no evidence in the ground. At the bailey entrance, a curving row of posts was sunk into the ground. It is not clear whether these represent a tower (tentatively called building LVI), or simply a revetment holding back the rampart material in a vertical wall flanking the entrance passage. Another large post-pit here may

represent a support for a fighting platform which bridged the entrance. The palisade defending the northern half of the bailey was not uniform throughout its length; in the north-west corner the rear posts supporting the fighting platform were some 3.5 m (11 ft) behind the front posts (building XXVIII); further east they lay only 1.5 m (5 ft) behind (building LV). This difference between the upper and lower halves of the bailey became more marked in later phases of the castle's development and subsequent palisades were of the narrower design. Despite this difference the evidence for all the posts was similar in that none stood in excavated post-holes. They stood directly on the laying-out bank (or the pre-castle field surface immediately behind), or in shallow depressions (perhaps the result of settling) or on pads of clay. The raising of the bank created a horizontal base for the front and rear posts, possibly indicating that the timbers were cut to pre-set lengths: perhaps the entire structure was prefabricated. There was no evidence on the ground of horizontal beams linking the front and rear posts; if they existed they were jointed in slightly higher up; if there were no such beams the uprights must have been supported in position while the rampart was piled around them. The rampart itself, dug from the surrounding ditch, was a largely undifferentiated dump of boulder clay and stones, in which tip lines were visible but no major periods of construction were apparent. Fence 17, located in the extreme north-west, and partially further east, may have been a revetment to control the tail of the rampart as it was dumped. From the rampart the palisade timbers must have risen at least 4 m (13 ft) to provide a breastwork tall enough to protect a man on the fighting platform and to allow access beneath.

The tail of the rampart did not long remain in this form. In the north-west corner, two small buildings (XXVI and XXVII) of which only the floor areas survived, were inserted.

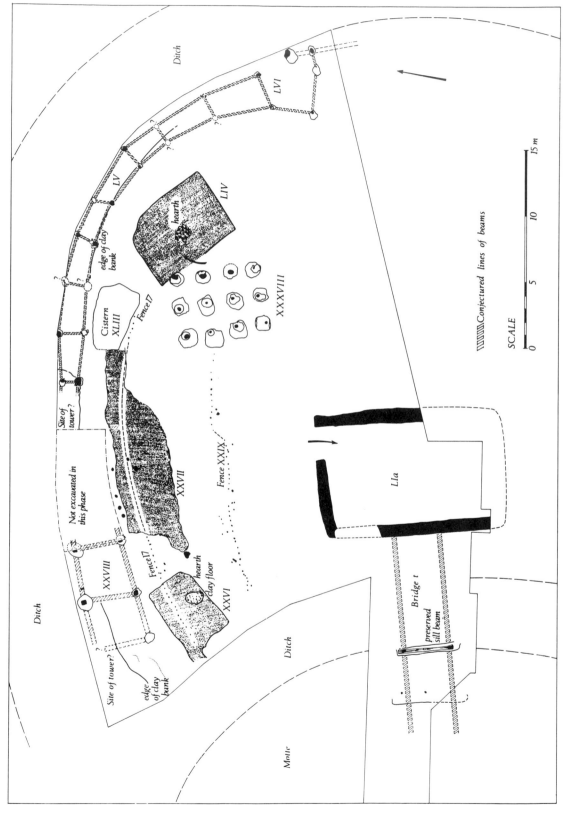

Ditch

Ditch

LVI

LV

LIV

hearth

edge of clay bank

Cistern
XLIII

Fence 17

XXXVIII

Site of tower?

Not excavated in this phase

XXVII

Fence XXIX

XXVIII

Fence 17

hearth

clay floor

XXVI

Site of tower?

edge of clay bank

Ditch

Motte

LIa

Bridge t

preserved sill beam

15 m

10

5

SCALE

0

Conjectured lines of beams

As illustrated, XXVII is represented by charred timbers, clay and charcoal from its destruction rather than a floor, but XXVI had a laid clay floor. The lack of wall foundations suggests that these were built of framed timbers. Further east lay building LIV, erected on a platform of clay and with walls represented by small post-holes whose timbers were perhaps clad in clay. Probably also belonging to this phase of additions was the digging of the first water cistern (XLIII) at the lowest point of the bailey. This was to remain, with alterations, throughout much of the castle's life.

Adjacent to building LIV was a massive structure with twelve deeply founded posts in four rows of three, set at close intervals. The post-pits of this building (XXXVIII) had been dug so that their bottoms were level to within 0.1 m (4 in), again suggesting some prefabrication of the timbers. Radiocarbon dating from the preserved bases of two of the posts produced results of 1054 ± 70 and 971 ± 70 (corrected dates) which may indicate the reuse of timbers from an earlier structure elsewhere. The close spacing of these timbers suggests that this building was not a domestic dwelling but a structure designed to resist the outward thrust of stored material, and a granary is the most likely interpretation. In addition, its proximity to the probable western entrance of building LIV suggests strongly that in this phase the twelve posts carried their superstructure high enough off the ground to allow access beneath it. This building had a long life, continuing through major reconstructions of the castle (see below).

Of similarly massive character was the building (LIa) occupying a central position in front of the motte ditch. This is represented by a foundation trench up to 1 m (3¼ ft) wide in places and cut deeper on the west (up slope) side so that its bottom was more or less level.

9.4 Hen Domen, the earliest castle.

This trench would have comfortably held horizontal timbers similar to a preserved example which lay in a trench at the bottom of the adjacent motte ditch. This sill beam, the foundation of the first bridge, was 4.5 m (15 ft) long and 0.3 m (1 ft) square. It had mortices near its ends to carry uprights for a bridge nearly 4 m (13 ft) wide. A timber slot and two post-holes on the motte side represented further elements of this bridge. A socket in the underside (and therefore redundant) of the preserved bridge timber is a further indication of the reuse of old timbers and prefabrication in the earliest castle's design, of which other evidence was quoted above. The proximity of the bridge to building LIa, as well as the comparable sizes of the preserved timber and its foundation trench suggest strongly that access to the bridge was via the building. The massiveness of the foundations also suggests that this building may have been of two storeys, perhaps a first-floor hall, the major residence within the bailey of the earliest castle. Fence XXIX, between this building and those behind the rampart, may represent an internal division of the bailey screening the main residence from lesser structures. Building LIa itself became the site of a further structure in the next phase and was of long-lasting influence in the site's development.

Restricted access to the motte bridge via building LIa would add another dimension to the defensibility of the motte, especially since the ground-floor entrance was in the northern wall of the building rather than facing the bailey entrance. If the motte tower to which the bridge led was constructed along similar lines as the rest of the earliest castle then, together with the bridge and building LIa and the palisade with its towers, it would have made a formidable sight in a landscape whose other buildings were of a much slighter character.

The twelfth-century castle
(figs 9.5 and 9.6)

The earliest castle underwent various modifications, with evidence of a new palisade and other structures dug into the top of the rampart in the north-west corner. The date of these changes is not known, nor is the date by which the bailey was transformed into the new layout for which we have the fullest plan, phase X, so far available. It is referred to here as mid-twelfth century and represents the de Boulers' castle. Fig. 9.6 is an attempt to show what the bailey looked like in this period, and is based as closely as possible on the excavated evidence. Some elements in the plan survived from the earliest castle, notably the granary building XXXVIII and the site of the cistern XLIII, but in many other respects the plan was different in detail, as well as being generally more built up. Phase X was principally composed of post-hole structures and there was evidence for extensive use of clay as solid walls (Buildings XII, XXII) or as cladding to thicken a skeleton of posts and wattles (the outer and inner palisades and the rooms beneath the inner fighting platform). The reconstruction and plan are here discussed progressively from the motte down to the bailey entrance.

There was virtually no evidence for the form of Bridge x, but the massive supports for the following Bridge y suggest that that bridge could be raised in some fashion as an early form of drawbridge. Accordingly, a leaf of the bridge in the reconstruction has been shown raised. Similarly, there is little evidence for the palisade and fighting platform shown encircling the base of the motte, except that when a chord was cut across the motte there were a number of large post-holes which seemed to have no other function, though they made no coherent pattern. It seems highly probable that there was some form of defence here since, if there were not, the motte would be defended only by the outer, more flimsy, palisade and whatever structures there were at its top, which would make it unacceptably weaker than the bailey.

In the earliest castle there was unequivocal evidence of a very large building at the foot of the motte, probably a hall which was, perhaps, of two storeys (see above). Building LIb seems to have been a post-hole building of the same dimensions and is here reconstructed as such. This building has been shown clad with a shingle roof.

Building XIV/XIII is here reconstructed as an apsidal chapel, on the grounds that it directly underlay the more convincing chapel of Phase Y and because from post-hole 13/48 came the remains of a limestone stoup for holy water. At the north-western end of the chapel is tower XVI on the thickened end of the bailey rampart. It is reconstructed as being of three storeys with a flat roof (as, for example, the southern tower at Stokesay castle, Shropshire) since, though it may have had a gabled roof, it is an awkward shape and a flat roof seems more probable.

The palisade which encircled the bailey is presumed to have been of clay, reinforced with a post and wattle skeleton, since the post-holes which make up its evidence are of many sizes, some quite small and dug in a wandering line along the rampart crest. The palisade itself is presumed to be some 4 m (13 ft) high, as it was in the earliest castle. In the reconstruction the lower part of the palisade is shown clay-clad, while the upper part is of vertical planking, jettied out over the ditch, with hoardings and, in places, various forms of roofing, chiefly to demonstrate the possibilities rather than be definitive, since there is no evidence for these elaborations. However, the jettied upper storey of the north tower at Stokesay has now been shown to be contemporary with the tower of about 1295–1305 and while the beginnings of jettying are unknown, it is interesting to see, for instance, an eleventh-century capital from the Abbaye aux Dames at Caen which depicts an elephant and castle in which the castle (which is nothing like a howdah) has a tower with a semi-circular headed door or window and a jettied crenellated upper storey (fig. 5.9c).

The roofing of the fighting platform is again purely conjectural, but there is, for example, clear evidence that the fighting platform at Goodrich Castle, though a good deal later, was roofed at the back with a pentice. In a small castle such as Hen Domen, there would be a real possibility of being hit in the back by an arrow shot from the other side of the castle, so that a roof would be a sensible precaution.

An unexpected discovery was that the bailey itself had been divided into two halves by a continuous series of buildings running south from Building XXII (ironically, almost exactly along the line of the baulk between the two stages of the excavation). The reconstruction of this line of buildings poses considerable problems but, as it seems intended for defence, rather than to be, for example, simply a social division (which it may also have been), we have incorporated a fighting platform across the whole complex. This fighting platform is suggested not only by the continuous barrier of buildings but also by a change in design from the first hall to Building LIb on the same plan, with its extra row of outer posts on its eastern side. Building XXII and the other structures to its west formed a group partly domestic, partly industrial in character. XXII, with its clay walls and central hearth, must have been a well insulated lodging (a nursery?) and the remains of a similar structure may be represented by XII. The floor of XV was littered with scrap iron, perhaps debris from a workshop and smithy.

To the east of the central division there are two prominent buildings – the granary, XXVIII, retained from the earliest castle and a lesser hall, XLVIII. The granary is reconstructed here as a sort of Dutch barn, with open or semi-open sides. The smaller hall had a hearth and two small attached rooms, L and

XLIX, at its northern end. Behind the granary lay the cistern, or static water tank, XLIII, set in the lowest part of the bailey, and fed from a gutter, 12.

The tower by the main gate, XLVI, is D-shaped on the plan, but was presumably round, since the evidence for its eastern side is lost in the trees on the front of the rampart. It is reconstructed with a clay-clad lower storey, a jettied upper floor and a conical planked roof, though other variants are, of course, possible.

There is little evidence for the form of the gate. The reconstruction shows a simple gate with a fighting platform forming a bridge above. It is worth noting that the existing earthworks on the other side of the gate's passage do not suggest that there was a second matching tower there. The situation is reminiscent of the modifications at Ludlow, Richmond and Exeter, where the entrance is altered so that the gate lies to one side of a single tower, though the parallel is perhaps more apparent than real. The entrance passage contained a cobbled area with some post-settings. It is not clear whether these represent simply a metalled surface or a building. Neither is shown on the reconstruction.

The evidence for the outer defences comes from the excavation of a short stretch of the outer rampart which showed clearly that there had been a palisade of small post-holes which presumably strengthened a clay wall, backed by a fighting platform lying on the ground surface, rather than raised above it. The outer ditch, which has been sectioned, showed no evidence of an outer bank, or a palisade on its counter-scarp.

Defenders trying to hold these outer defences would be in a desperate plight if the attackers managed to break through to the ditch, so we have tentatively suggested that plank bridges, capable of being quickly withdrawn, might have been provided and one of these is shown.

Whatever the merits of the details of this

Scale

0   5   10   15 metres

Ditch

Motte

Bailey

Bridge x?

Ditch

336

9.6 Hen Domen, reconstruction of Phase X, *c*.1150.

reconstruction, it must echo the realities in a number of ways. The bailey was certainly crowded with buildings – the interior would be claustrophobic – there would be no view into the surrounding open country except from the fighting platform or the towers – in this respect the present earthworks are quite misleading. There was very little open space except immediately within the entrance; the buildings were large, of two or three storeys in some cases and, most importantly, the castle was formidably defended. An attacker approaching from the fields to the north would be faced with concentric defences of quite massive proportions, reinforced by deep

9.5 Hen Domen, the northern half of the bailey, *c*.1150.

ditches, in places mud-, if not water-filled. We estimate that the distance from the bottom of the inner ditch to the top of the bailey palisade was some 10 m (33 ft).

Once an attacker got into the bailey the battle would then become like street-fighting – in many ways the most difficult and fearful kind of fighting – in which each building has to be taken separately, with the attackers surrounded on all sides. The evidence of this phase reveals clearly the dual nature of the castle, with its profusion of domestic buildings of all sizes and its provision of water supply and storage, within a heavily defended perimeter, overlooked by a formidable tower on top of the motte.

The later castle (fig. 9.7)

Either late in the de Boulers' occupation, or after their demise in 1207, the bailey underwent radical changes, partly in the structural techniques employed and partly in the general layout of its buildings. The new structures of this period (phase Y) made little use of upright posts set in pits, the evidence of timbers in the ground comprising shallow sockets outlined in stones where uprights stood and shallow gulleys in which sill-beams rested. In either case the buildings were supported by their own framing. The most striking illustration of the change came from the rampart, where there was little direct evidence of defences. At the north-west corner a pattern of shallow post-sockets and an outline created by intense burning revealed a D-shaped tower (IV) overlying the tower of the preceding phase. Between the bailey and the motte ditch lay a palisade set in normal post-pits (V). Near the bailey entrance the incomplete plan of an oval tower was recovered (XL). Between them, no structural evidence in the ground was apparent. But from the adjacent bailey ditch two timbers were recovered from a waterlogged deposit, each 1.2 m (4 ft) in length with a slot 7.5 cm (3 in) cut in them, pegged at intervals of 0.38 m (15 in). These were probably the base plates of a structure whose upright planks (0.38 m (15 in) wide and 7.5 cm (3 in) thick) would have made a formidable wall. If this sort of technique was used in the defences it would account for the lack of evidence on the rampart.

The impression within the bailey is that the castle was less crowded with buildings in this period. It must be remembered, however, that only half the bailey has been excavated so that we cannot know what changes were also being made elsewhere. The contrasts between phases X and Y may be more apparent than real, if in X the southern half was less crowded than the northern and if in Y vice versa.

Nevertheless there were certainly reductions in both the number and size of buildings. There were hardly any structures behind the rampart in the north-west corner, building VIII being the only obvious feature. The granary was reduced in size by half, to become a six-post building (XXXVIIIa). Most notably, the large hall in front of the motte ditch, which had stood in modified form from the castle's foundation, was removed and not replaced by any building of comparable size, at least not in the northern half of the bailey. Other features of this period were the counterparts of buildings in phase X. A second apsidal building (IX) stood on the site of the earlier putative chapel with the foundation (XI) of a possible bell tower to its north-west.

The cistern continued in use in modified form (LIII) and the massive foundations of a new bridge across the motte ditch lay slightly north of the earlier bridge axis. In the lower part of the bailey a new hall (LII), resting on ground sills in shallow gulleys, lay slightly east of its predecessor. At the bailey entrance the cobbled building (XLII) continued in use from phase X. There were three major additions, probably connected to each other. At the point where the bailey slope became more marked, a flight of crude steps (10) was constructed from pebbles and small boulders. This led to the site of a building (VI) of which only the western end was observed. But since this rested on sill beams it may have extended much further east. Immediately to its west lay a 3 m (10 ft) square rectangular pit (VII) whose un-eroded sides suggest permanent cover in a building formed by post-holes in the palisade along the motte ditch and others to their east. The environmental evidence from this pit will be described below and is of the greatest interest. Originally at least 6 m (20 ft) in depth, its digging had destroyed the foundation trench of the west wall of the hall

9.7 Hen Domen, Phase Y, late twelfth century to early thirteenth century.

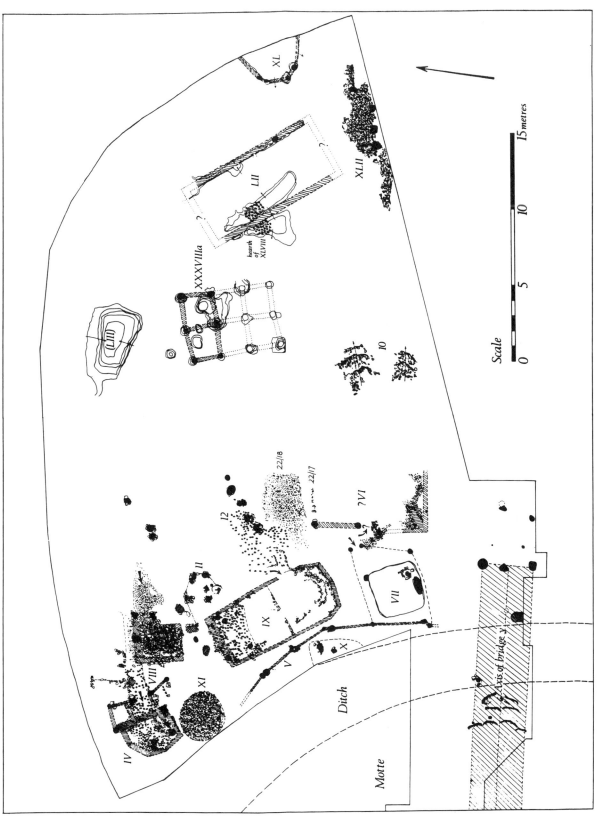

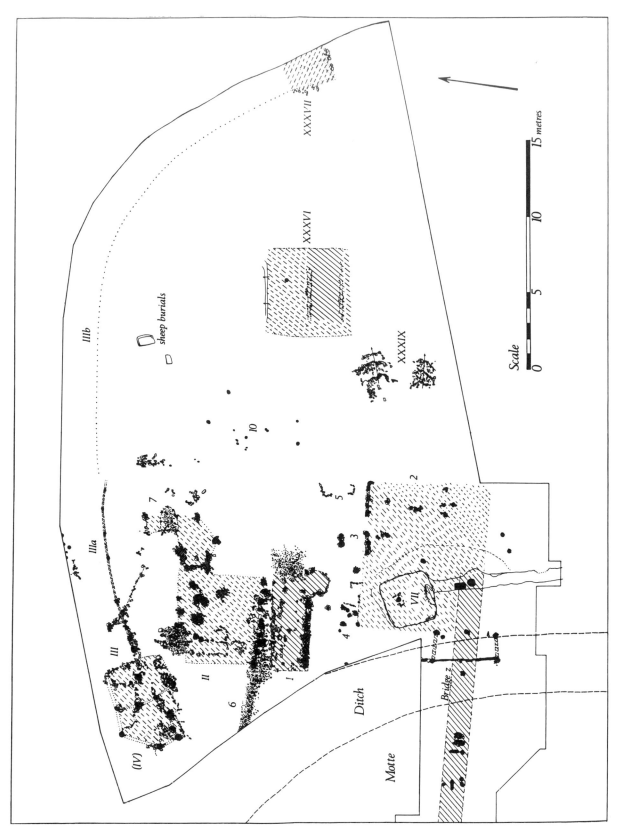

standing in front of the motte bridges. For much of its life it was probably a latrine pit, but it was eventually floored with clay, 1.5 m (5 ft) from its top, perhaps to become a cellar to a structure above. In its probable latrine use it is not clear whether it served only the adjacent building (VI) or the whole bailey. Its proximity to the chapel is somewhat curious, and it is certainly among the more enigmatic features.

The last castle *c.* 1223 – *c.* 1300.
(fig. 9.8)

In the lower parts of the bailey the surfaces of this period (phase Z) lay above a deep layer of silt, whereas in the upper parts they lay immediately above the surfaces of phase Y. The accumulation of this silt represents at least a period of relative disuse, perhaps total abandonment, and it has been suggested above in the history of the site that this was a result of Welsh control of the area from 1215 to 1223. In the subsequent rebuilding there was a major contraction of the built-up area and most of the structures identified lay in the western half, close to the motte. To the east lay a horizontal building platform with an internal partition, and a probable tower site by the entrance. Otherwise, the evidence lay west of the north-south division of the bailey which was most obvious in phase X but had its beginnings in the earliest castle and was also apparent in phase Y. As in phase Y there was evidence of a north-western tower but no sign of a palisade. This may therefore have been of framed construction, as in phase Y, though in the north-west corner the shallow sockets of the fighting platform supports were also located. The foundations of the motte bridge suggest a much narrower structure than any of its predecessors, much closer, in fact, to those gang-plank-like bridges shown

on the Bayeux Tapestry, than any of the earlier bridges here.

Apart from their obvious western concentration, the buildings of this period are difficult to describe. The evidence was wholly of very shallow post-sockets and stone alignments along the edges of buildings. A building of some form stood in front of the motte bridge and incorporated the sunken floor in the top of pit VII described in phase Y. To its north a rectangular structure or structures are indicated as buildings I and II with a pebble path (6) between them and a curiously shaped extension (7) at the north-east corner. The general impression is of a very different sort of bailey from that of the twelfth century though the slightness of the foundations may disguise an unexpected massiveness in the superstructure of the, presumably, framed buildings.

The motte (fig. 9.9)

In 1987 a contour survey of the motte was undertaken, revealing a mound with curves, slopes, straights and irregularities, presumably the product of original construction, alterations in use, demolition and subsequent erosion. Excavation since 1988 has shown that some parts, notably on the west and north, have eroded more than others, and that important evidence has been lost. It is also likely that the last period of occupation has disappeared completely: before the growth of turf stabilized the abandoned mound, erosion of its top and sides had produced the substantial material excavated in the motte ditch in earlier sessions. Beneath the turf lay a deposit of clay soil and stones. During its removal, two low banks of harder and cleaner clay emerged on the north and west. This evidence is tentatively interpreted as the heavily eroded remains of a clay-clad timber structure (building LVIII – not illustrated).

Beneath the latter were preserved the more

9.8 Hen Domen, Phase Z, *c.*1223–1300.

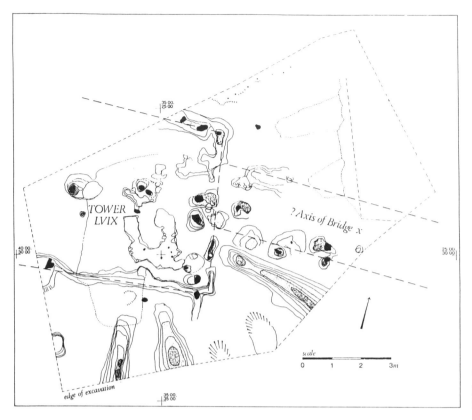

9.9 Hen Domen, provisional plan of motte top, phase X, *c*.1150.

obvious structural features of building LVIX, deliberately backfilled with clay soil and stones. This backfilling provides further evidence for the structural character of the overlying layers, since it would not have been necessary unless a new building was to be erected. Building LVIX was rectangular and occupied a level platform at what is now the western end of the motte top. But heavy erosion, or perhaps a collapse of the motte side, has partly destroyed it. Excavation of this building is still in progress. Evidence so far recovered suggests its walls consisted of timber uprights set in a trench and clad in clay to a thickness of approximately 0.75 m (30 in). It was probably a two-storey tower, providing both a high vantage point and a residence – the finds of pottery, metalwork and animal bones indicate more than occasional occupation. Although further excavation may disprove the idea, it is provisionally interpreted as part of phase X of the castle in which

similar construction techniques were employed. If this is correct, then the post-holes to the east of the building may represent a bridge connecting the motte tower to the large hall excavated in this phase at the west end of the bailey. Earlier features, including small postholes and burned areas, are also emerging, suggesting that a succession of towers or other structures may await discovery.

In contrast to the thin layers and occupation debris of the building platform, the perimeter of the motte comprises deeper deposits of more sterile clay. These are cut by a series of large gullies which extend beyond the limit of excavation on the south and east. They could have three possible explanations (or others as yet unthought of): a series of drainage gullies/garderobe chutes; a succession of bailey-motte bridge terminals; foundations for a fighting platform and revetment around the shoulder of the motte. Objections in detail, which are beyond the scope of this discussion, can be made to all three of these interpretations, and thus the problem awaits further excavation.

The finds

The impression given by the small objects recovered is not that of a rich community. Indeed virtually nothing at all from before *c*.1100 has been recovered. Like the rest of Wales and the Marches, the Montgomery area seems to have been without locally produced pottery from the Roman period until the early twelfth century. From the foundation period of the castle came a very few fragments of Stamford ware – fine glazed jugs from eastern England – and, from the later twelfth-century phase, other products of this industry were also found. Since it is unlikely that this was the result of marketing, the pottery probably came in the baggage of travellers to and from Yorkshire and Lincolnshire: Robert de Boulers had married into a family from this area. The bulk of the pottery recovered is from coarse cooking pots and simple glazed jugs. Study (by Pamela Irving and Alan Vince) has shown that some of these were made locally, others being identical to material found more widely in Shropshire and Hereford and Worcester.

Metal objects are not numerous and are generally functional pieces such as fragments of tools, arrowheads, locks and horseshoe nails. The impression given is of a community whose wealth was not displayed in the sort of possessions which might be found archaeologically and which was economic in its recycling of metal waste. On the other hand, since no rubbish pits have been located, we cannot be certain that the available finds are truly representative of the lifestyle of the inhabitants.

Numerous fragments of unworked wood were recovered from wet deposits in the ditches as well as the structural timbers described above. A well preserved stave-built tub of oak came from the bailey ditch near the castle entrance. Dendrochronological dating (by Ruth Morgan) showed that the tree from which it was made was probably felled in the late eleventh century. This object may have had a very long life before it was dumped in the ditch; alternatively, if it was discarded in the early twelfth century, it reveals that the inner ditch was never cleared out after that date, perhaps because the mud which collected at its bottom added to its defensibility.

Environmental evidence

A rich sample of material was recovered from the deep latrine pit (VII) situated by the motte ditch. Analysis (by James Grieg) revealed a wide range of local flora which had been growing in a variety of habitats: arable land, meadows, marshes, stream sides and woodland. The species included weeds, cereal crops, hedgerow plants, sedges from damp places and birch, hazel, alder, oak and willow from the woodlands. Peas and beans, known to have been an important element in medieval diet, are poorly represented probably because they preserve badly.

Most of the species represented are still found in the modern landscape of the area. In addition, the presence of the dung-feeding beetle and the biting stable fly suggest that some of the contents of the pit derived from stable sweepings, though interestingly no building within the excavated area has been identified as a stable. The pit itself seems to have fulfilled mixed functions as latrine and waste disposal pit. It seems probable that the latrine worked on deep-litter principles since there was a large proportion of charcoal, wood shavings and bracken in it which would have helped to compost the contents. Since it was always protected by a building (see above) the varied flora it contained must have been contained in the rubbish: it cannot have blown in.

Animal bone evidence

This material has been studied by Sue Browne, and came mainly from the ditches, the cistern and especially the latrine pit. Cattle, red and roe deer were well represented in the food remains but sheep were unexpectedly scarce and pig bones were very numerous indeed. Some dog and cat bones as well as marks of carnivorous gnawing on many bones, suggest that domestic animals were kept in the bailey. Plentiful butchery marks on bones of all species suggest that animals were brought to the site live for slaughter or as whole carcases. Fowl, goose, pheasant and woodcock added variety to the inhabitants' diet, but there was virtually no evidence of fish consumption. Since, however, the materials studied came from restricted areas and bone remains survived badly elsewhere on the site, great care must be applied in generalizing about two centuries of food supply and the excavation of a kitchen site might change the overall picture, especially as most of the evidence came from the latrine pit, which was a fairly late addition to the castle's development. Individual items were also of great interest. Green stains on the bones of a goshawk may suggest that it was a ringed hunting bird. The bones of eight new born piglets from the latrine pit suggest that their mother was kept within the bailey, and a complete boar skeleton in the ramparts must represent an animal which was for some reason considered unfit for consumption even by the dogs.

Discussion

Roger of Montgomery was one of William the Conqueror's greatest magnates and the castle which he built on the edge of Wales was sufficiently important to him to be named after his birthplace in the Calvados region of Normandy. On the fall of Robert de Bellême and the demise of the Earldom of Shrewsbury in 1102, the castle passed to a lesser family,

that of the de Boulers. The lordship attached to the castle was, nevertheless, quite extensive, comprising the lands in the immediate vicinity of the castle, the adjacent hundred of Chirbury, and outlying manors in Shropshire, and there were family possessions in other counties as far away as Yorkshire, Lincolnshire, Suffolk and Wiltshire, acquired through marriage during the course of the twelfth century. Moreover, the first head of the de Boulers family, Baldwin, was married to a woman, Sybil de Falaise, who was perhaps one of the bastard daughters of Henry I. Montgomery Castle (that is, Hen Domen, as it later came to be known) was the *caput* of the new marcher lordship, and remained until the early thirteenth century the military, social and judicial centre of the estates held by the de Boulers.

Since the beginning of the excavation, therefore, our understanding of everything found, from the plans of buildings to pottery, arrowheads to horseshoe nails, has been coloured by the knowledge that this was an aristocratic site of crucial strategic importance in this part of the Welsh border, since it is situated close to a major ford over the river Severn.

But there have been, even after 30 seasons of intensive excavation, no finds which could dispassionately be called 'aristocratic', nothing, apart from the defences themselves, to suggest that the site was occupied by a succession of wealthy and powerful families. It therefore occurred to the writer to wonder how, if we could clear our minds of all preconceptions, we would interpret Hen Domen? What conclusions would we draw about the people who lived here if we knew nothing of medieval life? What, in fact, distinguishes it from a small prehistoric defended site?

The presence of the motte precludes the earthworks from looking prehistoric but there are a number of ringworks in the region which cannot, on inspection, be dated more closely than within a bracket which includes the later Bronze Age at one end and the later thirteenth century at the other, and, if one stands with one's back to the motte, the bailey at Hen Domen could well be one of these.

The structural evidence revealed by the excavation is very varied, but none of it is different in kind from the methods of timber-building used in the previous thousand or more years. The most sophisticated structures implied by the Hen Domen evidence are timber-framed, with their sills lying on the ground or in sleeper-beam trenches. Such buildings require accurate joints, and two waterlogged timbers found in the outer ditch demonstrate this, though the preserved sill-beam of the earliest bridge (presumably built on the orders of Roger of Montgomery himself) has crude joints with unnecessarily large and therefore less efficient mortices. There is nothing here which could not have been fashioned at least from Roman times onwards – there are no suggestions of the highly elaborate joints of only slightly later date found in barns and church roofs.

Other forms of buildings, with post-holes and wattle walls, or clay walls strengthened with small irregularly-spaced posts are undatable in style, as were perhaps the buildings they represent. The writer always intended, when reconstructing the Hen Domen buildings, to have them bristling with dragons at the corners, like the motte towers on the Bayeux Tapestry or the stave churches of Norway, or the church at Kilpeck, only 80 km (50 miles) away. But, though a good deal of waterlogged worked timber has been found, none of it has any decorative carving, even of the simplest king – all is utilitarian. Nor have any of the pieces of leather found been tooled or punched decoratively.

In fact, the earliest levels on the site, those datable before c.1125, yield almost no finds at all. There are tiny scraps of pottery derived from pots thought to have been imported from elsewhere, probably the Midlands. The only finds of metal are nails, knives, arrow-heads and other less identifiable objects. The finds are, in fact, little different in quality or quantity from those found at a small defended Cornovian site at Sharpstones Hill, Shrewsbury, dug by the writer and others in 1965, and the Cornovii have been described by Graham Webster as 'a poor, backward rural community'. We seem to be getting close to Mortimer Wheeler's description of William the Conqueror as a 'scratch-mark-ware chieftain'.

Is this fair? Did Roger's men and Baldwin's family live like Cornovian peasants? (Or was the Iron Age site itself the home of a Cornovian aristocratic family? Their round houses were certainly bigger than any building yet found at Hen Domen, even if not so substantially founded.) It may be argued that a closer prehistoric parallel to Hen Domen is the hillfort on Fridd Faldwyn, only a few hundred yards away, excavated by B.H. St J O'Neil. Here the defences were built and rebuilt on an increasingly formidable scale, and the structural timbers, attested by the size of the post-pits, were massive. Although only a comparatively small proportion of the site was excavated, the area was as great as that at Hen Domen, yet only one sherd of Iron Age pottery was found, together with a very small number of other finds from a community which must, on any reckoning, have been large and flourishing.

The contrast with the Roman sites of the area, such as Forden Gaer and Wroxeter, sandwiched in time between Fridd Faldwyn and Hen Domen, is startling. At Wroxeter the quantities of pottery and small finds of all kinds are enormous – 86,000 sherds of pottery have been recovered, from the upper layers only, of an area approximately 140 m × 30 m (459 ft × 98 ft); the annual yield of coins is about 250 and there are hundreds of brooches, hairpins and beads, together with all kinds of decorative metalwork, carved objects of bone, shale and jet. There is also much evidence of trade with the continent and as far away as the eastern Mediterranean. From Hen Domen, by contrast, the only non-local sherds are fragments of Stamford Ware, both early and late types, and a sherd of the thirteenth century from northern France.

Yet both Wroxeter and Hen Domen lack one vital strand which we know was of the greatest significance in the lives of their inhabitants – at neither site is there any evidence of Christianity. If we knew nothing of Romano-British or Anglo-Norman culture we should have no inkling from these sites of that all-pervading influence. Yet there is every reason to believe that there was a bishop of Wroxeter from the fourth century onwards, that is, the period under excavation there, and the Normans were devout fighters who did penance for the souls of those they killed.

It should be pointed out that the building at Hen Domen identified, with some reservation, as a chapel is only considered to be so because of its tri- or quadri-partite apsidal shape and because, by analogy with so many surviving stone castles, one expects a chapel in a castle. A building of similar plan on a Romano-British site would be differently interpreted, since many apsidal Romano-British buildings seem to be purely domestic. As an extension of this somewhat tendentious way of thinking, the vessel from Hen Domen identified as a stoup for holy water was only thought to be so because it came from the 'chapel' area and because similar mortar-like vessels have elsewhere apparently been used in this way, for example, mortared into the porches of existing churches. In another context, this interpretation would probably not have occurred to us.

If so powerful a force as Christianity cannot easily be detected, other aspects of the spiritual and intellectual life of the site will be equally elusive. We may guess, from the deer and wild boar bones on the site, that Baldwin and his entourage enjoyed hunting, but we do not know their taste in poetry and music –

if any. And, though we can assume from what we know of castle life in general that Baldwin's wife and children lived with him, there is little, if anything, among the finds to suggest the presence of women and nothing, such as toys or feeding bottles (known elsewhere in pottery), to suggest children. It is probable that Roger's first castle was a garrison entirely manned by soldiers and that from 1102 onward the castle became residential, but there is at present no archaeological evidence to support this assumption except in the very general sense that there is much more occupation debris from the twelfth century.

This is rapidly becoming an essay on the limitations of archaeological evidence, which was not the original intention. What, therefore, can we say positively about the site in its earlier years and about the people who lived there?

Everything points to a life of great simplicity, shorn of extraneous trappings and ornament. The bailey is, at all times, crowded with buildings, but only two have any sign of heating (though the use of braziers, perhaps even in upper rooms, and therefore not archaeologically discernible, cannot be discounted). The impression one gets is of a life of great hardiness, lived mainly out of doors, except in the worst weather and at night – not unlike all-year-round camping. There is nothing to suggest literacy among any of the castle's inhabitants; they clearly used very little coin (one coin only has been found in 30 years' of excavation); they ate, as one would expect, beef, mutton and pork and some deer (though there is less antler, worked or unworked, than one would expect); there is very little bread wheat and no sign of cultivated fruits, such as plum or apple (though there are some wild blackberries) and no imported delicacies such as figs or grapes. The picture is, in fact, very close to that of the hard simple life, spent chiefly in the open, and with few social graces, that one would deduce from the excavation of prehistoric sites here or elsewhere on the border.

By the early thirteenth century all had changed. The new stone castle at Montgomery was decorated with stiff-leaf capitals as fine as the contemporary ones at Westminster, Wells or Worcester, and with elegant mouldings for the glazed windows, and it is reasonable to assume that the rest of the castle was in keeping. Even allowing for the fact that New Montgomery Castle was a royal foundation, and that the de Boulers were, by comparison, poor, nevertheless, Hen Domen is the site of their only castle and one might expect what movable wealth they had to be concentrated there. It has been suggested that the de Boulers and similar families might have had their wealth tied up in livestock rather than in

finery – if so, the comparison with prehistoric peoples is even closer. At Hen Domen, and particularly in the earlier decades, we seem to be in a quite different world from that of the courtly aristocratic life commonly envisaged in the medieval castle.

Nevertheless, the evidence excavated at Hen Domen demonstrates that timber castles could be permanent, substantial fortifications with impressive accommodation. Timber castles were not, as they are so often made out to be, temporary, second-rate erections, easily overcome and replaced in stone as soon as possible. This castle dominated its landscape for two centuries and was rebuilt, always in timber (and clay) several times. The earthworks of these monuments are only a pale reflection of their true character.

— 10 —

Epilogue

The evidence assembled here illuminates a feature of medieval life widely distributed in both time and space. Medieval timber castles belonged to a tradition of fortification which was already ancient and which has been continuously employed down to the present century. Some castles were always of timber. Some major castles, best known in stone, had timber origins. Though timber castles varied greatly in size, many were massive. All were conspicuous in their contemporary landscapes.

The evidence for timber castles is nevertheless deficient. The surviving earthworks are an impressive but structurally limited record. The excavated evidence comes from a tiny proportion of the known sites, and new discoveries could easily alter existing impressions. The documentary highlights come from sources largely written for specific purposes tangential to our needs. The pictorial evidence is restricted in quantity and so idiosyncratic as to make generalizations impossible. There is a degree of general harmony between these categories of evidence, but sometimes they provide divergent views of our subject. No excavation, for example, could ever indicate the complex superstructures described in the twelfth century at Ardres or Durham.

Another point of contrast concerns the character of a large number of the buildings which stood in timber castles. Some of the chronicle and administrative sources reveal the use of prefabricated timbers, especially in the twelfth and thirteenth centuries. Some archaeological evidence of this practice has also come from excavations. In some cases, for example the reuse of earlier timbers in the first phase at Hen Domen, this method of building may simply have been expedient, the new structures being improvised with timbers taken from other structures. But on the scale suggested by the documentary sources, the prefabrication of structures in general rather suggests that carpenters were working to designs whose main features were known in advance. There may well have been fairly standardized patterns of bretasches, which, as sometimes described, could be dismantled, transported and erected a second time. The excavated evidence, in contrast, reveals a picture of almost endless variation: no two sites have produced similar plans. It is impossible to suggest categories of timber castle buildings, other than those such as domestic halls which also occur in other contexts; the structures excavated on or in mottes are particularly diverse. Individuality was obviously a characteristic of timber castles no less than of stone ones.

This problem may partly be one of survival of evidence. Prefabricated structures, by their very nature, are likely to have used techniques of carpentry which made buildings more or less self-supporting and not dependent on ground-fast foundations. Such buildings would leave few traces detectable by excavation. The base-timbers from the bailey palisade at Hen Domen, preserved in the ditch below, had left no evidence on the bailey rampart itself. How many apparently featureless surfaces excavated elsewhere, including some motte-tops, may have been the sites of substantial buildings?

In more general terms also, the virtually complete non-survival of structures above ground is a major limitation on our appreciation of these sites. In medieval buildings generally, both secular and ecclesiastical, much changed between the tenth and fourteenth centuries. In the more visible remains of stone castles very striking changes in design and style can be seen, but the excavated ground-plans and the earthworks of timber castles cannot reveal this sort of information to us. Most of the documentary evidence, too, provides a fairly mundane view of timber castles. Only in a little of the literary and pictorial material do we have a hint of the more ornate aspects of the sites and of the more colourful side of their occupants' lives. The age of chivalry is not something we associate with timber castles because it is so much easier to reconstruct in the context of their better-preserved stone counterparts. But, temporary campaign castles apart, timber castles no less than stone ones were residences of the land-owning class, and the institutions of chivalric life were developing by 1100 at a time when timber castles were flourishing.[1] Timber castles were not necessarily plain in appearance, as the surviving fragments of carved woodwork, at Hereford, Leicester and Farnham indicate (see chapter 6). Their lifespan started in the Romanesque period and finished in the Gothic. It is reasonable to suppose that they were influenced in their appearance by contemporary developments in art and architecture, though in ways which we are unlikely ever to discover.

Timber castles were very adaptable, built on many scales, varying from massive to feeble. They were used by kings and princes, powerful barons, petty lords and knights and sometimes by men of lower status: all were following a long tradition of timber fortification. In 1912, Ella Armitage, whose contribution to the development of this subject was underlined in our first chapter, wrote:

It might be thought that the general expectation of the end of the world in the year 1000, which prevailed toward the end of the tenth century, had something to do with the spread of these wooden castles, as it might have seemed scarcely worth while to build costly structures of stone. But it is not necessary to resort to this hypothesis, because there is quite sufficient evidence to show that long before this forecast of doom was accepted, wood was a very common, if not the commonest, material used in fortification. The reader has only to open his Caesar to see how familiar wooden towers and wooden palisades were to the Romans; and he has only to study carefully the chronicles of the 9th, 10th, 11th and 12th centuries to see how all-prevalent this mode of fortification continued to be.[2]

The varied uses of timber castles continue to be the subject of analysis. Recent publications have illustrated that timber castles could be permanent or occasional residences, long-term fortifications or temporary campaign and siege bases, and could also be the means by which territory was colonized by an expanding indigenous society or by an invading one.[3] The speed with which they could be built has, however, often been exaggerated, by both contemporary and modern writers. A motte and bailey could not be completed in a matter of days, or even weeks. A defensible perimeter might be erected quickly, but the works which would then proceed within it would surely take several months, perhaps a number of building seasons, to complete. Nevertheless, a timber castle could be built more quickly and cheaply than a stone one.

Unfortunately, despite the occasional references to expenditure on timber castles (chapter 4) it seems impossible to estimate what the total cost might have been. In any case, especially in conditions of war, some of the labour may have been pressed rather than paid, and some of the materials requisitioned rather than purchased.

Timber was in general less strong than stone, but the continued use of timber castles shows that the increasing use of stone in the twelfth century did not render them all obsolete. Indeed, they were still of value centuries later at a time when stone castles were massive and sophisticated. Their earthworks, too, had a value of their own – steep to climb and resilient to impact (as later generations of artillery fort designers appreciated). But timber castles had one particular vulnerability: the hazard of fire. That this was a serious problem is revealed in various ways: on the scene at Dinan in the Bayeux Tapestry; in some documented contexts such as the attack on Le Puiset or the destruction of the motte tower at York; and in some excavated contexts such as the burnt-out tower on the bailey rampart at Hen Domen. On the whole, however, excavation of timber castles has not repeatedly revealed evidence of destruction by fire, deliberate or accidental, and the problem was evidently containable. Surprisingly, there is documentary evidence for thatch on domestic buildings on royal castles (see chapter 6), and at Okehampton (Devon) the motte ditch produced quantities of waterlogged straw, perhaps thatch from a late twelfth-century cob building excavated in the bailey.[4]

Fire-risk was reduced in various ways. First, massive timbers are themselves not easy to set alight, especially in temperate climates where they might be dampened by rain for much of the year. Second, buildings whose timbers were to any extent clad in clay would have their own extra immunity. Third, careful management of rain water at various points around a site – in ditches, cisterns and butts – would augment the supply available from a well, providing ready sources of control. It is, however, notable that while some castles, such as Old Sarum, New Montgomery and Beeston, had spectacularly deep wells others did not always possess them: Okehampton depended on a spring outside the castle and a rock-cut cistern within, and at Hen Domen, though a deep pit used for waste disposal may have been a failed well, the evidence for water supply in the excavated half of the bailey is confined to a cistern at the lowest part of the site and a possible water tank in the bailey rampart.[5] Fourth, the buildings, and particularly the defences, of timber castles may also have been protected by additional fireproof cladding, a point discussed as a possible interpretation of features shown on the Bayeux Tapestry and the Westminster capital. In the account of the attack on Le Puiset, coverings on the palisade were mentioned, and this practice, which would leave no evidence susceptible to excavation, may have been widespread. Like so many of the habits of medieval war – movable siege towers, battering rams, artillery engines – the provision of extra cladding of timbers was a device inherited from the ancient world.[6]

Jean Froissart, famous contemporary historian of fourteenth-century war, related in his *Chronicles* how in 1345 at the siege of La Réole (Gascony) the English army constructed two enormous three-storey siege towers (*berefrois*) of timber, each with four wheels. On the side facing the town each tower was covered with boiled hides (*cuir boulit*) as protection against fire and bowshot. These formidable belfries, with a hundred archers on each of their three stages, were rolled up to the town wall, whose ditch had been filled in preparation, and as the archers cleared the wall tops of defenders 200 men with picks undermined the wall.[7]

Whatever steps the occupants of timber castles took to defend themselves, they were clearly sufficiently effective for such sites to stand the test of time. It is important to note, however, that although many were still in use in the thirteenth century and some new ones also appeared at this time, the majority had been established in an earlier age, when siege warfare was less sophisticated. In military terms, timber castles had been conceived to meet mounted soldiers, who had to dismount to fight, and to resist violent, hand-fought attacks on gates and other parts of their perimeters. This helps explain why many are overlooked by higher ground not far away: access was more important to their builders than remoteness. In a later age, characterized by more massive siege engines and mining operations, situations on solid rock outcrops or within extensive water defences were more appropriate. Nevertheless, many stone castles of the later Middle Ages continued to occupy positions chosen by an earlier generation, their builders adapting the sites to meet new fashions.

Widespread though castles were, they did not appear everywhere in Europe to the same extent. The reasons for this lie in complex developments which are beyond the scope of this volume. As argued in the early chapters, the distribution of timber castles was heavily influenced by prevailing natural resources and building practices. Despite its great influence, however, the broader timber-building tradition does not explain all the details of timber castle distribution. This was also a product of political, social and economic circumstances. In southern Europe, where castles were plentiful, the thinning out of specifically timber castle-building is explicable environmentally: the necessary resources became scarcer and the entrenched tradition was one of stone technology. But in the far north, the situation was more complex. Despite its impressive defences of the Viking age and the appearance of castle-building among a restricted class from the twelfth century, Denmark did not experience a proliferation of castles until the later Middle Ages, especially the fourteenth century. It was only then that a sufficiently numerous class of squirearchy consolidated their landed

interests and set up permanent homes on their estates, frequently adopting variations on the motte and bailey theme. In the fifteenth century, the accumulation of a smaller number of extensive estates in the hands of a more powerful group brought a decline in the numbers permanently occupied, though some continued in use as farm sites.[8]

Further north, in Sweden and Norway, the conditions which encouraged the widespread use of timber castles by the land-owning class hardly developed. As in Denmark, some royal strongholds appeared in the twelfth century, at Stockholm, Bergen, Nidaros and elsewhere. In the following century castle-building developed, but remained restricted to a small and powerful class, by now familiar with the stone castle technology of more southerly countries. But the ready availability of a timber building tradition, which dominated secular architecture and is still splendidly displayed in the surviving stave churches of southern Norway, does not seem to have been sufficient in itself to promote the spread of timber castles.[9]

A theme emphasized at the start of this volume was the wider tradition of timber defences to which timber castles belonged. In this context, it is worth noting that a major feature of castle-planning was shared by a variety of sites of many periods: division into two parts, upper and lower or inner and outer, with varying differentiation of defensibility, social status or economic function. The motte and bailey, with its stone counterpart in the keep and curtained enclosure, is loosely paralleled in a very general way by other forms: late Roman towns in Gaul, where the walled area, a defended nucleus of public and administrative buildings, occupied perhaps only a quarter of the whole settlement; Scandinavian trading settlements, such as Birka and Hedeby, with their large enclosures alongside smaller, more defensible sites; the *Hauptburg* and *Vorburg* division found in some early medieval settlements; the fortified villages of Italy which developed through the process of *incastellamento*, in which there might also be an inner division occupied by a seignurial castle; medieval towns with castles, either imposed upon them or as part of a planned urban layout. The point is not to be exaggerated, because the physical details, as well as the dates and social functions of these sites, varied enormously. Nevertheless, bipartite plans, of which the motte and bailey – the best known of all timber castle forms – is an example, had widespread appeal.[10] In other circumstances, the process by which a bipartite castle plan dominated by a motte emerged from a simpler, undifferentiated site has been revealed by excavations in the Rhineland, northern France, England and Ireland.[11]

Happily, research into timber castles flourishes, and the subject now ranks with the long-established study of the stone monuments. In Great Britain and Ireland, fieldwork, excavation and historical study continue to illuminate the many sides of this fascinating, if sometimes enigmatic subject. The formation in 1987 of the Castle Studies Group has made communication between those involved in all aspects of castles research easier. The recent publication of John R. Kenyon's *Medieval Fortifications* (1990) has put timber castles firmly in the wider context of castle archaeology, a task which has long been overdue. In France, a lively debate is maintained on priorities in castle-studies, in which timber castles have a prominent role. One of the best known recent field projects in France, the excavation of the lakeside village site of Charavines-Colletière, has included a study of the surrounding landscape. Its numerous mottes, like the settlements around lake Paladru, resulted from a policy of rural colonization of this area pursued by the counts of Savoy and Dauphiné in the eleventh century.[12] More generally in Europe, the publications of the Château Gaillard conferences provide a means of communicating current work.

Undoubtedly, new research may make much of what is written here seem dated in the foreseeable future. New excavations might throw clearer light on the date of the first mottes, a major outstanding problem: their origins, subject to serious study for a century, are still not fully understood. Others might examine aspects of the subject which we have largely neglected. For example, the economic and social life of timber castle occupants could be analysed through the artefactual and environmental evidence recovered in excavation. Perhaps this was not significantly different from the life of occupants of other sorts of castle, but the subject is worthy of study. Also frequently neglected here have been the political and social circumstances of timber castle builders, which, particularly at the lower levels of castle-building society, deserve fuller research.

But, whatever the limitations of this volume, we must hope that it will achieve one purpose at least. 'Earthwork castles', to which secondary importance is attached in not only the older literature but also in some of the very recent, should disappear for ever. 'Timber castles', a much more meaningful notion, should be recognized as an important feature of the European landscape which persisted for many centuries.

— 11 —

Gazetteer of excavations in Great Britain and Ireland

Introduction

The following list includes sites in the British Isles from which some evidence of timber castles has been recovered by excavation. The sites are not necessarily open to the public. The difficulty of collecting even a remotely representative sample of European excavations has dictated our British coverage, though frequent reference to other material will be found throughout the main text.

Excavations included here vary enormously in extent, from long term research schemes and sizeable rescue projects to the smallest of explorations. No attempt has been made to distinguish one from another, though in many cases the length of the published item will give some indication, and many of the more informative studies are discussed above (chapter 8). This gazetteer is not analytical. It simply indicates the approximate extent of published work, and is to be regarded as a starting-point for further research rather than a definitive statement. The nature of the evidence recovered varies enormously, from substantial remains of timber buildings and defences to fragmentary traces, sometimes buried beneath later stonework. At some sites the evidence is simply of timber, at others it is of stone and timber side by side, and at others the evidence is of stone footings whose character suggested they carried timber superstructures. The gazetteer is therefore extremely heterogeneous, including not only wholly timber castles but also much else. This reflects the similar character of the volume as a whole. A few sites may seem somewhat out of place: Portchester castle is best known for its stone buildings (as well as its surrounding Roman stone defences), but it figures because evidence of timber buildings was also discovered in excavation. When the other timber history of Portchester is also considered – the excavated structures of Anglo-Saxon date and the documentary evidence of medieval works – it is clear how incomplete a view of a complex site can be provided by even such an impressive collection of stone buildings as survive here.

No attempt is made to classify the sites according to physical form, and a few of those included lie on the difficult borderland between castles and moated sites. The latter are, however, generally excluded. Also frequently omitted are excavations which have elucidated mainly earthworks rather than their timber structures. Some are included (for example, Castle Neroche, Somerset) where they have revealed important information on the site's development which has wider implications for the subject as a whole. No claim is made for total coverage and undoubtedly many omissions of all sorts of site will be noted, particularly of those mentioned in journals or newsletters which do not have a wide circulation. Some inclusions may be controversial. For example, the Norman date for the final phase at Dinas Powys

(Glamorgan) has recently been challenged, and a case made for including it in the site's earlier medieval phase (see N. Edwards, A. Lane, eds., *Early Medieval Settlement in Wales* (Cardiff, 1988), 58–61).

The numbers and distribution of excavated sites are not very significant (fig. 11.1). The situation is influenced heavily by the incidence of excavation which, for example, has been much higher in the smaller, northern part of Ireland, than in the larger, southern part. The largest number given is for England, which is also the largest country and has the largest number of sites, but many of its excavations have been small in extent. Differences in the density of castle distribution, within and between the five territories, are also important (see chapter 2). Scotland, for example, though larger than Wales, has few sites in its northern regions. Despite these limitations, the publications assembled here do provide a guide to the quantity and distribution of research up to about 1990, and readers can see at a glance what may exist for any particular area. The pre-1974 county names of sites excavated and/or published up to that date are given in brackets.

In addition to thanking individuals, notably J. Spurgeon (Wales), G. Stell (Scotland) and T. McNeill (Ireland), we would like to acknowledge the following publications, which have made the compilation of the Gazetteer easier:

1. D. Renn, *Norman Castles in Britain* (1968, 1973), in which useful entries on many of the sites in the list will be found in addition to

11.1 Numbers of excavated sites in Great Britain and Ireland (prepared by David Hill).

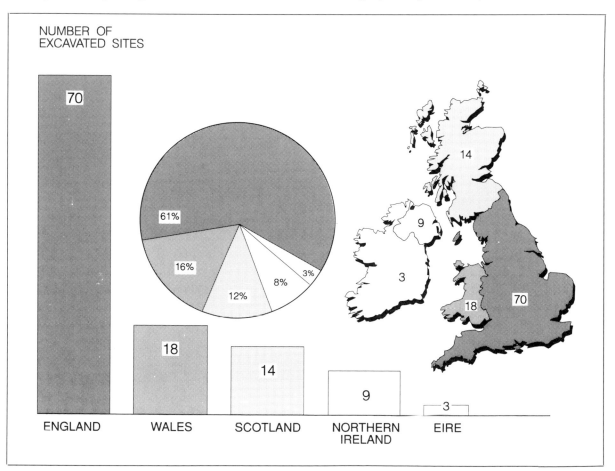

NUMBER OF EXCAVATED SITES

61%

16%

12%

8%

3%

70

18

14

9

3

ENGLAND WALES SCOTLAND NORTHERN IRELAND EIRE

14

9

3

18

70

those specifically quoted as the main source of information. Referred to as Renn 1973.

2. J.R. Kenyon, *Castles, Town Defences and Artillery Fortifications in Britain and Ireland* (3 vols., CBA Research Reports, nos. 25, 53, 72; 1978, 1983, 1990).

3. D.J.C. King, *Castellarium Anglicanum: an*

Index and Bibliography of the Castles in England, Wales and the Islands (2 vols., New York 1983).

4. Annual Notes on excavations published in the journal *Medieval Archaeology* are not quoted here comprehensively. They generally occur either where there is no other reference available or where the site has received only interim publication.

England

BEDFORDSHIRE

1. **Bedford** D. Baker, 'Bedford Castle: some preliminary results from rescue excavations', *Ch.G.*, VI (1973), 15–22.
2. **Biggleswade** P.V. Addyman, 'A Ringwork and Bailey at Biggleswade, Bedfordshire', *Beds. Archaeol. J.*, III (1966), 15–18.
3. **Chalgrave** A. Pinder, B. Davison, 'The excavation of a motte and bailey castle at Chalgrave, Bedfordshire, 1970', *ibid.*, 18 (1988), 33–56.
4. **Eaton Socon** P.V. Addyman, 'Late Saxon settlements in the St Neots area', *Proc. Cambs. Antiq. Soc.*, 58 (1965), 38–73.
T.C. Lethbridge & C.F. Tebbut, 'Excavations on the castle site known as "The Hillings" at Eaton Socon, Beds.', *ibid.*, 45 (1952), 48–60.
5. **Luton** Renn 1973, 355–6.

CAMBRIDGESHIRE

6. **Huntingdon** (formerly Huntingdonshire) *Med. Archaeol.*, XII (1968), 175.

CHESHIRE

7. **Warrington** (formerly Lancashire) Renn 1973, 340.
VCH Lancashire, vol. II (1908), 539–43.

CORNWALL

8. **Launceston** A.D. Saunders, Launceston castle, an interim report', *Cornish Archaeol.*, 3 (1964), 63–9.
A.D. Saunders, 'Excavations at Launceston Castle, 1965–69: interim report', *ibid.*, 9 (1970), 83–92.
A.D. Saunders, 'Excavations at Launceston Castle 1970–1976: interim report', *ibid.*, 16 (1977), 129–37.
Also, *idem, ibid.*, 18 (1979), 80; 19 (1980), 97–8; 20 (1981), 220–1; 21 (1982), 187–8.

CUMBRIA

9. **Aldingham** (formerly Lancashire) *Med. Archaeol.*, XIII (1969), 258–9.
Curr. Archaeol., 2 (1969–70), 23–4.

DERBYSHIRE

10. **Duffield**
T.G. Manby, 'Duffield Castle excavations 1957', *Journal of the Derbyshire Archaeological Society*, 79 (1959), 1–21.

DEVON

11. **Barnstaple** T.J. Miles, 'The excavation of a Saxon cemetery and part of the Norman Castle at North Walk, Barnstaple', *Proc. Devon Archaeol. Soc.*, 44 (1986), 59–84.

12. **Lydford I** *Med. Archaeol.*, IX (1965), 194.
ibid., X (1966), 196–7.
ibid., XI (1967), 263.

13. **Lydford II** A.D. Saunders, 'Lydford Castle, Devon', *ibid.*, XXIV (1980), 123–86.

14. **Totnes** S. Rigold, 'Totnes Castle, recent excavations', *Trans. Devonshire Ass.*, 86 (1954), 228–56.

DURHAM

15. **Barnard Castle** D. Austin, 'Barnard Castle: first interim report', *J. Brit. Arch. Ass.*, 132 (1979), 50–72.
D. Austin, 'Barnard Castle: second interim report', *ibid.*, 133 (1980), 74–96.
D. Austin, 'Barnard Castle, Co. Durham', *Ch.G.*, IX–X (1982), 293–300.

ESSEX

16. **Great Easton** *Med. Archaeol.*, X (1966), 190.
ibid., XI (1967), 284–5.
17. **Pleshey** *ibid.*, IV (1960), 145–6.
ibid., VIII (1964), 252–3.

F. Williams, *Pleshey Castle, Essex (XII–XVI century): excavations in the bailey, 1959–63* (BAR, 42, 1977).
18. **Rayleigh** E.B. Francis, 'Rayleigh Castle: new facts in its history and recent explorations on its site', *Trans. Essex Archaeol. Soc.*, XII (1913), 147–85.
Med. Archaeol., XIV (1970), 176.
S. Rigold, 'Structural aspects of medieval timber bridges', *ibid.*, XIX (1975), 48–91.

GLOUCESTERSHIRE

19. **Bledisloe** A. Dornier, 'Bledisloe Excavations, 1964', *Trans. Bristol Gloucs. Archaeol. Soc.*, LXXXV (1966), 57–69.
20. **Gloucester** T. Darvill, 'Excavations on the site of the early Norman castle at Gloucester, 1983–84', *Med. Archaeol.*, 32 (1988), 1–49.
21. **Holm Castle (Tewkesbury)** *ibid.*, XIX (1975), 239.
ibid., XX (1976), 184.

GREATER LONDON

22. **London** B.K. Davison, 'Three eleventh-century earthworks in England', *Ch.G.*, II (1967), 40–3.

HAMPSHIRE

23. **Bentley** P. Stamper, 'Excavations on a mid-12th century siege castle at Bentley, Hampshire,' *Proc. Hants. Field Club Archaeol. Soc.*, 40 (1984), 81–9.
24. **Portchester** B. Cunliffe, *Excavations at Portchester Castle*, Soc. Antiq. Res. Reps. 4 vols. (nos. 32, 33, 34 and 43, 1975, 1976, 1977 and 1985; 43 with J. Munby).
25. **Powderham** Renn 1973, 285.
26. **Silchester** M. Fulford, *The Silchester Amphitheatre: Excavations 1979–85* (Britannia Monograph Series, 10, 1989), esp. pp.59–65, 175–6, 193–5.
27. **Winchester** *Med. Archaeol.*, XV (1971), 147.
M. Biddle, 'Excavations at Winchester, 1971; tenth and final interim report: part I', *Antiq. J.*, LV (1975), 96–126.

HEREFORD & WORCESTER

28. **Kilpeck** *Med. Archaeol.*, XXVII (1983), 180.

HERTFORDSHIRE

29. **Anstey** Renn 1973, 50, 90.
30. **Hertford** *Med. Archaeol.*, XVI (1972), 185.
31. **South Mimms** (formerly Middlesex) *Med. Archaeol.*, V (1961), 318.
ibid., VI–VII (1962–3), 322.

ibid., VIII (1964), 255.
Curr. Archaeol., 5 (1967), 130.
J.P.C. Kent, 'Excavations at the motte and bailey castle of South Mimms, 1960–67', *Barnet District Local History Society Bulletin*, 15 (1968).
32. **Therfield** M. Biddle, 'The excavation of a motte and bailey castle at Therfield, Herts.', *J. Brit. Archaeol. Ass.*, 27 (1964), 53–91.

HUMBERSIDE

33. **Driffield** *Med. Archaeol.*, XX (1976), 184.

KENT

34. **Dover** *ibid.*, VI–VII (1962–3), 322.
ibid., VIII (1964), 254–5.
M. Biddle, 'The earthworks around St Mary-in-Castro', *Archaeol. J.*, 126 (1969), 264–5.
35. **Eynsford** S. Rigold, 'Eynsford Castle and its excavation', *Archaeol. Cant.*, 86 (1971), 109–71.
S. Rigold, 'Eynsford Castle: the moat and bridge', *ibid.*, 88 (1973), 87–116.
V. Horsman, 'Eynsford Castle: a re-interpretation of its early history in the light of recent excavations', *ibid.*, 105 (1988), 39–57.
36. **Tonge** D. Ford, 'Tonge: an early medieval manor house', *ibid.*, 79 (1964), 207–10.
D. Ford, 'Tonge medieval manor – summary of results, 1965', *ibid.*, 80 (1965), 265–9.

LANCASHIRE

37. **Penwortham** C. Hardwick, *History of the borough of Preston* (1857), 104–11.
Armitage 1912, 184.
Renn 1973, 276.

LEICESTERSHIRE

38. **Alstoe Mount, Burley** (formerly Rutland) G.D. Dunning, 'Alstoe Mount, Burley, Rutland', *Antiq. J.*, XVI (1936), 396–411.

LINCOLNSHIRE

39. **Goltho** G. Beresford, 'The excavation of the deserted medieval village of Goltho, Lincs.', *Ch.G.*, VIII (1977), 47–68.
G. Beresford, 'Goltho Manor, Lincolnshire; the buildings and their surrounding defences c.850–1150', *Proc. Battle Conf.* IV (1981), 13–36.
G. Beresford, *Goltho: the development of an early medieval manor* (English Heritage, 1987).

40. **Stamford** C. Mahany, 'Excavations at Stamford Castle', *Ch.G.*, VIII (1977), 223–33.

MERSEYSIDE

41. **Castle Hill, Newton-le-Willows** *Med. Archaeol.*, XXXII (1988), 261–2.
42. **Liverpool, West Derby** (formerly Lancashire) J.P. Droop & F.C. Larkin, 'Excavations at West Derby Castle, Liverpool', *University of Liverpool, Annals of Archaeology and Anthropology*, XV (1928), 47–55.

NORFOLK

43. **Burgh Castle** (formerly Suffolk) S. Johnson, *Burgh Castle, Excavations by Charles Green 1958–61* (East Anglian Archaeology, Report no. 20, 1983).
44. **Castle Acre** J. Coad, 'Excavation at Castle Acre, Norfolk, 1972–76, an interim report', *Ch.G.*, VIII (1977), 79–85.
J. Coad & A. Streeten, 'Excavations at Castle Acre, Norfolk, 1972–77: country house and castle of the Norman earls of Surrey', *Archaeol. J.*, 139 (1982), 138–301.
J. Coad, 'Recent work at Castle Acre castle', *Ch.G.*, XI (1983), 55–67.
45. **Castle Rising** *Med. Archaeol.*, XIX (1975), 239.
ibid., XX (1976), 185.
ibid., XXI (1977), 235.

NORTHAMPTONSHIRE

46. **Northampton** *ibid.*, VIII (1964), 257.
47. **Sulgrave** B.K. Davison, 'Excavations at Sulgrave, Northants., 1960–76: an interim report', *Archaeol. J.*, 134 (1977), 105–14.

NORTHUMBERLAND

48. **Nafferton** B. Harbottle & P. Salway, 'Nafferton Castle, Northumberland', *Archaeol. Aeliana*, 38 (1960), 129–44.
B. Harbottle & P. Salway, 'Nafferton Castle, Northumberland: second report', *ibid.*, 39 (1961), 165–78.
49. **Prudhoe** L. Keen, 'The Umfravilles, the castle and the barony of Prudhoe, Northumberland', *Proc. Battle Conf. (1982)*, V (1983), 165–84.

OXFORDSHIRE

50. **Middleton Stoney** S. Rahtz & T. Rowley, *Middleton Stoney: excavation and survey in a North Oxfordshire Parish,* 1970–1982 (Oxford University Department of External Studies, 1984).
51. **Wallingford** (formerly Berkshire) *Med. Archaeol.*, XVII (1973), 159–61.
N.P. Brooks, 'Excavations at Wallingford Castle, 1965: an interim report', *Berks. Archaeol. J.*, 62 (1965–66), 17–21.
T.G. Hassall, 'Wallingford Castle', *Archaeol. J.*, 135 (1978), 292–3.

SHROPSHIRE

52. **Pontesbury** P.A. Barker, 'Pontesbury Castle Mound Emergency Excavations, 1961 and 1964', *Trans. Shrops. Archaeol. Soc.*, LVII (1961–64), 206–23.
53. **Quatford** J.F.A. Mason & P.A. Barker, 'The Norman castle at Quatford', *ibid.*, 57 (1961–64), 37–62.
54. **Smethcott** *Med. Archaeol.*, I (1957), 157.
ibid., II (1958), 195.
55. **Woolstaston** T. Rowley, 'Excavations at Woolstaston Motte-and-Bailey Castle, 1965', *Trans. Shrops. Archeol. Soc.*, LX (1975–76), 75–80.

SOMERSET

56. **Neroche** B.K. Davison, 'Castle Neroche: an abandoned Norman fortress in South Somerset', *Proc. Somerset Archaeol. Nat. Hist. Soc.*, 116 (1972), 16–58.

STAFFORDSHIRE

57. **Stafford** E.C. Hill, *Stafford Castle: Interim Reports* (1980, 1982, etc., on behalf of Stafford Borough Council).
58. **Tamworth** R.A. Meeson, 'Tenth Tamworth excavation report, 1977; the Norman bailey defences at the castle', *Transactions of the South Staffordshire Archaeology and History Society*, XX (1980), 15–28.

SURREY

59. **Abinger** B. Hope-Taylor, 'The excavation of a motte at Abinger, Surrey', *Archaeol. J.*, 107 (1950), 15–43.
B. Hope-Taylor, 'The Norman motte at Abinger, Surrey, and its wooden castle', in R.L.S. Bruce-Mitford (ed.), *Recent Archaeological Excavations in Britain* (1956), 223–49.

SUSSEX (EAST)

60. **Hastings** P.A. Barker & K.J. Barton, 'Excavations at Hastings, 1968', *Archaeol. J.*, 134 (1977), 80–100.

SUSSEX (WEST)

61. **Lodsbridge Mill, Lodsworth** E.W. Holden, 'The excavation of a motte at Lodsbridge Mill, Lodsworth', *Sussex Archaeological Collections*, 105 (1967), 103–25.

WARWICKSHIRE

62. **Ratley and Upton** *Med. Archaeol.*, XVII (1973), 163.

WEST MIDLANDS

63. **Castle Bromwich** (formerly Warwickshire) *ibid.*, XV (1971), 148–9.
W.J. Ford, 'Castle Bromwich Castle', *Archaeol. J.*, 128 (1971), 214–15.
64. **Dudley** P. Boland *et al. Dudley Castle Archaeological Project. An Introduction and Summary of Excavations, 1983–85* (1985, on behalf of Dudley Borough Council). *Med. Archaeol.*, XXXII (1988), 286.
ibid., XXIX (1985), 203–5.

WILTSHIRE

65. **Ludgershall** P.V. Addyman, 'Excavations at Ludgershall Castle, Wiltshire', *Ch.G.*, IV (1968), 9–10.
P.V. Addyman, 'Excavations at Ludgershall Castle, Wiltshire, England (1964–72)', *ibid.*, VI (1973), 7–13.
Med. Archaeol. IX (1965), 192, and subsequent volumes to 1970.
66. **Trowbridge** *ibid.*, XXXI (1987), 168.
ibid., XXXII (1988), 289–90.

YORKSHIRE (NORTH)

67. **Huttons Ambo** (formerly North Riding, Yorkshire) M.W. Thompson, 'Excavation of the fortified medieval hall of Hutton Coleswain at Huttons Ambo near Malton, Yorkshire', *Archaeol. J.*, 114 (1957), 69–91.
68 **York (Baile Hill)** P. Addyman, 'Excavations at Baile Hill, York' *Ch.G.*, V (1972), 7–12.
P. Addyman, 'Baile Hill, York: a report on the Institute's excavations', *Archaeol. J.*, 134 (1977), 115–56.
69. **York (Clifford's Tower)** G. Benson, H. Platnauer, 'Notes on Clifford's Tower, York,' *Yorkshire Philosophical Society Report* (1902), 68–74.
RCHM York, vol. II: The Defences (1972), 59–86.
Renn 1973, 351–2.

YORKSHIRE (WEST)

70. **Sandal** P. Mayes & L. Butler, *Sandal Castle excavations, 1964–73* (1983).

Wales

CLWYD

71. **Hen Blas** (formerly Flintshire) G.B. Leach, 'Excavations at Hen Blas, Coleshill Fawr, nr. Flint', *Jnl. Flintshire Historical Society*, 17 (1957), 1–15.
72. **Rug, Corwen** (formerly Merionethshire) W. Gardner, 'The mound at Rug, near Corwen', *Jnl. Merioneth Historical Record Society*, 4 (1961–64), 3–6.
73. **Sycharth** (formerly Denbighshire) D. Hague & C. Warhurst, 'Excavations at Sycharth Castle, Denbighshire, 1962–63', *Archaeol. Camb.*, 115 (1964), 108–27.

DYFED

74. **Llanstephan** (formerly Carmarthenshire) G.C. Guilbert, J.J. Schweiso, 'Llanstephan Castle: an interim discussion', *Carmarthenshire Antiquary*, 8 (1972), 75–90.
Eidem, 'Llanstephan Castle: 1973 interim report', *ibid.*, 10 (1974), 37–48.
75. **Old Aberystwyth (Tan-y-Bwlch)** (formerly Cardiganshire) C.H. Houlder, 'Recent Excavations in Old Aberystwyth', *Ceredigion*, III (1957), 114–17.
R.A. Griffiths, 'The Three Castles at Aberystwyth', *Archaeol. Camb.*, CXXVI (1977), 74–87.
E.J. Talbot, Appendix II in L. Alcock, 'Castle Tower, Penmaen: a Norman ringwork in Glamorgan', *Antiq. J.*, 46 (1966), 207.

GLAMORGAN (SOUTH)

76. **Coed-y-Cwm, St Nicholas** E.J. Talbot, Appendix II in L. Alcock, 'Castle Tower, Penmaen: a Norman ringwork in Glamorgan', *Antiq. J.*, 46 (1966), 207.
77. **Dinas Powys** L. Alcock, *Dinas Powys: an Iron Age, Dark Age and Early Medieval Settlement in Glamorgan* (1963), 73–93.
78. **Llantrithyd** P. Charlton, J. Roberts & V. Vale, *Llantrithyd: a ringwork in South Glamorgan* (Cardiff Archaeological Society 1977).
79. **Pen-y-pill** E.J. Talbot, Appendix II in L. Alcock, 'Castle Tower, Penmaen: a Norman ringwork in Glamorgan', *Antiq. J.*, 46 (1966), 207.
80. **Rumney (Cae Castell)** K.W.B. Lightfoot, 'An interim report on the excavation of Cae Castell, Rumney, Cardiff', *Annual Report 1979–80, Glamorgan-Gwent Archaeological Trust Ltd.*, 1980, 9–12.
K.W.B. Lightfoot, 'Cae Castell, Rumney, Cardiff', *Annual Report 1980–81, ibid.*, 1981, 11–15.
K.W.B. Lightfoot, 'Cae Castell, Rumney, Cardiff: final interim report', *Annual Report, 1981–82, ibid.*, 1–7.
Med. Archaeol., XXV (1981), 203–4.
ibid., XXVI (1982), 225.

81. **Treoda** J. Knight & E.J. Talbot, 'The excavation of a castle mound and round barrow at Treoda, Whitchurch', *Trans. Cardiff Naturalists' Society.*, 95 (1968–70), 9–23.

GLAMORGAN (WEST)

82. **Loughor** J.M. Lewis, 'Loughor Castle', *Morgannwg*, 17 (1973), 60–2.
J.M. Lewis, 'Recent Excavations at Loughor Castle (South Wales), *Ch.G.*, VII (1975), 147–57.
Med. Archaeol., XIV (1970), 180.
ibid., XVI (1972), 186.
83. **Old Castle Camp, Bishopston** W.L. Morgan, 'Excavations at the Old Castle Camp, Bishopston, Gower', *Archaeol. Camb.*, 5th ser., 16 (1899), 249–58.
84. **Pennard** *Morgannwg*, IV (1960), 69–70.
ibid., V (1961), 81.
Med. Archaeol. VI–VII (1962–63), 326.
85. **Penmaen** L. Alcock, 'Castle Tower, Penmaen: a Norman ringwork in Glamorgan', *Antiq. J.*, 46 (1966), 178–210.
86. **Penrice** Renn 1973, 275–6.
E.J. Talbot, Appendix II in L. Alcock, 'Castle Tower, Penmaen: a Norman ringwork in Glamorgan', *Antiq. J.*, 46 (1966), 207.

GWENT

87. **Twyn-y-Cregen, Llanarth** (formerly Monmouthshire) B.H.St.J. O'Neil & A.H. Foster-Smith, 'Excavations at Twyn-y-Cregen, Llanarth, Monmouthshire', *Archaeol. Camb.*, 91 (1936), 247–58.

POWYS

88. **Hen Domen** (formerly Montgomeryshire) P.A. Barker, 'Hen Domen, Montgomery, Excavations, 1960–67', *Ch.G.* III (1969), 15–27.
P.A. Barker, 'Hen Domen, Montgomery, 1960–1977', *Archaeol. Jnl.*, 134 (1977), 101–4.
P.A. Barker & R.A. Higham, *Hen Domen, Montgomery: a timber castle on the Welsh Border* (R.A.I. Monograph, 1982).
P.A. Barker, 'Hen Domen Revisited', in *Castles in Wales and the Marches, Essays in Honour of D.J. Cathcart King*, eds. J.R. Kenyon, R. Avent (Cardiff 1987), 51–4.
P.A. Barker & R.A. Higham, *Hen Domen, Montgomery: a timber castle on the English-Welsh border. Excavations 1960–1988: a summary report* (Hen Domen Archaeological Project, 1988).
P.A. Barker, 'Hen Domen, Montgomery', *Curr. Archaeol.*, 111 (Sept. 1988), 137–42.

Scotland

BORDERS REGION

89. **Howden** (formerly Selkirkshire) *Med. Archaeol.*, II (1958), 196.

CENTRAL REGION

90. **Keir Knowe of Drum** (formerly Stirlingshire) *ibid.*, II (1958), 197.
RCAHM Stirlingshire, Vol. I (1963), 176–8.

DUMFRIES AND GALLOWAY

91. **Cruggleton** C. Tabraham *et al.*, 'Cruggleton Castle: motte', *Discovery and excavation in Scotland*, Scottish Group, CBA, 1980, 7; 1981, 4; 1982, 9.
G. Ewart, *Cruggleton Castle. Report of Excavations 1978–81* (Dumfries. Galloway Nat. Hist. Antiq. Soc. monograph, 1985).
92. **Lochmaben** (formerly Dumfrieshire) A. Macdonald & L.R. Laing, 'Excavations at Lochmaben Castle, Dumfrieshire', *Proc. Soc. Antiq. Scot.*, 106 (1974–5), 124–57.
R.C. Reid, 'Edward I's Pele at Lochmaben', *Trans. Dumfries. Galloway Nat. Hist. Antiq. Soc.*, 31 (1952–53), 58–73.
93. **Mote of Urr** (formerly Kirkudbrightshire) B. Hope-Taylor, 'Excavations at Mote of Urr; interim report: 1951 season', *ibid.*, 29 (1952), 167–72.

GRAMPIAN REGION

94. **Inverurie** (formerly Aberdeenshire) W.M. Mackenzie, *The Medieval Castle in Scotland* (Rhind lectures in Archaeology 1925–26), (1927), 6 & 12.
95. **Peel of Lumphanan** E. Talbot, 'Peel of Lumphanan', *Discovery and Excavation in Scotland* (CBA), 1980, 11–12.
96. **Strachan (Castle Hill)** P.A. Yeoman *et al.* 'Excavations at Castlehill of Strachan, 1980–81', *Proc. Soc. Antiq. Scot.*, 114 (1984), 315–64.

LOTHIAN REGION

97. **Peebles (Castle Hill)** H. Murray & G. Ewart, 'Two early medieval timber buildings from Castle Hill, Peebles', *ibid.*, 110 (1978–80), 519–27.

STRATHCLYDE REGION

98. **Dundonald** *Med. Archaeol.*, XXXII (1988), 307.
99. **Kilfinan** (formerly Argyllshire) *ibid.*, XIV (1970), 177–8.

100. **Portencross, Auldhill** *ibid.*, XXXII (1988), 307–8.

101. **Roberton** C. Tabraham, 'Norman Settlement in Upper Clydesdale – recent archaeological fieldwork', *Trans. Dumfries. Galloway Nat. Hist. Antiq. Soc.*, 53 (1977–78), 114–28.

G. Haggarty & C. Tabraham, 'Excavation of a motte near Roberton, Clydesdale, 1979', *ibid.*, 57 (1982), 51–64.

TAYSIDE REGION

102. **Kinnaird, Barton Hill** (formerly Perthshire) M. Stewart & C. Tabraham, 'Excavations at Barton Hill, Kinnaird, Perthshire', *Scottish Archaeological Forum*, 6 (1974), 58–65.

Northern Ireland

COUNTY ANTRIM

103. **Doonmore** V.G. Childe, 'Doonmore, a castle mound near Fairhead, Co. Antrim', *Ulster J. Archaeol.*, 3rd ser., I (1938), 124–35.

COUNTY DOWN

104. **Ballynarry** B.K. Davison, 'Excavations at Ballynarry Rath, Co. Down', *ibid.*, 24–5 (1961–62), 39–87.

105. **Castleskreen** D. Waterman, 'Excavations of a rath with motte at Castleskreen, Co. Down', *ibid.*, 22 (1959), 67–82.

106. **Clough Castle** D. Waterman, 'Excavations at Clough Castle, Co. Down', *ibid.*, 17 (1954), 103–63.

107. **Dromore** D. Waterman, 'Excavations at Dromore motte, Co. Down', *ibid.*, 17 (1954), 164–8.

108. **Duneight** D. Waterman, 'Excavations at Duneight, Co. Down', *ibid.*, 26 (1963), 55–78.

109. **Lismahon** D. Waterman, 'Excavations at Lismahon, Co, Down', *Med. Archaeol.* III (1959), 139–76.

110. **Piper's Fort, Farranfad** D. Waterman, 'Piper's Fort, Farranfad, Co. Down', *Ulster J. Archaeol.*, 22 (1959), 83–7.

111. **Rathmullan** C.J. Lynn, 'The Excavation of Rathmullan, a raised rath and motte in Co. Down', *ibid.*, 44–5 (1981–82), 65–171.

Republic of Ireland

COUNTY LOUTH

112. **Lurgankeel** Unpublished. Referred to in: T. Barry, E. Culleton & C. Empey, 'Kells motte, Co. Kilkenny', *Proceedings of the Royal Irish Academy*, 84 (1984), 157–70, esp. 159–60, and C.J. Lynn, 'The excavation of Rathmullan, a raised rath and motte in Co. Down', *Ulster J. Archaeol.*, 44–5 (1981–82), 65–71, esp. 112.

COUNTY KILKENNY

113. **Kells Motte** T. Barry, E. Culleton & C. Empey, 'Kells motte, Co. Kilkenny', *Proceedings of the Royal Irish Academy*, 84 (1984), 157–70.

COUNTY TIPPERARY

114. **Lorrha** E.J. Talbot, 'Lorrha Motte, Co. Tipperary', *North Munster Antiquaries Journal*, XV (1972), 8–12.

Appendices

Appendix A:
Timber castle vocabulary

In the discussion of timber castle origins (chapters 2 and 3), attention was drawn to the vagueness of much medieval terminology for castles as a whole. Words such as *castrum*, *castellum*, *munitio* and many others could apply to all manner of sites, stone as well as timber. The component parts of fortifications were also known by different terms, all of which have given rise to a wide range of modern equivalents, some derived from medieval words, others archaeological inventions.

The following list includes those terms most frequently encountered in medieval sources which relate more specifically, though not exclusively, to timber castles.

Mota, Motta From the twelfth century the word was used in Latin texts of an artificial or natural castle mound. Eventually, by extension of this meaning, it became (in English) 'moat', the ditch around an earthwork rather than the earthwork itself. This sense was developing by the late thirteenth century. At Caernarfon, for example, the ditch was described in Latin as *mota* (*KWI*, 381). In the Romance languages of France, Spain and Italy, as well as being applied to castles, *motta* (or some variation of it) also had an important meaning of an earthwork controlling water supplies for mills or irrigation. In these countries, where it was also a place-name element referring to both man-made and natural features, the word has continued to have a variety of applications in the vernacular, the simplest of which is a clod of earth or sod. In fourteenth- and fifteenth-century

France it was applied to the low ditched earth-works upon which *maisons-fortes* were built. In its castle sense, *motte* has also been absorbed into English usage.

Ballium This was used from the twelfth century of the defended courtyard of a castle with a motte or great tower. In Middle English it was *baile*, and in modern English bailey: hence the common phrase 'motte and bailey'.

Donjon The word derives from *dominionem*, the accusative case of low Latin *dominio*, meaning lordship. It was used to describe the major residential tower of a castle, which might be on a motte, and to which the symbolism of lordship was attached. *Dunjo*, as used by Lambert of Ardres as a synonym for *mota* (see chapter 4), might have the same derivation, though it has been suggested as more akin to *dun*, meaning a hill. *Donjon* also had a slightly looser meaning: at New Montgomery in 1249 it was used in reference to the stone gate-house and adjacent structures of the inner ward (*KWII*, 741). In Latin, *turris* or *magna turris* could equally mean a stone or a timber structure. In Middle English 'dungeon' appeared with the same meaning of a great tower. More recently it has been used incorrectly to indicate the supposed prison-like quality of castle ruins in the popular imagination. The English 'keep' had appeared by the sixteenth century, but its exact derivation, other than its obvious sense of a protective building, is not known.

Belfry This English word, which had assumed its familiar meaning of 'bell-tower' by the fifteenth century, had its equivalents in several languages:

medieval Latin *berfredus*; Old French *berfrei* or *belfroi*; and the Teutonic *bergfrid*, from which the other forms were derived. It indicated a place of safety, and had two applications. It could be the watchtower of a castle, particularly the *Bergfried* of a German castle. But it was commonly used in its Latin and French forms of the movable timber towers which were part of the machinery of sieges.

Bretasche, Bretagium, Brattice In its twelfth-century sense this was probably a timber tower, built on a motte, or at an entrance or on a perimeter. But from the thirteenth century century it also meant timber defences more generally, either palisades or hoardings on stone wall-tops. It has been suggested that its use for the latter, which projected, may indicate that the upper storey of the earlier timber towers had also projected. This is certainly implied by the description of Ardres (chapter 4). By the later Middle Ages, a brattice could, more rarely, be a stone structure, as at Berwick-on-Tweed in 1303 (*KWII*, 564). But its general meaning was a boarded or planked structure.

Palum, Palicium, Garillum These are general usages for timber walls or palisades. *Hérisson* was used for a hedge or fence of stakes on the counterscarp of a ditch, and *hurdicia, alures*, for the hourdes, or movable timber galleries on wall-tops.

Appendix B:
Castel

The description of certain English sites as castles associated with Frenchmen in the early 1050s is discussed in chapter 2. Normans had found favour at the court of Edward the Confessor, and whatever they built struck the English as noteworthy. The word used in this context in the Anglo-Saxon Chronicle 'E' for 1051–2 is *castel*. The same word is used in this source for castles built from 1066 onwards: Hastings was a *castel*, Odo of Bayeux and William FitzOsbern built *castelas* in 1067, and so on. In its account of 1051–2, the twelfth-century. Worcester chronicle (sometimes called, misleadingly, 'Florence') which drew on the Anglo-Saxon Chronicle rendered the word as *castellum*, by then a normal word for castle.[1]

This is the only pre-Conquest use of the word in the Chronicle, though not, as sometimes alleged, in Anglo-Saxon literature generally. *Castel* also appears, with a general meaning of town or village, in various texts, including Old English versions of the Vulgate, where it translates *castellum*.[2] The impression is, that from the 1050s, the English narrowed its usage to cover something distinctive, which they associated with the French, for which 'castle' is an appropriate rendering. But this narrower meaning did not immediately supersede the more general one. In ASC 'D' for 1051, *castell*, where the double 'l' is close to the Latin original, was also used of Dover. The consensus of opinion is that the reference here was to a defended town. ASC 'E' for 1051 called it a *burh*, and various post-Conquest Norman writers called it a *castrum*. It probably occupied the site of the later castle and included the pre-Conquest church which still survives.[3]

The Old English *castel*, which survived in Middle English and eventually became modern 'castle', is derived from Latin *castellum*. Old Saxon and Old High German had their equivalent, *kastel*, also of Latin derivation. The Romance and Celtic languages have their versions arising from the same root: château (from *chastel*) in French, *castillo* in Spanish, *castello* in Italian, *kastell* in Breton, *castell* in Welsh and Cornish. Opinions in the literature of castles have varied as to whether the Anglo-Saxon Chronicle of the 1050s simply employed an already available, Latin-derived English word, or whether, in the context of referring mainly to places associated with Normans, its use represents a borrowing from Norman French.[4] The published etymological explanation is that by this date there were two separate usages of the word, the general one deriving direct from Latin, the particular one, that is of the 1050s, deriving ultimately from Latin but more immediately from a borrowing of northern French *castel*, itself a derivative of *castellum*.[5] This theory is attractive, and may be correct, but it is impossible to prove because the French *chastel*, or its northern version *castel*, had yet to appear in any known sources. Its earliest occurrence is in the *Song of Roland*. This famous piece was composed just before 1100 by a continental author, and the earliest written version to survive is that copied by an Anglo-Norman scribe in the early twelfth-century Oxford manuscript.[6]

The French word may, of course, have been in spoken use for some considerable time before its appearance in the *Song of Roland*. On the other hand, Old English *castel* may well have been in spoken use before its appearance in the Anglo-Saxon Chronicle. Its application in a dative form (*castele*) in the latter ('E', 1052) may suggest it was already current rather than a first-time borrowing.

A Latin origin of all Old English forms of *castel* poses no such chronological problems. *Castellum* was well known to Anglo-Saxon writers of Latin from the eighth century onwards. The Anglo-Saxon *burh* at Wareham was a *castellum* to Asser, Alfred's biographer, for example, and there are many other instances.[7] On the available evidence, this derivation of *castel*, paralleled by its counterparts in other languages, seems just as likely as one arising from a French borrowing.

Notes

Chapter 1, pp. 17–35

1 H. Braun, 'Earthwork castles', *J. Brit. Archaeol.Ass.*, 3rd ser. 1 (1937), 28–156; B. Hope-Taylor, 'The excavation of a motte at Abinger in Surrey', *Archaeol. J.*, 107 (1950), 15–43; *idem*, 'The Norman motte at Abinger, Surrey, and its wooden castle', in R. Bruce-Mitford (ed.), *Recent Archaeological excavations in Britain* (1956), 223–49. For some brief but pertinent remarks on the subject, see also B. Little, *Architecture in Norman Britain* (1985), 23–4. For a recent preview of many of the themes discussed in the present volume, R.A. Higham, 'Timber Castles – a reassessment', *Fortress*, 1 (May 1989), 50–60.

2 These include: A. Herrnbrodt, *Der Husterknupp* (Cologne 1958); *idem*, 'Die Ausgrabungen auf der Motte "Hoverberg" bei Birgelen, Kreis Geilenkirchen-Heinsberg', *Bonner Jahrbücher*, 155–156 (1955–56), 343–54; *idem*, 'Stand der Frühmittelalterlichen Mottenforschung im Rheinland', *Ch.G. I* (1964), 77–100; *idem*, 'Die Ausgrabung der motte Burg Meer in Büderich bei Dusseldorf', *ibid.* II (1967), 62–72; M. Müller-Wille, *Mittelalterliche Burghügel ("Motten") im Nördlichen Rheinland* (Cologne 1966). More recent work has also been reported in *Bonner Jahrbücher* and the *Château Gaillard* conference proceedings.

3 Full details will be found in the Gazetteer.

4 A.D. Saunders (ed.), 'Five Castle Excavations: reports on the Institute's Research Project into the Origins of the Castle in England', *Archaeol. J.*, 134 (1977), 1–156; see also Chap. 2.

5 For an example of earlier work, J. Decaëns, 'Les enceintes d'Urville et de Bretteville-sur-Laize (Calvados)', *Annales de Normandie*, 18 (1968), 311–75. Among the later publications, *idem*, 'La motte d'Olivet à Grimbosq (Calvados): résidence seignurial du XIᵉ siècle', *Archéologie Médiévale*, XI (1981), 167–201; J. le Maho, 'Genèse d'une fortification seignuriale. Les fouilles de la motte de Mirville (XI-XII siècles)', *Ch.G.* XI (1982), 183–92; *idem*, 'Note sur l'histoire d'un habitat seignurial des XIᵉ et XIIᵉ siècles en Normandie: Mirville (Seine Maritime)', *Proc. Battle Conf.*, VII (1985), 214–23; *idem*, *Mirville* (Caen, 1984); the 1980 colloquium at Caen was published as A. Débord (ed.) 'Les fortifications de terre en Europe occidentale du Xᵉ au XIIᵉ siècles', *Archéologie Médiévale*, XI (1981), 5–123; see also Chap. 3.

6 B.W. Oliver, 'The Castle of Barnstaple', *Trans. Devonshire. Ass.*, 60 (1928), 215–23; G.D. Dunning, 'Alstoe Mount, Burley, Rutland', *Antiq. J.*, XVI (1936), 396–411; V.G. Childe, 'Doonmore, a castle mound near Fair Head, Co. Antrim', *Ulster J. Archaeol.* 3rd Ser., i (1938), 124–35; F. Jervoise, 'Norman motte at West Woodhay', *Trans. Newbury and District Field Club*, 10, no. 2 (1954), 65–7 (we are grateful to Mrs Norma Barker for this reference).

7 A.H.L.F. Pitt-Rivers, 'Excavations at Caesar's Camp, near Folkestone', *Archaeologia*, 47 (1883), 429–65; W. Morgan, 'Excavations at the Old Castle Camp, Bishopston, Gower', *Archaeol. Camb.* 16 (1899), 249–58; for Swansea, see W.L. Morgan, *The Castle of Swansea* (Devizes, 1914); for Penwortham, see C. Hardwick, *History of the Borough of Preston* (Preston, 1857), 104–11, *VCH Lancaster*, vol. 2 (eds. W. Farrer, J. Brownbill, 1908), 533–6, Armitage 1912, 183–5, and Renn 1973, 276; for Twmpath, see *Archaeol. Camb.*, 4 (1849), 301, 317–18. We are grateful to Jack Spurgeon for the references to Swansea and Twmpath. For Hilden, Düsseldorf, see R. von Uslar, *Studien zu Frühgeschichtlichen Befestigungen zwischen Nordsee und Alpen* (Cologne 1964), 5–7.

8 Recent RCAHM work described in C.J. Spurgeon, 'Glamorgan's first castles', *Fortress*, 8 (February 1991), 3–14.

9 Leland's castle descriptions are usefully listed as Appendix 2 in M.W. Thompson, *The Decline of the Castle* (1987).

10 For the background to Armitage's work, see J. Counihan, 'Mrs. Ella Armitage, John Horace Round, G.T. Clark and early Norman Castles', *Proc. Battle Conf.*, VIII (1985), 73–87; *idem*, 'The growth of castle studies in England and on the continent since 1850', *Proc. Battle Conf.*, XI (1989), 77–85; *idem*, 'Ella Armitage: castle studies pioneer', *Fortress*, 6 (August 1990), 51–9.

11 Dating problems associated with castles are discussed in R.A. Higham, 'Dating in Medieval Archaeology: problems and possibilities', in B.J. Orme (ed.), *Problems and Case Studies in Archaeological Dating* (Exeter, 1982), 83–107; the scientific aspects are further pursued in L. Alcock, 'Castle-Studies and the Archaeological Sciences: some possibilities and problems', in J.R. Kenyon, R. Avent (eds.), *Castles in Wales and the Marches: essays in honour of D.J. Cathcart King* (Cardiff, 1987), 5–22.

12 From the map of British mottes published in Renn 1973, 16.

13 D.J.C. King, J. Spurgeon, 'Mottes in the Vale of

Montgomery', *Archaeol. Camb.*, 114 (1965), 69–86; Barker and Higham 1982, chapter 3, from which the map is reproduced. On the Corbets, also I.J. Sanders, *English Baronies 1086–1307* (1960), 29.

14 P.A. Barker, 'Hen Domen re-visited', in Kenyon, Avent (see note 9), 51–4.

15 Wilton is in the *Life of S. Edith*, by Goscelin, *Analecta Bollandiana*, LVI (1938), 86–87; discussed in F. Barlow (ed.), *Vita Edwardi Regis* (1962), 46. We are grateful to Prof. Christopher Holdsworth for this reference. Athelney is discussed in *KW I*, 12; for a Domesday example of an *ecclesia lignea* see *DBi*, 320b (Old Byland, Yorks). For two excavated examples, see P.J. Huggins, 'Excavation of Belgic and Romano-British Farm with Middle Saxon Cemetery and Churches at Nazeingbury, Essex, 1975–76', *Transactions of the Essex Society for Archaeology and History*, 10 (1978), 29–117, where other documentary evidence is also summarized. We are grateful to Dr Simon Burnell for this reference.

16 For Old Windsor, *Med. Archaeol.* 3 (1958), 183–5; for Northampton, J. Williams, 'From palace to town: Northampton and urban origins', *Anglo-Saxon England*, 13 (1984), 113–36; J.H. Williams, *The Middle Saxon Palaces at Northampton* (1985); for Portchester and Sulgrave, D. Wilson (ed.), *The Archaeology of Anglo-Saxon England* (1976), 63–4, and below, chapter 2; for Mawgan Porth, R. Bruce-Mitford, 'A dark-age settlement at Mawgan Porth', in *idem* (ed.), *Recent Archaeological Excavations in Britain* (1956), 167–96.

17 For Yeavering and Cheddar, Wilson (ed.) (note 16), 65–8; on Asser, S. Keynes and M. Lapidge, *Alfred the Great* (Penguin Classics, 1983), 101; on *timber* and *timbrian*, J. Bosworth, T. Toller, *An Anglo-Saxon Dictionary* (1898 etc.), 986–7.

18 Wilson (ed.) (note 16), 120–41; C.A.R. Radford, 'The later preconquest boroughs and their defences', *Med. Archaeol.* 14 (1970), 83–103. For Chirbury, D. Whitelock (ed.), *The Anglo-Saxon Chronicle* (1961), 64.

19 Information on Norway from lecture (13.12.1984) to the Society for Medieval Archaeology by Øivind Lunde, partly published as 'Archaeology and the medieval towns of Norway', *Med. Arch.*, 29 (1985), 120–35. On Scandinavia generally, see for example, P. Foote, D. Wilson, *The Viking Achievement* (1970).

20 D. Buxton, *The Wooden Churches of Eastern Europe* (1982); A. and Y. Opolovnikova, *The Wooden Architecture of Russia* (Eng. ed. D. Buxton, 1989); M. Thompson (ed., trans.), *Novgorod the Great* (1967); see also H.-J. Brachmann, 'Research into the early history of the Slav populations in the territory of the German Democratic Republic', *Med. Arch.*, 27 (1983), 89–106; for the Kremlin, see J. Thompson and C. Wolinsky in *National Geographic*, vol. 177, no. 1 (Jan. 1990), 62–106; for Staraja Ladoga, P. Uino, 'On the history of Staraja Ladoga', *Acta Archaeologica*, 59 (1988), 205–22.

21 A useful summary of much European evidence is now available in J. Chapelot, R. Fossier, *The Village and House in the Middle Ages*, (Paris 1980, Eng. trans. Batsford, 1985).

22 *ibid.*, 183–97, 268–73; J. Lasfargues (ed.), *Architectures de terre et de bois* (Documents d'Archéologie française, No. 2, Paris, 1985).

23 Chapelot, Fossier (note 21) chap. VI.

24 J.R. Kenyon, 'A note on two original drawings by William Stukely depicting "The three castles which keep the Downs"', *Antiq. J.*, 58 (1978), 162–4 (these are illustrated in A. Saunders, *Fortress Britain* (1989), 38–9; on Russia, Opolovnikova 1989 (see n.20); on Ireland, G. Hill, *An Historical Account of the Plantation in Ulster, 1608–1620* (Belfast 1877; repr. 1970), 481; G.A. Hayes-McCoy, *Ulster and Other Irish Maps* (Dublin, Irish Manuscripts Commission, 1964). Thanks are due to Mr N. Brannon for these Irish references.

25 P. Bellwood, 'Fortifications and Economy in Prehistoric New Zealand', *Proceedings of the Prehistoric Society*, 37, (1971), 56–95; A. Fox *Prehistoric Maori Fortifications in the North Island of New Zealand* (Auckland 1976).

26 P. O'Neil, *The Old West: the Frontiersmen* (Time Life Books 1977); D. Nevin, *The Old West: the Soldiers* (Time Life Books 1974); H.M. Hart, *Old Forts of the Northwest* (New York 1963); I. Noël Hume, *Martins Hundred* (London & New York 1982); *idem*, 'First look at a lost Virginia Settlement', *National Geographic*, vol. 155, no. 6 (June 1979), 735–67.

27 On the social context of castle-building, see J.W. Hall, M. Jansen (eds), *Studies in the Institutional History of Early Modern Japan* (Princeton 1968), esp. J.W. Hall, 'The castle town and Japan's modern urbanization'; E.O. Reischauer, 'Japanese feudalism', in R. Coulborn (ed.), *Feudalism in History* (Connecticut 1965); P. Duus, *Feudalism in Japan* (1969); J.W. Hall, *Government and Local Power in Japan, 500–1700* (Princeton 1966); J.W. Hall, J.P. Mass (eds), *Medieval Japan: Essays in Institutional History* (Yale 1974). On the castles themselves, see P. Orui, M. Toba, *Castles in Japan* (Board of Tourist Industry, Japanese Government Railways, 1935); F. Guillain, 'Châteaux – forts japonais', *Bulletin de la Maison Franco-Japonaise*, XIII, no. 1 (1942), 1–216; P.M. Clayburn, 'Japanese castles', *History Today*, XV (1965), 20–8; in their general context of early modern warfare, see C. Duffy, *Siege Warfare: the Fortress and the Early Modern World 1494–1660* (1979), esp. 237–46.

28 S. Toy, *Castles: a short history of fortifications from 1600 BC to AD 1600* (1939).

Chapter 2 (pp. 36–77)

1 A. Allcroft, *Earthwork of England* (1908). 400–402; Armitage 1912, 80–5.

2 D. Pringle, 'Crusader Castles: the first generation, *Fortress*, 1 (May 1989), 14–25.

3 W. Anderson, *Castles of Europe from Charlemagne to the Renaissance* (1970), 167.

4 R.A. Higham, 'Early castles in Devon, 1068–1201,' *Ch.G. IX–X* (1982), 101–16; S. Toy, 'The round castles of Cornwall,' *Archaeologia*, 83 (1933), 203–26.

5 See Brown 1976, ch. I; Fournier 1978, chs. I–IV; R. Allen Brown, *Origins of English Feudalism* (1973).

6 Apart from Armitage 1912, the crucial publications were: J.H. Round, 'The castles of the Conquest,' *Archaeologia*, 58 (1902), 313–40; W.H. St. J. Hope, 'English fortresses and castles of the tenth and eleventh centuries,' *Archaeol. J.*, 60 (1903), 72–90; E.S. Armitage, 'The early Norman castles of

England,' *EHR*, 19 (1904), 209–45, 417–55; *idem*, 'The alleged Norman origin of castles in England,' *ibid*, 20 (1905), 711–18 (following T. Pryce, *ibid*, 703–11). A. Hamilton Thompson produced *Military Architecture in England during the Middle Ages* also in 1912.

7 For example, p. 78: 'If the Normans were late in adopting feudalism, they were probably equally late in adopting private castles, and the fortifications of William I's time were most likely copied from castles outside the Norman frontier'; she was also quite aware that the earliest castles in Normandy were enclosures rather than mottes (*ibid*, n.1).

8 R.P. Abels, *Lordship and Military Obligation in Anglo-Saxon England* (1988), and literature quoted there.

9 F. Barlow, *Edward the Confessor* (1970).

10 For example, D. Hooke (ed.), *Medieval Villages* (1985); M. Faull (ed.), *Studies in Late Anglo-Saxon Settlement* (1984).

11 R. Gem, 'The Romanesque rebuilding of Westminster Abbey', *Proc. Battle Conf.*, 3 (1980), 33–60.

12 J. le Patourel, *The Norman Empire* (1976), 304–18.

13 For West Saxon *burhs*, D. Hill, 'The Burghal Hidage: establishment of a text,' *Med. Archaeol.*, 13 (1969), 84–92; for Worcester, *EHD* I, 498; for theories of royal overlordship of castles, C. Coulson, 'Rendability and castellation in medieval France,' *Ch.G. VI* (1973), 59–67. Consideration of the pre- and post-conquest centuries together is a logical extension of regional studies: see R.A. Higham, 'Public and Private Defence in the Medieval South-West: Town, Castle and Fort', in R.A. Higham (ed.), *Security and Defence in South-West England before 1800* (Exeter Studies in History, 19, 1987), 27–49.

14 The castles debate was part of renewed study of the Conquest stimulated by its 900th celebration in 1966. See: B.K. Davison, 'The origins of the castle in England, *Archaeol. J.*, 124 (1967), 202–11; *idem*, 'Three eleventh-century earthworks in England: their excavation and implications,' *Ch.G. II* (1967), 39–48; *idem*, 'Early earthwork castles: a new model,' *Ch.G. III* (1969), 37–47; R.A. Brown, 'The Norman Conquest and the genesis of English castles,' *ibid*, 1–14; *idem*, 'An historian's approach to the origins of the castle in England,' *Archaeol. J.*, 126 (1969), 131–46, with reply from BKD, 146–8. The resilience of the orthodoxy, despite this debate, is seen in its repetition in the 1976 edition of R. Allen Brown's *English Castles*, in C. Platt's *The Castle in Medieval England and Wales* (1982), and in R. Allen Brown's *Castles from the Air* (1989).

15 D. Whitelock (ed.), *The Anglo-Saxon Chronicle* (1961), 30–1, 58–9. The actual date of the first incident was 786: see C.E. Wright, *The Cultivation of Saga in Anglo-Saxon England* (1939), 78–80. I am grateful to Prof. M. Swanton for comment on this item.

16 For the laws, *EHD* I, 364–380; for place-names, A.H. Smith, *English Place-Name Elements*, I (1956), 58–63; for an example of a local study, F.M. Griffith, 'Burh and Beorg in Devon', *Nomina*, 10 (1986), 93–103.

17 B. Hope-Taylor, *Yeavering: an Anglo-British Centre of Early Northumbria* (1977); P.A. Rahtz, *The Saxon and Medieval Palaces at Cheddar* (BAR, 65, 1979); for Doon Hill, see *Med. Archaeol.*, 10 (1966), 175–6.

18 *KW* I, 2, 42–8; P.A. Rahtz, 'The archaeology of West Mercian towns,' in A. Dornier (ed.), *Mercian Studies* (1977),

107–29; for Bamburgh, D. Wilson (ed.), *The archaeology of Anglo-Saxon England* (1976), 5, and *ASC* (E), s.a. 547; for the London background, A. Vince, *Saxon London: an archaeological investigation* (1990); for Gloucester, P. Garrod & H. Hurst, 'Excavations at Gloucester. Third interim report: Kingsholm 1966–75', *Antiq. J.*, 55 (1975), 267–94.

19 D. Whitelock (ed.), *The Anglo-Saxon Chronicle* (1961), 119–26; J.H. Round, 'Normans under Edward the Confessor', in *Feudal England* (1895, repr. 1964), 247–57; Brown 1976, 43–4; *idem*, *Origins of English Feudalism* (1973), 73–6. On the composition of the Anglo-Saxon Chronicle in this period, see S. Korner, *The Battle of Hastings, England and Europe, 1035–1066* (Lund, 1964), 14–20: although written in their present form after the Conquest, the extant versions of the Chronicle for the Confessor's reign had a pre-Conquest source for the years 1042–57.

20 P.E. Curnow, M.W. Thompson, 'Excavations at Richard's Castle, Herefordshire, 1962–64', *J. Brit. Archaeol. Ass.* 32 (1969), 105–27; R. Shoesmith, *Hereford City Excavations vol. I: Excavations at Castle Green* (CBA Res. Rep. No. 36, 1980), 56–60. *Domesday Book* (Record Commission, vol. I, 1783, fol. 186a,i) recorded that Ewyas had been rebuilt (*castellum refirmaverat*) by William fitzOsbern between 1066 and his death in 1071.

21 *EHD*, vol. I, 431–4. Printed in W. Stubbs, *Select Charters*, 88–90. It is sometimes known as 'Of people's ranks and laws'. On the social mobility implied, see also H.P.R. Finberg (ed.), *The Agrarian History of England and Wales, vol. I, pt. ii, AD 43–1042* (1972), 517–18.

22 For example B.K. Davison, 'The origins of the castle in England', *Archaeol. J.*, 124 (1967), 202–11.

23 R. Allen Brown drew attention to some of the difficulties outlined here in 'An Historian's approach to the origins of the castle in England', *Archaeol. J.* 126 (1969), 131–48; also *Origins of English Feudalism* (1973), 80–2. An example of the later survival of the phrase is Duke Henry's charter to Robert FitzHarding, 1153, granting lands at Bitton and Berkeley, Glos., and permission to build a castle there (H. Cronne, R. Davis (eds), *Regesta Regum Anglo-Normannorum*, vol. III (Oxford 1968, no. 309). The liberties and customs of these lands included 'tol et them et soch et sache et belle et burhgiete et infanckenethef'.

24 D.F. Renn, 'The first Norman Castles in England', *Ch.G. I* (1962), 127–32; D. Whitelock (ed.), *The Anglo-Saxon Chronicle* (1961); William of Poitiers, *Gesta Guilelmi* (ed. R. Foreville, Paris 1952); a summary of the castle entries in Domesday is given in vol. 4 of the Record Commission edition (1816), lxvii–lxxi; see also the list of Domesday and other late-eleventh-century castles in Armitage 1912, 396–9, and C. Harfield, 'A hand-list of castles recorded in Domesday Book', *EHR*, 106 (April 1991), 371–92.

25 The figures given by King and Alcock in 'Ringworks of England and Wales', *Ch.G. III* (1969) were updated in D.J.C. King, 'The field archaeology of mottes in England and Wales', *Ch.G. V* (1972), 101–11, and are approx. 740 mottes and 200 ringworks in England and Wales. Discrepancies between these figures and those in the table (p. 47) reflect the difficulty of identifying and classifying some of the sites.

26 Orderic Vitalis, *The Ecclesiastical History* ed. M. Chibnall, vol.

II (1969), 218–19. On the relationship of the text with William of Poitiers, see *ibid*, xviii, and on Orderic's parentage, *ibid*, xiii. Also, M. Chibnall, *The World of Orderic Vitalis* (1984), and 'Orderic Vitalis on castles', in C. Harper-Bill *et al.* (eds), *Studies in Medieval History presented to R. Allen Brown* (1989), 43–56.

27 S. Rahtz, T. Rowley, *Middleton Stoney: excavations and survey in a North Oxfordshire Parish, 1970–1982*. (Oxford Univ. Dept. External Studies, 1984), 49–53; B.K. Davison 'Castle Neroche: an abandoned Norman Fortress in South Somerset', *Proc. Somerset. Archaeol. Nat. Hist. Soc.*, 116 (1972), 16–58; C.M. Mahaney, 'Stamford: the development of an Anglo-Scandinavian borough', *Proc. Battle Conf.*, V (1982), 197–219, and *idem*, 'Excavations at Stamford castle, 1971–76', *Ch.G. VIII* (1977), 223–45; for Earls Barton, *RCHM: Central Northamptonshire* (1979), 40–2, Renn 1973, 31, 180 and B.K. Davison, 'The origins of the castle in England', *Archaeol. J.* 124 (1967), 202–11; on towers, D. Wilson, 'Defence in the Viking Age', in G. Sieveking *et al.* (eds), *Problems in Economic and Social Archaeology* (1976), 439–45. W.J. Ford, 'Castle Bromwich Castle', *Archaeol. J.* 128 (1971), 214–215, and *Med. Archaeol.*, 15 (1971), 148–9; A. Pinder, B. Davison, 'The excavation of a motte and bailey castle at Chalgrave, Bedfordshire, 1970', *Beds. Archaeol. J.*, 18 (1988), 33–56; J. Allan, C. Henderson, R. Higham, 'Saxon Exeter', in J. Haslam (ed.), *Anglo-Saxon Towns in Southern England* (Chichester 1984), 385–414.

28 B.K. Davison, 'Excavations at Sulgrave, Northamptonshire, 1960–76: an interim report', *Archaeol. J.*, 134 (1977), 105–14.

29 B. Cunliffe, *Portchester*, vol. II (*Soc. Antiq. Res. Rep.* no. 33, 1976), 1–6, 121–7, 301–4; *idem*, 'Excavations at Portchester Castle, Hants; second interim report', *Antiq. J.*, 46 (1966), 39–49; *idem*, 'Excavations at Portchester Castle, Hants; third interim report', *ibid*, 49 (1969), 62–74; B. Cunliffe, J. Munby, *Portchester*, vol. IV, (*Soc. Antiq. Res. Rep.*, no. 43, 1985), 64–71.

30 M. Biddle, 'Winchester: the development of an early capital', in H. Jankuhn *et al.* (eds), *Vor- und Frühformen der Europäischen Stadt im Mittelalter* (vol I, Gottingen 1973), 230–61; *idem*, 'Excavations at Winchester, 1971. Tenth and final interim report: Part II'. *Antiq. J.*, 55 (1975), 295–337; *idem*, 'The study of Winchester: archaeology and history in a British town, 1961–83', *Proc. Brit. Acad.*, 69 (1983), 93–135. On Exeter and York see n.27 and *RCHM York, vol. 2. The Defences* (1972), 9; on London, A. Vince, *Saxon London: An Archaeological Investigation* (1990), 20, 54–57.

31 V. Horsman, 'Eynsford Castle: a re-interpretation of its early history in the light of recent excavations', *Archaeol. Cant.*, 105 (1988), 39–57.

32 G. Beresford, *Goltho: the development of an early medieval manor* (English Heritage, 1987); *idem*, 'Goltho manor, Lincs.', *Proc. Battle Conf.*, IV (1981), 13–36; *idem*, 'The excavation of the deserted medieval village of Goltho, Lincs.', *Ch.G. VIII* (1977), 47–68; *idem*, *The Medieval Clayland Village: excavations at Goltho and Barton Blount* (Society for Medieval Archaeology, Monograph series, no. 6, 1975). The identification and chronology have received criticism from P. Everson, 'What's in a name? 'Goltho',

Goltho and Bullington', *Lincolnshire History and Archaeology*, 23 (1988), 93–9, and R. Hodges, 'The Danish contribution to the origin of the castle in England', *Acta Archaeologica*, 59 (1988), 169–72.

33 J. Coad, A. Streeton, 'Excavations at Castle Acre, Norfolk, 1972–77: Country House and Castle of the Norman earls of Surrey', *Archaeol. J.* 139 (1982), 138–301.

34 See the discussion in R. Morris, *Churches in the Landscape* (1989), ch. VI, where other potential sites of this sort are suggested; on Westminster and other royal palaces, see *KW* I, 42–8; *ibid*, II, 907–9.

35 For a recent summary, D. Bates, *Normandy before 1066* (1982), 111–21.

36 The foregoing information was much quoted in the publications by B.K. Davison, quoted above (n.14); for Hastings, P.A. Barker, K.J. Barton, 'Excavations at Hastings Castle, 1968', *Archaeol. J.*, 134 (1977), 80–100; for Neroche. B.K. Davison, 'Castle Neroche: an abandoned Norman fortress in South Somerset', *Proc. Somerset Archaeol. Nat. Hist. Soc.*, 116 (1972), 16–58.

37 M. Biddle, 'Excavations at Winchester, 1968; seventh interim report', *Antiq. J.*, 49 (1969), 295–329; *idem*, 'Excavations at Winchester, 1971; tenth and final interim report, Part I', *ibid*, 55 (1975), 96–126.

38 A.D. Saunders (ed.), 'Five Castle Excavations. Reports on the Institute's Research Project into the Origins of the Castle in England', *Archaeol. J.*, 134 (1977), 1–156; quotation, p. 5.

39 Discussed in C. Platt, *The Castle in Medieval England and Wales* (1982), 16–19; cf. the re-interpretation of Eynsford, one of the sites discussed in this context (above, n.31).

40 B.K. Davison drew attention to the Rhenish parallels in the publications given in n.14; on the Pas de Calais and England, see J.H. Round, 'The lords of Ardres' in *idem*, *Feudal England* (1964 reprint), 351–2.

41 M. Fulford, *The Silchester Amphitheatre, Excavations 1979–85* (Britannia Monograph, 10, 1989), 59–65, 175–76, 193–195.

42 W. Davies, *Wales in Early Middle Ages* (1982), 19–23.

43 *ibid*; also H.P.R. Finberg (ed.), *The Agrarian History of England and Wales, vol. I, pt. ii, AD 43–1042* (1972), 363–4.

44 *ibid*, 301–2, 358–63; for Rhuddlan, J. Manley, '*Cledemutha*: a late Saxon *burh* in North Wales', *Med. Archaeol.*, 31 (1987), 13–46, and N. Edwards, A. Lane (eds), *Early Medieval Settlement in Wales* (Cardiff 1988), 110–13; the attack of 1063 is in D. Whitelock (ed.), *The Anglo-Saxon Chronicle* (1961), 136; on the general background, L.A.S. Butler, 'Domestic Building in Wales and the evidence of the Welsh Laws', *Med. Archaeol.*, 31 (1987), 47–58.

45 What follows is from L. Alcock, 'The archaeology of Celtic Britain, fifth to twelfth centuries', in D. Hinton (ed.), *Twenty five years of Medieval Archaeology* (1983), 48–66, and Edwards & Lane 1988 (see n.43).

46 C.R. Musson, J. Spurgeon, 'Cwrt Llechryd: an unusual moated site in Central Powys', *Med. Archaeol.*, 32 (1988), 97–109; information on Forden Gaer, Clywd-Powys Arch. Trust, *pers. comm.*

47 For a full narrative see J.E. Lloyd, *A History of Wales* (2 vols. 1911, repr. 1939). The most recent synthesis is R.R. Davies, *Conquest, Co-Existence and Change. Wales 1063–1415* (1987),

esp. ch. 4. Also W. Rees, *An Historical Atlas of Wales from maps- early to Modern Times* (1951).

48 J.G. Edwards, 'The Normans and the Welsh March', *Proc. Brit. Acad.*, 42 (1956), 155–77.

49 For Welsh attitudes and castles, see Davies (n.47). J. Spurgeon in Kenyon and Avent 1987; also D.J.C. King, 'The defence of Wales, 1067–1283: the other side of the hill', *Archaeol. Camb.*, 126 (1977), 1–16; R. Avent, *Castles of the Princes of Gwynedd* (Cardiff 1983); P. Davis, *Castles of the Welsh Princes* (Swansea 1988). A list of documented examples is given in Armitage 1912, 299–301.

50 Ex info. J. Spurgeon, based, *inter alia*, on work done for RCAHM (Wales). And see, *idem*, 'The castles of Montgomeryshire', *Montgomeryshire Collections*, 59 (1965–6), 1–59.

51 Armitage 1912, chaps. VIII-IX, argued the Norman origin of Welsh mottes, as she had for England. Spurgeon, *ibid*, Appendix I, pp. 51–54; R. Haslam (ed.) *The Buildings of Wales: Powys* (1979), 188–96.

52 J. Spurgeon, 'The castles of Glamorgan: some sites and theories of general interest', *Ch.G. XIII* (1987), 203–26; see also D.J.C. King, L. Alcock, 'Ringworks of England and Wales', *Ch.G. III* (1969), 90–127.

53 Spurgeon in notes 50 & 52; D.J.C. King, 'The castles of Cardiganshire', *Ceredigion*, 3 (1956), 50–69; *idem*, 'The castles of Breconshire', *Brycheiniog*, 7 (1961), 71–94; for the Shropshire-Montgomery border, also L. Chitty, 'Subsidiary castle sites west of Shrewsbury', *Trans. Shrops. Archaeol. Soc.*, 53 (1949), 83–90, and D.J.C. King, C.J. Spurgeon, 'The mottes in the vale of Montgomery', *Archaeol. Camb.*, 114 (1965), 69–86; J. Spurgeon, 'Mottes and moated sites in Clywd', in *The Archaeology of Clywd* (forthcoming).

54 Barker and Higham 1982, 72; J. Spurgeon, 'Mottes and Castle-Ringworks in Wales', in Kenyon and Avent 1987, 23–49.

55 *ibid*. This essay contains a most useful summary of Welsh castle archaeology, providing the up-to-date figures (and map) quoted. See also the earlier studies by King and Alcock (see n.51) and A.H.A. Hogg, D.J.C. King, 'Early castles in Wales and the Marches', *Archaeol. Camb.*, 112 (1963), 77–124; *ibid*, 119 (1970), 119–24.

56 For the historical background, see for example G.W.S. Barrow, *Kingship and Unity: Scotland 1000–1306* (1981); *idem*, *The Anglo-Norman Era in Scottish history* (1980).

57 G. Neilson, 'The mottes in Norman Scotland', *Scottish Review*, 32 (Oct. 1898), 209–38; Armitage 1912, chap. X; the inquiry had been started in D. Christison, *Early Fortifications in Scotland* (Edinburgh 1898). The theme will be dealt with in a forthcoming article in *Proc. Soc. Antiq. Scot.* by G. Stell. On the early Norse contribution, S. Cruden, *The Scottish Castle* (1960), and C. Tabraham, *Scottish Castles and Fortifications* (Edinburgh 1986).

58 For Roberton and other sites quoted, see below, Gazetteer.

59 Armitage 1912, 307; W.M. Mackenzie, *The Medieval Castle in Scotland* (1927), 29–30.

60 L. Alcock, 'Early historic fortifications in Scotland', in G. Guilbert (ed.), *Hillfort Studies* (1981), 150–180; *idem*, 'The activities of potentates in Celtic Britain, AD 500–800: a positivist approach', in S.J. Driscoll, M.R. Nieke (eds.), *Power and Politics in Early Medieval Britain and Ireland*

(Edinburgh 1988), 22–39, including (pp.40–6) an appendix by E.A. Alcock, 'Enclosed Places, AD 500–800'; *idem*, 'The archaeology of Celtic Britain, fifth to twelfth centuries AD', in D. Hinton (ed.), *Twenty five years of Medieval Archaeology* (Sheffield 1983), 48–66; *idem*, 'Reconnaissance excavations on early historic fortifications...', *Proc. Soc. Antiq. Scot.*, 116 (1986), 255–79, and *ibid*, 117 (1987), 119–47. See also G. Ewart, *Cruggleton Castle. Report on excavations 1978–81* (Dumfries. Galloway Nat. Hist. Antiq. Soc. Monograph, 1985).

61 E. Talbot, 'Early Scottish castles of earth and timber – recent fieldwork and excavation', *Scottish Chronological Forum*, 6 (1974), 48–57; Crookston is illustrated in C. Tabraham, *Scottish Castles and Fortifications* (HMSO 1986), 32.

62 For what follows, Talbot 1974 (n.61) and *idem*, 'The defences of earth and timber castles', in D.H. Caldwell (ed.), *Scottish Weapons and Fortifications, 1100–1800* (Edinburgh 1981), 1–9; G. Simpson, B. Webster, 'Charter evidence and the distribution of mottes in Scotland', *Ch.G.*, V (1972), 175–92; G. Stell, 'Mottes', in P. McNeill, R. Nicholson (eds.), *An Historical Atlas of Scotland, c.400–c.1600* (St Andrews 1975), 28–9; S. Cruden, *The Scottish Castle* (1960).

63 C.J. Tabraham, 'Norman settlement in Galloway: recent fieldwork in the Stewartry', in D. Breeze (ed.), *Studies in Scottish Antiquity presented to Stewart Cruden* (Edinburgh 1984), 87–124; P. Yeoman, 'Mottes in north-east Scotland', *Scottish Archaeological Review*, 5 (1988), 125–33; for Strachan, see below, Gazetteer.

64 For the general background, M. Dolley, *Anglo-Norman Ireland* (Dublin 1972); and A. Cosgrove (ed.), *A New History of Ireland, vol. II, Medieval Ireland 1169–1534* (Oxford 1987).

65 Armitage 1912, chap. XII; G. Orpen's publications included 'Mote and Bretasche building in Ireland', *EHR*, 21 (1906), 417–44; and *ibid*, 22 (1907), 228–54; and 'Motes and Norman Castles in Ireland', *Journal of the Royal Society of Antiquaries of Ireland*, 37 (1907), 123–52; the historiography of this and earlier generations appears in a thesis currently being written on Irish mottes by Mr Kieran O'Conor.

66 Mr K. O'Conor (University College, Cardiff) and Dr T. McNeill (Queen's University, Belfast) have generously made available their (independent) unpublished work.

67 Orpen himself published *Ireland under the Normans* (4 vols., 1911–20); E. Curtis, *A History of Medieval Ireland, 1086–1513* (1938) was another major work. A more recent example is T. McNeill, *Anglo-Norman Ulster* (Edinburgh 1980). Among the periodical literature, combining documentation and fieldwork, is B.J. Graham, 'The mottes of the Norman liberty of Meath', in H. Murtagh (ed.), *Irish Midland Studies: essays in commemoration of N.W. English* (1980), 39–56.

68 A most useful summary of some of this, in the context of northern Irish excavation generally, is A. Hamlin, C. Lynn (eds.), *Pieces of the Past* (HMSO 1988); also T.B. Barry, *The Archaeology of Medieval Ireland* (1987), chap. 3.

69 There is a large periodical literature concerning the (often controversial) origins, date-range and functions of ring-forts, which it is not appropriate to cite here. For a general review, see G. Barret, 'Problems of spatial and temporal continuity of rural settlement in Ireland, AD 400–1169', *Jnl. Historical Geography*, 8 (1982), 245–60. The inspiration

of much of this work, as well as that on mottes and the problems of motte-ringfort relationship, was *An Archaeological Survey of County Down* by the Archaeological Survey of N. Ireland (HMSO 1966). For contrasting views on the twelfth-century use of raths, C.J. Lynn, 'The medieval ringfort – an archaeological chimera', in *Irish Archaeological Research Forum*, 11 (1975), 29–36; T.E. McNeill, 'Medieval Raths? An Anglo-Norman comment', *ibid*, 37–9.

70 T.B. Barry, 'Anglo-Norman Ringwork Castles: some evidence', in T. Reeves-Smyth, F. Hammond (eds.), *Landscape Archaeology in Ireland* (*BAR*, 116, 1983), 295–314; also T.E. MeNeill, *Anglo-Norman Ulster* (1980), 103; the recent estimate (and map) in T.B. Barry, *The Archaeology of Medieval Ireland* (1987), 45–53. In addition to Barry 1983 and 1987: B. Graham, 'Medieval Timber and Earthwork Fortifications in Western Ireland', *Med. Archaeol.*, 32 (1988), 110–29.

71 R. Glassock, 'Mottes in Ireland', *Ch.G. VII* (1975), 95–110, whose list has been extended, partly by the current field-work such as that referred to in n.66, and also by published studies such as T.E. McNeill, 'Ulster Mottes: a checklist', *Ulster. J. Archaeol.*, 38 (1975), 49–56; see also R.E. Glassock, T.E. McNeill, 'Mottes in Ireland: a draft list', *Bull. Group Study of Irish Historical Settlement*, 3 (1972), 27–51.

72 T.E. McNeill, *Anglo-Norman Ulster* (Edinburgh 1980), 65–9, 102–3; B.J. Graham 1980 (see n.67); T.E. McNeill, 'Hibernia Pacata et Castellata', *Ch.G. XIV* (1990), 261–75; I am grateful to Dr McNeill for access to his text in advance of its publication.

73 I am grateful to K. O'Conor for access to his forthcoming article in the *Kildare Archaeol. J.* entitled 'The later construction and use of motte and bailey castles in Ireland: new evidence from Leinster'.

74 For summaries, Barry 1987, Hamlin & Lynn 1988 (see n.68), and *Archaeological Survey of County Down* (1966), 185–206. For the individual sites referred to see: D.M. Waterman, 'Excavations at Lismahon Co. Down', *Med. Archaeol.*, 3 (1959), 139–76; C.W. Dickinson, D.M. Waterman, 'Excavation of a rath with motte at Castleskreen, Co. Down', *Ulster J. Archaeol.*, 22 (1959), 67–82; D. Waterman, 'Excavations at Duneight, Co. Down', *ibid.*, 26 (1963), 55–78; C.J. Lynn, 'The excavation of Rathmullan, a raised rath and motte in Co. Down', *ibid.*, 44–5 (1981–82), 65–171; B.K. Davison, 'Excavations at Ballynarry Rath, Co. Down', *ibid.*, 24–5 (1961–62), 39–87; T. McNeill, *Anglo-Norman Ulster* (Edinburgh 1980), 84–5, for Dunsilly; C.J. Lynn, 'Excavations on a mound at Gransha, Co. Down, 1972 and 1982: an interim report', *ibid.*, 48 (1985), 81–90 (summary in Hamlin & Lynn 1988, 38–41); Big Glebe, summary in Hamlin & Lynn 1988, 41–4; Deer Park Farms, Glenarm (Antrim), summary in Hamlin & Lynn 1988 (n.67), 44–7; D. Waterman, 'Excavations at Clough Castle, Co. Down', *Ulster J. Archaeol.*, 17 (1954), 103–63.

75 See for example the discussion (pp.112–16) in C. Lynn's Rathmullan report (n.74); for further discussions of the vernacular building tradition see H. Murray, 'Documentary evidence for domestic buildings in Ireland, *c.*400–1200, in the light of archaeology', *Med. Archaeol.*, 23 (1979), 81–97.

76 Armitage 1912, 323, n.1; T.B. Barry, *The Archaeology of Medieval Ireland* (1987), 54–5; Graham 1988 (see n.70).

77 Graham, *ibid*, with references to recent historical work quoted there.

78 Roger of Howden's *Chronica*, quoted in P.F. Wallace, 'Irish Early Christian "wooden" oratories – a suggestion', *North Munster Antiq. Jnl.*, 24 (1982), 19–28 (esp. 27). This article is more relevant to the wider theme of Irish timber buildings than its title suggests.

Chapter 3, p. 78–113

1 G. Schmidt, 'Le fortificazioni altomedievali in Italia vista dall 'aero', *Settimane di Studio del Centro Italiano di Studi sull'alto medioevo*, 15 (1968), pt. 2, 859–928; A.A. Settia, 'Tra Azienda agricola e fortiezza: case forti, "motte" et "tombe" nell'Italia settentrionale. Dati e Problemi', *Archeologia Medievala*, 7 (1980), 31–54; A.A. Settia, conference discussion in *Archéologie Médiévale*, XI (1981), 23–4, 68–9; A.A. Settia, 'Motte e castelli a motta nelli fonti scritte dell'Italia settentrionale. Dati e problemi', in *Mélanges d'archéologie et d'historie médiévales, en l'honneur du Doyen Michel de Boüard* (Paris 1982), 371–83.

2 Armitage 1912, 80–2.

3 A.J. Taylor, 'Three early castle sites in Sicily: Motta Camastra, Sperlinga and Petralia Soprana', *Ch.G.* VII (1975), 209–14.

4 M. de Boüard, 'Quelques données françaises et normandes conçernant le problème des origines des mottes', *Ch.G.* II (1967), 19–26; also noted in Armitage 1912, 81.

5 R. Comba, A.A. Settia (eds.), *Castelli: Storia e Archeologia* (1984). Also, G. Noyé, 'Féodalite et habitat fortifiée en Calabre dans la deuxième moitié du XIe siècle et le premier tiers du XII siècle', in *Structures Féodales et Féodalisme dans l'Occident Mediterraneen (Xe-XIIIe siècles)* (École Française de Rome, 1980), 607–630. For Scribla, G. Noye, 'Le château de Scribla et les fortifications normandes du bassin du Crati de 1044 à 1139', and G. Noye and A.-M. Flambard, 'Le château de Scribla: étude archéologique', both in *Societa, potere e populo nell'eta di Ruggero II* (Bari 1979), 207–38.

6 M. Riu, 'Probables Huellas de los primeros castillos de la Cataluña Carolingia', *San Jorge*, 47 (1962), 34–39. A motte in northern Spain at Mota del Torrejon, where 12th–14th century occupation was excavated, was reported at the First Congress of Medieval Archaeology in Spain in 1985. Thanks are due to Dr Philip Banks for this information and to Dr Richard Hitchcock for translation assistance.

7 P. Banks, J. Zozoya, 'Excavations in the Caliphal Fortress of Gormaz (Soria), 1979–81: a summary', in T. Blagg, R. Jones, S. Kay (eds.) *Papers in Iberian Archaeology* (*BAR*, internat. series, no. 193).

8 W. Anderson, *Castles of Europe from Charlemagne to the Renaissance* (1970), 29–32.

9 D. Herlihy (ed.), *The History of Feudalism* (1970), 228–9; P. Aragnas, 'Les châteaux des marches de Catalogne et Ribagorce', *Bulletin Monumental*, 137 (1979), 205–24; T.N. Bisson, 'Feudalism in twelfth-century Catalonia', in *Structures Féodales* (1980) (see note 5), 173–92.

10 E. Roesdahl, *Viking Age Denmark* (1982), 147–55; *idem*, 'The end of Viking age fortifications in Denmark, and what followed', *Ch.G. XII* (1985), 39–47; *idem*, 'The Danish

geometrical Viking fortresses and their context', *Proc. Battle Conf.*, IX (1986), 209–226.

11 R.A. Olsen, 'Danish medieval castles at war', *Ch.G. IX–X* (1982), 223–235; H. Stiesdal, 'Die altesten dänischen Donjons', *Ch.G. VIII* (1977), 279–86.

12 H. Stiesdal, 'Die motten in Dänemark', *Ch.G. II* (1967), 94–99; idem, 'Late earthworks of the motte and bailey type', *Ch.G. IV* (1968), 219–20; N.K. Liebgott, 'An outline of Danish castle-studies', *Ch.G. XI* (1983), 193–206; V. La Cour, H. Stiesdal, *Danske Voldsteder frå Oldtid og Middelalder* (Copenhagen, 2 vols., 1957, 1963).

13 J. Hertz, 'The excavation of Solvig, a Danish Crannog in Southern Jutland', *Ch.G. VI* (1973), 83–105.

14 See review of M.K. Karger, *Drevni Kiev* (Ancient Kiev) by M.W. Thompson, in *Med. Archaeol.*, 10 (1966), 227–31.

15 For some early medieval background, J. Hermann, 'Wanderungen und Landnahme in Westslawischen Gebeit', *Settimane di Studio del Centro Italiano di Studi sull'alto Medioevo*, 30 (1983), 75–102; P. Skubizewski, 'L'Art des slaves occidentaux autour de l'an mil', *ibid*, 745–99.

16 For general surveys, W. Hensel, 'Types de fortifications slaves du haut moyen-age', *Archaeologia Polona*, 2 (1959), 171–84; W. Hensel, *La Naissance de la Pologne* (1966); W. Hensel, 'Fortifications en bois de l'Europe Orientale', *Ch.G. IV* (1968), 71–136.

17 R. Theodorescu, 'Byzance, Balkans, Occident dans la civilisation roumaine aux Xe–XIIe siècles', *Cahiers de Civilization Mediévale*, 15 (1972), 259–282; G. Anghel, 'Les premiers donjons en pierre de Transylvanie (Roumaine)', *Ch.G. VIII* (1977), 7–20.

18 Hensel 1966 (see note 16), 154 ff; K.W. Struve, *Die Burgen in Schleswig-Holstein; Band I: Die slawischen Burgen* (Neumunster 1981), 69–74; H.J. Brachmann, 'Research into the Early History of the Slav populations in the territory of the G.D.R.', *Med. Archaeol.*, 27 (1983), 89–106.

19 L. Leciejewicz, 'Medieval archaeology in Poland', *Med. Archaeol.*, 20 (1976), 1–15; J. Zak, 'Mittelalterliche kegelförmige Burghügel in Polen', *Ch.G. XI* (1983), 289–91. For the Plemięta excavation, see A. Nadolskiego (ed), *Plemięta* (Warsaw 1985). On late use of earthworks, see L. Kajzer, 'Recent excavation and survey at Zduny, Wrzęd and Kliczków Maly: earthworks of the modern period', *Antiquity*, 65, no. 248, Sept. 1991, 716–21. A general survey of Polish castle problems was given by Dr L. Kajzer as a lecture, 'The major problems of archaeological and architectural researches on defensive architecture in Poland', at the Lund conference on medieval archaeology, 1990. I am indebted to Dr Kajzer for much helpful correspondence and access to his lecture prior to its delivery, as well as to Dr W. Piotrowski for the benefit of a lecture on Polish castles given in Exeter in 1990 and much valuable discussion arising from it.

20 For the Unterregenbach and Xanten excavations see H.M. Taylor (*Med. Archaeol.*, 17 (1973), 192–195) and C.A.R. Radford (*ibid*, 18 (1974), 232–3). For Koepfel, see Salch 1979, 872. For the background to what follows, H. Hinz, *Motte und Donjon* (Cologne 1981) and G.P. Fehring, *Einfuhrung in die Archäologie des Mittelalters* (Darmstadt 1987).

21 English summary in W. Schlesinger, 'Early medieval fortifi-

cations in Hesse: a general historical report', *World Archaeol.*, 7, no.3 (1976), 243–60. R. von Uslar, *Studien zu Frühgeschichtliche Befestigungen zwischen Nordsee und Alpen* (Cologne 1964) is reviewed by M.W. Thompson in *Med. Archaeol.*, 9 (1965), 224–7. Other literature cited in the summary of recent and current research in southern Germany by J. Zeune, 'Castellology in Bavaria', *Fortress*, no.5 (May 1990), 27–34. Thanks are due to Dieter Barz for assistance with current work.

22 See M. Müller-Wille, *Mittelalterliche Burghügel ('Motten') im Nordlichen Rheinland* (Cologne 1966); reviews by M.W. Thompson, *Med. Archaeol.*, 11 (1967), 336–7; and M. de Bouard, 'Recherches récentes sur les mottes de Rhénanie', *Annales de Normandie*, 17 (1967), 359–64.

23 A. Herrnbrodt, *Der Husterknupp: eine Niederreinische Burganlage des frühen Mittelalters* (Cologne 1958). Useful reviews by B. Hope-Taylor, *Antiquity*, 34, no.135 (Sept. 1960), 227–30; and L. Alcock, *Med. Archaeol.*, 3 (1959), 332–4.

24 A. Herrnbrodt, 'Die Ausgrabung der motte Burg Meer in Büderich bei Düsseldorf', *Ch.G. II* (1967), 62–72; W. Janssen, 'Neue Grabungsergebnisse von der frühmittelalterlichen Niederungsburg bei Haus Meer', *ibid* V (1972), 85–99; M. Müller-Wille, *Rheinische Ausgrabungen, I: Beitrage zur Archäologie des Mittelalters* (Cologne 1968), 1–55; W. Janssen, K-H Knorzer, *Die Frühmittelalterliche Niederungsburg bei Haus Meer, Stadt Meerbusch, Kreis Grevenbroich* (Grevenbroich, n.d.).

25 H. Parker, 'Feddersen Wierde and Vallhagar: a contrast in settlements', *Med. Archaeol.*, 9 (1965), 1–10. For background, S.J. de Laet, *The Low Countries* (1958), 153–7, and H. Halbertsma, 'Les mottes Frisonnes', *Ch.G. VII* (1975), 111–25.

26 J.C. Bestemann, 'Mottes in the Netherlands: a provisional survey and inventory', in T.J. Hoekstra, H.L. Janssen, I.W.L. Moermann (eds.), *Liber Castellorum: 40 variates ophet thema kasteel* (Zutphen 1981), 40–59; idem, 'Mottes in the Netherlands', *Ch.G. XII* (1985), 211–24.

27 H.L. Janssen, 'The archaeology of the medieval castle in the Netherlands. Results and prospects for future research', in J.C. Bestemann, J.M. Bos, H.A. Heidinga (eds.), *Medieval Archaeology in the Netherlands* (Assen 1990), 219–64.

28 For Berg van Troje, Bestemann 1981 (see note 26), 46; for other excavations, see J.A. Trimpe-Burger, 'Onderzoekingen in vluchtbergen Zeeland', *Berichten van de Rijksdienst voor Oudheidkundig Bodemondezoek*, 8 (1957), 114–57. I am grateful to June Strong for assistance with Dutch translation.

29 Bestemann 1985 (see note 26); J. Renaud, 'Quelques remarks concernant le 'Hunneschans' au lac d'Uddel', *Ch.G. IV* (1968), 191–9; H.A. Heidinga, 'The Hunneschans at Uddel reconsidered', *ibid*., XIII (1987), 53–62; J.A. Trimpe-Burger, 'The geometrical fortress of Oost-Souburg (Zeeland)', *ibid*., VII (1975), 215–9.

30 J. le Meulemeester, 'Mottes castrales du Compte de Flandre', *Ch.G. XI* (1983), 101–15; D. Callebaut, 'Le Château des comtes à Gand', *ibid*, 45–54. A van der Walle, 'Excavations in the ancient centre of Antwerp', *Med. Archaeol.*, 5 (1961), 123–36.

31 M. Rouche, 'Vinchy: le plus ancien château à motte', in *Mélanges d'Archéologie et d'Histoire Médiévales, en l'honneur du*

Doyen Michel de Boüard (Paris 1982), 365–9.

32 A. Débord (ed.), 'Les fortifications de terre en Europe occidentale du Xe au XIIe siècles (Colloque de Caen, 2–5 Octobre 1980)', *Archéologie Médiévale*, XI (1981), 5–123; J-M. Pesez, 'Approches méthodologiques d'un recensement géneral des fortifications de terres médiévales en France', *Ch.G. XII* (1985), 79–90; E. Zadora-Rio, 'Les essais de typologie des fortifications de terre médiévales en Europe: bilan et perspectives', *Archéologie Médiévale*, XV (1985), 191–6.

33 J. Soyer, 'Les fortifications circulaires isolées en France', *Annales de Normandie*, 15 (1965), 353–414.

34 M. de Boüard, 'Les petites enceintes circulaires d'origine médiévale en Normandie', *Ch.G. I* (1964), 21–35, was a turning-point for non-motte studies in France. M. Bur, *La Maison Forte au Moyen Age* (Paris 1986) is a recent survey.

35 Fournier 1978, 79–80; M. de Boüard, *Manuel d'Archéologie Médiévale* (Paris 1975), 94.

36 A. Débord (ed.) 1981 (see note 32), 18–19. The same problem occurs in establishing the significance of 'motte' names and attributions in Salch 1979, where there are over a hundred under 'A' alone.

37 A. Débord (ed.) 1981 (see note 32), 8.

38 See the bibliography, particularly the items of local and regional study, in M. de Bouard, *Manuel d'Archéologie Médiévale* (Paris 1975), 96 ff.

39 C. Enlart, *Manuel d'Archéologie Française*, vol. II (Paris 1904), eg. 457 ff.

40 P. Héliot, 'Les châteaux-forts en France du Xe au XIIe siècle à la lumière de travaux récents', *Journal des Savants* (1965), 483–514.

41 For instance, de Boüard, 1975 (see n.35), 48–108; Fournier 1978, *passim*.

42 Fournier 1978, 266–74; on the background, C. Gillmor, 'The logistics of fortified bridge-building on the Seine under Charles the Bald', *Proc. Battle Conf.*, XI (1989), 87–106.

43 Armitage 1912, ch. V; Brown 1976, 22–8; Fournier 1978, Part I.

44 J. Verbruggen, 'Note sur le sens des mots *castrum, castellum,* et quelques autres expressions qui désignent les fortifications', *Revue Belge de Philologie et d'Histoire*, 28 (1950), 147–55; on the early eleventh-century Aquitanian chronicler, Ademar of Chabannes, see B. Bachrach, 'Early medieval fortifications in the "West" of France: a revised technical vocabulary', *Technology and Culture* 16 (1975), 531–69, and A. Débord, '*Castrum* et *castellum* chez Ademar de Chabannes', *Archéologie Médiévale*, IX (1979), 97–113.

45 For a summary of the development of French ideas see A. Débord (ed.) 1981 (see n.32), under 'Châteaux et pouvoirs de commandement', 72–80; also G. Fourquin, *Lordship and Feudalism in the Middle Ages* (Eng. trans. I. Sells, 1976), 87–96.

46 Armitage 1912, 72–5.

47 eg. M. de Boüard, *L'Archéologie du Village Médiévale* (Louvain, Gand, 1967), "La Motte", 35–55.

48 Fournier 1978, 65–80; A. Débord (ed) 1981 (see n.32), 8–11.

49 M. de Boüard, Quelques données françaises et normandes concernant le problème de l'origine des mottes', *Ch. G. II* (1967), 19–26.

50 Mortet and Deschamps, i, 113.

51 Such instances found, for example, in M. Bur, *Vestiges d'habitat seignurial fortifié du Bas-Pays Argonnais* (Reims 1972), 6–7.

52 M. de Boüard, 'De l'aula au donjon. Les fouilles de la motte de la Chapelle à Doué-la-Fontaine', *Archéologie Médiévale*, iii–iv (1973–74), 5–110.

53 M. Deyres, 'Le donjon de Langeais', *Bulletin Monumental*, 128 (1970), 179–93; *idem*, 'Les châteaux de Foulque Nerra', *ibid*, 132 (1974), 7–28; Fournier 1978, 69. For a critical view of Deyres's argument, and an unnecessarily disparaging view of timber fortifications, see B. Bachrach, 'The Angevin Strategy of Castle-Building in the reign of Fulk Nerra, 987–1040,' *American History Review*, 88 (1983), 533–60.

54 For an excellent English coverage of the background, see M. Jones, 'The defence of medieval Britanny', *Arch. Jnl.*, 138 (1981), 149–204; the most recent Breton survey is A. Chedeville, N. Tonnère, *La Bretagne Féodale, XIe–XIIIe siècle* (Rennes, 1987), esp. chapter 3.

55 Examples of regional motte studies include: R. Sanquer, 'Les mottes féodales du Finistère', *Bulletin de la Société Archéologique du Finistère*, 105 (1977), 99–126; P. Lanos, 'Les mottes castrales de l'arrondissement de Saint Malo', *Dossiers du Centre Régional Archéologique d'Alet*, 10 (1982), 73–105.

56 For the Leskelen motte, (for which several other publications relate only to the excavation of the chapel), see J. Irien, 'Le site médiévale de Leskelen en Plabennec: le castel Saint-Tenenan', *Bulletin de la Société Archéologique du Finistère*, 109 (1981), 103–19.

57 I am very grateful to Dr M. Jones for discussion of his recent work on manoirs and their relationship with mottes, as well as for more general guidance on Breton matters. See also X. Barral i Altet, 'Motte et maison forte en Bretagne au moyen âge', in M. Bur (ed.) *La Maison Forte au Moyen Age* (Paris 1986), 43–51.

58 Sources quoted in Brown 1976, 25, 27, 28, 35; for Dudo, see A. Renoux, 'Châteaux Normands du Xe siècle', in *Mélanges* 1982 (see note 31), 327–46.

59 M. de Boüard, 'Fouilles au château de Bonneville-sur-Touques', *Annales de Normandie*, 16 (1966), 351–78.

60 F. Delacampagne, 'Seigneurs, fiefs, et mottes du Cotentin (Xe-XIIe siècles); étude historique et topographique', *Archéologie Médiévale*, XII (1982), 175–207.

61 Fournier 1978, 66–7, and references there, esp. A. Renoux, 'Le château des ducs de Normandie à Fecamp (Xe–XIIe)', *Archéologie Médiévale*, 9 (1979), 5–36.

62 E. Zadora-Rio, 'L'enceinte fortifiée du Plessis Grimoult (Calvados)', *Archéologie Médiévale*, 3–4 (1973–74), 111–243; B.K. Davison, 'A survey of the castle of Arques-la-Bataille, Seine-Maritime', *J. Brit. Archaeol. Ass.*, 36 (1973), 100–2.

63 B.K. Davison, 'Early earthwork castles: a new model', *Ch. G. III* (1969), 37–47.

64 J. Decaens, 'Les enccintes d'Urville et de Bretteville-sur-Laize (Calvados)', *Annales de Normandie*, 18 (1968), 311–75; A. Renoux, 'L'enceinte fortifiée d'Audrieu (Calvados), XIIe–XIVe siècles', *Archéologie Médiévale*, 2 (1972), 5–65; J. Decaens, 'L'enceinte de la Chapelle-

Colbert dans la forêt de Saint-Gatien', in *Mélanges* 1982 (see note 31), 91−102.

65 M. de Bouard, 'Les petites enceintes circulaires d'origine médiévale en Normandie', *Ch. G. I* (1964), 21−35; M. Fixot, *Les Fortifications de Terre et les Origines Féodales dans le Cinglais* (Caen 1968); idem, 'Les fortifications de terre et la naissance de la féodalite dans le Cinglais', *Ch. G. III* (1969), 61−6.

66 J. Decaens, 'L'enceinte fortifiée de Sebecourt (Eure)', *Ch. G. VII* (1975), 49−65.

67 On Mirville: J. le Maho, 'Genèse d'une fortification seigneuriale. Les fouilles de la motte de Mirville (XIe−XIIe siècles)', *Ch. G. XI* (1982), 183−92; idem, *Mirville* (Rouen, 1984); idem, 'Note sur l'histoire d'un habitat seigneurial des XIe et XIIe siècles en Normandie: Mirville (Seine Maritime)', *Proc. Battle Conf.*, VII (1985), 214−23; on Gravenchon: idem, 'Notre-Dame-de-Gravenchon (Seine Maritime)', *Archéologie Médiévale*, 17 (1987), 247−50; J.-J. Bertaux (ed.), *Les Châteaux Normands de Guillaume le Conquerant à Richard Coeur de Lion* (Caen 1987). Both sites are also discussed in P. Halbout & J. le Maho, *Aspects de la Construction de Bois en Normandie du I au XIV siècle* (Centre Archéologique de Normandie, Caen, 1984).

68 J. Decaens, 'La motte d'Olivet à Grimbosq (Calvados): résidence seignuriale du XIe siècle', *Archéologie Médiévale*, 11 (1981), 167−201.

69 Thanks are due to J. le Maho for this information and helpful discussion of recent and current work in Normandy. For Gaillefontaine, see also his contribution to *Les Châteaux Normands de Guillaume le Conquerant à Richard Coeur de Lion* (note 67); cf. the earlier rejection of Gaillefontaine by B.K. Davison in *Château Gaillard*, III (1969), 39−42.

70 Armitage 1912, 78; D. Bates, *Normandy before 1066* (1982), 111−21. For a popular review of Norman castle archae-ology, including reconstruction models, see J.-J. Bertaux, J.-Y. Marin, 'Les châteaux Normands', in *Dossiers histoire et archéologie*, 117 (June 1987), 50−5, and J.-J. Bertaux (ed.) 1987 (n. 67). J. le Maho has briefly reviewed the evidence for Carolingian fortification in pre-Norman Normandy in 'Châteaux d'époque franque en Normandie', *Archéologie Médiévale*, 10 (1980), 153−65.

71 On Montgomery, J. Yver, 'Les châteaux-forts en Normandie, jusqu'au milieu du XIIe siècle', *Bulletin de la Societé des Antiquaires de Normandie*, 53 (1955−56), 28−115, esp. 53−4, and B.K. Davison in *Château Gaillard*, III (1969), 41; on the family, see J.F.A. Mason, 'Roger de Montgomery and his sons (1067−1102)', *Transactions of the Royal historical Society*, 5th ser. 13 (1963), 1−28; K. Thompson, 'The Norman aristocracy before 1066: the example of the Montgomerys', *Bulletin of the Institute of Historical Research*, 60 (1987), 251−63.

72 An excellent exception, which deserves acknowledgement, is the discussion in W. Anderson, *Castles of Europe from Charlemagne to the Renaissance* (1970), chap. I.

Chapter 4, p. 114−46

1 For the practices of medieval chroniclers, see B. Smalley, *Historians in the Middle Ages* (1974); A. Gransden, *Historical Writing in England* c.*550 to* c.*1307* (1974); N.F. Partner,

Serious Entertainments − the Writing of History in Twelfth Century England (1977).

2 Alexander Neckham, *De Utensilibus*, in T. Wright, (ed.), *A Volume of Vocabularies* (1857), 96−119, esp. 103−5; quoted in translation in W. Anderson, *Castles of Europe from Charlemagne to the Renaissance* (1970), 97.

3 The text of Lambert's chronicle is in *Monumenta Germaniae Historica*, XXIV (1879), 550−642; the relevant passages are at pp. 613, 624; also in Mortet and Deschamps, i, 180−5; useful discussions in Fournier 1978, 286−92; Brown 1976, 32, 36 (including this translation); Armitage 1912, 89−90. For the political background to Ardres, Guisnes, Merchem and other places in Flanders discussed in this chapter, see H.E. Warlop, *The Flemish Nobility before 1300* (1968; Eng. ed., J.B. Ross, 1975−76, 4 vols.). For Lambert's place in the development of twelfth-century family histories, and his treatment of his patron's careers, see M. Keen, *Chivalry* (1984), 19−20, 32−33, and G. Duby, 'Youth in Aristocratic Society', in idem, *The Chivalric Society* (trans. C. Postan, 1979), 112−22. For the archaeological background to Ardres, see M. Cabral, 'Le Site archéologique d'Ardres, Pas de Calais', *Revue du Nord* 1973, 17−28. The survey of Ardres (British Library Cott. Aug. I, ii, 74) is the work of Giovanni Rosetti, an Italian in Henry VIII's employment from 1543 who may earlier have been in French service − see *KW IV*, pt. II, 393, 700−1. I am grateful to Mr H.M. Colvin for advice on this item.

4 The text of the *Life* is in *Mon. Germ. Hist.*, XV, ii (1888), 1145ff; the relevant passage is in Mortet and Deschamps, i, 312−15; useful discussions in Fournier 1978, 326−8; Brown 1976, 60−1 (including this translation); Armitage 1912, 88−9; G.T. Clark, *Medieval Military Architecture in England* (1884), vol. i, 33−4. On the identification, see Warlop vol. II, n.228, p. 423 (see n.3); also B. Hope-Taylor, 'The excavation of a motte at Abinger in Surrey', *Archaeol. J.*, 107 (1950), 15−43, Appendix A, and J. de Meulemeester, 'Mottes Castrales du Comté de Flandre', *Ch.G. XI* (1982), 101−15. For the plan of Merckeghem, see Salch 1979, 745. For Merchem and Ardres in the wider context of building history in their region, see A. Verplaetsem, 'L'architecture en Flandre entre 900 et 1200', *Cahiers de Civilization Médiévale*, 8 (1965), 25−42.

5 The text is in 'The Dialogues of Laurence of Durham', ed. J. Raine, *Surtees Society*, LXX (1878), 8−15. The relevant passage is translated in Armitage 1912, 147−9, reproduced here with some additions and changes. The site's history and development is in *VCH Durham*, vol. III, ed. W. Page (1928), 64−93, and a useful recent summary, including the quotation, in R. Allen Brown, *Castles from the Air* (1989), 107−9. For an unconvincing argument that the description refers to a wholly stone castle, see S. Toy, *Castles: a short history of fortifications from 1600 BC to AD 1600* (1939), 54.

6 For the *aggeres* of the Norman duchy, above chapter 2; for the *Anglo-Saxon Chronicle* see D. Whitelock's edition (1961), and for the *Gesta Stephani*, the edition by R.C.H. Davis and T. Potter (Oxford Medieval Texts, 1976). On the back-ground to 1154−5, see W.L. Warren, *Henry II* (1973), esp. 51−3, 59−61. Robert of Torigny is quoted in Brown 1976, 82 and 215. For Vreden, see J.C. Bestemann, 'Mottes in the Netherlands', *Ch.G. XII* (1984), 211−20, esp. 213 and n.7,

quoting a description from Albert of Metz.

7 For Ivry, see Brown 1976, 25, 30; also P. Heliot, 'Les origines du donjon résidentiel et les donjons-palais romans de France et d'Angleterre', *Cahiers de Civilization Médiévale*, 17 (1974), 217–34, esp. 230. Orderic's account is in BK.VIII of his *Ecclesiastical History* (ed. M. Chibnall, Oxford, vol. iv, 1973, 290) and in Mortet and Deschamps, i, 276. For the present site, Salch 1979, 621. Jean de Garlande's mid-thirteenth-century *Dictionnaire* is quoted in J.F. Fino, *Forteresses de la France Médiévale* (Paris 1977), 84 and n.3. In a text of *circa* 1005, *architectus* is associated specifically with a *turris lignea* (Mortet and Deschamps, i, 7).

8 For example it is highly likely that Lambert of Ardres' description of the *dunio* or *munitio* built at Guisnes in the mid-tenth century was coloured by the practices and vocabulary of the later twelfth century (*MGH*, XXIV, 564–5). It cannot be used, as some have used it, as evidence of a motte and timber tower of that date. Guines (and Calais) eventually had a circular stone donjon, like Ardres: see L.R. Shelby, 'Guines Castle and the Development of English Bastioned Fortifications', *Ch.G. III* (1969), 139–43; *KW* I, 423–4. That at Guisnes may have been the *domus rotunda* built of stone also referred to by Lambert of Ardres (*MGH* XXIV, 596).

9 M.J. Hubert, 'L'ancien château de Montereau-fault-Yonne', *Bull. Soc. Nat. Antiq. de France* (1954–55), 56–7.

10 The text is in Mortet and Deschamps, i, 78; useful discussion in Brown 1976, 32, 39; Fournier 1978, 77–8. Armitage 1912, 73 and n.4, observed the difficulty of its translation long ago. For Fulk's castles, see M. Deyres, 'Les châteaux de Foulque Nerra', *Bulletin Monumental*, 132 (1974), 7–28.

11 The sources are discussed in Brown 1976, 39 and n.67; Armitage 1912, 73 and n.1 (using a corrupt text); Fournier 1978, 68.

12 Text from the *Miracles of S. Benedict*, quoted in Mortet and Deschamps, i, 10–11; also in Brown 1976, 36, and J.-F. Fino, *Forteresses de la France Médiévale* (Paris, 1977), 110–11.

13 From the *Chronicle* of Guy de Bazoches, monk of Châlons. Text in Mortet and Deschamps, ii, 126–7; discussed with other examples in P. Héliot, 'Les Châteaux forts en France du Xe siècle à la lumière de travaux récents', *Journal des Savants* (1965), 483–514, esp. 498–9.

14 Quoted in J. Richard, 'Châteaux, châtelains et vassaux en Bourgogne aux XIe et XIIe siècles', *Cahiers de Civilization Médiévale*, 3 (1960), 433–47, esp. 435.

15 From a charter of Savigny Abbey, quoted in D. Herlihy, *The History of Feudalism* (New York, London, 1970), 230–1.

16 E. Searle, *The Chronicle of Battle Abbey* (Oxford, 1980), 34–5. The site is further discussed below. For the *Life* by Matthew Paris, see *La Estoire de Seint Aedward le Rei*, ed. K.Y. Wallace (Anglo-Norman Text Society, 1983), esp. p.122.

17 For Torrington, *Gesta Stephani*, 82, and R.A. Higham, S. Goddard, 'Great Torrington Castle', *Proc. Devon. Archaeol. Soc.*, 45 (1987), 97–103. For Brough, *KW II*, 582; for York, *ibid*, 889. For Brough, also *Jordan Fantosme's Chronicle* (ed. R.C. Johnston, Oxford 1981), 110–12.

18 Gerald of Wales, *The Journey through Wales and the Description of Wales* (ed. L. Thorpe, Penguin 1978), 147–9, 195–6;

19 *Bruts*, quoted in E.J. Talbot, 'The defences of earth and timber castles', in D.H. Caldwell (ed.), *Scottish Weapons and fortifications, 1100–1800* (Edinburgh 1981), 1–9, esp. 5.

20 *Bruts*, quoted in Armitage 1912, 280–1; Renn 1973, 131; *KW II*, 590–1.

21 Abbot Suger, *Vie de Louis VI le Gros* (ed. H. Waquet, Paris 1964), 136–40, 158–64; discussed in Brown 1976, 173–4; Fournier 1978, 70, 76–8, 89–90. See also W. Anderson, *Castles of Europe from Charlemagne to the Renaissance* (1970), 80–3.

22 G. Fournier, 'Le Château du Puiset au debut du XIIe siècle et sa place dans l'évolution de l'architecture militaire', *Bulletin Monumental*, 122 (1964), 355–374, from which the plan is taken. Fournier rightly points out that the *murus* of the inner defences could have been a rampart and palisade as easily as a stone wall.

23 For Aumerval, see *MGH*, XXIV, 588–590; also Mortet and Deschamps, ii, 50–2; discussed by Fournier 1978, 71, 79, 328–30. For Bamburgh, D. Whitelock (ed.), *The Anglo-Saxon Chronicle* (1960), 172.

24 The account of Mategriffon 'the Greek-killer', is put together largely from the chronicles of Roger of Howden and Richard of Devizes. Roger was a royal clerk (from Howden, Yorkshire) who accompanied the Crusade but had returned to England by the end of 1191 when he began to write his work. His testimony is therefore that of an eye-witness. Although he did not specifically say the castle was of timber, its speed of erection and dismantling indicate that it was. It was also Roger who said Richard and Philip spent Christmas there: see *Chronica*, vol. III (Rolls Series, ed. W. Stubbs, 1870), 55ff, esp. 67, 92–3, and 105. For Roger generally, F. Barlow, 'Roger of Howden', *EHR*, lv (1950), 352–60. Richard of Devizes, a monk of St Swithun's, (the Old Minster) Winchester, mentioned the (fairly obvious) fact that Mategriffon was timber-built, and refers to its dismantling, transport by boat and later use as a siege tower by Richard's archers at Acre: see *Chronicle of Richard of Devizes* (Nelsons Medieval Texts, ed. J.T. Appleby, 1963), 25, 27, 43. Richard's chronicle (covering the years 1189–92) was not based on any other known written account. His version of events in Sicily and Palestine was presumably based on the testimony of returning Crusaders. The very full account of the Crusade in the *Itinerarium* of Richard I gives few details of the castle but does relate the king's celebration of Christmas there with Philip of France (ed. W. Stubbs, Rolls Series, 1864, 172–3). For the background to the incident, see J. Gillingham, *Richard the Lionheart* (1978), 149–63, and *idem, The Life and Times of Richard I* (1973), 64–9, 81–91.

25 *Chronica Monasterii de Melsa*, ed. E. Bond (Rolls series, 1866), I, 104–5; discussed in A.J. Taylor, 'Military Architecture', in A.L. Poole (ed.), *Medieval England* (1958), I, 98–127, esp. 104; also F.H. Crossley, *Timber Building in England* (1951), 92. For the fate of stone castle fabric at a later date, M.W. Thompson, *The Decline of the Castle* (1987). For Magny-les-Villiers, see Fournier 1978, 80 and n.16.

26 The text is in C.II. Haskins, 'The Norman "consuetudines et iusticie" of William the Conqueror', *EHR*. xxiii (1908), 502–8; *idem, Norman Institutions* (1918), Appendix D. The

text presumably implies that no staging for the removal of spoil from ditches was permitted, and has given rise to suggestions of a maximum depth of about 3 m, though certainty is impossible: e.g. C. Enlart, *Manuel d'archéologie francaise* (Paris, 1904), II, 418–26, and M. de Bouard, 'Les petites enceintes circulaires d'origine médiévale en Normandie', *Ch.G.* I (1964), 23–3.

27 *The Laws of Henry I*, ed. L.J. Downer (Oxford Medieval Texts, 1972), 108, 116, 323. See also Brown 1976, 7 and n.16, where the equation with double banks and ditches is argued.

28 On licences generally, C. Coulson, 'Structural symbolism in medieval castle architecture', *J. Brit. Archaeol. Ass.*, 132 (1979), 73–90; for Basing, *Cal. Pat. Rolls, 1258–66*, 172, and Melton, *ibid, 1292–1301*, 70. For contrasts between Angevin and Capetian policy on castle control, see C. Coulson, 'Fortress policy in Capetian tradition and Angevin practice: aspects of the conquest of Normandy by Philip II', in *Proc. Battle Conf.*, VI (1983), 13–38; on Gascony, J. Gardelles, *Les Châteaux du Moyen Age dans la France du Sud-Ouest* (Geneva 1972), esp. 19 (Ahetze); on Champagne, C. Coulson, 'Castellation in the county of Champagne in the thirteenth century', *Ch.G.* IX–X (1978–80), 347–64, esp. 351–2 (Gurcy); for Gironville, J.M. Poisson, 'Recherches archéologiques sur un site fossoyé du XIVe siècle: la bastide de Gironville', *Ch.G.* XII (1985), 225–36; J.M. Poisson, 'Une fortifications de terre et de bois edifiée en 1324: le bastide de Gironville à Ambronay (Ain)', in M. Bur (ed.), *La Maison Forte au Moyen Age* (Paris 1986), 253–60. For *maison fortes* generally, Fournier 1978, 209–15, and M. Bur, *op. cit.*

29 H.-M. Maurer, 'Burgen', in *Die Zeit der Staufer*, vol. III (Stuttgart 1977), 119–28, esp. 126–7.

30 Quoted in J.C. Bestemann, 'Mottes in the Netherlands', in *Liber Castellorum* (eds. T.J. Hoekstra, H.L. Janssen, I.W.L. Moerman, Amsterdam 1981), 40–59, esp. 42–4.

31 Quoted in R. Fossier, *La Terre et les Hommes en Picardie jusqu' à la fin du XIIIe siècle* (Paris 1968), II, 679.

32 Quoted in P. Héliot, 'Les Château-forts en France du Xe au XIIe siècle à la lumière de travaux rècents', *Journal des Savants* (1965), 483–514, esp. 486; and C. Coulson, 'Structural symbolism in medieval castle architecture', (see n.28).

33 N. Brooks, 'The development of military obligations in eighth and ninth century England', in *England before the Conquest* (eds. P. Clemoes, K. Hughes, 1971), 69–84; D. Hill, 'The Burghal Hidage: establishment of a text', *Med. Archaeol.* 13 (1969), 84–92; R.H.C. Davis, 'Alfred and Guthrum's Treaty', *EHR*, 97 (1982), 803–10; *KW II*, 6–11.

34 *KW I*, 24–6.

35 S.R. Blaylock, 'Exeter Castle Gatehouse: architectural survey', *Exeter Museums Archaeological Field Unit* (1987); S.R. Blaylock and R.A. Higham, 'Exeter Castle', in *The Exeter Area* (Royal Archaeological Institute Summer Meeting Proceedings, Supplement to Archaeol. J., 147 (1990), 35–9).

36 G. Zarnecki, '1066 and Architectural Sculpture', *Proc. Brit. Acad.*, L11 (1966), 87–104 (reprinted in *idem, Studies in Romanesque Sculpture*, 1979).

37 *KW I*, 24–6: A. Ballard, 'Castle Guard and Barons' Houses', *EHR*, XXV (1910), 712–15; Barker and Higham 1982, 13–20.

38 Ballard, *ibid*; R.A. Higham, S. Goddard, M. Rouillard, 'Plympton Castle, Devon', *Proc. Dev. Arch. Soc.*, 43 (1985), 59–75, esp. 61–3.

39 *Gesta Stephani*, 102–4; for Plympton, see previous note; for Devon generally, R.A. Higham, 'Early Castles in Devon, 1068–1201', *Ch.G.* IX–X (1982), 101–16; R.A. Higham, 'Public and Private Defence in the Medieval South-West: town, castle and fort', in R.A. Higham (ed.), *Security and Defence in South West England before 1800* (Exeter Studies in History, no. 19, 1987), 27–49.

40 For the contents of the Treaty of Winchester, see *Gesta Stephani*, 238–40, and *EHD, II*, 404–6; for its aftermath, R. Allen Brown, 'A List of Castles, 1154–1216' *EHR*, 74 (1959), 249–80, esp. 250–1. For Pleshey and Saffron Walden, *ibid*, 251 and n.10; for Stamford, Armitage 1912, 216–17. For documented siegeworks, see *KW I*, 40–2, and Renn 1973, 48–9. For Corfe and the Rings, see *RCHM South East Dorset* (1970), 96–8; for Barley Pound, etc., see D. Renn, D.J.C. King, 'Lidelea castle: a suggested identification', *Antiq. J.*, 51 (1971), 301–3; for the excavation at Bentley, see P. Stamper, 'Excavations on a mid-twelfth century siege castle at Bentley, Hampshire, *Proc. Hants. Field Club Archaeol. Soc.*, 40 (1984), 81–9.

41 For the background, see W.L. Warren, *Henry II* (1973), esp. 140–2; R. Allen Brown, 'A List of Castles' (see n.40), esp. 252–4; for the Assize of Northampton (1174), *EHD, II*, 411–13; for Framlingham, R. Allen Brown, 'Framlingham Castle and Bigod, 1154–1216', *Proc. Suffolk Inst. Nat. Hist. Archaeol.*, 25 (1950), 127–48. For Tutbury, Armitage 1912, 227–8; Mrs Armitage's contention that the timber domestic buildings mentioned in the sixteenth century were survivals from the twelfth is questionable: they could also have been part of the royal works of the fifteenth century: see *KW II*, 847–849. For Axholme, see R. Allen Brown (quoting Ralph Diceto), 'Royal Castle Building in England, 1154–1216', *EHR*, 70 (1955), 353–398, esp. 365. For the siegework at Huntingdon whose destruction is recorded on the Pipe Roll of 1174 (20 Henry II, 50, 63), R. Allen Brown, 'A List of Castles' (see n.40), 252.

42 R. Allen Brown, 'A list . . .' (see n.40), esp. 254–6; *EHD*, III, 332–7 (Magna Carta, 1217 issue, Clause 47). For the new works of the civil war, R. Allen Brown (quoting Walter of Coventry),' Royal Castle-Building . . .' (see n.41), esp. 365; for Anstey, see Renn 1973, 90, and R. Allen Brown, *Castles from the Air* (1989), 38–9; for Barnstaple and Great Torrington, see R.A. Higham, 'The Origins and Documentation of Barnstaple Castle', *Proc. Devon. Archaeol. Soc.*, 44 (1986), 74–81; R.A. Higham, S. Goddard, 'Great Torrington Castle' (above, n.17). The order for the reduction of both was contained in a single royal instruction of 1228 (*Close Rolls, 1227–31*, 69–70). The destruction of Malmesbury (Wilts) in 1217–18 had already been arranged by king John and should not be placed in this category (Pipe Roll 2 Henry III, 9 and Introduction, XV and n.1).

43 F.M. Powicke, *The Loss of Normandy* (2nd ed. 1961), 179, 201.

44 O. Rackham, *Trees and Woodland in the British Landscape* (1976); *idem, Ancient Woodland: its history, vegetation and uses in England* (1980); M. Taylor, *Wood in Archaeology* (Shire

45 Archaeology, 1981); J. Munby, 'Wood', in J. Blair and N. Ramsay (eds) *English Medieval Industries* (1991), 379–405.

45 Abbot Suger quoted in J.-F. Fino, *Forteresses de la France Médiévale* (Paris 1977), 85; on Suger's bias, see C. Coulson 1983 (see n.28), esp. 20 and n.13. For Calais and Guisnes, *KW I*, 426–7; for Dover, *KW II*, 638; Tintagel, *ibid*, 846; Montgomery, *ibid*, 742; Kenilworth, *ibid*, 685; *ibid*, *passim*, for purchase and acquisition of timber in building works at stone castles.

46 Much of what follows is drawn from vols. I and II of *KW*.

47 For Aumerval, above (n.23); for Ardres *c*.1200, see Mortet and Deschamps, II, 188–91, translated in G. Coulton, *A Medieval Garner* (1910), 170–2. For nightwork at Queenborough in the fourteenth century, see *KW II*, 796.

48 For Dover and York, and the problem discussed here, see Brown 1976, 155–7.

49 *KW I*, 26–7.

50 *KW I*, 57–9; on masons and carpenters generally, see various works by J. Harvey, including *English Medieval Architects* (1954); on carpenters specifically, *idem*, 'The medieval carpenter and his work as an architect', *Jnl. Royal Institute of British Architects*, 45 (1938), 733–43; *idem*, 'The King's chief carpenters', *J. Brit. Archaeol. Ass.*, X (1945–47), 13–34.

51 For carpenters, ditchers and *hurdatores*, see *KW I*, 59–62.

52 North Wales, *KW I*, 67 and n.2; Shropshire, quoted in Brown 1976, 82; Sauvey, *KW II*, 829; Chirk, R.W. Eyton, 'The castles of Shropshire and its borders', *Trans. Shrops. Archaeol. Soc.*, X (1886–87), 10–32, esp. 18.

53 For the various meanings of *bretasche*, see below, Appendix A; for Warwick, Armitage 1912, 230–2; Southampton, *ibid*, 840; Eye, *ibid*, 649.

54 Newcastle under Lyme, *KW II*, 748; Wallingford, *ibid*, 850; Skenfrith, *ibid*, 837; Windsor, *ibid*, 865; Worcester, *ibid*, 888, and Armitage 1912, 240–2.

55 *KW II*, 555; Harbottle, P. Salway, 'Nafferton Castle, Northumberland', *Archaeol. Aeliana*, 38 (1960), 129–44; *idem*, 'Nafferton Castle, Northumberland: second report', *ibid*, 39 (1961), 165–78.

56 Montgomery, *KW II*, 740; Vale of Montgomery, Barker and Higham 1982, 19–20; Coleshill (Flint), D.J.C. King, *The Castle in England and Wales: an interpretative history* (1988), 54; *idem*, *Castellarium Anglicanum*, (1983), I, 153. For Rhuddlan, A.J. Taylor, *Rhuddlan Castle* (1956), 4; *KW I*, 318 and n.8. For the Isle of Ré, see *Cal. Pat. Rolls 1232–47*, 340, 343, 352; *Close Rolls 1242–47*, 6; Armitage 1912, 82; *KW I*. 118; Fournier 1978, 79.

57 York, *KW II*, 889–91; Shrewsbury, *ibid*, 835–6 (from which the quotation is taken); Armitage 1912, 207–9; C.A.R. Radford, 'The medieval defences of Shrewsbury', *Trans. Shrops. Archaeol. Soc.*, lvi (1957–60), 15–20.

58 It is likely that an extensive search through certain classes of thirteenth- and fourteenth-century sources in the Public Record Office would provide further evidence of timber defences and buildings on non-royal castles (particulary *inquisitions post mortem*, Ministers Accounts and Enrolled Accounts). Such a search, which is beyond the scope of this work, would probably only amplify the impression given by the evidence quoted.

59 G. Simpson, B. Webster, 'Charter evidence and the distribution of mottes in Scotland', *Ch.G. V* (1970), 175–92; Armitage 1912, 305 and n.3.; W.M. Mackenzie, *The Medieval Castle in Scotland* (1927), 9, 32; E. Talbot, 'Early Scottish castles of earth and timber', *Scottish Arch. Forum*, 6 (1974), 48–57; for Strathbogie, W.D. Simpson, 'The architectural history of Huntly Castle', *Proc. Soc. Antiq. Scot.*, 56 (1922), 134–63, esp. 148–54.

60 *KW I*, 409–22; R.C. Reid, 'Edward I's Pele at Lochmaben', *Trans. Dumfries Galloway Nat. Hist. Antiq. Soc.*, 31 (1952–3), 58–73; A. Macdonald, L.R. Laing, 'Excavations at Lochmaben Castle, Dumfriesshire', *Proc. Soc. Antiq. Scot.*, 106 (1974–5), 124–57. On Edward's Welsh and Scottish wars in their wider context, M. Prestwich, *Edward I* (1988). For Haywra, *KW II*, 671–3; on Edwardian castles in Wales, *KW I*, ch. VI; Emlyn, *KW II*, 646–7; St Briavel's, *ibid*, 822–3; Liddell, D. King, *Castellarium Anglicanum* (1983), I, 88; Fretun, *KW I*, 451.

61 Quoted in W. Douglas Simpson, 'The Tower-Houses of Scotland', in E.M. Jope (ed.), *Studies in Building History* (1961), 229–42, esp. 241–2.

62 'The Chronicle of the Isle of Man', in *The Church Historians of England*, vol. V, pt. I, ed. J. Stevenson (1858), 385–405, esp. 389.

63 *Pipe Roll 17 Henry II*, 29; discussed in *KW I*, 70 and note 6; the expenditure was recorded under Lancashire, from whose coast the timber components were presumably despatched. The evidence of 1211–12 is in *The Irish Pope Roll of 14 John (1211–1212)*, published by *Ulster J. Archaeol.*, Supplement to vol. 4 (1941) with Index and Corrigenda in vol. 6 (1943).

64 For Durrow, see Gerald of Wales, *Opera*, V (*The Conquest of Ireland*), ed. J. Dimmock (Rolls Series, 1867), 387 and note 2; for Dublin, *Cal. Docs. Ireland, vol. I, 1171–1252*, no. 116; for Roscrea, see *Cal. Docs. Ireland, 1171–1252* (ed. H. Sweetman, 1875), 411–12; for King John and the March, *Rotuli Chartarum*, 98–9.

65 J.T. Gilbert (ed.), *Historic and Municipal Documents of Ireland, A.D. 1172–1320* (Rolls Series, 1870), 103–4; *Close Rolls Henry III, 1242–47*, 336–7, 341–2, 343–5, 362–5; *Cal. Docs. Ireland, 1171–1252*, 408.

66 T.B. Barry, E. Culleton, C.A. Empey, 'Kells motte, County Kilkenny', *Proceedings of the Royal Irish Academy*, 84 (1984), 157–70, esp. 162–4.

67 *Ibid*, 164 and note 41; for the documentation on moated sites, see T.B. Barry, *Medieval Moated Sites of S.E. Ireland* (BAR, 35, 1977), 78, 95–7.

68 Quoted in M. Bloch, *Feudal Society* (Eng. Trans. L.A. Manyon, 1965), II, 293; also Brown 1976, 173–4.

69 *L'Histoire de Guillaume le Maréchal, Comte de Striguil et de Pembroke, régent d'Angleterre de 1216 à 1219: Poème historique*, ed. P. Meyer (Société de d'histoire de France, 3 vols., 1891–1901), lines 3929–60; discussed in S. Painter, *William Marshall* (Baltimore 1933), 41–2, and Fournier 1978, 79–80.

70 A.J. Holden, *Le Roman de Rou de Wace* (3 vols. Paris, 1970–73), II, 23, 44–54, 125–133; the connection between the passage quoted and Hastings was noted in Armitage 1912, 159; for a critical view of Wace's reliability, see J.H. Round, *Feudal England* (1895), 399–418. See also *idem*, 'Wace and his authorities', *EHR*, VIII (1893), 677–83, and D.C.

Douglas, 'The companions of the Conqueror', *History*, 28 (1943), 129–47 (cf. *idem*. *William the Conqueror* (1964), 203, 209, where Robert of Eu is included without comment). For an attempt to rescue Wace from the criticism of Round and Douglas, emphasising the contribution of oral tradition, see M. Bennett, 'Poetry as history? The 'Roman de Rou of Wace' as a source for the Norman Conquest', *Proc. Battle Conf.*, V (1982), 21–39, and *idem*, 'Wace and Warfare', *ibid*, XI (1988), 37–59. The normal practice has been to dismiss Wace on this point as anachronistic, e.g. *KW I*, 20, and note 3, Renn 1973, 27, and Bennett *op. cit.* See also the discussion of Hastings in the Bayeux Tapestry, below Chapter 5.

71 W.M. Mackenzie, *The Medieval Castle in Scotland* (1927), 9; *idem*, 'Clay castle-building in Scotland', *Proc. Soc. Antiq. Scot.*, lxviii (1933–4), 117–27 (for Hakon's saga); Mackenzie's view was heavily criticized by W.D. Simpson, 'The architectural history of Rothesay Castle', *Trans. Glasgow Archaeol. Soc.*, ix, pt. iii (1939), 152–83, esp. 165–72; R.L.G. Ritchie, *The Normans in Scotland* (1954), 307–9, quotes the Roman von Guillaume le Clerc, where the castle built by Somerled of Argyll, though described in terms contemporary with its composition, was set in the Arthurian period. For Stirling in the fourteenth century, see *KW I*, 422 and note 1.

72 Translation from A. Conran, *The Penguin Book of Welsh Verse* (1967), 153–4; for a more literal translation, as well as the site's history and excavation, see D. Hague, C. Warhurst, 'Excavations at Sycharth Castle, Denbighshire, 1962–63', *Archaeol. Camb.* 115 (1966), 106–27. On the late medieval traditions of Welsh poetry, see T. Parry, *A History of Welsh Literature* (1955), chap. VI, and G. Williams, *An Introduction to Welsh Poetry* (1953), chaps. V, VI. For the historical background, J.E. Lloyd, *Owen Glyn Dwr* (Oxford 1931), including Appendix II, 'The Poetry', 154–7. For a poetic description of another Welsh house, in Montgomeryshire, where a similar poetic device with multiple building elements is found, see D.R. Thomas, 'Llandrinio in the fifteenth century: two poems by Gutto'r Glyn, *circa* 1430–1470', *Montgomeryshire Collections*, 33 (1904), 143–54. The emphasis on multiple units may refelect much earlier building traditions, seen in the law codes which describe the nine buildings erected at royal properties for kings by their bondmen. Although by the later middle ages these separate functions were probably under one roof, their literary description may have been anachronistic: see I.C. Peate, *The Welsh House* (Liverpool, 1944), 112–33.

Chapter 5, pp. 147–170

The sources discussed in this chapter are listed in one composite note for each subject discussed in the text.

1 The literature on the Bayeux Tapestry is extensive, and the debate about its interpretation continues. It has recently been suggested by R. Chenciner as an eighteenth-century reproduction of the original, though the idea has not found general favour. The major issues are discussed in its most recent edition, *The Bayeux Tapestry*, ed. Sir D. Wilson (1985). Also useful is the earlier version, ed. Sir F. Stenton (2nd ed. 1965), which contains a commentary on the buildings by R. Allen Brown. In the 1985 edition the arguments for its date and origin are on pp.201–12, the discussion of building evidence on pp.213–18, and the relevant plates are nos. 21–5 and 49–50. Especially useful is N.P. Brooks and the late H.E. Walker, 'The authority and interpretation of the Bayeux Tapestry', *Proc. Battle Conf.*, I (1978), 1–34. On the building of William's fleet, see C.M. Gilmor, 'Naval logistics of the cross-channel operation, 1066', *ibid*, VII (1984), 105–31. For bow-sided building construction and convex roof-lines, see P. Schmidt, 'The Trelleborg house reconsidered', *Med. Archaeol.*, XVII (1973), 52–77. See also U.T. Holmes, 'The houses of the Bayeux Tapestry', *Speculum*, 34 (1959), 179–83; H. Hinz, 'Zu zwei Darstellungen auf dem Teppich von Bayeux', *Ch.G. VI* (1972), 107–19; H. Hinz, *Motte und Donjon* (Cologne, 1981).

For plans of the later medieval defended towns of Dol, Dinan and Rennes, see Salch 1979, 415, 417, 965. For the possible destroyed motte at Dol, see P. Lanos, 'Les mottes castrales de l'arrondissement de Saint Malo', *Les Dossiers du Centre Régional Archéologique d'Alet*, 10 (1982), 73–105, esp. 77–9. For Rennes and Dinan, see A. Chédeville & N. Tonnère, *La Bretagne Féodale, XI–XIII siècle* (Rennes 1987), 409–16. For Rennes (including a plan showing the position of a motte), Dinan and Dol, see also M. Jones, 'The defence of medieval Britanny', *Archaeol. J.*, 138 (1981), 149–204, esp. 153–5, 158. For the possible construction of Hastings from bags of sand, see A.J. Taylor in *Archéologie Médiévale*, XI (1981), 29. For discussion of the possibly stilted construction of motte towers and the possible use of external protective plates, see B. Hope-Taylor, 'The Norman motte at Abinger, Surrey, and its wooden castle', in R. Bruce-Mitford (ed.), *Recent Archaeological Excavations in Britain* (1956), 223–49. An early Asiatic portrayal of a tower hung with shields is in A. Mersier, 'Hourds and Machicoulis', *Bulletin Monumental*, 82 (1923), 117–29, esp. 118–19. For the *operturae* at Le Puiset see the passages quoted above in chapter 4. For 'targes' see *KW I*, 364–5, 453 and *KW II*, 747, 823. Timber protection is discussed generally in W. Hermann, *Le Château Préfabriqué* (Strasbourg 1989).

2 For the association of Humphrey of Tilleul with the campaign and with Hastings castle, see J.F.A. Mason, 'The companions of the Conqueror: an additional name', *EHR*, LXXI (1956), 61–9; the crucial passage in Orderic Vitalis, 'Humphrey of Tilleul, who had held the castle of Hastings from the day of its foundation', is in his *Ecclesiastical History*, ed. M. Chibnall, vol. II, 220. On Hastings itself, see A.J. Taylor, 'Evidence for a pre-conquest origin for the chapels in Hastings and Pevensey castles', *Ch.G. III* (1969), 144–51; P.A. Barker and K.J. Barton, 'Excavations at Hastings castle, 1968', *Archaeol. J.*, 134 (1977), 80–100; *KW II*, 669–70. For the motte stratigraphy quoted see Renn 1973, 259 (Norwich), 131 (Carisbrooke), 336 (Urr); T.G. Hassal, 'Excavations at Oxford castle, 1965–73', *Oxoniensia*, XLI (1976), 232–308, esp. 243; P.V. Addyman, 'Baile Hill, York', *Archaeol. J.*, 134 (1977), 115–56; R.A. Higham, 'Excavations at Okehampton castle, Devon, Part I: the motte and keep', *Proc. Devon Archaeol. Soc.*, 35 (1977), 3–42. Mrs Armitage, whose discussion of the sources for Hastings was characteristically perceptive, rendered the

Pipe Roll entries for 1181–2 and 1182–3, *in operatione castelli Nove Hasting*, as 'the new castle' which may be strictly speaking incorrect if the capital 'N' is deliberate, though the overall meaning in the context is much the same (*PR 28 Hen II*, 88 and *29 Hen II*, 138).

3 For Westminster palace, see *K.W.I*, 45–7, and W.R. Lethaby, 'The palace of Westminster in the eleventh and twelfth centuries', *Archaeologia*, LX (1906), 131–48. The discoveries of 1834 were reported by S. Smirke in *Archaeologia*, XXVII (1838), 135–9, and became more widely known through their inclusion in *RCHM (England), London, vol. ii: West London* (1925), 121–3 and plate 177, when the pieces were in the Victoria and Albert Museum. Now housed in the Jewel Tower, Westminster, they have been commented upon in various publications by G. Zarnecki: *English Romanesque Sculpture 1066–1140* (1951), 17–18, 29 and plates 25–6; '1066 and Architectural Sculpture', *Proc. Brit. Acad.*, LII (1966), 87–104; 'Romanesque sculpture in England and Normandy in the eleventh century', *Proc. Battle Conf.*, I (1978), 168–89; the most recent commentary, from which the passage quoted in the text comes, is in *English Romanesque Art 1066–1200* (Hayward Gallery Exhibition Catalogue, 1984), 147, 154–5. Thanks are due to Dr Lindy M. Grant for allowing access to her unpublished M.A. thesis, 'Romanesque Sculptural Decoration at Westminster Hall' (Courtauld Institute of Art, 1976), which contains a valuable description and discussion. Long recognized as some sort of castle, the piece in question was used by Hope-Taylor (1956) in his interpretation of Abinger (see n.1), but the assumption that it represents a timber building was questioned by R. Allen Brown in the 1965 edition of the Bayeux Tapestry, 87 and n.55. The basic assumption is still, however, much repeated, for example in the 1985 edition of the Tapestry, 214. For Plympton, see R.A. Higham, S. Goddard, M. Rouillard, 'Plympton Castle, Devon', *Proc. Devon Archaeol. Soc.*, 43 (1985), 59–75.

4 The sculpture has been the subject of extensive commentary by R.S. Loomis, who favoured a very early twelfth-century date and wrote the following works. The best reproduction of the piece is in his *Arthurian Legends in Medieval Art* (1938, Kraus reprint 1975), 8–10, 32–6 and plates 7–8. See also 'An Italian sculpture and a Breton tale', in *Celtic Myth and Arthurian Romance* (New York, 1927), 3–11; 'The date, source and subject of the Arthurian sculpture at Modena', in *idem* (ed.), *Medieval Studies in memory of Gertrude Schoepperle Loomis* (Paris and New York, 1927), 209–28; 'The Modena sculpture and Arthurian romance', *Studi Medievali*, IX (1936), 1–17; *Arthurian Literature in the Middle Ages* (1959), 60–2 and plate 2. For more recent opinion, allowing for a date up to about 1150, see R. Salvini, *Il duomo di Modena* (Modena 1983) and A. Peroni & E. Castelnuovo in *Lanfranco e Wiligelmo. Il duomo de Modena* (Modena 1985). The contrasting views are usefully discussed in W. Hermann, *Le Château Préfabriqué* (Strasbourg 1989), 29–38. The relevance of the carving in our context was kindly pointed out by Drs C. Currie and R. Rogers.

5 The two depictions are from British Library Add. Ms. 10293, fols 157, 160. They were first discussed in T. Wright,

'Illustrations of domestic architecture,' *Archaeol. J.* i (1844), 301–7. One was reproduced in T.H. Turner, *Domestic Architecture of the Middle Ages*, vol. II (1853), 14, and again in T.B. Barry, *Medieval Moated Sites of S.E. Ireland* (BAR, 35, 1977), 79 (incorrect manuscript reference in both cases). The context and date of the three related Mss. (10292, 10293, 10294) are discussed in R.S. Loomis, *Arthurian Legends in Medieval Art* (1938), 97–8.

6 For the *Armorial* of William Revel see the publications by G. Fournier: *Châteaux, Villages et Villes d'Auvergne au XV siècle, d'après l'Armorial de Guillaume Revel* (Geneva, 1973); 'Les fortifications de la Basse Auvergne au milieu du XV siècle, d'après l'Armorial de Revel', *Ch.G. V* (1972), 55–64; 'La maison forte en Auvergne', in M. Bur (ed.), *La Maison Forte au Moyen Age* (Paris, 1986), 261–88.

7 First published in H. Braun, *The English Castle* (1936), 53 and plate 13. On the relationship of Old and New Buckenham, see M. Beresford, *New Towns of the Middle Ages* (1967), 468; Brown 1976, 78, 215; *idem, Castle Rising* (HMSO, 1978), 13–14; P. Rutledge & S. Rigold in *Archaeol. J.*, 137 (1980), 352–5. On New Buckenham, see D. Renn, 'The keep at New Buckenham', *Norfolk Archaeology*, XXXII (1960), 232–5; R.P. Wilcox, *Timber and Iron Reinforcement in Early Buildings* (Society of Antiquaries, 1981), 15–17. The foundation charter of New Buckenham priory is given in W. Dugdale, *Monasticon Anglicanum*, vol. VI, part i (1830), 419. E.J. Rose (Norfolk Archaeological Unit) supplied further material about the two sites, and P. Rutledge (Norfolk Record office) most helpfully supplied the information quoted here on the date and context of the carving and on the significance of the flanking animals. M. Myhill kindly took some working photographs. For aerial views of Old and New Buckenham see R. Allen Brown, *Castles from the Air* (1989), 58–61.

8 This piece has been much reproduced in general works on castles and warfare. For the general background to Martini, see J. White, *Art and Architecture in Italy 1250–1400* (Pelican History of Art, 1966), 233–43. The best edition of Martini's work is G. Contini and M. Gozzoli, *L'Opera Completa di Simone Martini* (Milan, 1970). The authenticity of this fresco was challenged a few years ago, and it has been suggested as the work of a later artist. The radial marks on the second piece illustrated result from a (presumably revolving) world map which once covered it. On the local context of Martini's works at Siena, see A. Cairola, *Simone Martini and Ambrogio Lorenzetti in the Town Hall of Siena* (Florence, n.d.), where the associated collection of maps and globes is also explained.

9 See P.A. Barker, *Techniques of Archaeological Excavation* (1977), 219–21. For the general background to Campagnola and his contemporaries, see S.J. Friedberg, *Painting in Italy 1500–1600* (Pelican History of Art, 1970), 236–42.

10 Illustrated and discussed in M. Bur, *Vestiges d'habitat seignurial fortifié du Bas- Pays Argonnais* (Reims, 1972), 6–7, 39–45. The author has kindly provided further comment which is incorporated in the text. For a historical note on the site, see C. Coulson, 'Castellation in the County of Champagne in the thirteenth century', *Ch.G. IX–X* (1982), 347–64, esp. 355, n.35.

11 See M. Merriman, 'The Platte of Castlemilk, 1547', *Trans.*

Dumfries. Galloway Nat. Hist. Antiq. Soc., 44–5 (1967–68), 175–81; also in G. Stell, *Dumfries and Galloway* (1986), 91. The suggestion of clay construction is in W.M. Mackenzie, *The Medieval Castle in Scotland* (1927), 32–5, where a sketch of the site based on the platte also occurs. For the twelfth-century origin, see Renn 1973, 138.

12 British Library Cotton Augustus I, vol. ii, 106; the drawing belongs to the same group of material as the surveys of *c.*1540 which included Ardres and Guisnes (above, chapter 4, n.3,8).

Chapter 6, pp. 171–93

1 Robert of Torigny, quoted in chapter 3; the building may be depicted on the Bayeux Tapestry: see Brown 1976, 33.

2 William of Poitiers, *Gesta Guillelmi* (ed. R. Foreville, Paris, 1954), 18; Orderic Vitalis, *Eccles. Hist.* vol. 4 (ed. M. Chibnall, Oxford 1973), 208–10; Fournier 1978, 300 and n.1; the existing keep is illustrated in Salch 1979, 204. On this and other passages in Orderic relevant to castle building-materials, see M. Chibnall, 'Orderic Vitalis on castles', in *Studies in Medieval History presented to R. Allen Brown* (eds. C. Harper-Bill, C.J. Holdsworth, J.L. Nelson, 1989), 43–56.

3 For Amboise, see Mortet and Deschamps, i, 113 and n.2; for la Bussière, Fournier 1978, 81 and n.18; for Paris, see J.-F. Fino, *Forteresses de la France Médiévale* (Paris 1977), 106–7.

4 P. Héliot, 'Les origines du donjon résidentiel et les donjons-palais romans de France et d'Angleterre', *Cahiers de Civilization Médiévale*, 17 (1974), 217–34, esp. 218; A.L.J. Van der Walle, 'Le Château des Comtes de Flandre à Gand,' *Ch.G. I* (1964), 161–9; D. Callebaut, 'Le Château des Comtes à Gand', *ibid*, XI (1982), 45–54.

5 F.M. Powicke, *The Loss of Normandy* (2nd ed., 1961), 184–96, 204–6; for Gisors, also Y. Bruand, 'Le Château de Gisors', *Bulletin Monumental*, 115–16 (1957–58), 243–65.

6 *KW II*, passim.

7 Arundel, *KW II*, 554; Carlisle, *ibid*, 596; Gloucester, *ibid*, 651 and n.11 (Armitage 1912, 156–8, was apparently mistaken in identifying these works as a wholly timber keep).

8 The evidence for these references will be found in the alphabetical list of entries in *KW II*; for Carisbrooke, *ibid*, 591–5.

9 Kidwelly, *KW II*, 685–7; for Marck, *KW I*, 455.

10 For the toy castles of the royal family, see A.J. Taylor, 'Military architecture', in A.L. Poole (ed.), *Medieval England* (1958), vol. I, 98–127, esp. 98; on the period generally, A.J. Taylor, 'Castle-building in Wales in the later thirteenth century: the prelude to construction', in E.M. Jope (ed.), *Studies in Building History* (1961), 104–33; J. Goronwy Edwards, 'Edward I's castle-building in Wales', *Proc. Brit. Acad*, 32 (1946), 15–81; *KW I*, ch. VI; for the hall from Ystumgwern at Harlech see *Archaeol. Camb.*, vol. 2, 3rd series (1856), 176–7.

11 The evidence for these references will be found in the alphabetical list of entries in *KW II*; for Montgomery see the survey of 1592–93 printed in appendix I to J.D.K. Lloyd and J.K. Knight, *Montgomery Castle* (HMSO, 1973); for Windsor see W.H. St J. Hope, *The Architectural History of Windsor Castle* (2 vols. and plans, 1913), esp. vol. II, 501–4,

544–7. I am most grateful to Mr B. Kerr and Mr J. Pidgeon for providing information from their unpublished research at Windsor, carried out on behalf of English Heritage, and to Mr O. Everett, Royal Librarian, for providing the seventeenth-century illustrations.

12 *Sir Gawain and the Green Knight*, trans. W.R.J. Barron (1974), 12–13, 67–71; see also M.W. Thompson, 'The Green Knight's Castle' in *Studies in Medieval History presented to R. Allen Brown* (see n.2), 317–25.

13 Renn 1973, 85, 187–9; N. Pevsner, I. Nairn, B. Cherry, *The Buildings of England: Surrey* (2nd ed., 1971), 233; C. Hewett, *English Historic Carpentry* (1980), 38–41; for the castle generally see M.W. Thompson, 'Excavations in Farnham Castle keep, Surrey, England, 1958–60', *Ch.G. II* (1967), 100–5; idem, 'Recent excavations in the keep of Farnham Castle, Surrey', *Med. Archaeol.*, IV (1960), 81–94; idem, Farnham Castle Keep (HMSO, 1961).

14 N.W. Alcock, R.J. Buckley, 'Leicester Castle: the Great Hall', *Med. Archaeol.*, XXXI (1987), 73–9, with references to earlier work; see Renn 1973, 223, for the castle generally.

15 J. Blair, 'The twelfth century Bishop's Palace at Hereford', *Med. Archaeol.*, XXXI (1987), 59–72, with references to earlier work.

16 R. Meeson, 'The Timber Frame of the Hall at Tamworth, Staffordshire, and its contents', *Archaeol. J.*, 140 (1983), 329–40.

17 For Conway, A.J. Taylor, *Conway Castle and Town Walls* (HMSO, 1968); for Kidwelly and a general discussion of hourdes, D.J.C. King, *The Castle in England and Wales* (1988), 85–6, 97; for the other examples see the alphabetical sequence of entries in Renn 1973 (with Warkworth on p. 71). The drawings of hourdes and other details commonly reproduced in books, for example, A. Hamilton Thompson, *Military Architecture* (1912, 1975 reprint), 79, originate from Viollet-le-Duc's *Dictionnaire de l'Architecture* and owe much to the latter's creativity. See also A. Mersier, 'Hourds et Machicoulis', *Bulletin Monumental*, 82 (1923), 117–29. On Viollet-le-Duc see T. Ball, 'Castles on paper', *Fortress*, 2 (Aug. 1989), 2–15.

18 For Heidenreichstein (Austria), where a timber gallery survives beneath the conical roof of a cylindrical tower, see W. Anderson, *Castles of Europe from Charlemagne to the Renaissance* (1970), 160; for fortified churches and castles in Romania, see G. Anghel, 'Les premiers donjons en pierre de Transylvanie (Roumanie)', *Ch.G. IX–X* (1982), 13–33; for other examples of surviving timberwork in the upper storeys of castle and town walls in Germany and Switzerland, see W.F. Schuerl, *Medieval Castles and Cities* (English trans. F. Garvie, 1978); for Woël, see Salch 1979, 1258.

19 M.E. Wood, *Thirteenth Century Domestic Architecture in England* (*Archaeol. J.*, vol. 105, supplement, 1950), 65–70 (where the dating of much of the site is earlier than that now generally accepted); for much of the argument presented here, see R.A. Cordingley, 'Stokesay Castle, Shropshire: the chronology of its buildings', *The Art Bulletin*, 45 (1963), 91–107; see also J.F.A. Mason, *Stokesay Castle, Shropshire* (undated guidebook, *c.*1966). Mr B. Morley, Ms G. Chitty and Mr R. Tolley kindly offered comments on the current conservation work.

20 R.P. Wilcox, *Timber and Iron Reinforcement in Early Buildings*

(Soc. Antiquaries Occasional Paper, New Series, II, 1981), 12−21, 28−35; *idem*, 'Timber reinforcement in medieval castles', *Ch.G. V* (1972), 193−202; R.A. Higham, S. Goddard, M. Rouillard, 'Plympton Castle, Devon', *Proc. Devon. Archaeol. Soc.*, 43 (1985), 59−75; for York, Renn 1973, 351−2; G. Benson and H. Platnauer, 'Notes on Clifford's Tower', *Yorkshire Philosophical Society Report.* (1902), 68−74; *RCHM York, vol. II: The Defences* (1972), 74.

21 W. Hermann, *Le Château Préfabriqué* (Strasbourg 1989), 24−8, where other published discussions of the site are quoted.

22 C.J. Lynn, 'The excavation of Rathmullan, a raised rath and motte in Co. Down', *Ulster J. Archaeol.*, 44−5 (1981−82), 65−171, esp. 99−112.

23 D. Hague, C. Warhurst, 'Excavations at Sycharth castle, Denbighshire, 1962−63', *Archaeol. Camb.*, 115 (1964), 108−27.

24 But note that the suggestion by S. Rigold, 'Eynsford Castle and its excavation', *Archaeol. Cant.*, 86 (1971), 109−171, of a Norman timber tower on stone footings at Eynsford (Kent) has been disproved by more recent excavation at the site: see above, chapter 2.

25 Renn 1973, 50, 90.

26 S. Rigold, 'Totnes Castle: recent excavations', *Trans. Devonshire Ass.*, 86 (1954), 228−56.

27 For a preliminary statement, see M.W. Thompson, 'Motte Substructures', *Med. Archaeol.*, V (1961), 305−6.

28 M.W. Thompson, 'Recent excavations in the keep of Farnham Castle, Surrey', *Med. Archaeol.*, IV (1960), 81−94; *idem*, 'Excavations in Farnham Castle keep, Surrey, England, 1958−60', *Ch.G. II* (1967), 100−5.

29 B.K. Davison, 'Three eleventh century earthworks in England', *Ch.G. II* (1967), 39−48, esp. 40−3.

30 J. Coad, A. Streeton, 'Excavations at Castle Acre, Norfolk, 1972−77: country house and castle of the Norman earls of Surrey,' *Archaeol. J.*, 139 (1982), 138−301; *idem*, 'Excavation at Castle Acre, Norfolk', *Ch.G. VIII* (1977), 79−85.

31 Interim Notes in *Med. Archaeol.*, VI−VII (1962−63), 326; *Morgannwg*, IV (1960), 69−70, V (1961), 81.

32 P.A. Barker, 'Pontesbury Castle Mound emergency excavations, 1961 and 1964', *Trans. Shrops. Archaeol. Soc.*, 57 (1961−64), 206−23.

33 Interim Reports by D. Austin in *J. Brit. Archaeol. Ass.*, 132 (1979), 50−72 and 133 (1980), 74−96; *idem*, 'Barnard Castle', *Ch.G. IX−X* (1982), 293−300; other information kindly supplied by Mr Austin.

34 S.R. Blaylock, 'Exeter castle gatehouse: architectural survey, 1985', *Exeter Museums Archaeological Field Unit Report* (1987); S.R. Blaylock, R.A. Higham, 'Exeter Castle', in *The Exeter Area* (Royal Archaeological Institute Summer Meeting, Supplement to *Archaeol. J.*, 147 (1990), 35−9.

35 F. Williams, *Pleshey Castle, Essex (XII−XVI Century): excavations in the bailey, 1959−63* (BAR 42, 1977), esp. 37−40; other information in the annual notes in *Med. Archaeol.*, *passim.*

36 K.W.B. Lightfoot, 'Cae Castell, Rumney, Cardiff: final interim report', *Glam-Gwent Arch. Trust Ltd., Annual Report* (1981−82), 1−7.

37 Interim Notes in *Med. Archaeol.*, XII (1968), 181−2; XIV (1970), 179; XVI (1972), 186.

38 P.V. Addyman, 'Excavations at Ludgershall Castle, Wiltshire, England, 1964−72', *Ch.G. VI* (1973), 7−13; other information in the annual notes in *Med. Archaeol.*, passim.

39 B.K. Davison, 'Excavations at Sulgrave, Northants, 1960−76: an interim report', *Archaeol. J.*, 134 (1977), 105−14.

40 B. Cunliffe, *Portchester*, vol. II (Soc. Antiq. Res. Rep., no. 33, 1976).

41 For Durham, see chapter 4. For Winchester, see M. Biddle, 'Excavations at Winchester, 1971; tenth and final interim report: part I', *Antiq. J.*, LV (1975), 96−126. For Dover, see *Med. Archaeol.*, VI−VII (1962−63), 322 and VIII (1964), 254−5.

42 J. Decaens, 'L'enceinte fortifiée de Sebecourt (Eure)', *Ch.G. VII* (1975), 49−65.

43 J. Decaens, 'Les enceintes d'Urville et de Bretteville-sur-Laize (Calvados)', *Annales de Normandie*, 18 (1968), 311−75.

44 E. Zadora-Rio, 'L'enceinte fortifiée du Plessis-Grimoult (Calvados)', *Archéologie Médiévale*, iii−iv (1973−74), 111−243; *idem*, 'L'enceinte fortifiée du Plessis-Grimoult, résidence seigneuriale du xi siècle', *Ch.G. V* (1972), 227−39.

45 P. Halbout, J. le Maho, *Aspects de la Construction de Bois en Normandie du I siècle au XIV siècle* (Centre Archéologique de Normandie, Caen, 1984), 96−8; J. le Maho, 'Notre-Dame-de Gravenchon (Seine Maritime)', *Archéologie Médiévale*, 17 (1987), 247−50.

46 R. Borremans, 'Fouille d'une motte feodale a Kontich', *Ch.G. I* (1964), 9−20.

47 For Windsor, see *KW II*, 868.

48 B.K. Davison, *The Observer's Book of Castles* (1979), 123−5.

49 M. Beresford, J.G. Hurst (eds.), *Deserted Medieval Villages: Studies* (1971), 93−4; for a review of the European evidence, complicated by wider regional variation in climate and available building materials, see J. Chapelot, R. Fossier, *The Village and House in the Middle Ages* (English trans. H. Cleere, 1985), 277−84.

50 These points have been discussed by various authors. See, for example, A. Chatelain, *Donjons Romans des Pays d'Ouest* (Paris 1973), 18−19, 28; *idem*, 'Essaie de typologie des donjons romans quadrangulaires de la France de l'Ouest', *Ch.G. VI* (1973), 43−57.

Chapter 8, pp. 244−325

1 Published references to French and German sites will be found in notes 2 and 5 to chapter 1, and notes 23 and 67 to chapter 3. Those for British sites will be found in the Gazetteer of Excavations, chapter 11, and the Gazetteer number is given in brackets after the site name.

2 Weoley: A. Oswald, 'Excavation of a thirteenth-century wooden building at Weoley castle, Birmingham, 1960−61', *Med. Archaeol.*, 6−7 (1962−63), 109−34.

Chapter 10, pp. 326−46

1 See M. Keen, *Chivalry* (Yale 1984).

2 Armitage 1912, 78.

3 For example in Britain by D.J.C. King in the opening chapters of *Castellarium Anglicanum* (2 vols 1983) and in *The Castle in England and Wales: An Interpretative History* (1988); and in France by A. Débord, 'A propos de l'utilization des

mottes castrales', *Ch.G. XI* (1983), 91–9, and 'Les fortifications de terre en Europe occidentale du Xe au XIIe siècles', *Archéologie Médiévale*, XI (1981), 5–123.

4 R.A. Higham, J.P. Allan, S.R. Blaylock, 'Excavations at Okehampton Castle, Devon. Part 2: the Bailey', *Proc. Devon Archaeol. Soc.*, 40 (1982), 19–151, esp. 27–38.

5 Higham *et al.*, *ibid*; Barker and Higham 1982, 36, 59–71. Castle water supply is currently the subject of research by Nigel Ruckley, to whom thanks are due for discussion. See his 'Water supply of medieval castles in the United Kingdom', *Fortress*, No. 7 (Nov. 1990), 14–26.

6 They are all to be found, for example, in the writings of Gaius Julius Caesar. At the siege of Marseilles in 49–48 BC a tower of brick and timber was roofed in shingles and tiles, with hides to finish it off: *The Civil Wars, Book II* (Loeb Classical Library, A.G. Peskett, 1928, esp. 133–9). On the general background, Sir J. Hackett (ed.), *Warfare in the Ancient World* (1989).

7 S. Luce (ed.), *Chroniques de Jean Froissart*, vol. III (Paris 1872), 81–2; for the general background, A.H. Burne, *The Crecy War* (1955), chap. V; other medieval documentary references given in W. Hermann, *Le Château Préfabriqué* (Strasbourg 1989).

8 R.A. Olsen, 'Big manors and large-scale farming in the late middle ages', *Ch.G. XIII* (1987), 157–67; see also above, chapter 3.

9 For the general background, K. Larsen, *A History of Norway* (Princeton 1948), and I. Anderson, *A History of Sweden* (1956); see also above, chapter 1. This subject is now one of active research in these areas, and the generalizations offered here may in due course become obsolete.

10 The literature on these topics is considerable. See, for example: on towns in Gaul, S. Johnson, *Late Roman Fortifications* (1983), chap. V; on the Scandinavian sites, P. Foote, D. Wilson, *The Viking Achievement* (1970); on *incastellamento*, J. Chapelot, R. Fossier, *The Village and House in the Middle Ages* (Eng. trans. 1985), esp. 133, 186–97; on Slavic sites, above, chapter 3.

11 For details, see chapters 2 and 3. For general discussion in a French context, see J. le Maho, 'De la *curtis* au Château: l'exemple du pays de Caux', *Ch.G. VIII* (1977), 171–83,

and *idem*, 'L'apparition des scigneuries châtelaines dans le Grand-Caux a l'époque ducale', *Archéologie Médiévale*, 6 (1976), 5–148.

12 See A. Débord, 'Châteaux et résidence aristocratique: réflexions pour la recherche', *Ch.G. XIII* (1987), 41–51; on Charavines, see *Dossiers Histoire et Archéologie*, no. 129 (July–August 1988), and M. Colardelle and C. Mazard, 'Premiers résultats des recherches sur les mottes médiévales en Dauphiné et en Savoie', *Archéologie Médiévale*, IX (1979), 65–95. Thanks are due to Michel Colardelle and Eric Verdelle for discussion of this work.

Appendix B, p. 362

1 The relevant extracts are conveniently collected in R.A. Brown, *The Origins of English Feudalism* (1973), 99–102.

2 J. Bosworth & T. Toller, *An Anglo-Saxon Dictionary* (1898 *etc*), 146. On the various post-Conquest forms and meanings, see H. Kurath, M.K. Sherman, *Middle English Dictionary* (Michigan 1959), vol. III, 80–3. I am grateful to Prof. M. Swanton for comment on the Anglo-Saxon aspects of this discussion.

3 Brown (see n.1), 76, 99, and references quoted there.

4 See, for example, Armitage 1912, 22–5; H. Braun, *The English Castle* (1936), 13; Renn 1973, 2; Brown 1976, 42–4; M.W. Thompson, *The Decline of the Castle* (1987), 1; D.J.C. King, *The Castle in England and Wales* (1988), 34.

5 The (1921) *Supplement* to Bosworth & Toller 1898 (see n.2), 118; *The Oxford English Dictionary* (2nd ed., 1989), vol. II, 956; *The Oxford Dictionary of English Etymology* (1966), 151.

6 A. Tobler & E. Lommatzsch, *Altfranzösisches Wörterbuch* (vol. II, Berlin, 1936), 303–5; in the edition of the *Song of Roland* by F. Whitehead (Oxford, 1942 etc) it occurs in lines 4, 236, 704, 2611, 3783. Here the word was normally used in the plural, in contrast to cities (*chastels, citez*). For the different French forms of *chastel* in use in England, see L.W. Stone & W. Rothwell (eds.), *Anglo-Norman Dictionary* (Fasc. I, 1977), 93a. I am indebted to Dr D. Trotter for assistance with the French aspects of this discussion.

7 A selection is given in Armitage 1912, 25.

Further Reading

Chapter 1

E. Armitage, *Early Norman Castles of the British Isles* (1912).

J. Counihan, 'The growth of castle studies in England and on the continent since 1850', *Proc. Battle Conf.*, XI (1989), 77–85.

R.A. Higham, 'Timber castles – a re-assessment', *Fortress*, 1 (May 1989), 50–60.

Chapter 2

E. Armitage, *Early Norman Castles of the British Isles* (1912).

B.K. Davison, 'The origins of the castle in England', *Archaeol. J.*, 124 (1967), 202–11.

D.J.C. King & L. Alcock, 'Ringworks of England and Wales', *Ch.G.*, III (1969), 90–127.

G. Simpson & B. Webster, 'Charter evidence and the distribution of mottes in Scotland', *Ch.G.*, V (1972), 175–92.

R. Allen Brown, *English Castles* (3rd ed. 1976).

A.D. Saunders (ed.), 'Five castle excavations. Reports on the Institute's Research Project into the Origins of the Castle in England', *Archaeol. J.*, 134 (1977), 1–156.

G. Beresford, *Goltho: the development of an early medieval manor* (1987).

T.B. Barry, *The Archaeology of Medieval Ireland* (1987).

Chapter 3

E. Armitage, *Early Norman Castles of the British Isles* (1912).

B.K. Davison, 'Early earthwork castles: a new model', *Ch.G.* III (1969), 37–47.

W. Anderson, *Castles of Europe from Charlemagne to the Renaissance* (1970).

A. Débord (ed.), 'Les fortifications de terre en Europe occidentale du Xe au XIIe siècles', *Archéologie Médiévale*, XI (1981), 5–123.

D. Bates, *Normandy before 1066* (1982).

A. Chédeville & N. Tonnère, *La Bretagne Féodale, XIe–XIIIe siècle* (Rennes 1987).

Chapter 4

E. Armitage, *Early Norman Castles of the British Isles* (1912).

R. Allen Brown, H.M. Colvin, A.J. Taylor, *The History of the King's Works: the Middle Ages* (2 vols 1963).

R. Allen Brown, English Castles (3rd ed. 1976).

Chapter 5

There are no general discussions of the pictorial evidence. See the publications given for each item discussed in the notes to the chapter. The most accessible is Sir D. Wilson (ed.), *The Bayeux Tapestry* (1985).

Chapter 6

Some of the documentary evidence is brought together in H.M. Colvin *et al.*, *The History of the King's Works. The Middle Ages* (1963), and one aspect of the archaeology is discussed in R.P. Wilcox, *Timber and Iron Reinforcement in Early Buildings* (Soc. Antiquaries 1981).

Chapter 7

D.J.C. King, L. Alcock, 'Ringworks of England and Wales', *Ch.G.* III (1969), 90–127.

Hugh Braun, 'Earthwork castles', *JBAA*, 3rd series, i 91937), 128–56.

R.A. Higham, 'Early castles in Devon, 1068–1201', *Ch.G. IX–X* (1982), 101–16.

D.F. Renn, 'Mottes: a classification', *Antiquity*, 33 (1959), 106–12.

D.J.C. King, 'The field archaeology of mottes in England and Wales', *Ch.G. V* (1972), 101–12

D.J.C. King, J. Spurgeon, 'Mottes in the Vale of Montgomery', *Arch. Camb.*, 114 (1965), 69–86.

On boroughs and castles, see M. Beresford, *New Towns of the Middle Ages* (1967), I. Soulsby, *The Towns of Medieval Wales* (Chichester, 1983), and on castle destruction in English towns at the Norman Conquest, H.C. Darby, *Domesday England* (1977), 304ff.

On castles and dispersed settlement patterns, see

Higham 1982 (above), *idem*, 'Castles in Devon', in S. Timms (ed.), *Archaeology of the Devon Landscape* (Exeter 1980), 70–80, and J. Spurgeon, 'The Castles of Montgomeryshire', *Montgomeryshire Collections*, 59 (1965–66), 1–59.

Chapter 8

J.R. Kenyon, *Medieval Fortifications* (Leicester 1990).

Chapter 9

P.A. Barker and R.A. Higham, *Hen Domen, Montgomery: a Timber Castle on the English-Welsh Border* (Royal Archaeological Institute Monograph, 1982).

Appendix A

The Oxford English Dictionary (2nd ed. 1989).

E.S. Armitage, *Early Norman Castles of the British Isles* (1912).

D.J.C. King, *The Castle in England and Wales* (1988).

H.M. Colvin *et al.*, *The History of the King's Works. The Middle Ages* (2 vols. 1963).

M. de Bouard, 'Quelques données françaises et Normandes concernant le problème de l'origine des mottes', *Ch.G. II* (1967), 19–26.

J.-M. Pesez, 'Maison forte, manoir, bastide, tour, motte, enceinte, moated-site, Wasserburg, ou les ensembles en archéologie', in M. Bur (ed.), *La Maison Forte au Moyen Age* (Paris 1986), 331–9.

Index of places

Page numbers in *italics* indicate illustrations

Abbaye-aux-Dames, Caen 158–9, 161, 334
Abbekinderen, Zeeland 93
Aberffraw 62
Aberllynfi Castle, Gwennyfed 228
Aberystwyth 173
Abinger 17, 58, 152, 187, 201, 245, 273, 293, 294, 295, 295, 296, 296, 357
Acre 125
Acton Bank, Lydbury North 208
Aggersborg 79, 80
Ahetze 128
Aigle 102
Aldermanbury 53
Aldingham 61, 61, 355
Alençon 102, 144
Alstoe Mount, Burley 21, 356
Amaston, Alberbury 207
Amboise 97, 171
Ambrières 102
America 33, 34
Anglesey 47, 62
Anjou 60, 97, 98
Anstey 134, 187, 356
Antrim 73, 74, 360
Antwerp 92
Ardres, Calais 29, 115–16, 117, 135, 136, 193, 245, 348
Århus 79
Arques-la-Bataille 101, 101, 102
Arundel 105, 129, 172, 199, 201, 245, 310
Ascot Doilly 187
Athelney 30
Audricq 125, 135
Audrieu 101
Aumerval 125, 136

Baginbun Head 72
Baile Hill, York 20, 60, 154, 358
Ballynarry 74, 360
Bamburgh 42, 125, 129, 137
Bari 159
Barley Pound 133, 133, 278
Barnard Castle 58, 189, 278, 278, 355
Barnstaple 21, 134, 355
Barton Hill, Kinnaird 315, 317, 317, 318, 360
Barton-on-Humber 50
Basing 128
Bayeux 102, 147, 149, 150, 151, 153
Beaumaris 173
Beaumont le Roger 102
Bedford 134, 355

Bedfordshire 47, 355
Beeston 172, 350
Behren-Lübchin 84
Belgium 122
Bellême 102
Bentley 133, 133, 356
Berg van Troje 91
Bergen 351
Berkeley 59
Berkshire 47
Big Glebe 74
Biggleswade 355
Birka 351
Birket 245
Bishop's Moat, Castlewright 202, 214, 215
Bishopston 21, 22, 23, 206, 359
Biskupin 86
Blackdown Rings, Loddiswell 25, 220
Bledisloe 356
Bonneville-sur-Toques 100, 147
Bordeaux 138, 173
Bothwell 140
Bramber 20, 60, 129
Brecknockshire 47
Breteuil 102
Bretteville-sur-Laize 101, 104, 191
Bridgnorth 185, 185
Brionne 100, 102, 171, 185
Briquessard 102
Britanny 60, 98ff.
British Camp, Malvern 61, 197, 200, 239
British Isles 20, 27, 36ff., 96, 122
Brix 102
Brockhurst Castle 196
Brookland 245, 258, 259
Brough 122, 184
Buckinghamshire 47
Builth 173
Bur 172
Burgh Castle 200, 357
Burghead 67
Byzantium 85

Cae Castell, Rumney 190, 303, 305, 306–7, 308, 309, 358
Caen 20, 93, 100, 144, 334
Caer Penrhos 200, 236
Caernarfon 18, 62, 63, 142, 173, 361
Caernarvonshire 47
Caesar's Camp, Folkestone 21, 22, 22
Calais 135, 167, 172
Caldern 88
Caldicot 181

Calvados 101, 195, 344
Cambridge *59*
Cambridgeshire 47, 355
Camp des Rouets, Bodieu 99
Canterbury 147, 200
Cardiff 63, 66, 200
Cardigan 122, 123
Cardiganshire 47
Carisbrooke 154, 172, 200
Carlisle 140, 172
Carmarthenshire 47
Carrickfergus 72, 142
Castell Cadwaladr *see* Caer Penrhos
Castell Collen 200
Castell Crugerydd 201, *222, 223*
Castell Cym-Aron, Llanddewi *243*
Castell foel Allt 199, *234, 235*
Castle Acre 57, 58, 184, 187 , 357
Castle Bromwich 49, 296, *297*, 298, 358
Castle Cary 133
Castle Hill, Newton-le-Willows 357
Castle Hill, Peebles *see* Peebles
Castle Hill of Strachan 312, 313, *314*, 359 *see also* Strachan
Castle Neroche 49, *49*, 60, 198, 200, 353
Castle Pulverbatch 200
Castle Rising 163, 185, 357
Castle Tower, Penmaen 187, 198, 308, 310, 311, 359
Castledykes 68
Castlemilk 167, *169*
Castleskreen 74, *75*, 76, 360
Catalonia 79
Caus castle 27, 28, 66, 195, 200, 201, 202, 229, 236, *237*, 265
Cefn Bryntalch, Llandyssil *209*
Chalgrave 49, 355
Champagne 120
Charavines-Colletière 352
Chartley 196, *240*
Château Gaillard 172, 185
Châtillon-sur-Seine 185
Cheddar 31, 41, *42*, 54, 57
Chepstow 58, *59*, 63
Cherbourg *102*
Cherrueix *102*
Cheshire 47, 172, 355
Chester 27, *59*
Chilham 184
Chirbury 31, 344
Chirk 137
Church Stretton 196
Clavering 42
Cledemutha see Rhuddlan
Clifford *59*, 184
Clifford's Tower, York 138, *138*, 184, 358
Clones 142
Clough 20, 74, 76, 187, 318, 319, *319*, 360
Clun 196, 202
Clungunford 194
Clwyd 358
Clyde 140
Coed Caeau, Erwood *204*
Coed-y-Cwm, St Nicholas 358
Coitbury 53
Colchester 58, 172
Coleshill 138
Colwyn Castle, Glascwm 200, *238*
Conway 173, 181
Conwy Castle 64
Corfe Castle 132, 133, 172, 184
Cork 72
Cornwall 31, 47, 132, 195, 355

Cotentin 100, 172
Coucy-le-Château 185
Cripplegate, London 53
Crookston 67, *69*
Cruggleton 67, *68*, 311–12, 359
Cumberland 47, 140
Cumbria 355
Cwm Camlais Castle, Trallerg 211
Cwrt Llechryd 62, *63*

Dampierre le Château 167, *168*
Dauphiné 352
Deal 32
Deer Park Farms 74
Deganwy 61, 62, 63, 143
Denbighshire 47
Denmark 20, 37, 79ff., 111, 351
Derbyshire 47, 355
Devon 47, 132, 355
Dinan 99, 147, *148*, 150, 151, 152, 153, 158, 350
Dinas Emrys 62
Dinas Powis 62, 352, 358
Dinbych see Tenby
Dinorben 62
Dol 99, 147, *148*, 150, 151, 152, 153, 158
Domen Castell 64
Domfront *102*, 144
Doon Hill 41–2
Doonmore 21, 360
Dorestad 32
Dorset 47
Doué-la-Fontaine 97, 171
Dover 58, 59, 129, 135, 136, 137, 153, 172, 191, 356
Down 74, 320, 360
Downpatrick 198
Driffield 356
Dromore 142, 360
Dublin 77, 143
Dudley 200, 201, 245, 310, 358
Duffield 355
Dumbarton 67
Dumfries 140
Dunadd 67
Dunbar 41
Dundonald 359
Dundrum 142
Dundurn 67
Duneight 74, 360
Dunollie 67
Dunsilly 74, 76
Dunster 133
Durham 47, 115, 118–20, *119*, 139, 190, 348, 355
Durrow 143
Düsseldorf 21
Dyfed 358

Earls Barton 50, *50*, 51
East Anglian dykes 31, 129
Eaton Socon 355
Echauffour *102*
Edinburgh 42, 67
Eglwys Cross, Bronington *212*
Eketorp 32
Elmley Castle 200
Emlyn 140
England 38ff., 103, 127, 128, 129, 151, 172, 352
Eriksvolde 83
Essex 47, 132, 355
Etreux 128
Eu *102*
Evreux *102*

Ewyas Harold 43, *45, 59*
Exeter 40, 50, 53, 58, *59*, 61, 129, *130*, 189, 194, 200, 274, 337
Exme *102*
Eye 137
Eynsford 31, 53, *54*, 57, 60, 184, 356

Falaise *102*
Farnham 177–8, *178*, 187, *190*, 197, 349
Fécamp 100
Feddersen Wierde 91
Ferrycarrig 72
Finistère 99, *99*
Flanders 60, 92
Flint 47, 173
Forden Gaer 62, 345
Forest of Dean 202
Forth 142
Framlingham 133
France 32, 37, 38, 57, 93ff., *94*, 123, 128, 143f., 159, 352
Frétun 140
Fridd Faldwyn 345
Fyrkat 79, *80*

Gallefontaine *102*, 103
Galloway 70, 142
Gard 128
Gascony 128
Germany 32, 37, 61, 88ff., 128
Ghent 92, 171
Gironville 128
Gisors 172, 185
Glamorgan 24, 47, 63, 65, *65*, 195, 303, 358, 359
Glasgow 140
Gloucester 42, 57, 172, 356
Gloucestershire 47, 356
Gniezo 86
Goltho 49, 53, 54ff., *55, 56*, 57, 60, 61, 127, 198, 203, 265, 273, *281, 282–3, 284, 285, 286*, 356
Goodrich 184, 335
Gormaz 79
Gournay *102*
Gransha 74, *76*
Gravenchon, Nôtre-Dame de 20, *102*, 103, *107, 108, 109*, 191, 192, *267, 267*
Great Easton 355
Great Torrington 122, 134
Greenstead 30
Grimbosq 20, *102*, 103, *111*
Guildford 172
Guines 135
Gurcy-le-Châtel 128
Gwent 359
Gwynedd 62, 64

Hampshire 47, 356
Hanley 172
Haraldsborg 79
Harlech 173, *174*
Harptree 133
Hastings 20, 58, *59*, 60, 122, 129, 142, 144, 153, 154–6, *154, 156*, 195, 357
Haus Meer 20, 90
Havrum 83
Hawcock's Mount 27, 72, 195, 201, 202, *205 see also* Caus
Hay-on-Wye 184
Haywra 140, 172, 175
Hedeby 32, 79, 351
Hen Blas 358
Hen Domen Montgomery 20, 27, 29, 34, 60, 63, 66, 135, 137, 144, 166, 197, 199, 201, 202, 206, *217*, 254, *263*, 265, 310, 318, 326–47, 348, 349, 350, 359

Hereford 27, 43, *43*, 44, *172, 178, 179*, 192, 349
Herefordshire 43, 47, 57
Hertford 356
Hertfordshire 47, 356
Highlands 70
Hilden 21
Hockleton, Chirbury 199, 200, *218, 219*
Hodnet 329
Hofe 88, *89*
Hogg's Mount 43, *44*
Holm Castle 356
Hope 173
Hopton 196
Hoverberg, der 20, 273, *274*
Howden 359
Hungary 85
Hunneschans 91
Huntingdon *59*, 133, *134*, 355
Huntingdonshire 47
Huntly Castle 140
Husterknupp, der 20, 88, 89, *91*, 198, 203, 265, 268, *268, 269, 270, 271, 272*, 273
Huttons Ambo 358

Inch 143
Inverurie 359
Ireland 20, 37, 38, 70ff., *72, 73*, 89, 139, 142, 143, 194, 352
Isle of Axholme 133
Isle of Man 47, 142
Isle of Ré 138
Italy 20, 32, 37, 78ff., 96, 351
Ivry *102*, 104, 121

James River 33
Jamestown, Virginia 33
Japan 33–4, *35*
Jersey 144
Jewel Tower, Westminster 156, 157
Jomfruhoj 83
Josselin 99
Jumièges 40
Jutland 79, 84

Kaersgaard 83
Keir Knowe of Drum 312, *313*, 359
Kells 143, 360
Kengfig 172
Kenilworth 135, 176
Kernec 99
Kerry Ridgeway 202, 214
Kidwelly 173, 181
Kiev 84
Kilfinan 359
Kilpeck 345, 356
Kinardferry 133
King's River 143
King's Wood 135
Kingsland 212, *229*
Kington 172, 223
Kinnaird *see* Barton Hill
Knaresborough 172
Knockgraffon *74*
Koepfel 88
Kontich 191

La Bussière 171
La Chappelle-Colbert 101, *105*
La Cour-Marigny 121
La Ferté en Bray *102*
La Garnach 99
La Réole 350
Lady's Mount 202, *242*

Lancashire 47, 172, 356
Langeais 97, 171
Langley Park 176
Launceston 58, 60, 130, 175, 274, *275*, 276, *276*, 355
Le Cinglais 101, 102
Le Homme *102*
Le Puiset 122, *124*, 125, 136, 150, 151, 152, 350
Leeds 176
Leicester 178, *179*, 192, 349
Leicestershire 47, 356
Leinster 73
Les Andelys 95, 172
Leskellen en Plabennec 99
Lewes 129, 184
Liddell 140
Limerick 72
Lincoln *59*, 133, 184, 200
Lincolnshire 47, 343, 344, 356
Lingen *230, 231*
Linlithgow 140, *140*, 142
Lismahon 20, 74, 76, 187, 199, 200, 245, 303, 320, *321, 322, 323*, 360
Liverpool, West Derby 357
Llandovery 122, 123
Llanstephan 190, 358
Llantrithyd 303, *304*, 308, 310, 358
Lochmaben 140, 142, 167, 359
Lodsbridge Mill, Lodsworth 358
Loire valley 93, 122
London 42, 47, 53, 58, *59*, 156, 172, 200, 356 *see also* Tower of London
Longtown 181
Lorrha 360
Loughor 359
Louth 24, 360
Low Countries 32, 37, 90f., 96, 128
Ludgershall 174, 185, *185*, 190, 191, 358
Ludlow 58, 133, 337
Lumphanan 67, 359
Lundy Island 47
Lurgankeel 76, 360
Luton 355
Lydford 58, 60, 277, *277*, 278, 355
Lynn 142

Magny-les-Villiers 125
Maiden Castle 197
Maine 98
Malesmains 185
Malvern Hills 61, *239*
Mamble *256, 257*
Manéhouville *102*
Marburg 88
Marck 172
Marlborough 172
Martin's Hundred, Virginia 33, *34*
Mathrafal 62, *63*
Mawgan Porth 31
Meath 73
Meaux 125
Melton 128
Merchem 115, 118
Mercia 31, 47, 62, 129
Merckeghem 115, 118
Merckem *see* Merchem
Meretun 41
Merionethshirc 47
Messina 125
Meuse 121
Middleton Stoney 49, 357

Mirville 20, 102, 103, *106, 264, 265, 266*, 267, *267*, 273
Moat, Llandinam *226, 227*
Modena cathedral 158–9, *160*, 245
Moel Frochas, Llanrhaeadr-ym-Mochnant *220*
Moncontour 185
Monmouth 59
Monmouthshire 47
Montacute *59*
Montaigu *102*
Montboyau 121
Montbran 99
Montemasso 164
Montereau-fault-Yonne 121
Montfort-sur-Risle *102*
Mont-Glonne 121, 122
Montgommeri *102*
Montgomery, New 27, 29, 62, 135, 137, 174, 202, 329, 350
Montgomery, Old (Hen Domen) 27, 66, 129, 137, 172, 195, 202, 329
Montgomery, Vale of 27, 218, 221, 328
Montgomeryshire *28*, 47
Montreuil l'Argillé *102*
More 198, *232–3*
Morman 98
Mortain *102*
Mortemer *102*
Moscow 32
Mote of Mark 67
Mote of Urr 67, *69*, 359
Moulins la Marche *102*
Mount Ferrant 125, *126*

Nafferton 137, 357
Nagoya, Japan *35*
Nantes 98
Navestock *258*, 303
Neauffles *102*
Neufmarché *102*
Near East 37
Neath 172
Nes stave church, Norway 2467, *247, 248, 249, 250, 251, 252*, 301
Netherlands 91, *92*
Nevers 128
New Buckenham 161, 163–4, *164*, 184, 185 *see also* Old Buckenham
New Montgomery *see* Montgomery, New
New Zealand 33
Newcastle under Lyme 137
Newcastle upon Tyne 129, 137
Nidaros 351
Nollich 185, *186*
Norfolk 47, 357
Normandy 28, 36, 43, 58, 60, 89, 98, 100ff., 122, 126, 134, 150, 155, 172, 195, 326
Nørrevolde 83
North America *see* America
Northampton 31, 133, 172, 357
Northumberland 357
Northumbria 42, 45, 47
Norway 31–2, 246, 351
Norwich 154, 172
Nottingham *59*, 172
Nottinghamshire 47
Novgorod 32

Odense/Nonnebakken 79, *81*
Odiham 172, 176
Offa's Dyke 31, 129
Okehampton 58, 154, 187, 191, 201, 350

Old Aberystwyth 358
Old Buckenham 163, *164*
Old Montgomery *see* Montgomery, Old *and* Hen Domen
Old Sarum 172, 184, 350
Old Windsor *see* Windsor
Oost-Souburg 91
Orford 172, 196
Orkney Islands 142
Oxford 154
Oxfordshire 47, 357

Pain's Castle *216*
Paladru, lake 352
Palestine 125
Pan Pudding Hill, Bridgnorth 201
Paris 171
Pas de Calais 60, 122
Pays de Caux 28, 172, 195, 205, 265
Peebles 315, *316*, 359
Pembridge 245, *254*, *255*, 258, 259, 260, *263*, 303
Pembroke 63, 122, 123
Pembrokeshire 47
Pen Llystyn 62
Pen-y-pill 358
Penard 187, 359
Penmaen *see* Castle Tower, Penmaen
Penrice 359
Penwortham 21, 356
Peran 98
Petralia Soprana, Sicily 78
Pevensey 58, *59*, 122, 129, 153, 156, 172
Pickering 172
Pilleth 199
Pinkie 167
Piper's Fort, Farranfad, 360
Pirton *253*, 303
Pîtres (Pistes) 95
Plemięta *87*, 88
Pleshey 132, 190, 355
Plessis-Grimoult 101, *102*, 191
Ploumoguer 99
Plympton 130, 131, *131*, 132, 184, 185, *186*
Poitiers 48
Poitou 134
Poland 20, 86, 88, 111
Pontesbury 187, 288, 357
Portchester 31, 50, 51, *52*, 53, 54, 172, 190, 353, 356
Portencross, Auldhill 360
Powderham 133, *133*, 356
Powis castle 65, 202, *242*
Powys 27, 31, 62, 63, 64, 65, 146, 359
Poznan *86*
Prudhoe 49, 284, 285, *287*, 288, 357

Quatford 357

Radnorshire 47
Rathmullan 74, *75*, 76, 187, *188*, 265, 273, 360
Ratley and Upton 358
Rayleigh 355
Rea-Camlad valley 199
Redon 99
Rennes 98, 99, 142, *144*, 150, 151, 152
Restormel 181
Rhineland 20, 60, 88, 90, *90*, 96, 352
Rhuddlan 62, 63, 64, 66, 122, 123, 138, 142, 173, 202, 241
Rhyd Whyman 202, 329
Rhyd yr Onen, Llangurig *225*
Richard's Castle 43, *44*, 196
Richmond 58, 184, 337
Rings, The *132*, 133

Roberton 67, 68, 360
Rochester 120, *172*, 173, 181, 185
Romania 85, *85*
Roscrea 143
Rothesay 144
Rouen 100, 171
Rougemont 50
Rougiers 32
Rue en Marquenterre 128
Rumigny 122
Rug, Corwen 358
Rumney Castle *see* Cae Castell
Russia 32
Rutland 21, 47

Saffron Walden 132
St Aubin *102*
St Briavels 140, 172, 173
St Cénéri *102*
St Denis (Paris) 135
St Evroul 46
St Florent-le-Vieil 121
St Foy de Montgomery 104, *112*
St Germain de Montgomery 104, *112*, 195
St James de Beuvron *102*
St Valery-sur-Somme 144
St Verain 185
San Marco Argentano (Cosenza) 78
Sandal 58, 186, 201, 245, 298–9, *299*, *300*, 358
Sandown 32
Sassoforte 164
Sauvey 137
Savigny 122
Savoy 352
Scandinavia 32
Scharstorf, Holstein 86
Scilly Isles 47
Scotland 38, 66ff., *70*, 139, 140, 142, 144, 167, 359
Scribla 78
Seafin 142
Sebecourt 102, *105*, 191
Segontium *see* Caernarfon
Seine 95
Selkirk 140, *141*
Severn 63, 65, 202, 328, 329
Sheffield 184
Shirlet 135
Shrewsbury 27, 28, 47, *59*, 105, 138, *139*, 175, 195, 201, 202
Shropshire 47, 135, 137, 265, 344, 357
Sicily 78, 125
Siena 164
Silchester 61, 356
Sjørrind 79
Skenfrith 137
Smethcott 357
Snead 135
Solvig *83*, 84
Solway Firth 144
Somerset 47
Somerton 175
South Mimms 187, 197, 198, 201, 279, *279*, 356
Southampton 137
Spain 79
Stafford 19, *19*, *59*, 196, 199, 201, 245, 288, 289, *289*, *290*, 291, *291*, 293, 310, 357
Staffordshire 47, 357
Stamford 47, 132, 330, 343, 346, 357
Staraja Ladoga 32
Stockholm 351
Stokesay 181–2, *182*, *183*, 184, 334

Strachan 67 *see also* Castle Hill
Strathbogie 140
Suffolk 47, 344
Sulgrave 20, 31, 49, 50, *50*, *51*, 53, 54, 56, 57, 60, 61, 72, 127, 190, 357
Surrey 47, 357
Sussex 47, 328, 357, 358
Swansea 21
Sweden 32, 351
Sycharth 144–6, *145*, 187, 201, 301, *302*, 358

Tamworth 24, 42, 180, *180*, *292*, 293, *294*, 357
Tandslet 245, *246*
Tarrega 79
Tenbury Wells 194, *210*
Tenby 61
Ter Horst 128
Therfield 279, 280, *280*, 281, 356
Threave 185
Tilleda 32
Tillières-sur-l'Avre *102*
Tintagel 135
Tomen Bedd Ugre, Llandewi Ystradenny *224*
Tomen Castell, New Radnor *213*
Tomen y Rhodwydd 64, *217*
Tonge 356
Totnes 58, 130, 187, *189*, 355
Tours 121
Tower of London 58, 172, 187, 200
Trans 98
Transylvania 85
Trelleborg 32, 79, *81*
Trematon 130
Treoda 359
Tretower 185
Trim 72, 142
Trowbridge 358
Tutbury 133
Twmpath, Rhiwbina 21
Twt Hill, Rhuddlan *241*
Twyn-y-Cregen, Llanarth 359

Unterregenbach, Germany 88
Urquhart 67
Urr 154
Urville 101, 191

Vale of Montgomery *see* Montgomery, Vale of
Vernon *102*
Vinchy 93

Waardenburg 128

Wales 24, 37, 38, 61ff., *66*, 72, 123, 137, 142, 173, 195, 201, 358 *see also* Welsh border
Wallingford *25*, 133, 137, 357
Walmer 32
Wansdyke, East 31, 129
Wansdyke, West 31, 129
Wareham *25*
Warendorf 32
Warkworth 181
Warrington 355
Warwick *59*, 137, 201
Warwickshire 47, 358
Waterford 72, 142
Wells 347
Welsh border 27, *41*, 43
Welshpool 64, 65
Wembworthy *24*
Weoley 265, 321, 323, *324*, 325, *325*
Wessex 31, 41
West Woodhay 21
Westbury (Old Caus) 27, 172, 236
Westminster 40, 42, 152, 347, 350 *see also* Jewel Tower
Westminster Abbey 137, 301
Westminster Hall 57, 158
Westmorland 47
Wigmore *59*
Williamstown, Virginia 33
Wilmington, Chirbury *228*
Wilton 30
Wiltshire 47, 344, 358
Wimbourne 41
Winchester 31, 42, 53, *53*, 57, 58, *59*, 60, 191, 356
Windsor 31, 137, 175, *175*, 176, *176*, *177*, 191, 199, 200, 201, 245, 310
Wöel 181
Wolstenholme Town, Virginia 33, *34*
Woolstaston 357
Worcester 40, *59*, 133, 137, 158, 200, 347
Worcestershire 47
Wroxeter 345

Xanten (Lorraine) 88

Y Gaer, St Nicholas *203*
Yarpole 245, 258, 259, *260*, *261*, *262*, 303
Yeavering 31, 41, 42, *42*
York 45, 53, *59*, 60, 122, 136, 138, 175, 184, 200, 350, 358
Yorkshire 47, 328, 343, 344, 358
Ystumgwern 173, *174*

Zeeland 91